ONCE WITHIN BORDERS

ONCE
WITHIN
BORDERS

Territories of Power,

Wealth, and Belonging

since 1500

CHARLES S. MAIER

THE BELKNAP PRESS *of*

HARVARD UNIVERSITY PRESS

Cambridge, Massachusetts

London, England

2016

First printing

Library of Congress Cataloging-in-Publication Data

Names: Maier, Charles S., author.

Title: Once within borders : territories of power, wealth,

and belonging since 1500 / Charles S. Maier.

Description: Cambridge, Massachusetts : The Belknap Press of

Harvard University Press, 2016. | Includes bibliographical references and index.

Identifiers: LCCN 2016014044 | ISBN 9780674059788 (alk. paper)

Subjects: LCSH: Political geography—History. | Territory, National—History. |

Boundaries—History. | Boundary disputes—History.

Classification: LCC JC323 .M34 2016 | DDC 320.1/2—dc23 LC record available at

https://lccn.loc.gov/2016014044

To the memory of Pauline

And to our children,
Andrea, Nicholas, and Jessica,
whose pride in their mother helped sustain her

CONTENTS

PREFACE

FROM AUGUST 13, 1961, UNTIL NOVEMBER 9, 1989, the Berlin Wall served as the world's most conspicuous border. It separated two halves of the city, two halves of Germany, in fact, two global domains that were both territorial and ideological. Next to the urban Friedrich-straße railroad station, which served as one of its sanctioned crossing points, stood an annex building known as the Tränenpalast or Palace of Tears. It got this nickname because it was where visitors from the West who were returning home bid good-bye to their relatives and friends immured in the East. Traveling in the opposite direction before the wall fell, I would cross to the East on the S-Bahn line, get out of one train, watch as stone-faced border guards sequestered my U.S. passport for a disquieting interval, then board another train into "Berlin: Capital of the German Democratic Republic." After the fall of the wall, the Tränen-palast became a nightclub for more than a decade; today it is a museum installation about what had been a serious border, one at which perhaps more than a hundred East Germans lost their lives attempting to cross.

That German-German frontier has disappeared, but today states the world over are building walls to keep travelers out, not in. They, too, produce tears. Thinking of these new barriers, Pope Francis has summoned us, rightly I believe, to build bridges, not borders. But borders are more than just barriers; for some they guarantee community and belonging. In each case their persistence lends the following work a timely relevance. They organize the spatial structure of our collective life, and this enduring but changing construction of territory is what this book attempts to chronicle and illuminate.

The work has claimed a long period of study and writing. To borrow a term from Hollywood, it represents a "prequel" to my studies *Among Empires: American Ascendancy and Its Predecessors* (2006) and *Leviathan 2.0: Inventing Modern Statehood* (2012). It is hard to know where intellectual quests begin. Over thirty years ago, within the framework of the Joint Committee on Western Europe of the SSRC and ACLS, a wonderful group of colleagues and friends—Suzanne Berger, Gerald Feldman, Jürgen Kocka, Claus Offe, Alessandro Pizzorno, Charles Sabel, Michele Salvati, and Philippe Schmitter among them—helped stretch my thinking. In our second cycle of discussions, I edited a volume, *Changing Boundaries of the Political,* and wrote an essay on the ways in which the passage of time appeared within different ideological frameworks. The exercise prompted me to ask in what ways different sociopolitical regimes and ideas might also influence the spatial organization of society. Although initially I classified temporal frameworks in terms of left versus right, I later came to think of spatial orientation as less responsive to ideology (though it sometimes is) than as varying by historical epoch—a change in perspective that helped me engage with Foucault as well as Marx and Weber. Along the way, prodded by current issues and controversies, I yielded to intellectual detours to explore the historiography of the Holocaust and the Cold War. By the late 1990s, I proposed some suggestions about the historical stages of political space in an article published in the *American Historical Review* in June 2000: "Consigning the Twentieth Century to History: Alternative Narratives for the Modern Era." But again I pointed this research in a different direction after 2001, once U.S. policies seemed to make the issue of empire compelling to me as both citizen and historian. Empires had already seized my attention as a characteristic organization of territory with specific properties, and as such they claim a chapter in this book. After writing *Among Empires,* I was recruited for an extended essay on state making in the modern era for a multivolume global history, *World Connecting* (2012), which has also appeared as a stand-alone book: *Leviathan 2.0: Inventing Modern Statehood* (2014). It does not center on the transformations of territory per se, but some of the topics covered there also play a role in this work, to which I finally returned.

Readers, I believe, will find here an unconventional history. It has no set of core events to structure a narrative; it focuses on no single geographical unit. It does not endeavor to paint the traits of an age. It represents a significant shift of focus from the earlier part of my scholarly career. I started my research a half century ago seeking to explain, first, how societies could remain so cohesive in the presence of great degrees of inequality; second, how they might suddenly explode into violence or revolutionary change and then just as quickly settle down to stable patterns of continuity. I still believe these are important issues, although they may seem old-fashioned concerns next to those focusing on environmental history or issues of personal identity. But the history offered here speaks more directly to another set of problems that have long occupied me: the loyalties and forces that lead human communities to war and conflict. I would like to think that I have supplemented my earlier work on the "vertical" structures of society, with all their differentiation and potential for conflict, with a complementary investigation into how communities are organized "horizontally" in the world. At the end I propose that these two principles of collective orientation, those based on territory and those reflecting social inequality, have come to mesh in the contemporary world.

Let me add a word about sources. This book is based on printed primary sources and substantial reading in several secondary literatures, not on archival documentation. Given the diversity of topics covered in this study—among them the history of fortifications, cartography and cadastral development, the development of international law, early modern agrarian economic theory, railroad development, disentail of the countryside, geopolitical doctrine, geography texts, and so on—I have not assembled a general alphabetical bibliography of works cited. The reader should consult the endnotes on each of these themes as they occur in the separate chapters. Scholars who are expert in these respective topics may well feel that the research in each falls short of what they would find in a monographic study. There are trade-offs between mastery and synthesis. Readers must judge whether they were justified.

———

Of course, I have more specific debts of gratitude. The Woodrow Wilson Center for Scholars in Washington supported me as a distinguished fellow for a semester in 2011; I repaid them with a different book from the one I promised, but *Once Within Borders* advanced under their auspices and I benefited from the mix of abstract and policy-oriented ideas that flourished in their quarters. The Harvard History Department and the Minda de Gunzburg Center for European Studies have long been my intellectual milieu and an unequalled environment for engagement with ideas, supportive colleagues, and continually challenging students, many of whom have become close friends and have been immensely sustaining over the years. Two teaching collaborations in the past years have stimulated my intellectual metabolism: for almost a decade Niall Ferguson and I have taught a fantastically motivated and intelligent set of students in international politics and economics; and Sven Beckert and I have developed a program of global history, supported by the Weatherhead Center for International Affairs, which has helped expand my horizons of interest beyond the European and U.S. topics with which I began my career. I had the chance to benefit from presentation of chapters to my own department's International and Global History Seminar, the Berkeley History Department, the Yale Institute of Strategic Studies, and the Harvard Seminar in the History of Capitalism—and long ago at the outset of the project to the UCLA Geography Department, where John Agnew and Edward Soja engaged me in particular. Sadly, two of my long-term intellectual mentors died in the course of my work on this book—Stanley Hoffmann and Ernest May. Their questioning would no doubt have helped improve it.

Several students have helped at particular junctures with research (as did earlier ones on previous projects). At the Wilson Center in Washington, Whitney Wallace and Johnnie Lotesta helped with bibliography; Joshua Kucera, an MA candidate in the Harvard program on Russian and Eurasian studies, researched Russian railroad enthusiasms (now in Chapter 5); Benjamin Sacks, currently a doctoral candidate at Princeton, contributed to my work on early-modern cartography; and Stefan Link, now teaching at Dartmouth, sent research notes from Europe. Most signally, Daniel Sargent, now a faculty member at the University of California in Berkeley, provided precious research help and orientation in the early stage of the work, and Steven Press, now on the faculty of Stanford University, read through chapters and helped refine ideas in the final stages. I owe them both an immense debt. David Weimer and the curators of the Harvard Map Collection assisted with visual material as did Eric Mulder at Harvard University Press. The anonymous readers for the Press prodded some key rewriting. Most recently, Julia Kirby supervised production and Mikala Guyton took in hand the demanding task of being the production editor of a complex manuscript. Joyce Seltzer, my long-term general editor, this time as earlier, provided continuing encouragement through a long intellectual journey. Turning toward family, I have always benefited from the questions, suggestions, and unconditional support of my children: Andrea, a civil servant of the European parliament; Nicholas, who keeps me in touch with the trans-territorial world of electronic information; and Jessica, a historian of Renaissance art who shares my interest in what maps "do."

As some of my readers will know, during the long work on this book, my wife of half a century, Pauline Maier, died from the rapid and harsh onset of lung cancer. Aside from more intimate memories, I have often thought during the period since her death of her achievement as a wonderful and widely respected historian of revolutionary America. Besides the highest standards of scholarship, she possessed gifts of empathy with her protagonists, of narration, and of communication with a wide public that loved her work, which far transcend my talent in these areas. I miss the continuing reports from the historiographical front that she provided on a daily basis. Her initiative also bequeathed our family a weekend and summer home and gardens in Rhode Island that I have grown to cherish. It was a rare collaboration. But I have been fortunate in the last period to find a new partner, Anne Saadah—an old family friend, a student of contemporary Europe and, more recently, of Middle Eastern politics, and a professor of politics—who engages in similar dialogue and has stepped into a great gap. The cycle of loss and recovery is hard to fathom, but it does affirm that doing history, every sort of history, must answer some deep curiosity about human endurance through time.

Cambridge and Little Compton, February 2016

INTRODUCTION

A History of Political Space

TERRITORY—AN IDEA that seemed to have fallen into genteel disuse—has intruded into our lives with a renewed and menacing urgency. It refers to a geographic space, set apart from others by law and boundary. Until recently we could take territory for granted; it was protective and offered security and belonging, with less and less self-conscious effort. After the end of the Cold War, Europeans and Americans tended to believe that territorial priorities had become anachronistic, subsisting mostly among stubborn peoples in the Balkans or the Middle East or as a stake in East Asia. Now the security that territory once offered seems precarious everywhere and to be maintained only with constant surveillance.

The new sense of vulnerability rarely arises from traditional international rivalries as it used to. Rather, all our customary homelands seem assailed by global trends that transgress once reassuring borders and spatial stability—by threats of terrorist attacks, uprooted refugees, tidal flows of international capital, the scary spread of new diseases, and the threat of climate change oblivious to frontiers. Peoples who have long enjoyed territorial security no longer feel sheltered. Some seek new and nonspatial defenses; others mobilize to reaffirm boundaries under threat. And in many places, groups that have never possessed territorial security are prepared to kill and die for it. Territory is not what it was, but it remains indispensable.

Territory is not just land, even extensive land. It is global space that has been partitioned for the sake of political authority, space in effect empowered by borders. Territories allow people to be governed or taxed or imbued with loyalty by virtue of their shared spatial location, not their race or their kinship ties or their faith or their professional affiliation.[1] Territory has been a major sociopolitical invention.

We have a sense of why territory has become precarious in recent times. But how did this spatial sheltering of group life emerge, flourish, and then perhaps decay? Can we write a history of territory as a central attribute of human society? Certainly we can research and write the history of particular territories, small or extended: of city-states and vast empires, Luxemburg or Russia. But until recently territory as such has had little attention from historians, although geographers and political scientists have reflected on its evolution.[2]

One reason for neglect is that except for those moments when borders are made explicit—by having to flash a passport, or viewing via CNN the desolation of the displaced or another interminable, faraway war—we have taken for granted the fact that territorial divisions exist. They have been an unremarkable constant of life. The specific boundary lines might change, whether by peaceful means or by violence, but the fact of territorial division has seemed as permanent as political organization. In fact, territory and the properties that territory entails—so-called territoriality—have changed over time and continue to change profoundly. They have had a history.

This book attempts to write that history of territory as such, of its idea and, just as important, its social practice and manifestations in the last half millennium. It traces how territory was endowed with critical attributes, became a major resource for state and economic development, thereafter an obsession in some cases, and has now perhaps irreparably weakened in efficacy, leaving some citizens with a great sense of political melancholy and others with a determination to revalorize its capacities.

Reconstructing that history allows significant insights into human development. Jean-Jacques Rousseau identified the importance of territory for property: "The first man who, having enclosed a plot of land, thought of saying, *this is mine,* and found people simple enough to believe him, was the real founder of civil society."[3] Max Weber underlined its role for politics: "The state is the community that successfully claims a monopoly of legitimate capacity for force within a defined area—and the area is integral to the definition."[4] Most of Weber's commentators have dwelled on the ideas of violence and legitimacy. Until recently, they have taken the criterion of "defined area" or territory for granted, giving it little more attention than the air that all historical subjects must breathe. But frontiers control the entry and sometimes exit of residents or travelers, of goods, of money, and even occasionally, though less successfully, of ideas. People tend to divide over whether they should be made more absolute or more porous. Robert Frost thought that "something there is that doesn't love a wall," but the farmer next door stubbornly believed that "good fences make good neighbors." We have usually divided over that alternative, sometimes raising the fences, sometimes making them more permeable.[5]

The tendencies we lump together under the idea of globalization suggest that the attributes of territory are changing rapidly. Over the last quarter century, globalization has impinged on the public imagination as an unprecedented and irresistible force, undermining a stable geopolitical ordering of the world.[6] What has weakened is precisely a traditional sense of territory. The political rights that came with territory included determination of who belonged and who was foreign, how wealth would be generated and distributed, how the domain of the sacred must be honored, how families reproduced themselves. Territory is thus a *decision space*. It established the spatial reach of legislation and collective decisions. At the same time, territory has specified the domain of powerful collective loyalties. Political and often ethnic allegiance has been territorial. "Breathes there the man with soul so dead, / Who never to himself hath said, / This is my own, my native land!"[7] Territory has thus also constituted an *identity space* or a space of belonging.[8]

Through the first three quarters of the twentieth century, excepting experiences of wartime or emigration, most adults in the West understood their decision space and their identity space to be congruent. The areas that claimed their loyalty also organized their labor, provided security, and ensured family continuity. Today these domains no longer coincide so pervasively. Territoriality seems less a resource for guaranteeing livelihoods, excluding foreigners, or maintaining coherence of values. It no longer provides the same capacity for control, even if territories remain the nexus of primary allegiance. Identity space and decision space have diverged.

In fact, they were not always identical. The age of territory was not part of the natural order but historically bounded. The common assumption is that before globalization there was little transformation. Most commentary, whether journalistic or academic, has taken territory to be a permanent and reassuring fixture of social and political organization that has come suddenly under attack—much like the great polar ice shelves, only now after millennia of frozen solidity melting into the sea. Historians, however, are rightly suspicious of conditions that have remained unquestioned and supposedly unchanging. In fact, the idea of territory has evolved over the last half millennium as societies, sometimes states and nations, imagined and organized the segments of the globe's surface on which they lived. These concepts and practices—call them constructions of territory or the territorial imagination—have continually changed along with the other major variables of human history, such as environment, technology, class divisions, attributes of gender, principles of faith and politics and science, and forms of political organization.

Globalization may undermine the capacity for territorial governance, that is, erode decision space, but it does not necessarily weaken identity space, the grip of the territorial imagination, and perhaps not the stubborn persistence of frontiers.[9] Recall the Middle Eastern refugees seeking entry into Europe, the recurrent border conflicts, most recently in Ukraine, and the dismaying surge of national and ethnic violence since the 1990s, including the murderous conflicts in Bosnia, the slaughter of Tutsi in Rwanda, the ethnic cleansing in Kosovo, the resistance of Chechnya, the marauding bullies in East Timor, the long misery in Darfur, and the seemingly intractable confrontation of Palestinians and Israelis. Even if we leave violence out of account, nationalism still prospers. Peoples still seek nationhood, and they continue to win recognition as national states.

Within states globalization has shattered accustomed political-party frameworks. It has created a major new principle of political division that has both cut across the party systems of Left and Right with which most of the countries of the Americas and Europe have tried to regulate the allocation of state power and public goods for about two centuries. "Globalists," who believe in and benefit from the new flows of capital and employment, confront "territorialists," who fear that their jobs and traditional values are being sacrificed. Each of these camps has its own Left and Right. The globalist Left urges state intervention to create new employment and assist those displaced; the globalist Right, often labeled neoliberal, stresses the imperatives of market competition and is confident that the further the process goes the wealthier societies become. The territorialist Left believes that the removal of trade barriers has destroyed jobs and urges government intervention to sustain employment at home while the territorialist Right tends to emphasize strengthening borders against migration and often includes the groups we think of as "Populist." Our traditional parties contain both globalists and territorialists. The result has been two or three decades of often muddled politics and the rise of more xenophobic parties and candidates.

But this inquiry is not about globalization per se or the persistence of ethnic loyalties and nationalist passions. Rather it concerns the capacity and the resources for effective governance that national space and frontiers once provided but seem to no longer. No one can overlook the lurid fires of communal loyalties, religious passion, and the advances of a global populism. But these forces do not restore national industry, confidence in economic growth, or familiar cultural homogeneity. They do testify to the search for primitive bonds as the more abstract loyalties of territorial inclusiveness slowly disintegrate. The question here is not which new claimants will get a state or who will dominate a state. Neither is it how ethnically pure a state, old or new, will become. It is, rather, what can one do with the territory at the basis of statehood? What livelihood or psychic belonging will it provide; what self-sufficiency can it claim? The answers can help resolve more policy-oriented questions concerning the consequences for domestic politics, for international order, and for capitalist economies.

Not every people has thought it useful or important to establish fixed and clear-cut borders. There are alternative concepts for claiming shares of global space and seeking territorial stability without fixed frontiers. Nomadic peoples have staked out territories, in effect, with varying perimeters, homelands sometimes with an ancestral core but often shifting, whether seasonally or long term. Such confederated peoples can live in a parallel relationship with their more settled neighboring communities, sometimes extracting tribute, slaves, women, and animals in fierce warfare. Sometimes they are described as tribal, but not always. When they have had military talent—as did the Mongols, Turks, Comanche, and ambitious nineteenth-century African chieftains—their polities have achieved vast extensiveness in space. But they have also tended to change character rapidly, sometimes fragmenting, sometimes becoming absorbed into the more regulated states they conquered. And for those tribal communities that persisted, their geographic range and possibilities for legal autonomy were progressively reduced in the late nineteenth century outside of remote forest or desert environments. Living with a frontier and within a frontier has tended to carry the day.[10]

———

As an examination of territory, this must be an inquiry into political space, not a history of landscape or natural environment. Some of the greatest histories written in the past century, such as Marc Bloch's study of rural France or Fernand Braudel's survey of the Mediterranean basin in the sixteenth century, organize great swaths of human life in terms of the geographical regions that contain them. The land on which people settle, which they transform by cultivation or environmental abuse, remains the theme of much history—sometimes close studies of micro-localities, sometimes vast panoramas. Simon Schama has written a monumental study of particular landscapes—forests, mountains, rivers. Scholars such as John McNeill, the late John F. Richards, Richard White, Mark Elvin, and David Blackbourn (to cite only a few writing in English) have focused on the records of ecological transformation or despoliation.[11] Along with anthropologists, historians have related such changes to economic systems—plantation slavery or commercial farming, overfishing and forest clearances, slash-and-burn agriculture designed to respond to the demands of colonial powers for cash commodities. There are studies, too, of land as a scarce resource, of landscapes and wilderness as finite goods, whether naturally rare or socially coveted. This book, however, attempts something different. It is not so much a history of places—real or imagined, nurturing or ravaged—but a history of the organization of the earth's surface by law, war, commerce, and technological change. Neither is it a history of the state, but rather of an underlying framework that makes states and economies possible. The narratives overlap and intertwine but are not identical.

Nonetheless, the relationship of territory to the state or to a national economy requires specification. Territoriality in the world as we experience it does not present itself apart from the qualities of politics or economics or social connections that are organized with respect to their spatial extent. We ascribe territorial qualities to social and political organizations to make them function. René Descartes, who followed the territorial struggles of his era up close, proposed that the common attribute of things in the material world was their "extension," a foundational basis for their sensory manifestations of mass, size, and shape. In a similar sense, territoriality is manifested less as a quality in its own right than as a property implicated with historical phenomena that change, whether frontiers, states, sovereignty, or economic resources. So the history of territoriality must remain an investigation into the activities in which territory has a formative presence: military strategy, cartography, property claims, economic production, and exchange. Critics may object that I am telling the story of these latter phenomena, like beads strung on a chain that cannot itself be seen within the stones. The claim is stronger, however. It is that the historical phenomena discussed below would not characterize aspects of human experience without the common thread of territoriality. Not all historical subjects need involve spatiality directly; the ones described in the chapters that follow do. They testify to the potential of bordered space even as they are made possible by its existence.

Still, the story is not really causal. Territoriality does not play the generative role that Marxists assign to class conflict, Freudians to the Oedipus complex, or biologists to genes. Wars for territory result from conflicting ambitions or collective insecurity, not geography per se. The economic exploitation of territory involves the organization of labor and technology; output does not just flow from the earth. But social scientists better comprehend these ambitions or arrangements for production and exchange by tracing how their protagonists have understood the geographic space in which they take place.[12] Territory is usefully thought of as a domain in which geographic space is ordered by certain rules or properties that are ascribed to it, perhaps somewhat the way mathematical fields express the logical possibilities for combining numbers. Examining the logic of territoriality throws a new light on the history unfolding in spatial frameworks.

It is intriguing to probe this logic and analyze how territory "works." To date, it is geographers who have naturally focused on this question, as have ethologists or students of animal species who have recognized that territorial behavior plays a large role in the relations between and within species. As a resource by virtue of which societies enforce important collective outcomes, territory confers its value precisely because it is scarce—limited absolutely by the size of the global surface, and limited just as fundamentally in social or political terms by the number of societies or elites and rulers who covet it. In this sense territory remains a zero-sum asset: one power can accumulate territory only at the cost of others, whether external challengers or internal rivals. (This is not to deny that institutional ingenuity has allowed shared sovereignty regimes over contested regions, whether by assigning extraterritorial enclaves or by cessions of financial or judicial rights.)

But if the finite nature of territory renders it valuable to those possessing or controlling it, its benefits are not solely exclusive. Theory and history both suggest that territoriality, or the properties of exclusivity and control that territory confers, provides some of the qualities of a public good and others that are restricted in nature. The classical test of a public good is whether it can exclude so-called free riders or those who benefit from its existence without having to share the costs of making it possible, such as a road maintained privately but open to all users. The stability and peace that can be achieved *within* territories is a public good. On the other hand, territoriality requires the capacity both to exclude possible beneficiaries and to legally constrain those within who might wish to opt out of obligations. It comes into existence only when particular groups or individuals wrest control of global surface vis-à-vis other claimants. To be sure, they can subdivide territory or assign some of the governmental capacities it creates to subordinate authorities for more efficient functioning. Analogously, governments have created private wealth for the sake of economic development by allocating formerly free or plentiful goods. The United States and Canada distributed frontier territory to railroad companies; later, Americans auctioned off rights to "spectrum space" or electromagnetic frequency bands to radio and television stations. In sum, establishing and developing territory allows private benefits even as it generates public goods, It thus provides the spatial foundation for differentially benefiting subjects within but sufficiently for the general resident (at least those not forcibly subjected to servitude or colonial conquest) to nurture consent, loyalty, and legitimacy. The history of territorialization incorporates a continuing dialectic of public possibilities and private appropriation.

Successive epochs of territoriality in the last half millennium have been characterized by their changing approaches for appropriating resources from spatial enclosure—ideological and moral resources as well as claims on labor and material rewards. It may help the reader to have a rough map of the chapters that follow and that are organized around these evolving ambitions and capacities. Chapters 1 and 2 distinguish between competing manifestations of delimiting territorial space: the spaces of expanding empire, a historical feature since ancient times, and the newer space of the early modern sovereign state. Modern territoriality developed alongside, indeed as a component of the ideas of modern sovereignty, which in the West, at least, involved claims for the supremacy of political over religious authority. (In the Islamic and Confucian worlds, these could not readily be separated.) Sovereignty and territory emerged as twinned concepts in the seventeenth century, associated today primarily with the writings of Jean Bodin and Thomas Hobbes and the partially new European state system implied by the Treaties of Westphalia, which ended the Thirty Years' War. The treaties gave their name to so-called Westphalian sovereignty, characterized (albeit somewhat misleadingly) by its regime of separate states each fully empowered within a given territory.[13]

The focus of these chapters, though, is not primarily on theory, but on the practices associated with establishing territorial sovereignty, above all in the seventeenth century those concerned with drawing and sometimes fortifying frontiers. Bordering state space established the domain of law and control. It determined the transactions between subjects within and peoples outside: their trade, their coexistence, their right to cross or transport in each direction, the tribute that might be collected. Thus the emergence of state space began with a discussion of what one French writer has called "the invention of the frontier."[14]

Territorial security is a fundamental resource for political authority. But it is not the only asset. The size of a population, its education, and its capacity to draw wealth from agriculture, mining, and forest products are also resources. So is the power to extract wealth and labor and skills from families and individuals and local communities or religious associations. The second thrust of developing territorial control consisted of organizing space *within* borders, and that story comprises Chapters 3 and 4 of this study. Developments in the eighteenth and nineteenth centuries in particular added the capacity of economic productivity to the resources of political sovereignty. Social-science analysis and common usage alike distinguish between the political role played by territory and the role of land as property, which is global surface (and sometimes subsurface and air rights, too) that has been partitioned for the sake of income and wealth. In fact, these two assets conferred by establishing territory—power and wealth—flow into each other. Since political authority usually requires revenue, territorial control often entails control over property as well, or at least conflict over revenues.

At stake in the early modern period were both the legal and constitutional relationship of landownership to political authority and the relationship of peasants to landowners. Changes in these relationships, analyzed below, were among the fundamental historical transitions of the early modern and modern eras. Just as the emergence of modern maps testified to the concern with state boundaries, so the increased production of cadasters, that is, maps of property holdings, revealed the rationalization of the countryside and its economic potential, whether for the state fisc or for private landowners. The "cadastral century"—in Europe, a period we might trace from about 1680 to 1820—signaled in turn the great movement that freed up the land, and the labor that worked the land, which is described in this study as the commodification of the countryside. Efforts to substitute general rules of movement and of markets for land and labor rather than to rely on personal control over individuals allowed both great periods of enrichment and great movements of unrest. The upheaval in the agrarian world associated with the substitution of market relations for patrimonial or "feudal" extraction is a change sometimes described in terms of the end of the ancien régime and the freeing of agricultural labor—although this transition often degenerated into the substitution of debt relations for legal servitude.

This profound rural transformation has been described in many works as a chapter of political economy. The treatment here, however, seeks to understand the changes within the matrix of a competitive territorial order. Reforming the productivity of the countryside was not just a transnational exercise but an imperative of territorial governance. Changes were spurred in part by doctrines that focused on agricultural productivity—ideas epitomized by eighteenth-century Physiocracy, although with a global influence far broader than those who write on the French theorists sometimes realize. At their center was the relationship of the productive peasant to well-bordered land, land often wrested from religious property holders (secularization) and from customary collective control.

The Industrial Revolution brought significantly new capacities for augmenting control of large expanses of territory. These included, of course, the development of the railroad, steamship, telegraph, and all the mechanisms that immensely speeded communication of people, goods, and ideas. But they did more, as Chapter 5 seeks to demonstrate. They let extensive territories be governed, so to speak, in real time: they conveyed the sense that national space was a realm of relatively simultaneous application of control. Troops could be moved swiftly, instructions instantaneously. Such permeation of territory by central authorities foreclosed sooner or later of nomadic or tribal alternatives, which henceforth could survive only in remote peripheries of large or underdeveloped empires. The national territory became envisaged as an energy field, where the power of the state could be transmitted to any point along lines of force. The technological innovations accompanied a vast new capacity for social knowledge, for enumerating peoples and resources. Modern states as we knew them until very recently emerged from this quantum leap in technologies in the nineteenth century.[15]

Finally, for many rulers and peoples, the very extent of territory often constituted an almost fetishized measure of state success, powerful enough certainly to motivate aggression or costly defense and war in general. Size mattered; inviolability was crucial. By the late nineteenth century and often earlier, the extent of territory itself frequently seemed the overriding index for measuring national welfare. If a state could not easily expand its share of the saturated European terrain, it might acquire vast possessions in other continents. Late nineteenth-century and early twentieth-century leaders, sometimes prodded by adventurers and entrepreneurs, developed an obsession with enclosing territory in overseas empires, where hitherto trading rights or legal extraterritorial access and control of river mouths had satisfied imperial powers. Enthusiastic intellectuals contributed to theories of strategy based on control of continental space and communications. So-called geopolitics, discussed in Chapter 6, supposedly promised the key to the rise and fall of empires according to the size, shape, location, and industrial infrastructure of great landmasses. Its almost cultlike devotees became all the more influential when political commentators assumed that geographical space must be associated once again (as during the age of religious wars) with ideological properties. The world wars and the Cold War saw the territorialization of ideologies as a central stake in global survival.

The successive transformations of territoriality recounted in the chapters that follow have accompanied other major historical transitions. This study does not claim that changes in the properties attributed to territory have produced these political and economic watersheds. But it is based on the idea that profound shifts in our ideas of territory accompany fundamental political and economic changes—and are accompanied, too, by shifting scientific and philosophical concepts of space (and time). At the end of this research, we can argue for epochs of historical development that differ from conventional narratives. Modern territoriality emerged in the seventeenth century. It came to involve systematic exploitation of economic resources in the eighteenth, and it triumphed as the principle for organizing collective life (at least among Europeans and their American offshoots) in the second half of the nineteenth century and the first two thirds of the twentieth. The changes that took place from the Renaissance onward augmented its persuasive hold on the imagination of states and rulers by adding new economic and technological possibilities for the political organization of global space. They also helped render alternatives unviable. Only since the 1970s has this ineluctable territorialization seemed to falter.

For all the formidable objections raised by postmodern analyses, I persist in believing in the value of causal narratives. If compelled to choose, I would point to the material and technological possibilities of each epoch, fully aware that the latter emerge from intellectual advances. Ultimately, the historical world is simultaneously overdetermined (given the inextricability of causal logics) and underdetermined (given the horizons of knowledge) in its openness to surprise and contingency.

At the end of the Cold War, with its overhanging menace of nuclear catastrophe, it appeared to some that territorial rivalries along with ideological ones would no longer hold the great powers in their grip. A post-territorial era seemed conceivable along with a consensus on human rights and democratic government. That happy future has dissipated in the current century, buffeted by the long shadow of 9/11 and the economic troubles that have lasted for most of a decade now. Territorial consciousness and institutions still maintain a grip, as revealed by struggles for statehood and sovereignty, claims to citizenship, and the challenge of migration. Territorial thinking is not still confined by dependence on the limited landed surface of the globe. The open seas, as we shall see, came to be defined as a portal for all. Likewise, outer space is not yet subject to the exclusive claims that constitute territory. The "space" of electronic communication has been partitioned; just turn your radio dial to be reminded. But these assigned wavelengths can have unlimited receivers; the spectrum is semiterritorial. Ambiguities attend the Internet and World Wide Web and e-mail, as they have traditional information and media. "Cyberspace is not a public commons; it is not like international waters or the moon," a recent expert has claimed. "It is not a collection of territories that governments or militaries could effectively control—even if we were to ask them to."[16] But, she goes on to suggest, it is nonetheless a domain of potential conflict and damage—thus perhaps like an ocean infested by pirates, some licensed by sovereigns. For the moment cyberspace is both pre-territorial and post-territorial. Meanwhile we are faced, too, with earlier conundrums, such as who gets to regulate international corporations or call human rights violators to account. Historical inquiry cannot resolve these puzzles, but it can illuminate earlier tensions between common and proprietary space. Human societies have not liberated themselves from territoriality, but they continue to transform it. What follows aspires to show how and why. We all share the sense that we live in a transformative moment of territoriality. The ground is shifting under our feet—never a reassuring feeling—but hopefully this work will provide some perspective on the process.

1

Spaces of Empire
(1500–1650)

THE SPACE OF EMPIRE IS RESTLESS and contested at its perimeter. Sometimes the soldiers at the edge of empire despair at its extent. It cannot go on forever, but it pulls them ever outward. Marguerite Yourcenar, the French writer who conjured up the world of Rome from her aerie on the Maine coast, imagines the Roman emperor Trajan weeping on the shore of the Persian Gulf: "for the first time the immensity of the world overwhelmed him. . . . The supreme commander who had borne the Roman eagles to hitherto unexplored shores knew now that he would never embark upon that sea so long in his thoughts: India, Bactria, the whole of that vague East which had intoxicated him from afar, would continue to be for him only names and dreams."[1] Expanding empires have an extensive boundary region or contact area: an open borderland—so the Chinese frontier poets, the soldier literati, write—stretching "until the end of the sky." This is land beyond the Great Wall, which was constructed in antiquity and then restored under the Ming (1368–1644) as a defensive rampart. But the expansionist dynasties, the earlier Tang and the later Qing, leave the Wall behind to decay, to stand "lopsided as if high costs exhausted the old dragon's heart. In the very end what was it constructed for, by what people?"[2] The German soldiers invading Russia from 1915 to 1917, then again in the summer and fall of 1941, advance rapidly across a charred and primitive landscape, but the land stretches on and on and sometimes they confide their uneasiness to their diaries.

Two Spatial Imaginaries

Political communities suggest to their citizens, their adversaries, and their observers a characteristic geography; they evoke broad-brush visions of territory or what can be called recurring spatial imaginaries. For units larger than the independent cities of antiquity or the Renaissance, two major alternatives can be contrasted: the *space of empires* and the space of less extensive and usually more cohesive territories—termed here the *space of states*. The space of empire is characterized by chronic unrest at the periphery and the often uneven grip of central authority within. Empires have tolerated enclaves of local autonomy and relatively loose frameworks for adherence of tributary communities. Some claimants to empire, such as the Russian tsars and Ottomans, developed ideas of a coherent territory only relatively late and thought primarily in terms of tribal overlordship.[3] The space of states aspires to frontiers stabilized by treaty—often as well by the so-called natural barriers of rivers and mountains—and to a more direct, uniform, and pervasive administration at home.

Granted, the distinction between the space of empires and the space of states is never absolute, nor are the types of polity always distinct. The empire, after all, is a type of state, and some rulers whom historians describe as governing "mere" states had imperial pretensions, claimed multiethnic territories, and adopted imperial images and claims. Henry VIII and his advisers saw Britain in these ambitious terms; so did Sweden's Gustavus Adolphus, who depicted himself in imperial laurels, held German and Finnish territory, humbled the Danes, contained Muscovy, and was Protestant champion.[4] The title of the Japanese ruler, *tenno,* is translated as "emperor," but until Japan took up Western-style imperialism in the late nineteenth century, the *tenno* was monarch of a recognizable national state, as was the German kaiser after 1870.

The United States, officially forswearing the title of empire, continually expanded into regions populated by indigenous peoples, and in so doing created a de facto imperial frontier. British and French colonial authorities had recognized Native American communities as polities with whom treaties should be struck, even as it tucked them into its expanding territory. With independence came the recognition by former colonists that in terms of size their new nation would be an empire that would be as extensive as Macedon's or Rome's or, in Jefferson's words, an "empire of liberty."[5] During the course of the nineteenth century, Washington increasingly treated the western territories as a colonial domain where early treaties could be revised at will and whose reserves of land might be taken, purchased, or leased from other powers with prior claims—all this before trans-Pacific annexations took place at the end of the nineteenth century. With expansion came the traditional rhetoric of empire. American apologists talked about a great underlying value or purpose—enforcing peace and law, transmitting a unifying and supposedly superior culture, including often Protestant religions and public health, later a mission couched in terms of spreading democracy and economic progress. Its ruling groups thought and continue to think in terms of a regional or global vocation.

———

Other territorial understandings existed, both just as ancient but increasingly vulnerable in the modern era. One was the space of the city-state, the other the space identified with so-called nomads or tribes. The sovereign or independent city-state—whether the Greek polis, the later medieval Italian republic, or Central European principality (both sometimes confederated into Leagues, Lombard, or Hanseatic), or even the South Asian sultanate—remained a focused theater of civic participation with a symbolically fraught municipal center or *urbs,* and a small agricultural hinterland. Even when cities could not retain autonomy, their concentrated spaces served as representations of wider domains. Princes reconstructed their walls and gates, fortifications and street grids, parks and arches, to display their broader authority within a confined arena.[6] And with skillful leadership and favorable geography, many succeeded in preserving their independence into the early modern era—in a Switzerland hard to conquer, as coastal enclaves in the Adriatic, or along Arabian seas and the Indian Ocean. So, too, religious authorities, whether electoral archbishops in the Holy Roman Empire, or the pope, or Buddhist monasteries in East Asia, often claimed their own temporal and territorial rights.

Nomad space was occupied by tribal confederations that often sustained their communal life by their pronounced ecological characteristics: in some cases a highland environment, in others steppe and grassland, and in some places coastal wetlands and forests. The polities based there maintained a strong sense of entitlement to the areas in which they lived or migrated with the seasons. Often they preserved a sense of religious communion with its natural landmarks, but they did not necessarily claim exclusive control of its space unless reacting to encroaching empires. Borderlands where empires contended but had not yet established unchallenged territorial control allowed indigenous peoples the chance to negotiate their tribal survival.. Indian leaders could seize a political role by opportune alliances with the imperial claimants, especially if they controlled a desirable economic resource such as the fur trade in the North American Great Lakes region. Indeed warring tribal confederations might mobilize rival European claimants against their own enemies, a tactic, however, that could end with their own subordination. Where possible, the native peoples tried to negotiate with multiple European authorities, for "an accommodation that relied solely on a single European power was an almost . . . certain path to extinction."[7] Thus as sheltering borderlands where sovereignty remained ambiguous were succeeded by clearly demarcated territories, tribal communities faced ethnic cleansing and quasi genocidal perils. The Algonquian and Iroquois confederations in the "middle ground" of the Great Lakes where French and British claims collided preserved a politically influential role until the advancing United States staked its own claims in the early nineteenth century. The Seminole and Creeks in the Florida region found an international role until the Spanish ceded to the United States.[8] Between the 1680s and 1757 the Zhungar people of western China, led by the ambitious political leader Galdan, lost their political autonomy, their male cadres, their communal existence to the expanding Qing empire and its allies in firming up an agreed on border.[9]

Where old or new imperial rulers could not really penetrate local power structures, nomadic remnants could persist in the great interior landmasses even after they were finally regulated and confined by the expanding empires and nations of the eighteenth and nineteenth centuries. The Persian state was in no position to suppress tribal organization and identity until the Pahlavi dynasty after 1926, but tribal leaders became mediators of state power even while they were spokesmen for their own polity.[10] The Europeans who moved into Africa late in the nineteenth century sometimes sought to preserve political intermediaries even as they might ruthlessly exploit tribal labor. In Central Asia and Africa, some maintained their quasi autonomy into the twentieth century and indeed still do so.

Empires and states, however, increasingly dominated the patterns of territorial organization, and their territorial attributes need to be analyzed in turn. For each group the nature of the frontier remained a critical property. Precarious, and often provisional, expanding or eventually shrinking, frontiers dominated the political contests within empires. They had to be continually negotiated, drawn and redrawn. The formidable antiliberal German theorist of power and law Carl Schmitt (1888–1985) connected the epoch of European imperial expansion in the sixteenth century with the first effort at "global boundary thinking" *(globales Liniendenken)*. "Immediately after the discovery of the new world the struggle begins for the appropriation of this new world's land and seas. The partitioning and allocation of the earth increasingly becomes a common affair for the people and powers who exist alongside each other on the very earth they are dividing."[11] But Schmitt was theorizing a common European imperial effort that allegedly led its ambitious participants to negotiate a pluralist international order among themselves as they appropriated non-European land. He did not look within each empire and, it hardly needs mention, ignored the conquered peoples, who made no appearance in his treatise. From the perspective of the expanding empire, the expanding frontier appeared less of a sanctified border than a geographic respite of convenience, a provisional resting point for yet another thrust outward.

During their eras of expansion, conquerors and colonizers exploited characteristic geographic features, long recognized by scholars. They left the old walls behind, as the Chinese warrior poets recognized, and advanced over great grassy plains or deserts or wide seas and on far shores to penetrate up the long rivers into the interior. Marc Bloch noted how Norse warriors used the Seine and other French rivers to establish their states, as they exploited communication by the sea to seize Sicily as well.[12] But geography (interacting with the circumstances of succession) also imposed institutional constraints after conquest. Large land empires might have to be divided, as was the case for Rome and even more quickly for the vast conglomerates conquered by Alexander in the fourth century

B.C.E., Charlemagne's Central Europe more than a millennium later, and the realms from the Black Sea and Fertile Crescent to the Pacific accumulated by Chinggis Khan before 1270.

Stabilizing empire is difficult; it is no accident that "rise and fall" or "decline and fall" furnish the narrative tropes. Even without division, administering the far perimeters of empire led to characteristic territorial expedients that often escaped control from the center. One pattern comprised the semiautonomous military domains, the Marks or Marches or voivods of Central and southeastern Europe, or even, as it turned out by 1931, by the Japanese military occupiers of Manchuria. Another paradigm was the cloned settlement replicating, but without full independence, the local and regional governments of the home country, such as British settler colonies, or the U.S. "territories" in the annexed interior of North America. The local elites, especially the "creoles" of the mother country's ethnic stock or even subjects of mixed race, will rarely accept a subordinate status for long. Programs for full incorporation—for example, Caracalla's extension of Roman citizenship in 212 to all freemen in the empire, or long afterward the Americans' blueprint for elevating western U.S. territories into statehood—were needed.

So long as an empire was successful, that is "rising," its space tended to be dynamic. To dig in at the frontier intimated decline. The Turkish historian Suraiya Faroqui reports that the Ottomans during their heyday in southeastern Europe negotiated linear borders really as temporarily acceptable halting points. "Ottoman land borders were imagined, in early modern Europe, to be broad, porous, and impermanent," Palmira Brummett similarly observes.[13] In the sixteenth century, efforts to negotiate boundaries with Venetian or Polish-Lithuanian territories yielded no definitive results. Only by 1681 did a Polish-Ottoman border commission start to establish a demarcated boundary. It is not that empires do not have walls; indeed they do, but the walls tend to emerge as structures of defensive consolidation when the energy of expansion flags, or when prudence prevails over ambition as the peoples encountered in the intermediate trading zone become threatening, whether as ethnic immigrants or hostile soldiers.

Frontiers at the edge of an expanding empire were thus zonal, not linear—more regions of cultural and ethnic osmosis than firm barriers.[14]

One segment or another of the imperial perimeter, whether at the edge of its landmass or overseas, was usually contested and the site of rebellion and resistance. Enthusiasts at home believed the fighting invigorated the commonwealth and helped maintain civic health. Opening new territory supposedly provided a "safety valve" to relieve domestic tensions. Frederick Jackson Turner famously argued that the openness of the American frontier, which as of the 1890 census could no longer be represented as a continuous line of settlement, had nurtured democracy. For the generation of 1890 in Europe, America, and Japan that carried colonialism (along with such related projects as Alpinism, big-game hunting, organizing Boy Scouts, and the revived Olympic games) to a climax of annexationist and manly enthusiasms, the project of empire would also integrate a potentially revolutionary proletariat into a national consensus even as it prevented liberalism and prosperity from degenerating into mere civic indolence. The peace within empire—Pax Romana, Pax Britannica, or Pax Americana—allegedly existed symbiotically with the continuing and invigorating tension at the militarized frontier.[15]

The zonal frontier often cited as one distinguishing property of empire—the frontier as a "march" or as a strip of ethnic exchange—usually was found only in the farther reaches of its territory, such as the Russian steppe, the American great plains, the Ottomans' Danubian marches or Mesopotamian perimeter, the northern forests or arid western highlands of the Qing realm, or the new lands claimed by European powers across the seas. Earlier historians stressed their brutal and violent properties; recent researchers like to emphasize the cultural and commercial mixing that took place. American historians have paid a great deal of attention to the zones of contact in North and South America from the sixteenth through the nineteenth centuries.[16] In an understandable effort to stress the agency of indigenous peoples, historians now deploy the catchword *negotiation;* it recurs over and over again, as if every accommodation was reached after a peaceful parley.[17] Many of these negotiations, of course, were deals that could not be refused, or, if refused, triggered violent coercion before settlements (or surrenders) were reached.

Turbulent imperial frontiers existed on the margins of European settlement in the Americas, the Caribbean, and Australia, but also at the margins of Qing and Muscovite expansion (which ultimately served each other's interests in suppressing the Zhungar confederations in between), and in the regions where Ottomans, Persian Safavids, and Mughals had to sort out each other's conflicting aspirations. Ottomans and German Habsburgs confronted each other in another major early modern frontier zone, the Danubian regions of today's Hungary, and Croatia. In the same eras, Spanish Habsburgs faced Ottomans along the North African coasts while Venetians defended their island holdings in the Mediterranean. Whether a zone of cultural and commercial contact or the site of frightening acts of violence—or often the one punctuated by the other—the frontier of empire that faced outward remained, in effect, an extended glacis that separates the realm of law from the barbarian.

But sparsely populated frontiers, however, were not the only border; empires bordered on other empires, where frontiers might be clearly inscribed, but contested over centuries. Empires also abutted on organized states whose sovereignty they recognized, even if they sometimes wanted them in tributary status. Europeans who came to the Americas in the sixteenth and seventeenth centuries recognized some indigenous confederations as treaty partners (the Creek and Seminole and Cherokee in the southern United States and Iroquois in the north) but sometimes claimed that they were expanding into territories they could appropriate for their own sovereign use because they did not confront what they understood to be organized states or a native sense of property—the "new world" was *terra nullius*. But in South Asia the same national actors understood that they were entering a region of highly complex, layered sovereignties with whose rulers formal treaties had to be concluded.[18]

Empires also confronted more structured regions of conflict in their own front yards or backyards: facing the French on the Pyrenees, Charles V envisaged a state frontier that was hardly vague. He erected fortifications vis-à-vis Francis I, just as Francis's late seventeenth-century successor, Louis XIV, was to build them against the Habsburgs. So, too, in their viceroyalty of Naples, the Duchy of Milan, or confronting their rebellious subjects in the Lowlands, the Spanish Habsburgs adopted the mentality and architectural practices of competitive and crowded state space in general. The Mughal emperor Aurangzeb (1658–1707) warred continually along relatively static lines against the Maratha states to his south, even as the British East India Company officials inserted themselves into a crumbly but highly developed political framework and thought it important from the viewpoint of international law to be awarded the high Mughal administrative office of diwani as they became sovereign (if not suzerain) over Bengal, Bihar, and Orissa in the northeast of the subcontinent. For all these diverse reasons, the aspirations of empire often bog down in the contentious acreage analyzed in Chapter 2 as the space of states.

Empires and lesser states can morph into each other. Empires are often assembled by the conquest of well-organized states, not just the absorption of tribal confederacies. Conversely, the territorial entities that have seceded from the overarching framework of empires or have managed to preserve their time-honored independence jealously guard an international status no less sovereign than empires claim. In Europe after 1648 their rulers were also recognized as possessing supreme political authority over their own territory—subject to agreed-on "Christian" norms that bound them collectively.[19] For these nonimperial sovereigns, territory remained a scarcer commodity and often required a firmer container. Their state frontier became more "linear," even though abutting states might postpone exact mapping along remote stretches.

For all the properties of interior authority and frontier enclosure that they might share, the space of empires and the space of states evoked different enough mental maps to suggest alternative missions and strategies for ruling. Conceptualizations of the frontier played a major role in implanting these two spatial imaginaries. Empires were indeed often created from the outside in, or at least emerged from the interaction of frontier with the historical center. Caesar had to cross the Rubicon to challenge the Senate and people of Rome. Various historical interpretations attribute preeminence to the frontier in the creation of institutions. The Ghazi warrior, or crusading Islamic soldier of the Ottoman frontier, was alleged to have stamped his character on the Ottoman Empire. James Billington wrote his magisterial interpretation of Russia in terms of icon and ax: religion and the forest frontier. A major interpretation of British imperial expansion has been based on the turbulence of the frontier and the inability to stabilize it. Imperial republics supposedly had their political culture as well as their voracious expansionism forged at the undefined borderlands of settlement: Frederick Jackson Turner attributed America's democratic values to vast accessible lands, closing as he wrote. Argentine historians stressed the role of the gaucho and the pampas (not really the frontier, but the opposite of the metropolis). The drawing of frontiers in faraway colonies became an obsessive component of Europeans' late nineteenth-century imperialism, and found a classic justification in Lord Curzon's notable lecture on frontiers in 1907, inspired by his long preoccupations about the Himalayan boundary of the Raj.[20]

But the yearning for a stable frontier, for an idealized *limes* marked by a river or a mountain ridge or a formidable wall, is rarely fulfilled in a vigorous empire. How can it be when imperial dreams call for continuing expansion! And there, where borders are less clear-cut and military or proconsular authority less circumscribed—whether because passage at sea is essential, or imperial claims extend upriver into vast forest realms of the interior, or because tribal confederations rather than organized ongoing states confront the metropole's expansionary ambitions—the space of empire prevails and its edge is always a restless zone, prone to violence and contested legal claims. Size was the reward for unrest at the frontier. Size mattered; territorial extension remained compelling and fascinating both for contemporaries and those who followed. Empire builders were both megalomaniac and awesome. They would conquer long-standing peoples and empty lands alike. As Christopher Marlowe had Tamburlaine (Timur) declare to his betrothed:

> Were Egypt Jove's own land,
> Yet would I with my sword make Jove to stoop.
> I will confute those blind geographers
> That make a triple region in the world,
> Excluding regions which I mean to trace,
> And with this pen [reduce them to a map,
> Calling the provinces, cities, and towns,
> After my name and thine, Zenocrate. . . .
> We mean to travel to th' antarctic pole,
> Conquering the people underneath our feet,
> And be renown'd as never emperors were.[21]

Epochs of Empire

There is a time as well as space for empires. They possess typical temporal trajectories as well as territorial patterns. Individual empires, historical comparison suggests, require ruthless vigor, conquest, and reform to become established and notable. Then they excite rivals on the margins; their elites absorb revenues on the local level that are needed by the central administration; imperial succession produces repeated crises, contestation, and often rebellion. No wonder their vicissitudes encourage grand theories about rise and fall, whether Mediterranean notions of *fortuna,* Ibn Khaldun's sense of Nomadic inner softening, Marxist-derived ideas about the exhaustion of surplus value, or Paul Kennedy's notion of imperial overstretch. The historical and social-science explanations find equivalents in poetry, novels, and painting—for instance, Thomas Cole's cycle of canvases created in the mid-nineteenth century. Whether historical or aesthetic, these are meditations about the rise and fall of individual empires.

Traditional histories of imperial expansion also propose a model of successive hegemonic bids and their ultimate defeat. The German historian Ludwig Dehio wrote a brief classic that treated Philip II of Spain, Louis XIV, Napoleon, and Hitler as case studies of successive megalomaniacs cut down to size by the opposing coalitions their ambitions conjured up.[22] But what was happening was not so simple a drama. Examining successive epochs of empire, a different question intrudes: Why are there periods that seem relatively favorable to the rise of imperial organizations across large areas of the globe, and periods that seem more adverse? There are always imperial contenders, but some eras stand out by virtue of the many that seem to thrive together.

Taking a metaphor from accounts of climate change and the advance and retreat of the glaciers during the last ice age, can we provide, in effect, a theory of imperial glaciation? Three or four epochs of territorial consolidation and disaggregation on a global scale stand out during recorded history—in particular those marked by Han Chinese and Roman ascendancy, circa 220 B.C.E./560 C.E.; the Turkic-Mongol conquests of 1220–1420; the confluence of global empires (circa 1490–1650) described above, followed by the extension of maritime colonies into the eighteenth century; and then the age of modern imperialism, 1870–1950. The dates in each case are very approximate markers for when early individual dynastic initiatives emerge as major trends.

Major empires had arisen and fragmented from the fourth to the second century B.C.E. Alexander's conquests prolonged by the Seleucids in the Middle East and the Mauryan Empire in northern India comprised a major constellation across south central Asia during the third century B.C.E. Qin Shi Huang, "the first emperor" (221–210 B.C.E.), had established the tradition of a unified Chinese imperial state at a time the Mediterranean world remained fragmented under rival rulers. But if a global geographer had arrived a century to three centuries later, the global state of play would have congealed. In the first two centuries of the Common Era, he or she would have found two vast imperial aggregations at the opposite ends of Eurasia. One unified much of mainland East Asia and the other the diverse peoples of Europe and the Mediterranean world. They were hardly the first large empires, and neither was qualitatively more extensive than the brief personal state created by Alexander. But Rome and Han China had sustained institutional histories; they rested on foundations of law, civil religion, bureaucratic and historical records, and orderly procedures for recruiting cooperative elites. The East Asian state was already long in existence, having been forged and broken and reforged from river-valley and provincial kingdoms over several centuries. It maintained a large army, a conviction of an encompassing culture, binding diverse language and geographical groupings, and an ideology of patriarchal and ethical rule that aligned families, villages, and the imperial state into a hierarchical structure of loyalties. It collected taxes, ensured commerce across long-distance canals, and recruited officials on the basis of an examination system that rewarded merit as well as family wealth.

The empire at the other end of Eurasia likewise recruited a professional army, secured communication by road and ship, and stressed a concept of political and legal belonging that came to be known as citizenship. Smaller imperial or monarchical entities also organized the north and south of India, Southeast Asia, and Mediterranean Africa. But the degree of territorial consolidation in Rome and China was unparalleled in extent. The Roman structure lasted centuries but proved unsustainable. The Chinese structure was subject to periodic long-term crises, invasions from outside, and bureaucratic sclerosis, but as a frame of collective reference it continued to endure.

Perhaps it was a consequence of pressures originating in the Altaic highlands and steppes lying between Rome and China that sent the peoples living in these immense central regions to the west and to the east; perhaps it was harsher conditions for the agrarian masses; perhaps the spreading influence of more subjective and less civic spiritual orientations—in any case both these entities faced disintegrative pressures from the third century on, such that economies became more local, cities were depopulated, and ambitious local strongmen claimed independent local or regional rule. Various efforts were made to reconstitute them. In Western Europe the Carolingians would unite the Germanic and Frankish kingdoms that succeeded Rome for about fifty years, claiming the historic dignity of emperor from the pope, even as the Greek-based inheritor of the Roman Empire survived in reduced territory for many centuries and Arab confederations charged by Muslim religious zeal welded a dynamic and expansionist political structure through the Middle East, the southern littoral of the Mediterranean, and Iberia. Ambitious states emerged in large but relatively self-contained geographical arenas: northern and southern India, Africa, Japan, and Meso-America.

Can we plausibly generalize about the multitude of large state structures that emerged, expanded, and then stabilized or were displaced by new leaders? Before the development of maritime empires, say, from the voyages of Vasco da Gama and Columbus on, two basic patterns of imperial expansion seemed to dominate. The units that could project power and construct institutions across continents arose either at the two edges of Eurasia or on the basis of rapid conquests in its interior landmasses that built on their own momentum to demoralize resistance. Continuous communication for camels and horses served successive generations of warriors. The Arab victories of the seventh and eighth centuries, which also curved around the shores of the southern Mediterranean, were followed by the ascent of vigorous Turkic dynastic states around the millennium and then by the spectacular conquests of the Mongols under Chinggis Khan and his successors, who from about 1100 rode across the steppe lands of Central Asia to China in the east, Persia in the southwest, and the Black Sea littoral in the west, penetrating as far as today's Poland.

In contrast to the legal and state structures constructed by Rome and Han China, each with its awareness of long historical precedent and legal development, inner-Asian imperial bricolage took place under charismatic military leadership in one or two generations and fastened on to the fragile shells of previous conquests or the institutions of neighboring empires. In this respect it resembled more the older achievement of Alexander. The Mongols sought to preserve their conquests by princely decentralization, and the heirs of Chinggis Khan divided his realm into Khanates from the Black Sea to Baghdad, Central Asia, and China and gradually lost their fierce expansionary thrust.[23] Conquerors of settled cultures, they were themselves assimilated by the civilizations they set out to rule. New combinations then asserted themselves: dynasties emerging from the Iranian tribes and the plateaus of today's Afghanistan and northern Pakistan and India.

In the fourteenth and fifteenth centuries, the new vigorous Ottoman state would establish itself as a regional superpower south of the Black Sea, cross to the Balkans, capture the remnants of the Byzantine Empire, and claim the leadership of Islam. To the east another Turkic confederation under Timur (Tamburlaine) would subdue Baghdad, Persia, and Central Asia, and threatened to repeat the earlier Mongol conquest of China, cut short only with the sudden death of its leader; while finally by the mid-sixteenth century a third Turkic people (whom the Persians mistakenly labeled Mongols) would expand from Afghanistan to conquer the Indus and Ganges Valleys and establish the Mughal Empire, even more populous than the Turkish realms.[24]

Just as in earlier epochs, advances in military technology played a major role. The mounted archer whose animals were sustained by the grasslands had served Central Asian expansion from the Parthians to the Mongols. Gunpowder and artillery and long-distance sail after 1450 let the Portuguese, later the Dutch and British, become major players. For Marshall G. S. Hodgson the mid-sixteenth century responded to the innovative power of artillery and firearms, thus the appellation of gunpowder empires.[25] The extended grassy plains of Eurasia also allowed the formation of clan-based confederations that by dint of conquest could build on the culture and wealth and experience of the more settled edges. Tribal "empires" worked on different principles from those that had become sedentary: rapid mobilization over vast areas thanks to horses and archery, intense personal loyalties, and myths of common origin that substituted for the ideological universals that the fixed empires built on. Tribal confederations needed the adjacent settled states from which to draw their resources, slaves, animals, and trade. Locked in rivalry, nomads and consolidated states together created vast constructs of empire on different but complementary principles. Peter Turnchin has thus sought to explain the formation of large ancient empires by the proximity of a steppe frontier, which places one people into sedentary units, and others into arid lands or grasslands.[26] But his model still seeks to explain why and how individual empires arose, what he calls imperiogenesis. The question raised here is why this state form became relatively prevalent at particular moments of time, and could not be maintained at others.

If the global traveler arrived in the first half of the sixteenth century, she or he would find again an epoch of imperial glaciation, like the era of Han and Rome, or the epochs of Chinggis Khan and Timur, in which great imperial structures seemed to prevail and in which size—or at least the reputation of rapid conquest—seemed to confer advantages for state organization. The Ottoman polity had established its ascendancy in Anatolia and the Balkans by this date and defeated the remnant of the Byzantine Empire in 1453. Half a world away, Incas and Aztecs established their imperial regimes in the same decades. The Ming dynasty was at its height and established its capital at Beijing. Eighty years after Timur's death and a century before Marlowe's play, the Europeans rounded Africa to penetrate the Indian Ocean and within another couple of decades understood that they had arrived on a new continent. A world encompassed by great empires seemed closer to fulfillment in the next century and a half than it had for more than a thousand years. The Portuguese, Spanish, Dutch, British, and French established trading colonies and sometimes zones of interior settlement on the coasts of the Atlantic, Caribbean, and South Atlantic, around the Arabian Sea, Indian Ocean, and the archipelagos of Southeast Asia. The Muscovite dynasty extended its domain south and east to the edge of Europe, even as the Polish-Lithuanian Commonwealth united a dominion from the Baltic to the Black Sea and the Austrian Habsburgs asserted themselves along the Danube and in Italy. The once tribally organized peoples of the Asian highlands organized huge imperial domains that reached heights of expansion and cultural attainment—the Ottoman's under Süleyman I, the Persian Safavids, and the Mughals from Afghanistan to Bengal. China's Ming dynasty, preoccupied by bureaucratic rivalries, ecological adversity, and growing rebellion, declined precipitately from the 1620s on and was defeated by a recently organized federation of northeast Asian horsemen. Across the Sea of Japan, a succession of talented military leaders created a stable and stratified polity after decades of "feudal" devolution and civil war.

Scanning the regions of the globe, our sixteenth-century geographer would find the principles of empire—the incorporation of diverse ethnicities and religions, the affirmation of an imperial ideology, and the continuing contestation of the frontier—at their zenith. The Ming and Qing states in China incorporated different modalities of rule, fixed on different perimeters, but each in turn affirmed Chinese imperial unity. The emerging Mughal rulers extended their control from Afghanistan over northern and central India, adding a massive Hindu population to its Muslim core; the Ottoman state was organizing its diverse religious adherents into tolerated consistories or millets even as it claimed the leadership of Islam.

Each empire found itself in continuing warfare, precisely because it confronted ambitious imperial rivals. The Ottomans had encircled the eastern Mediterranean, now as a formidable naval power, and also moved up the Danube, even as they battled the Persians on their eastern borders. Muscovy was pressing back the Tartars and claiming the legacy of Byzantine Rome. The Austrian Habsburgs were seeking to recover their influence in the religiously and territorially fragmented Holy Roman Empire and to stabilize the Hungarian frontier. After Charles V abdicated and the aspiration of universal monarchy slipped, the Austrians remained cousined to the Spanish Habsburgs, who conquered the relatively recently established Mexica (Aztec) and Inca imperial states in Mesoamerica and the Andes. The Portuguese established large land holdings in Brazil as well as their trading post colonies in China, Africa, and India; the Dutch (like the Portuguese) briefly held northeast Brazil and Manhattan but were more durably penetrating the Indonesian archipelago. Once again rulers found that extensive territory and the resources of men and wealth they provided were advantageous to rule. Empire beckoned as a form even where it was not formally institutionalized: the English and the Swedes used its formulae and imagery in the north. It helped that a succession of remarkable monarchs and advisers could hold power for long decades of institution building and relentless military campaigning: Charles V, Maximilian, Philip II, Elizabeth of England, Ivan IV of Russia, Süleyman I, later Shah Abbas of Persia and Akbar of India, even later in the seventeenth century Kangxi and Aurangzeb. But the contingency of favorable life spans can explain only so much, and we still face the puzzle of what conditions favored from time to time the extensive territorial assemblages of rule under a central authority.

The critical historian might suggest that the alleged imperial clustering was illusory, and a detailed census of regimes across the centuries would even out the proportion of empires. Likewise, the very distinctiveness of empire as a polity might seem less salient. The usual objection that every unit in history is unique so that comparison has little purpose will also arise; likewise that the category of empire vis-à-vis other state forms breaks down. These are issues of significance—for example, which characteristics are more important?—and can be answered only subjectively. But I would maintain that imperial clustering is a real phenomenon, and the reason lies precisely in the circumstance that the emergence of an empire favors the development of other empires.[27]

Political scientists have recognized that regime types often come in waves. The interwar period saw the rise of dictatorships and single-party governments. The transformation of Spain, Portugal, Greece, and authoritarian Latin America in the 1980s, then of formerly communist Europe, has been described as a third wave of democratization following on the late eighteenth-century American and French Revolutions, and the 1918–1919 breakup of empires in Central and Eastern Europe. The reasons for multicountry transformations are often underspecified, attributed often to underlying economic conditions or the example of preceding revolutions.[28] The world empires that clustered together were not precipitated simultaneously, but over decades and even centuries tended to reinforce one another's structures and spatial ambitions.

Empire involves at least a double-stranded process of self-reproduction. Once Central Asia became a major strategic as well as commercial axis between the political units of the Mediterranean and East Asia (whether in the third to fifth centuries C.E. when both Rome and the Han were under pressure or under the Mongols or the Timurids), global empires rise and often prosper in groups or systems. Their ascent and survival or faltering and transformation take place in terms or pairs. The study has to be of the system and not just of the individual unit. Historians accept this logic for nonimperial states, but it is as important for imperial states.

In the great landmasses of Asia, such systemic pairing arose from the interplay of nomadic confederations and sedentary civilizations. The rude vigor of the former conquer the rich prey of the latter, create a glorious imperial synthesis, and eventually lose their vitality. This is the dynamic arising in the case of what Thomas Barsfield has called "shadow empires," identified as a cyclical pattern by Ibn Khaldun.[29] That pattern recurred with the Turkic conquests of the fifteenth century: under Timur with the Mughals (who were Turkic), Ottomans, Safavids, and Qing. Martial dynasties batten on wealthy states that have run into domestic resistance to their fiscal extraction or clientelism.

Sometimes the military and expansionist energy of new contenders could bring forth a surge of defensive organizational energy and evoke a surge of administrative and military vigor on both sides. Rival ambitions and confrontations—Hellenic and Persian, Roman and Carthaginian, Habsburg and Ottoman, or Spanish Habsburg and Mexican or Andean, later French and British, Soviet and American—summoned up reciprocal energies. Empires created the opportunity structures for other empires. In the modern era of maritime empires, implicit or explicit alliances characterized several centuries of expansion. Pairs of empires tended to confront each other throughout: Portuguese and Spanish versus English and Dutch; later English and Dutch versus French and Spanish. In the twentieth century, English and American imperial confederations confronted Japanese, German, and Soviet contenders. Survival, expansion, and sometimes exhaustion took part within a framework of cooperative alliances. Sometimes the logical pairings failed to materialize since rivalries were too great to overcome for the sake of strategic rationality. The German-Soviet tandem that might have successfully countered the Anglo-American partnership functioned only tentatively and halfheartedly (at Rapallo in 1922 and under the Ribbentrop-Molotov Pact from 1939 until 1941). Still, successful empires in the modern period tend to prevail in pairs.

The old story of successive hegemons each finally brought low by opposing coalitions thus needs amendment. Global or regional territorial organization is as crucial to the understanding of these structures as what happens at home (or in the new home). China perhaps has been the great and enduring exception, persisting and reorganizing on the basis of its own institutional and cultural momentum, even across the dynastic cycles and conquests. But even its expansion under the Qing can be seen as taking place in tandem with the Russian surge across north central and

East Asia. In Europe, Russia, Austria, and Prussia cooperated to liquidate the Polish Commonwealth and partition its territory even as Russia and the Habsburgs effectively reduced Ottoman holdings in common. The space of empires leads empires to act in partnership as well as to incur enmities. And the acceptance of partnership is another factor that lends fluidity to imperial borderlands. But so, too, do the oceans.

Empires at Sea

"Here the land ends and the sea begins." Portugal's great soldier-poet Camões writes in his epic of maritime empire: *Os Lusiadas* in 1572.[30] The empire sought and won lay on the other side of those seas—but could the oceans themselves constitute an empire or part of an empire? Were they a shared and common realm or a particular domain? These were the issues opened up in the wake of the voyages of Vasco da Gama and Columbus. Empires acquired across the oceans raise some questions in common with the great landed assemblages of the Chinese, the Russians, Ottomans, or Habsburgs, in particular what rights come with conquest? But they open up others, as well: the nature of "discovery," the rights of aboriginal first peoples, the claims of commerce. Overseas empire in antiquity developed from the cloning of colonies on distant shores as city-states sought to reproduce themselves. Colonization from the late fifteenth century originally involved the drive to mobilize wealth through trade or extraction often accompanied by the effort at religious conversion. The Iberian colonizers acted directly in the name of monarch and church; the Dutch and British were to organize trading companies, although the Tudors and Stuarts also conferred huge proprietary grants on ambitious favorites. In the New World, where the imperial powers aspire to acquire the land as such, the captains who administer it are given vast landed holdings and privileges over indigenous labor.[31] In the crowded eastern seas, overseas empire allows powers with little European hinterland to gain great prosperity: Portugal, the Netherlands, and an England torn by religious and dynastic conflict.

The open sea provides the portal to territories on distant shores, but it is *not* a territory. It is in effect one of the frontiers for overseas empire, but for different empires at the same time. If relations among them were amicable, tradition, soon codified into international norms, suggested that it should be a shared site of passage and of fishing—a maritime commons. When relations were competitive and hostile, it became an oceanic no-man's-land. The intercontinental voyages prompted discussion of legal rights and the mobilization of what the lawyers and scholars retrieved from antiquity as the law of nations, jus gentium—common usages and understandings that Spanish scholastics in the sixteenth century, such as Francisco Vitoria, claimed were derived from Christian doctrines of natural law. Most commentators agreed that absent a true world empire—that is, one that spoke for all Christianity—no nation or state could claim exclusive rights to control ocean traffic. To violate the rights of passage and trade in peacetime amounted to piracy, recognized as an international scourge since antiquity and one that could be combated by any power in the name of all—a notion akin to today's idea of universal jurisdiction. Religious rivalry complicated the norms, and Christian and Muslim theorists divided over the protection to be accorded the other community. For the theorists writing in the natural law tradition—Vitoria and Hugo Grotius above all—the right to peaceful commerce followed from the need of all men to ensure their survival.

Nonetheless, maritime or coastal powers often violated the usages of peace, many simply de facto and some citing different legal understanding. The Portuguese, Grotius charged, illegitimately claimed dominium over the seas and the right to control commerce.[32] Moroccan corsairs felt no need to respect Christian shipping. Christians often took advantage of the papal line of arbitration of 1495, dividing Portuguese and Spanish colonial territorial spheres in the New World, and subsequent treaties to suggest that by establishing a defined zone of peace they left much of the oceans in a Hobbesian state of nature: there was "no peace beyond the line." "Beyond the line there are no more friends, and everything afloat is a prize," Étienne de Flacourt wrote from the forlorn French settlement in Madagascar in the mid-seventeenth century. And even in wealthier Malabar across the Indian Ocean, Hendrik van Rheede reported in 1670, "One is at the frontier here and never assured against the cunning of white and other nations and does not know when they will implement some devious plot."[33] The sea, therefore, had the same fuzzy legal status as an imperial border region, separating European concepts of lawful behavior from the treacherous usages of Asian rulers, and, even more dangerous, from the ambitions of their own Christian rivals. For overseas empires the oceans could not remain just a maritime commons: naval conflict was always a possibility, and naval power, expensive and continually to be refined in terms of its technology, was a prerequisite.

From the viewpoint of the Asian powers, Camões famous line could be reversed: "Here the sea ends and the land begins." Rulers of the coastal states and cities in Kerala or along the Oman and Yemen coast and the merchant communities in Surat might draw significant proportions of their revenue from interstate maritime trade, but the major Asian empires did not, even if domestic coastal trade *(cabotage)* was active.[34] For Safavids and Mughals, Qing, and Tokugawa, the important economic activity and tax base was largely internal, overwhelmingly based on the peasant labor force and the production of staples. Maritime trade was for them largely a source of rents and protection money. Outside the Mediterranean (also a theater of contending empires par excellence) Europeans, above all the Portuguese, Spanish, and Dutch in the sixteenth century, controlled the eastern seas, whereas the Asian realms—Mughal, Chinese, Japanese—largely defaulted in terms of countervailing naval power. So did the Ottomans, for reasons that scholars have debated. After one attempt at midcentury by their celebrated navigator and cartographer Piri Reis, they abdicated in the Arabian Seas, somewhat as the Ming had turned its back on the Indian Ocean a century and a half earlier. The lords of the horizon envisaged the expanses of desert, not ocean: overland caravans and new responsibilities as guardians of the holy cities seemed important.[35]

According to Vitoria in the early sixteenth century or Grotius in his early plaidoyer *Mare Liberum* (the chapter published from his 1605 anti-Portuguese polemic *De Iure Praede*) and his mature *Law of War and Peace,* the oceans are a global commons, open to all, whereas the rights to land remain subject to exclusive claims, often contested, to be sure. But here's the rub: the high seas—open to all under the usages of *liberum maris*— were not the same as coastal waters, where local rulers often claimed control of passage and certainly of entrance to their own ports. Ottomans, Mughals, the diverse sultanates and merchant associations of southern Asia, the Chinese and Japanese all sought to control their ports and access to trade, even as the Europeans battled among themselves. But they had less a stake in the trade itself than in the licenses and duties it yielded. In South and Southeast Asia the landed empires had little effective sovereignty over the coasts. Before the British reorganized Bengal and Orissa, the Europeans did not deal with masses of Asian peasants, but with local quasi sovereigns of the South Asian coast, often willing to defect from the relatively weak suzerainty or rather theoretical overlordship of the Mughals, or with the even more autonomous sultans and rulers in the Indonesian archipelago. Once the Europeans arrived the legal privileges had to be negotiated, especially when the Portuguese, Dutch, and English were rivals. Sometimes the privileges involved just the right to trade or even an exclusive right to trade that excluded national rivals. When they could, the Europeans sought their own extraterritorial enclave with a defined and fortified land frontier. Within several decade of passing the Horn of Africa the Portuguese had a string of coastal fortresses. The stakes were high. In volume the Asian trade was dwarfed by Europe's coastal trade, but the money value of the commodities from the Indies was great, and single ships could carry a fortune of bullion or silk or indigo. An accessible port was the gateway to wealth. But local rulers did not yield privileges easily. The European trade was intimately tied to violence or the threat of havoc: "If no fear, no friendship, if no force, no trade."[36]

When Europeans acquired overseas bases they also claimed the right to grant or withhold trading privileges and licenses. The most famous was the *asiento* or the right granted by Madrid from 1543 to 1834 to convey slaves to Spanish holdings. The Portuguese attempted to control Indian Ocean trade by requiring merchant ships to stop at a Portuguese settlement to acquire a *certaz* or maritime passport that stipulated both cargo and armaments or to face the penalty of having their ships confiscated. International usage allowed capture of enemy ships, but the Portuguese claim was illegitimate. Tables were turned by the Dutch. When they first penetrated the eastern seas in 1596, they were still at war with the Spanish. Portugal and its territories had passed to Spanish control in 1580 and would remain so until 1640. In 1602 Hugo Grotius's cousin Jacob van Heemskerck, captured a Portuguese ship, the Santa Catarina, laden with Japanese copper, Chinese silk and porcelain, and bullion from Peru and Mexico, worth three million guilders or about half the capitalization of the Dutch East India Company, the VOC (Verenigde Oost-Indische Compagnie), which was to be consolidated from mergers a year later. Two years later the Dutch also took the fort of Amboyna, whose ruler had given the Portuguese a monopoly on the local spice trade in 1600.

The Portuguese denounced the seizure of the ship as piracy and demanded return of the goods; denunciation of the fort's capture also followed. The brilliant young Grotius stepped in to justify the capture of ship and fort in his tract on *De Iure Praedae,* on the law of prize and booty.[37] At one level he had to defend the right of a chartered private trading company to take military action, all the more controversial since the pre-1603 companies were chartered only by the "States" (for example, estates or government) of Holland, the major governmental component of the United Provinces (today's Netherlands), but not the national unit. The united VOC after 1603 was to receive its charter from the United Provinces, but even then the country was still unrecognized by the Spanish (then sovereign over Portugal) with whom they were struggling in a long war of independence. Grotius argued that private associations could employ coercive measures for the public good where no constituted civil society existed. The Dutch like all men—Grotius followed Vitoria here—were by virtue of natural law entitled to pursue self-preservation so to "it shall be permissible to acquire for oneself, and to retain, those things which are useful for life."[38] He further insisted that Asian states, regardless of their rulers' non-Christian faith, enjoyed full international status as sovereign actors and could conclude valid trade treaties with whomever they wished. Portugal had sought to prevent the sultan of Johore from trading with the Dutch; retaliation against the Portuguese constituted a sanction necessary to pursue Dutch rights. The claim verged on self-contradiction: the sultan supposedly had the sovereign right to trade with the Dutch, but apparently he did not have the right not to trade with the Dutch, although he had the right to prohibit trade with the non-Dutch, since the treaties the VOC negotiated with local rulers in Southeast Asia limited their sultans' right to sell to other countries' trading companies.[39] Clearly Grotius was engaged in special pleading, but the issues echo in today's EU disputes with Google or Microsoft. How did one create bounded jurisdictional spaces (or defy others' efforts to challenge them) in an arena that was supposedly nonterritorial and open to all? The ocean sea raised the questions posed successively by domains that have been held to be universally open in defiance of territorial claims.

Objections to the right to unhindered trade soon followed. The Portuguese churchman Serafim de Freitas agreed that Muslim states could claim the rights of freedom of the seas, but that they must also be willing to allow Christians to preach the faith or they could be treated as enemies. More to the point of the controversy, he argued that even if given the vastness of the seas, Portugal could not claim dominium over the whole, Portugal could partially "impose our imperium" over its particular interests. Their de facto control justified their de iure claim. Pace Grotius, the Portuguese had "discovered" the far coasts of Africa and of the Indian Ocean, had occupied strong points, and had planted stone pillars to show their presence. Portugal had been the first to Christianize the natives and bring them into history.[40] Portugal's efforts to restrict trade with recalcitrant Muslim sovereigns on the part of other Europeans was thus justified by virtue of this higher imperative.

The British originally tended to side with Grotius—Spain, along with the Portugal it controlled until 1640, was the enemy, and Anglo-Dutch disagreements were resolved by negotiations (in which Grotius took part) in 1613. But a few decades later, the Spanish threat seemed diminished, the Dutch rivalry more menacing. English writers were to accuse the Dutch of seeking to acquire the dominion of the sea that the Portuguese had sought. The Dutch sent a fishing fleet of two thousand ships protected by an armed squadron to the North Sea waters off the east coast of Britain; and John Selden argued that the ocean's bounty of cod was no more a public good, replenished by nature, than the land, and like the land it could be assigned to particular owners. In particular, his tract *Mare Clausum* announced two theses: "In the First, is Shew'd that the Sea, by the Law of Nature, or Nations, is Not Common to All Men but Capable of Private Dominion or Proprietie as well as the Land; in the Second, is Proved That the Dominion of the British Sea, or That Which Incompasseth the Isle of Great Britain, is, and Ever Hath Been, a Part or Appendant of the Empire of that Island."[41] Where did the British Sea end? For Selden the territory of empire remained elastic and allowed continued acquisition of common space even at the cost of war. Societies might covenant with each other not to seize far regions, but absent an agreement, "all men had a right to all things."[42] Close to home, therefore, the British could claim the right to limit access to "their" ocean, while far away they could justify exclusive maritime privileges in pursuit of empire, not so different from the rights Portugal claimed on behalf of Christian proselytizing. Despite a law of nations that protected man's common realm, empire justified unlimited acquisition.

Carl Schmitt was to argue that a new international legal order, or global *Nomos,* which would provide the foundation for modern international law, emerged to accommodate the European expansion into the Americas, Asian waters, and later Africa.[43] International law, such was the implication, became codified as a convenience for avoiding conflicts among Europeans as they carved up the wider globe. According to Vitoria and Grotius and Freitas, international law, as an expression of natural law, justified freedom of the seas but also sanctioned the right to conclude exclusionary monopolies with local sovereigns. Where did the sovereign rights, whether to grant maritime passports or to restrict trade, end? *Liberum maris* and *mare clausum* might be claimed for different zones, but there were no clear lines in the water; they would have to be fought over or negotiated. In the eighteenth century what became codified was the right of a state to control waters within cannon shot of land, soon to be known as the three-mile limit. This would be formally extended to twelve miles in the 1982 UN Convention on the Law of the Sea, which also allowed states the right to extract undersea resources, say, fish or oil, out to two hundred miles and to conduct bathyscapic or seabed exploration out to three hundred miles—subject to the concurrent permission of other states whose own two-hundred-mile or three-hundred-mile privileges happened to overlap. Given a Chinese government currently enlarging reefs into air bases, these issues will not go away. The commons has always been hard to defend—on the other hand, as the conclusion takes up, information and data may confound the trend.[44]

———

So the high seas, supposedly in times of peace accepted as a zone of free passage and unlimited fishing, became a contentious portal for the lands that bordered them. Ottomans, Mughals, the diverse sultanates and merchant associations of southern Asia, the Chinese, and the Japanese all sought to control their ports and access to trade, even as the Europeans battled among themselves. They confronted extraordinary agents of Western power: the Dutch VOC and the British EIC (East India Company), as well as royal fleets under Portuguese and Spanish flags. In April 1612 Henry Middleton, whose small trading fleet was frustrated by an apparent Mughal clampdown on the merchants of Surat in Gujarat, captured fifteen Indian ships including a vessel of a thousand tons, with a crew and passengers of about fourteen hundred persons belonging to the emperor's mother. By September he obtained his license to trade *(firman)*. James I's ambassador to the Mughals advised his king that he was "Lord of all the Seeas" and could win by force what he had sought in vain by courtesy.[45] EIC agents even pressed the emperor at Agra to provide reparation for non-Mughal attacks on their caravans and extracted further concessions.

The aggressiveness of local agents was not always appreciated at home. What today are called principal-agent problems arose: how should the company control rapacious captains abroad? The directors of the VOC in Europe worried that the feisty attitude of the governor of Batavia or their company representatives in Persia endangered their wider interests. The agents on the scene, however, claimed that they faced treacherous locals: "By nature the kings in India are unreliable," the Portuguese councilors in Goa explained, "and if we suffer but the slightest reverse they will immediately side with our opponents."[46] Colonial officials differed on what legal norms might be expected. Of course the Asians were not Christians, but did that invalidate all their oaths? The issue was not only religious but ethnic. "We have had ample occasion to learn that people in the East Indies are in general of an evil and treacherous nature" willing to break commitments. Departing from his 1604 defense of their sovereignty, Grotius argued by 1625 that they lacked respect for legality and commitments, which made it impossible to include them in the system of natural law. Officials were prone to complain that local rulers were simply despots seeking bribes and thus had no claim on European commitments; more thoughtful observers such as van Rheede argued that despite corruption at court, an unwritten constitutionalism still prevailed, as at Kerala.[47]

These views hardly provided a guideline for resolving conflicts among the colonial powers and could prove a disaster for the situation of the natives, who might or might not possess rights. The question of whether the inhabitants of the Americas might or might not be enslaved led to celebrated debates between the Spanish monastic orders, resolved by the compromise that they might be assigned as laborers to the grantees of *encomiendas*. But the more consequential issue in real terms was whether the Indians had any claim on the land.[48] (Outright slavery waited until

Europeans could buy natives already in a condition of chattel, which in a mass sense applied only to Africa.) French and Spanish appropriation of land might be justified on the basis of conquest, but the British colonizers waffled on this question: formally conquest would have meant the overseas domains belonged to the king; instead commentators preferred to refer to the natives' own lack of individual property and their unwillingness to "improve" the land they occupied.[49] As Robert Tray argued with respect to Virginia, "There is not a meum or teum amongst them: so that if the whole lande should bee taken from them, there is not a man that can complaine of any particular wrong done unto him." So too John Donne told the Virginia Company, when he was not asking God to batter his heart or summoning his girlfriend to bed, the land like the sea could belong to no group: states must legislate for the best advantage of the state and to improve its endowments; colonizers must act for the advantage of men in general. If parts of a country are uninhabited, Samuel Purchas argued, they are open to those who come—"every man by Law of Nature and Humanitie hath right of Plantation."[50]

These claims, which flowed from the doctrine of *terra nullius* (land without owners) are well known, but the implications for concepts of territory as such have been less discussed than the impact on native peoples. The debates, and the actions that followed, could not but erode the distinction between property and political control. Was sovereignty actually being purchased when rights to property were bought from the natives? Peter Minuit acquired more than a private island in 1624, when he traded trinkets for Manhattan, but was there a shared understanding of what public rights came with the purchase? For the next 250 years, Europeans were prone to claim that private dominion and political authority were acquired as a package. The ambiguity persisted where non-state trading companies bought political dominion, as in the New World or in Africa, or when military commanders claimed it in the name of their sovereign, as did the Spanish and the Portuguese and the French. The acquisitions of empire were thus fuzzy in a second sense—ambiguous not just in terms of how far they extended geographically, especially at sea, but as to what entitlements they provided. These were always debated—and the relative defenders of indigenous rights were largely overruled from the conquest of the New World to the scramble for Africa four centuries later.[51]

Contemporary chattel slavery, however, presented similar dilemmas: the new owner bought control over a person who could provide an income through his or her productive and reproductive powers. The control was despotic—short, perhaps, of inflicting death—but the transactions were subsumed under commercial concepts. After major debates mentioned above, the Spanish drew the line: the indigenous population was to be Christianized but not to be enslaved—although slaves might be purchased from African chieftains. Later the North Americans debated from 1820 until 1860 whether territorial jurisdiction was central to the criteria for personal ownership—could the United States designate lines beyond which slavery was forbidden? The legislators of 1820 said yes; the Supreme Court of 1857 said no. *Imperium* originated as a Roman term to define unlimited power over people; it was to become a term for sovereignty over territory. But this augmenting of the concept was logical, for territory itself was intimately tied up with the control of human labor power as property. "No peace beyond the line," but no immunity from domination either, whether by physical or economic constraint within territorial borders or on the waters needed to reach them.

Nor finally was the religious realm to be excluded from territorialization. The duty to proselytize justified the seizure of territory, but within the New World conquests Franciscans and Dominicans were to be awarded exclusive zones for missionary activity. Underlying natural law, when inflected by religion, was still the notion of a Christian commonwealth. The Muslims had their own mission to expand the people of Islam, the Ummah, which also gave a right to conquest. Natural law and divine ordinance alike provided justifications for extending the claims of empire beyond almost any given boundary of public domain, rights, and space.

Crises of Imperial Governance

The diversity of peoples ruled by an emperor or "king of kings," to cite the Persian designation, was as much a title of pride as the size of the realm. Palmira Brummett summarizes for the Ottomans, "The mental maps of the time seemed not to require such drawing of state boundaries. The narrative did, however, characterize territory as occupied by either enemies or supporters of the sultan."[52] Valerie Kivelson emphasizes that in maps of the Russian realm toward 1700, the Tsar's subjects to the north of the Amur River border are depicted by onion-towered churches, the Mongols to the south by Yurts.[53] Recent summaries of empire stress "the management of diversity."[54]

But, of course, diversity was a source of tension. The Venetian ambassador reporting to the doge in the sixteenth century stressed both the diversity and the unhappiness of the Ottoman domain: "More than two thirds of the country is inhabited by Christian Greeks, Bulgars, Slavs, and Albanians in Europe, and Armenians in Asia, all discontented with the Turks because of extortion, rape, violence and unjust administration . . . their neighbors, who are Arabs, Persians, Georgians, Mongrellians, Circassians, Russians, Moldavians, Hungarians, Germans and Your Serenity, are likewise discontented with the Turks because, in truth, this their neighbor who shares a border with them is always attacking, always robbing, and making excuses as it is wont to do."[55]

Large though they were, infatuated with their own extensive spaces, empires did not cover a homogenous territory and size itself invited vulnerability. Empires usually faced resistance in one territory or another, and often in several places at the same time from adversaries without. The end of a Chinese dynastic cycle saw internal rebellion and invasion at the borders jointly undermining the Mandate of Heaven: external military pressure required tax exertions that provoked uprisings at home. Managing imperial territory involved a constant geographical balancing act, which at the same time increased social tensions and often challenged the religious or secular principles of legitimacy. One region or place did not have the same obligations and rights as another: the empire was a collection of peoples, faiths, and often privileged spaces more than a single cohesive one. Many enjoyed special rights: churches, abbeys, Islamic religious foundations, and Buddhist or Christian monasteries might owe their allegiance to a spiritual leader; cities retained self-government and tax immunities. In terms of territory, empire was a spongy construction.

The Spanish Habsburg realm, which by marriage came to rest under the imperial crown of Charles V in 1519, exemplified the challenges. As Carlos I of Spain, the young king/emperor arrived in 1516 with an unpopular coterie of Flemish nobles to govern state and church. Angered by infringements on their traditional rights, new fiscal demands, and the descent of Flemish administrators, the city communes of Castile entered into open revolt in April 1520, and an outright civil war began during 1521. Ultimately the Populist violence unleashed split the patrician leadership, the uprisings petered out, and Charles V restored a certain amount of autonomy across his Spanish domains in the 1520s.[56] The tenacity with which the regions and cities of Spain held on to their privileges remained; when in 1640 the Count-Duke Olivares proposed a "union of arms" to Phillip IV in order to widen the tax base for prosecution of the wars against France and the Netherlands, the idea provoked an uprising in Catalonia. In Naples the only recourse was selling offices, but by the 1640s, "everything was sold," and revolt soon followed in 1647.[57] By this time much of Europe, indeed much of the globe, was in upheaval.

The war of the *comuneros* and the great revolts in Catalonia and Naples more than a century later illustrated not only the dynamic of early modern revolution in Europe but the recurring tensions of all political units with agrarian tenancy—the threefold division between the state and its administrators, territorial magnates who resisted financial demands in their local assemblies, and the rural and urban workers, who desperately sought to moderate their own taxes, rents, and feudal dues. Politics involved a continuing struggle among all three elements for whatever surplus could be generated among working people on the land and in towns. Revolt could flare in units of all size from city-state republics to dynastic states to far-flung imperial assemblages. But empires brought their own particular political fragility by virtue of the costly ambitions of their princes and the separation of local distress from remote central decision making. Intermediaries had to be employed and given large degrees of police and revenue-raising power.

Conflicts of faith were also acute in the early modern era, and became inseparable from the restless nature of territorial tensions. Empires and nonimperial states alike presented themselves as protectors of a territorially organized religion that had at least to be supported at home and in the case of empire propagated beyond the boundaries of the faith that had prevailed hitherto. The sultan was a descendant of the founder Osman; he was a holy warrior (ghazi); and after the capture of Constantinople, he was the legatee of the Roman Empire. Selim I's conquests (1512–1520) were represented as a struggle for Muslim orthodoxy against Shi'ite Persians and Mamluk allies. With his conquest of the Hijaz and Egypt, the Sultans became Servants of the Two Sanctuaries and assumed the title of caliph.[58] But then followed the Mediterranean struggles with the Venetians and Spanish, thereafter the long Hungarian wars, and by the seventeenth century further exhausting campaigns against the Safavids, who successfully defended Baghdad in the 1620s. The titles increased in grandiosity. The Ottoman commander Mustafa Ali's description of Cairo calls Mehmed III (1595–1603) "the successful king of the horizons, the fortunate world ruler of absolute power, the namesake of his Highness the Prophet." When Süleyman III announced his accession in 1687 to Louis XIV, he was described as master of the world, a lord whose name is read in the Friday prayer sermon in all the mosques of the believers.[59]

Nevertheless, the world of which the sultan was master was not primarily, or at least not exclusively, based on Islamic universalism. After the Mongols conquered Baghdad in 1258, the idea of a universal Islamic empire allegedly lost its luster. Caliph became a rather generic title for a Muslim ruler, expressing his religious leadership within his domains. The Ottomans assumed it in 1517; the Mughals assumed an equivalent in 1578 to quash the assertion of sharia law by the Muslim religious elite (including execution of a Brahmin for insulting the name of Mohammad). By the fifteenth and sixteenth centuries, Ottoman legitimacy drew equally on the imputed lineage of the Mongol and Turkic conquerors of Central Asia of whom the founder was Chinggis Khan and Timur an emulator.[60] Sovereignty in the gunpowder or steppe empires emphasized Islamic religious duties, but also obscure lineages from the great Khan and grandiose territorial claims. The Mughal emperor Akbar (ruled 1556–1605) claimed the legacy of the Timurids and even Chinggis Khan; and according to his court historian, Abu'l Fazl, his maintenance of religious tolerance was a source of authority and would be initially for Aurangzeb (1658–1707), as well. The emperor ruled in Afghanistan and Hindustan, spoke Persian, and understood that the mass of his subjects were Hindu; gradually a geographical concept of Hindustan emerged as a peninsula with outliers in Sri Lanka, parts of Sumatra, and Malaysia.[61]

Religious duties varied according to circumstance. When an empire was extended over large populations with a preexisting alternative faith, it usually pursued a policy of accommodation: such was the case for the Ottomans after the conquest of Constantinople and the Balkans and for the Mughals as they moved east into "Hindustan." But when, as under the Habsburgs, a new schism rocked a preexisting empire, the dynasty sought to enforce orthodoxy, provoking war throughout German and Dutch domains. Only exhaustion sanctioned territorial partitions to resolve issues of faith: *Cuius regio euis religio,* the principle of territorializing confessions was not necessary in Ottoman or Mughal realms. The Ottomans dealt with religious communities on a nonterritorial basis, allowing them to worship and have their own courts, but obligating them to pay a special tax. The Mughals conquered northern India as a Muslim empire, but Akbar kept Islamic authorities at a distance and claimed, again according to Abu'l Fazl, to be a religious light unto all peoples, adopting some Hindu rites of charity and ceremonies. He also abolished the property tax on non-Muslims. The pendulum was to swing back under later rulers, but the empire was not identified with an Islamic religious cause.

Religious unrest arose often from the peripheries of empire to challenge the hierarchies of ritual on which empires relied: Religious inwardness—Sufi or Protestant or even Arminian—challenged the hierarchies of the center. These confrontations over faith often took place in times when empires were challenged by frontier wars and internal rebellion and indeed helped aggravate the violence. Between 1520 and the mid-1550s, the German lands underwent a civil war arising from Protestant challenges to the upholders of the Holy Roman Empire.[62] In the successive decades the confessional conflicts had spread to France with a civil war among great and lesser feudal families. The German quarrels resumed in the second decade of the seventeenth century over the precarious and contested balance of power between the Habsburg dynasty and its Catholic loyalists on the one side, suspicious Protestants on the other. Although relative calm had settled over the Habsburg-Ottoman frontier regions while the Ottomans were preoccupied by ongoing war with the Safavid dynasty in the Arab borderlands. Vienna still faced serious military challenges from the Swedes at the zenith of their power and zeal, and then from the French. The unslaked ferocity of the Central European conflicts continued through the late 1640s.

By the 1630s and 1640s, much of the world seemed caught up in simultaneous wars and rebellions, as states faced financial exhaustion, and became prey to aristocratic factions, committed often to religious reform or reaffirmation and seeking to dominate monarchs who insisted on obedience but were seriously overstretched. The French nobility took advantage of a child monarch to revolt against Mazarin; parliamentary defenders and Scottish Presbyterians fought and executed a monarch who insisted on full power; Catalans revolted against the Castilian state that sought to end their special tax privileges; Portugal recovered its independent status after eighty years, but lost possessions to the Dutch navies, which at least briefly held Manhattan and the Hudson Valley and northeastern Brazil, as well as West Indian, South African, and Batavian outposts. Cossacks ravaged the Ukraine in their uprising against the claims of an overextended aristocratic republic and an ambitious Russian absolutist state. The newly unified Manchurian tribal federation swept away the rulers of what had been the world's densest and most highly organized empire, but one weakened by ecological strain, provincial administrative breakdown, and factional disputes that trapped recent short-lived emperors in a cocoon of court officials, eunuchs, concubines, and favorites.

In terms of their global power, empires, as noted above, often flourished in dyadic relationships. They prospered alongside another empire: over the centuries a Spanish-Portuguese, an Anglo-Dutch, Franco-Spanish, Russo-Chinese, eventually an Anglo-American tandem. In terms of their domestic politics, the key to successful rule in the early modern era lay in preserving an equilibrium with local elites. To support their military force, successful empires must allow commanders and administrators the resources ultimately produced by peasants, whether the manpower for direct military service or for agrarian production. The Chinese began their dynastic renewals as partial exceptions to feudal devolution. They managed to sustain a bureaucratic/great-family ruling class that lived off the privileges they got for loyal service. But balancing effective administration of the provinces with effective oversight of provincial officials was difficult. The Mongol Yuan dynasty reinvigorated provincial administration, and the Ming built on their innovations. But the reformed administration broke down by the seventeenth century with the familiar consequences of rebellion, warlordism, and the involvement of ambitious external federations, in this case the newly consolidated Manchu state that founded the Qing dynasty.[63] The Habsburgs in the Americas, as Sanjay Subrahmanyam has emphasized, were able to impose a uniformity of institutions in the new world that proved impossible in their European realms.[64] In Europe the Spanish had to resort to loans to pay their manpower, and there were frequent desertions and mutinies; across the

Atlantic they could provide land and labor grants, the *encomiendas*, to their soldiers. The Ottomans dragooned one set of soldiers under direct control at the center by sweeping Christian youth up for life in the Balkans, and they settled another force on fiefs (timars) in the conquered Balkans. Expanding Muscovy introduced peasant servitude by decree.[65] The Mughals in Delhi and Agra erected a formidable military power by carving out fiefs from their conquests in northern India and creating a class of military servants, mansabars, whose collective income claimed up to 85 percent of imperial revenues. It was assigned from particular fiefs or jaghirs, keyed for the individual to a dual numerical scale based both on their personal ranking and their obligations in terms of military men and horses to be mustered. But it was the headmen of village groups, the zamindars, who collected rents in the first instance, not as landowners but as long-sanctioned intermediaries. They offered that staple of semiparasitic bosses the world over, "protection," and in return siphoned off a significant share of the society's domestic product.[66] Historians of early modern India have debated the extent of the feudal crisis, recapitulating the British historians' "storm over the gentry" in terms of the ascent of zamindars and the squeeze on the mansabars and jaghiri resources.[67] In any case, the Mughals moved south from Afghanistan no earlier than the Portuguese on the west coast and the Dutch, British, and French on the east coast also implanted themselves in the subcontinent. These offshore powers added to their difficulties, which become acute by the 1730s in the years after the last powerful emperor, Aurangzeb, overstrained his sources of revenue and soldiers with two decades of warfare along the southern borders of his empire.

———

In the early modern period, empire is prevalent but always vulnerable. Large continental territories must be run by those powerful on the land. Territorial control for the center remains conditional and precarious, reassured perhaps by tribute, ceremony, and deference, but undermined by the difficulty of tapping resources, and the new costs of warfare imposed by effective artillery, firearms, fortresses, and sieges. Decisive confrontations, whether between states in general and often within them, now occur often in terms of sieges. Akbar overwhelms the Rajput fortress of Chitor in 1568; the Ottomans will besiege Baghdad unsuccessfully in 1623–1624; Richelieu blockades the Huguenot stronghold at La Rochelle a few years later and will go on to compel the destruction of fortresses within the kingdom, as will the new Tokugawa rulers of Japan.

Landed empire is imposing but precarious. *Decline* is a teleological term to avoid. There are moments of expansion, moments of retrenchment. Early modern landed empires comprise a few zones of heartland where revenue collection and ritual seem to function, many inner zones of continuing struggle over extraction and loyalty, and a perimeter of endemic and costly conflict as well as emergence of new dynastic rivals. Empires can decompose either at the center or in the provinces. At the court, corruption, favoritism, the politics of the harem, or the rivalry of advisers can undercut the emperor. And if the emperor is flawed, the whole system is in trouble. The historian Mustafa Ali recounts the rapid decay of the Ottoman state under Murad III near the end of the sixteenth century: the sultan was crediting calumny about virtuous officials at face value; he was undermining his Vezir and becoming the pawn of the eunuchs and concubines of the harem; he had descended to accepting bribes. Ali attributed perhaps too many of the realm's woes to the sultan's personal flaws, and he was resentful of successful adversaries at the court.[68] But lest we think the perspective too fixed on the ruler, let us recall our own attributions of American difficulties to the deficiencies of our presidents and sometimes their chief advisers.

We can find more institutional or structural sources of difficulty if we analyze the dilemmas posed by extracting surplus from peasant production—ultimately a Marxist-oriented analysis—or from the very conditions of imperial territoriality.[69] Empires find it challenging to penetrate territory "deeply." Like every organized enterprise they face rival go-betweens, united only in seeking their own rents, whether magnates and grandees or estate managers and village zamindars. Landlords and/ or officials who should protect household producers and pass along what custom has sanctioned become exploitative and self-enriching. Perhaps the Chinese slow the process of "feudal" decay most successfully over the long term by virtue of their meritocratic bureaucracy, but every two or three centuries their ponderous mechanisms slip into crisis—the most recent as of 1650 having been the implosion of the Ming order: "The body of tenets that Confucius and Mencius had intended some two thousand years earlier to inspire and lead, became an instrument for repressive conformity . . . mediocrity was encouraged in the name of morality and intellectual dishonesty remained a fixed characteristic of bureaucratic life."[70]

Historians have focused, therefore, on multiple tensions: the infighting at courts, peasant immiseration and rebellion, religious dissent, regional conflicts, and the general divisions between a sophisticated elite plugged into the capital and provincial landlords (court versus country), often under the influence of religious zealotry. Territorial resources were needed to satisfy the elite with fiefs and prebends and pay for the military that safeguarded the borders. Empires had to demonstrate control of the frontiers, but preoccupation with the border could subtly undermine as well as excite the "spirit" of empire. The space of empire was by its very nature conceived of as a restless realm, contested at its edges, enticing to expansion or compelling defense. Inevitably, safeguarding imperial territory required stabilizing its boundaries, a strategy that had to inhibit the ideologies of ever grander space that was so important for its very raison d'être. Rome's leaders divided over the wisdom of retrenchment: Tacitus thought it undercut the virtues of state; the emperor Hadrian believed it would guarantee peace and stability.[71] In any case the spokesmen for empire aspire to rule peoples, not just acreage, and their maps depict the communities of those who belong and those who do not, often with reference to their characteristic architecture of churches and settlements. Still, the peoples they depict are those with homelands that have been or must be annexed. Thus the multiethnicity of empire means that territorial specificity enters by the back door. And when it does it raises as many problems as it solves. There will always be hawks in the capital who insist that not an inch can be yielded lest the structure collapse. Empires should transcend territory, but they become hostage to it instead. Perhaps Trajan had good reason to weep on the shores of the Persian Gulf.

2

Spaces of States
(1550–1700)

IT IS HARD TO IMAGINE France's Louis XIV weeping when in 1681 he reached the Rhine and annexed Strasbourg. A major achievement based on debatable legal procedures and the continuing threat of force, it decisively expanded state space—his space. To get a sense of state space, start in the attic of the Invalides, the grandiose baroque structure Louis had built as a hospital and home for old soldiers. High up under the roof, today's visitor finds the intriguing Musée des Plans-Reliefs. Displayed in large glass cases up to ten feet square in a long darkened corridor are twenty-eight beautifully detailed models on a 1/600 scale of French military fortifications depicted in their physical environments, whether on offshore islands, river mouths, urban waterfronts, or isolated hills. The Sun King authorized construction of these maquettes ostensibly for studying military engineering and siege defenses, at the suggestion of Michel Tellier, the Marquis de Louvois, his minister of war. The designer of the frontier forts, Sebastien le Prestre de Vauban (1633–1707), was a brilliant and productive official, promoted by merit from his modest Burgundian landowning origins into the highest aristocratic circles of state service. Vauban and his boss were both compulsive workers: Tellier badgered his skilled subordinate constantly for data, and Vauban wrote that if he didn't have to field so many inquiries, he might get more done.[1]

Both sieges and the construction of fortifications required elaborate plans and models. Year after year for almost two centuries, skilled engineers and officers were assigned to enlarge the collection, deemed useful for teaching the strategy of royal defense. First installed in the Tuileries, at the end of the reign the models were moved to the Grand Gallery of the Louvre, to be showed to select viewers such as Peter the Great during his 1717 visit or the Turkish ambassador in 1721. Today's visitor sees only about a third of the hundred or so models. Chosen for display are the forts that guarded the maritime and mountain perimeter against the Spanish and the English, from Toulon on the Mediterranean to the Spanish border, then across the Pyrenees, and continuing up the Atlantic coast to the Channel.[2]

The effort lavished on the models suggests how important a role fortification played in the psychology of national defense, if not always its practice. The forts were not merely deterrents, since they hardly prevented the almost constant warfare that embroiled France in the early modern era. They testified to the power of a concept, that of the border or frontier—the line of protection that enclosed the sovereign space of the kingdom, envisaged as a hexagon by the time of Vauban's death in 1707. The space, of course, was constantly to be pressed outward and its fortifications augmented, but wherever the frontier might be established it separated France from highly organized rival entities. France had soldiers stockaded in remote Saint Lawrence settlements and priests living among the Hurons, but the state frontier faced the house of Habsburg and its allies. Two days after congratulating himself on a site visit to the newly conquered fortress of Luxembourg on May 21, 1687, the king reconnoitered the nearby village of Traben on the Moselle and decided to expand the fortifications of Trarbach on the facing heights across the river *"pour faire trembler toute l'Allemagne."*[3] As it turned out, the site would be surrendered as part of the next peace settlement. Nonetheless, French policy makers had a fixation on the borders, one that suggested how decisive would be the possible battles at the perimeter, all the way to the battle of the frontiers in September 1914 and construction of the Maginot Line in the 1930s.

Not all forts, of course, coincided with a national border line, not even in Europe's crowded space. An expanding frontier could leave them in the hinterland, or they might be situated strategically along an enemy's line of march as at Verdun on the Meuse. One of Vauban's talents was to fit the accumulating two-centuries-old departures in military technology into the appropriate natural sites. Location established the valence of the fortification—its political message as well as its military utility. Some princes intended the citadel to dominate an interior region or control an important city. It represented a locus of political power, a nodal point of sovereignty to be affirmed or a rival subordinate claim to be overcome. Territory—both within and at its edge—was envisaged in terms of the potential for military resistance. Just as the French state was erecting its necklace of frontier fortifications, it had been tearing down fortified strongholds within the kingdom.[4] The fortifications of the early modern period establish the primacy of strategic location, emphasize inner and outer domains, define and augment the commitment to the competitive state securely bounded and supreme at home. They are where sovereignty crystallizes in the assertion of military control.

Descartes and Vauban at War

Military technology and ideas of global space have always lived under the same roof. The relationships modeled under the eaves of the Invalides in particular had been developing since the close of the Middle Ages, and an account of militarized state space must go back at least two centuries before Vauban. But the full conceptual consequences developed slowly. "I was then in Germany, to which country I had been attracted by the wars which are not yet at an end," Descartes, one of the great theorists of spatiality, writes in the 1630s about the dreams that had overcome him at age twenty-three on November 10, 1619, and that had led him to seek the sources of axiomatic knowledge. Descartes had already taken time off from formal academic study to learn from "the book of the world." He gravitated particularly toward the military world. A year earlier, in 1618, he had enrolled in the informal military school run under the auspices of the preeminent Dutch leader Mauritz of Nassau (Maurice of Nassau) at Breda, studying the engineering connected with sieges and ballistics, and entering into an intense six-month intellectual friendship with the mathematician and educator Isaac Beeckman. These life changes intervened just as the precarious confessional balancing of the Holy Roman Empire was falling out of control, the ten-year truce (1609–1619) between Spain and the Netherlands was expiring, and the United Provinces in particular was racked by the dispute between Arminians and predestinarians. A year later, as open war resumed in the Low Countries and rebellious Bohemia, Descartes enrolled with the Catholic armies of Maximillian of Bavaria, attended the coronation of Emperor Ferdinand II at Frankfurt, perhaps witnessed the emperor's army crush the Bohemian nobility at the White Mountain, and in 1627 may have added a visit to Richelieu's siege of the Huguenot stronghold of La Rochelle: all in all he studied the lessons of war for almost a decade during the years of Catholic military success.[5] He left the world of war at age thirty-two to study and write in the Protestant haven of the Netherlands, often touchy and spiteful when accused of being derivative, fearful, too, of church condemnation though outside its reach, but for all the prudent conformism, determined to search for incontrovertible assurance of the external world based on "all that is best in geometrical analysis and algebra."[6] "Take for example this piece of wax that has just been drawn from the hive," he writes in his famous discussion of "extension," the primary property of matter. The warm and fragrant wax changes shape but retains the fundamental property of taking up space—the defining quality of bodies, which "are not properly speaking known by the senses or by the faculty of imagination, but by the understanding only."[7] At stake was what we know and how we know it; Descartes progressed by stripping down the sensory world to the conceptual underpinning of creator and of what existence entails in space and time.

Descartes lived in a world in which two-dimensional mapping had become as crucial as perspective and three-dimensional depiction were in Italy two hundred years earlier. He devised the assignment of x and y coordinates for points in a Euclidean plane; in effect treating the map and the surface of the earth as sharing the geometry of what mathematicians in the nineteenth century would describe as a two-dimensional manifold, a surface that may curve but whose neighborhoods we can map point for point on flat surfaces which can then be assembled as an atlas. The challenge of projection for mapmaking had been understood at least since Ptolemy (circa 100–170), but was made urgent in the fifteenth and sixteenth centuries with the advent of global exploration. How do we depict our earth once we venture beyond the local? The larger the area, the more transformation takes place in the translation of earth's surface to flat rectangular sheets.

Prevailing Ptolemaic representation curved the parallels and meridians to suggest the earth's sphere, but guidance for sailors was approximate at best. Innovative maps with "rhumbs," or lines of constant compass orientations from landmark to landmark, became important by the end of the thirteenth century. The mathematician and geographer Pedro

Nunes (1502–1578), working in Coimbra and Lisbon, laboriously calculated tables of rhumb lines (also known as loxodromes) in the 1530s and 1540s. On maps they could be drawn in the form of a compass rose and the crisscrossing lines on so-called portolan maps. Gerard Mercator (1512–1594) included some on his globe of 1541 and in 1569 projected the spherical coordinates onto a cylinder wrapped in effect around the equator and thus aligned north and south. Areas were thereby distorted, but navigators could have charts that anticipated the locations they would encounter as they used a straight-edge to plot their course at a constant bearing.[8] And for the crowded European territories where empires rubbed against states halfway "up" the globe, the distortion of area was even less important than for global, imperial distances. Every place within the frontiers of the state had an assignable location, which by adding coordinates could be related to every other place.

Different maps serve different needs. Nunes and Mercator were subjects of Portugal and the Habsburgs, respectively, attentive to global geography and the requirements of long-distance voyagers. Landed empires had different cartographic agendas: sixteenth- and seventeenth-century Russian rulers were preoccupied with the peoples their state encountered at the far frontiers.[9] By the eighteenth century, Sunderland insists, a new territorial consciousness took place. The Russian state commissioned new cartographic representations: a geodesic survey, then Ivan Kirilov's atlas of 1734, revealing "the expanse of a great empire," and the second atlas produced by the Academy of Sciences in 1745. The mid-1700s maps would serve as the basis for the extraction of material resources as well as the vivid depiction of national territory.[10]

Frontiers gradually became a standard feature of European state maps after Westphalia. Before the mid-sixteenth century they were a minor feature; Ortelius's *Theatrum Mundi* of 1570 included borders on about half the maps, whereas Joan Blaeu's *Theatre du monde ou novel atlas* marked the frontiers on almost four fifths of the maps. Internal frontiers also took a prominent place especially in French maps.[11] For Chinese and Japanese maps of the interior, in contrast, boundaries seemed less critical than the urban artifacts of rule and landscape markers: the message was that of state activity, and less of perimeters unless contested. But over time the demands of travel technology and the role of Western European navigators, and then conquerors and missionaries, diffused and imposed the European-style map. The frontispiece for the Asian volume of Joan Blaeu's great twelve-volume world atlas of the mid-seventeenth century shows six putti measuring the angles of a mountainous landscape through a gate, even as they transfer the map of China from a large globe to flat map on which a Mercator projection of the country has been printed. The maps inside were territorial; the Chinese maps of the time remained both territorial and topographic, showing landscape and peopling.[12]

Recent historians of cartography have showed us how considerations of power influenced the representations of territorial possession; projections and orientations privileged the world-view of the mapmaker or his client. Indeed, as recently argued, the maps themselves contributed to the sense of territorial sovereignty.[13] This does not mean, however, that subjectivity ruled. The representations were constrained by the useful rules of mathematical projection, by what might be considered as proto-topology; they were efforts at rational analysis and not just blueprints of hierarchy. A map is not just a Panopticon of territory built at will; at this time and place it was a search for useful representations, and these representations must take account of the international rivalries between states as well as produce images to convey domination within them. Within the frontiers of the state, the sovereign was not seeking to eliminate indigenous inhabitants or establish land up for grabs by cartographic convention— rather the opposite, to understand human and material resources.

The Renaissance and early modern maps in Europe had many sources. Making an image precise and fixing its location often derived from a common ambition. The Stoic ideal of contemplation that had motivated the Antwerp producers of cityscape and early landscape around 1500 had evolved via the map into an allegory of power.[14] In the sixteenth and seventeenth centuries they were conceived in terms of fortified space; by the 1700s the need to take account of the resources of the state would call for maps of economic and financial productivity; whether the mission be to defend or to appropriate it. Two centuries after the innovations unleashed in artillery and fortification, the mapping of territory and the fortification of territory possessed the minds of those entrusted with competitive statecraft. Elaborate views of sieges and citadels become a staple of baroque art just as city views had evolved over two centuries, combining art and science. Descartes observed them; half a century later Vauban perfected them.

———————

"Place défendue par Vauban, place impregnable, place attaquée par Vauban, place prise"—any site Vauban defended was impregnable; any site he attacked would fall.[15] Vauban would construct a bristling new citadel within four years of the French conquest of Lille in 1697, suspending private masonry construction to commandeer the brick makers and materiel. Lille was designed to survive as a self-contained garrison city of up to twenty-five hundred soldiers for sixty-four days. Its inner line of fortifications was pentagonal, a design that followed from the logic of a convex perimeter, which enabled the artillery atop and on the face of each rampart to cover its neighboring walls and to eliminate any approaches that were free from defensive fire. Three of its faces looked east to deter an enemy coalition; two looked into the city to ensure obedience from its population. South of Strasbourg, the elaborate fortifications of Neuf Brisach would protect Louis's late seventeenth-century acquisitions on the Rhine frontier in Alsace. Vauban organized a corps of engineers that grew to more than three hundred men under Louis XIV and continually incorporated the suggestions of other designers to overcome the difficulties of technology, for instance, casemates within the bastions that filled with smoke, and budget constraints—double walls were incredibly costly. Still, the fortifications would always be vulnerable, and no one knew that better than their designer, who spent a major part of his time and mental energy devising siege procedures that would overcome his own fixed ramparts. Even the forts and fortress cities Vauban designed were not designed to hold out forever in isolation, but to allow time for reinforcements to arrive and relieve the siege. The fortifications protected the territory of the realm; the territory provided the spatial unity that rendered frontier defense a coherent strategy. The border membrane, in a very practical as well as theoretical way, established the space of the state.

During the course of fifty sieges, Vauban perfected not only the architecture of the defensive but the system of attack. He calculated that he could compel surrender in the course of a forty-eight-day advance. Besiegers were to construct a first ring of trenches beyond range of the walls for assembling equipment and cannon and then a second ring behind them to protect from counterattack in the rear. Next a third, inner ring would be built, supplied from the original circle by radial zigzag trenches ("saps")—which impeded the defenders' fire from raking through a long line of attackers. Vauban estimated that a thousand men or more would be needed to advance the trenches. The light wicker cover to protect the first diggers or sappers would be replaced with more substantial ceilings. Trenches would be progressively widened and buttressed so that they could accommodate the attacker's advancing artillery, which toward the year 1500, seems to have had an effective range capable of battering masonry of two hundred to four hundred yards.[16] From this closest trench, the final assault would be mounted.

Such an elaborate and stately pace of warfare had been evolving for at least two centuries before Vauban. It transformed not only strategy and combat but earlier intuitive notions of territory, as well, endowing the latter with a far greater sense of determinate place and giving borders, strong points, and locations in general a fixity that the flux of imperial possessions had not required. Seventeenth-century thinkers, rulers, mapmakers, and military leaders were preoccupied by the quality we can call positionality, the determination of points in space, aware, of course, that they change. It was over the nature of what changes and what remains constant that they continually debated. Their concepts varied, and major insights were achieved alongside obscurities and what seem misconceptions. Descartes famously defined space and time in terms of relational positions between objects, and he envisaged the inertial tendency of a tethered body moving in a circle, that is, centrifugal force, not as tangential to the circumference but radially from the center. That is, he saw it flying outward, not forward when released. Newton objected and insisted that space and time were absolutely preexisting qualities; both agreed in abandoning the Aristotelian idea that there was a natural center to which bodies must fall. The point is that ideas of state territoriality emerged in a period in which the scientific description of force and motion in time and space was a consuming philosophical and intellectual obsession. To analyze them rigorously, so the tasks of mapmaking suggested at the same time, required mathematical methods; one must slice up motion into infinitesimal changes, first by repeated calculations of trigonometric functions as Pedro de Nunes had to do, then at last in the seventeenth and eighteenth centuries with the conceptual shortcuts of differential and integral calculus. Falling bodies, changes in velocity, the trajectory of cannonballs, what would be defined as the conservation of momentum, the establishment of territorial jurisdiction, and the representation of authority were all problems of an epistemic world fraught with controversy over control—including the church's efforts to keep its authority from being undermined.[17]

Spain's ambitious imperial claims in southern and northern Italy and in the lower Rhineland ensured a proliferation of mapping and treatises on fortification in both theaters. Iberia's acquisition of overseas territories in realms unknown only half a century earlier had encouraged a revival of global mapping. But a generation later, even as its soldiers of fortune were organizing their empires in Mexico and the Andes, this global monarchy had to defend its possessions in very crowded regions of Europe. Marriage gave the Habsburg heir the crowns of Spain and the duchies of Naples, Milan, and the Low Countries at a moment when religious dissent and the rivalry with powerful abutting lands imposed the crowded constant frictions of the state. Catholic rulers had to defend their coasts and Danubian territory against the Ottomans and their Central European frontiers against Protestant princes.[18] The rush to fortify, the capacity to map, the mathematical knowledge needed for viewing and hurling projectiles all developed rapidly. The costs of the enterprise were huge; quickly outrunning the new wealth that their conquered indigenous American subjects could be forced to dig out of the silver deposits half a world away. States remained at war or preparing for war, consuming great quantities of supplies, demanding far more artillery for both defense and offense, and keeping mercenaries in the field for long campaigns. The consequence, as is well known, was a continuing struggle for fiscal resources from which state institutions were to emerge more bureaucratic and more exigent—no matter whether the contest for control of these resources would be won in successive centuries by monarchs or by oligarchical assemblies.[19]

The Transformation of the Fortress

Vauban's fortifications culminated two centuries of defensive development that responded to decisive improvements in the use of gunpowder and artillery. Fortification and enclosure, on the one hand, siege "engines," on the other, had been consequences of competitive statehood since antiquity.[20] Recall Troy and Jericho and the kingdoms of Sumeria, then the long walls from Athens to its port of Piraeus, and the successive walls of Rome, both the city and its distant frontiers on the Rhine or in north Britain. Ancient Indian fortifications from the Indus Valley and the northwest coastal region (pre-1000 B.C.E.) have left archeological remnants, as have the citadels built in the Ganges Valley system and the south of the subcontinent by the regional states that emerged from the debris of the Mauryan Empire after about 200 B.C.E.[21] The Great Chinese Wall in its present form was a Ming dynasty reconstruction of a crumbling barrier erected two thousand years earlier. But the Chinese also pioneered the trebuchet or catapult by the twelfth century, which became the most effective pre-gunpowder launcher of projectiles. By the later Middle Ages, "Frankish," that is, European besiegers were undermining castle walls and building siege towers and counterfortifications designed to prevent defenders from making effective sorties. The great fortifications on a key border of the medieval Christian and Muslim world, the crusader kingdom of Jerusalem, had a particular and fraught history. The historiography of these often massive fortifications—perfected as "concentric" castles in the Levant and in the west between roughly 1180 and 1280—has been laden with controversies: Did the crusaders bring the concepts for these structures from the west, or did they absorb an Islamic architecture itself influenced by Byzantium?[22] As for Jerusalem, the iconic walls of the Old City were constructed by Süleyman the Magnificent in the sixteenth century, a millennium and a half after the Roman wall crumbled, itself almost a thousand years after David fortified his capital.

The decisive transformation of the long progress of fortification in fact originated in Italy in the fifteenth century. Ancient and medieval city walls, relatively high and thin, designed to withstand infantry attacks (as at Carcassonne), could not resist the improvement of artillery. Cannon had been used from around 1340, but as early stone projectiles often shattered harmlessly against the ancient city walls. In contrast, the cast-iron cannonball introduced by French artillery engineers after about 1450 could reduce traditional fortifications to rubble. Early cannonballs also fit irregularly into the barrels and allowed the propellant's pressure to dissipate and diminish the force of the charge, but the technique of inserting a tighter-fitting wooden plug between powder and ball alleviated this problem. Bronze cannon were less likely to explode; wheeled mountings increased mobility. The French invasion of Italy under Charles VIII in 1494 stunningly demonstrated the devastating impact of the new ordnance. Bombardment overwhelmed the static defenses designed to resist the attacker. Artillery was still too cumbersome to be decisive in the field, but it became mobile enough for siege warfare.

Of course, defense and offense play leapfrog over time. Italians learned the lesson meted out by the French artillery, and their celebrated architects and artists rewrote the rules of the defensive even as their mathematicians and metallurgists caught up on the sciences of ballistics and offensive weapons, which they had largely neglected for a century. By the early and mid-sixteenth century they were redesigning high vulnerable walls according to what became known as the *trace italienne*—low and slanted ramparts, masonry-faced, and filled with earth and rubble, wide enough to accommodate platforms at different levels for countervailing cannon. Ditches and sometimes lower forward walls were also constructed. Nevertheless, the new doctrine of the defense accepted that outer breaches were likely, so that characteristically the fortifications were laid out with projecting bastions allowing diagonal lines of artillery and small arms fire that eliminated the relatively protected areas directly under any walls and towers. Italian military engineers were engaged by the French and the Habsburgs, who contested the peninsula, and they recruited its talent for work in faraway theaters. Military designers debated the merits of the round bastion, which accommodated only a few cannons that had to cover a large terrain, versus triangular projections, ultimately developing intricate arrowhead-shaped platforms for mounting the defensive artillery. As elaborated in theory and then construction over the course of the sixteenth century, these designs would lead to the star-shaped fortifications so striking in architectural treatises, models, and today's aerial photographs. The plans for fortifications became elaborate geometric exercises of calculating the distances between bastions and of inscribing circular cities within polygons formed by walls running between the bristling triangular and arrowhead vertices.[23] By the end of the sixteenth century, the pentagonal inner walls of the fortress (protected by a profusion of projecting bastions) had become the canonic form for the citadel, although other geometric variations were appropriate when natural features, such as rivers or bluffs, could be utilized.[24] (See illustrations.)

———

"The strength of a fortress depends upon the quality of its plan rather than the thickness of its walls," argued Francesco di Giorgio Martini (1439–1501), the Sienese-born architect who codified the new doctrine in his *Trattato di architettura, ingegneria e arte militare,* finished sometime after 1482 (thirty years after Leon Battista Alberti's general treatise on architectural types and techniques, which also included a chapter on fortification). Francesco contributed to the emerging bastion forts of the Romagna in central Italy in the 1460s and 1470s, and then constructed some of the most significant Aragonese fortresses of southern Italy. The key was the ability to bring flanking fire to bear along a straight line of a city wall from another projecting bastion from left or right.[25] The range of the cannon—perhaps two hundred to three hundred meters—determined how far apart the bastions could be placed. Albrecht Dürer, who traveled south of the Alps in the late fifteenth century; the military engineer Gebriello Busca of Milan; Antonio da Sangallo the Elder, designer of the canonic fortification at Nettuno in 1501; and Sangallo the Younger, who designed Florence's Fortezza da Basso; among other architects, including Michelangelo and Leonardo, all drafted plans and refinements.

Francesco di Giorgio Martini worked from the 1470s for Federico da Montefeltro, condotierre from Urbino, whose Uffizi profile with its hooked nose and red cap was painted so memorably by Piero della Francesca around 1465. In the companion profile of Federico's consort, Battista Sforza, who returns his gaze across the frames, the viewer discerns in the background one of the new bastion towers that were being constructed in the 1460s and 1470s in Montefeltro's domains—squat, solid, and topped with loopholes for defending firearms.[26] Francesco's first Montefeltro commission was redesigning the imposing promontory fortress of San Leo, which commanded the Adriatic plain. Perhaps he discussed the idealized cityscapes and the art of fortification at the ducal court with Piero, whose *Flagellation of Christ,* hanging still in the palace of Urbino, was a fundamental exploration of the laws of perspective as well as a cool and enigmatic depiction of two philosophers too absorbed in conversation to cast a glance at the abandoned victim. One of Francesco's paintings of an ideal city hangs there, as well (an even more austere one is in Berlin).

Military and civilian architecture had not yet fundamentally diverged, and landscape and urban plans were also kin. Through the political alignments of Montefeltro and Duke Alfonso di Calabria, Francesco di Giorgio had taken on Neapolitan projects by the 1480s and was seconded to Aragonese service in light of an expected Turkish invasion. He could see the ruinous impact of the French artillery on the Neapolitan Castel Nuovo in late 1494, but by engineering a spectacular underground explosive mine helped the Duke of Calabria retake the key stronghold. The bleached plains of southern Italy possessed Hohenstaufen and Angevin forts in the old walled style. The urgent task seemed to be protection of the ports of Gallipoli (the Apulian, not Turkish city), Taranto and Otranto from the Turks even as the politics of the peninsula was being transformed by the French intervention. Stout bastions erected to protect the Apulian coastal cities from Manfredonia to Matera to Brindisi and Taranto reveal Francesco's concept and handiwork throughout, before he retired to his native Siena, where he died in 1501.[27] The clash of Spanish and Ottomans and Venetians and Ottomans led to massive and costly programs of fortress building on the sea coasts. Pursuing Morisco forces, now in exile from Granada, Ferdinand established half a dozen *fronteras* on the North African coast between 1509 and 1511. The Ottomans, who assumed the suzerainty of Algiers, responded with their own program of fortifications as a century of naval warfare began to embroil the Mediterranean. The viceroys in Naples and Palermo continued to add forts; Antonio da Sangallo the younger designed a complete angle-bastioned *enceinte* or enclosure at papal Civitavecchia in 1515.[28]

Fortress architecture reflected the transition from the still viable tradition of urban republicanism in the sixteenth century to the gradual subjection of the peninsula by local strongmen and the encroaching Habsburgs in the seventeenth. Both the logic of artillery and the new prevalence of territorial states organized around *condotierri* engaged in recurrent warfare, introduced new concepts of territory and political space. The entry of the French into Italy, fatefully invited by the Sforza rulers of Milan, was not only the sign of significant ramping up of warfare, but as recognized ever since Guicciardini's *History of Italy,* constituted a political dividing line, as well. Louis XII followed Charles VIII, and Emperor Charles V, heir to the Spanish possessions of southern Italy, decided to take on the French hold over Milan, notably invading Rome in the 1520s. Baldassare Peruzzi equipped Siena with new bastions and massive gates (inner and outer with a barbican in between) to protect the vulnerable ridges projecting from the urban center between 1527 and 1532, as the city faced attacks from the Florentines, its own exiled aristocratic faction, and the imperial troops who had savaged Rome.[29] By the mid-1550s, however, following a generation of civil strife and outside interventions, Spanish and other forces of the empire joined with the Medici dukes to absorb the Republic. Unsurprisingly, but not without civil strife repeated in city after city, the republican traditions that had seemed well rooted through much of the northern half of the country fell victim to the ambitions of military leaders who established their own dynasties and to the oligarchies that supported them.[30] The state as it was being reorganized in Italy was increasingly the domain of the prince, who knew how to attract his own court of artists and intellectuals.[31] Italy was one of the global zones where empire and ambitious non-empires collided and transformed the artifacts and principles that played against each other. It was both periphery and heartland at the same time: the center of an imperial religion, whose own institutions in the world were buffeted by the civil conflicts and the religious upheaval beyond its borders.

The new fortress architecture drew further inspiration from the idealized radial city plans developed in Renaissance art and utopian political tracts. The ideal radial city inside the polygonal fortifications of bastion and barbican were complementary: "The fortress must be the principal component of the city," Francesco di Giorgio wrote in his *Trattato,* "because it is like the head of the body. When it is lost, so is the body, likewise when the fortress is lost, so is the city it rules.[32] Francesco and other planners envisaged streets running from the gates to the main piazza at the center with smaller circular streets and decorative squares (in contrast to other urbanists including Pietro Cataneo and later Palladio, who played with checkerboard arrays). Cataneo, who published his massive treatise on architecture in 1554, seventy years after Francesco's

Trattato, identified fortification against artillery as a chief requisite of contemporary urbanism.[33]

In the 1530s Pope Paul III convened the leading urbanists and military architects to discuss rebuilding the walls of Rome, a city traumatized by the Habsburg invasion in 1526. The seminars seem to have provided a common formation for the architects, who went on to draft radial urban plans for fortress cities.[34] The star of the seminars (to be repeated when the initial plans needed modification for economic reasons in the 1540s) was Antonio da Sangallo the Younger—heir to his father's fortress expertise—who served as general director of the Roman projects until his death in 1546, when he was succeeded by Michelangelo, who had challenged both his Roman and Florentine plans.

Radial city planning always invited utopian elements; drafting ideal fortress towns allowed concepts that reinforcing medieval towns could not. By the mid-sixteenth century Francesco de Marchi (1504–1576), who developed ideas from Alberti and Francesco di Giorgio, divagated on the centralization of public buildings, the virtues of wide streets, sewage systems, and nearby agricultural zones. Only one such radial utopian site would be built in Italy in the sixteenth century: Palmanova, on the eastern frontier of the Venetian republic, was initiated in 1593.[35] A decade later Tommaso Campanella, the feisty Calabrian Dominican who would die in French exile, still described his "City of the Sun" as a fusion of military fortification and virtuous regime:

> It is divided into seven rings or huge circles named from the
> seven planets, and the way from one to the other of these is
> by four streets and through four gates, that look toward the
> four points of the compass. Furthermore, it is so built that if
> the first circle were stormed, it would of necessity entail a
> double amount of energy to storm the second; still more to
> storm the third; and in each succeeding case the strength and
> energy would have to be doubled; so that he who wishes to
> capture that city must, as it were, storm it seven times. For
> my own part, however, I think that not even the first wall
> could be occupied, so thick are the earthworks and so well
> fortified is it with breastworks, towers, guns, and ditches.[36]

Campanella's radial city plan was in fact less the plan for a utopia than an anachronism. It evoked the city-state republicanism that was already withering by the end of the century and would seem positively old-fashioned in the seventeenth. Urban forts, such as the pope's Castel Santo Angelo (1490s) or the Medici's Belvedere (1511) on the southern heights of Florence and Sangallo's Fortezza da Basso in the north (1534), had been calculated to dominate as well as to protect. The enemy was as often within as without. For that reason, as a leading military architect wrote, urban citadels could provoke town dwellers—"like the bridle in the mouths of wild horses" and were "dangerous in cities or places used to living free."[37] Later sixteenth-century architects separated the planning for the perfect fortress from the rest of the city. While the city as a whole was to be fortified, an enclosed polygonal citadel was designed to anchor at least one or another end. Antwerp provided one model, Milan and Turin two others. Two of the sides faced inward and were designed to deter revolt and inhibit the populace; three faced outward to resist besiegers. Vauban added a citadel to the earlier Burgundian fortifications at Lille. (See illustrations.) The citadel testified to the separation of prince and population; as in the Florentine forts, it signaled absolutist, not republican, state forms. The fortified city with the citadel as its head confronting potential enemies within as well as enemies without, departed from republican radial concepts but had a gridlike center, where the cathedral and civic administration welded military concepts to the politics of the absolutist state. The long, straight avenue served the ruler and elites for display purposes. Turin would be constructed by the Savoy monarchs in the early eighteenth century as perhaps the most elegant garrison city of the continent, with grand squares, arcades, and a massive central citadel heroically defended in 1706.[38]

Italian models of fortification became the international style of military architecture. This is evident from the beginnings of the new Italian designs in the late fifteenth and early sixteenth centuries. Renaissance thinkers and artists had transformed concepts of spatiality, intimate and global. Painting and cartography began to go separate ways. By the mid-sixteenth century, the orthographic map (the view onto a flat plane) emerging from the charts that marine navigators required was beginning to displace the city view, although the Braun and Hogenson prints of

European cities, which combined pictorial and maplike features, became prize possessions.[39] (Indeed the Google maps, GPS projections, and computer games that combine elevations and orthographic plans testify to the continuing appeal of combining orthographic and topical features.)

Italian military architects could not all find employment at home, and they took up contracts in France and elsewhere in Europe, including Hungary and the east. Those engineers in the employ of the Habsburgs who controlled Milan and Naples took their designs from the peninsula and Sicily north to Milan and then to the wealthy provinces of the Netherlands, likewise a prize imperial possession. Toward the end of the sixteenth century, treatises on military architecture spread throughout Habsburg possessions: Cristóbal de Rojas and Diego Gonzáles de Medina Barba published studies in 1598 and 1599. The Spanish engineer Fernández de Medrano, stationed in Flanders, brought the new designs back to Madrid, where he would start an engineering division on the model of Vauban's. By the end of the century, the Spanish had fortified the port of Havana, Cartagena de las Indias in today's Colombia, and Mexico's Veracruz, and fortification followed throughout Latin America through the next two centuries.[40]

By the mid-seventeenth century treatises and manuals and engraved site plans proliferated throughout Europe. The Prussian-born Adam Fritag (variant Freitag), who followed the long Dutch war of independence, published perhaps the most influential of the northern treatises on fortifications in 1630. Fritag and the German Spekler would have an impact on Vauban, as he elaborated their ideas for the French frontier. The treatise of Alonso de Cepeda y Andrada appeared in Brussels in 1669, and two years later Pedro Antonio Ramón Foch de Cardona's manual was issued in Naples. In 1672 Andrés Dávila y Heredia published monographs on the fortified sites (plazas) of Picardy and of Lorraine—both provinces then still in the Empire while Jose Cafrion contributed his *Planos de Fortificaciónes de Ciudades* in 1687. Medrano, who emerged in this milieu, emphasized the geometric rules that underlay military architecture in his *Rudimentos Geométricos y Militares* with its chapter on *Fortificación Moderna o Arquitectura militar.*[41] Medrano's fortification designs resembled Vauban's: the technology of artillery suggested common solutions. Medrano would also press for a corps of military engineers on the French model, which would be established, with a new world branch, as well.

The Spanish and Dutch had modified the designs during their long war in the Netherlands: "the biggest, bloodiest and most implacable . . . since the beginning of the world," according to a frustrated Spanish councilor of state.[42] In the densely populated topography of the Low Countries, crisscrossed by waterways and muddy buffers, the science of static war became ever more highly developed. Decades of fighting in the estuaries of the Rhine, Waal, Meuse, and Schelde began to reverse the technological edge of the defensive, but at tremendous cost. To lay siege to a fortress involved a major quasi-architectural effort of its own. Frederick Henry of Nassau used twenty-eight thousand troops to besiege Spanish-held's-Hertogenbosch from May 1, 1629, until its fall four and a half months later. The siege works included many miles of walls, nine bastioned forts, 116 cannons, and six entrenched camps.[43] By the 1620s, France's Marshal de Tavannes could reflect that while thirty years earlier the defensive seemed impregnable, the adversaries in the Netherlands, Antonio Spinola of Genoa, commander for the Spanish, and Maurice of Nassau, Holland's paladin, had so refined the art and science of siege craft that they might overcome the resistance of the strongest fortress and calculate its fall to within a matter of days.[44] (Recall that it was to Maurice's military academy that Descartes had come to learn the arts of war in 1618 and 1619' and where he was overcome by his life-transforming "dreams.") Attackers learned to trench their way toward the walls under continually erected cover, and often to combine artillery fire with massive mines at their base. But this only spurred on the designers to attempt more resistant citadels.

Forts, however, were not just a construction for the frontier, although that coupling would become intuitive by the seventeenth century. Fortification determined territory in general just as pairs of integers or Cartesian coordinates were coming to define a Euclidean plane. Even before Vauban started on his bastioned necklace of the kingdom, Cardinal Richelieu was tearing down the strong places within it. The fort was an instrument of sovereignty, and state space was designed to reduce local power and resistance. In contrast to the defensive walls that enclosed the city, the fortification designed to dominate space was to be constructed in the "middle" or on a significant passage in a conquered territory. A city might grow around it—witness the settlement of San Antonio that serviced the Spanish fortification on the northwestern frontier of Mexico.

But the distant stronghold served primarily to house the forces that asserted a claim to imperial conquests beyond the metropolitan state.

Far to the east in India, artillery had imposed a similar logic. The first of the Mughal conquests were in the north. The major siege involved Emperor Akbar's investment and capture of the Hindu Rajput fortress of Chitar from October 1567 until February 1568. Chitar occupied a massive hill site; the fortress was finally overcome by sapping operations and climaxed with a defense to the death by eight thousand defenders, the suicide of many of the women, and Akbar's slaughter of twenty to thirty thousand peasants who had found themselves on the resisting side. The fortress of Ranthambor fell a year later when an initial artillery barrage and the covered passage had reached the walls. Like Vauban a century later, the Mughal ruler built fortifications even as he overcame others, erecting a quadrilateral of massive citadels at Agra, Allahabad (guarding river junctions in the Gangetic Plain), Lahore (protecting the approaches from Afghanistan), and Ajmer. These enjoyed heavy artillery and massive walls, although not the elaborate geometries of the European forts.[45] As they gained control of northern India the Mughals built their large forts to dominate the Ganges plain and made them the site of government centers.[46]

Siege warfare continued as the Mughals became involved in their long wars of the seventeenth and early eighteenth centuries against the Muslim kingdoms of the Deccan—the belt of south central India running east of today's Mumbai—with a pattern of small sultanates jealous of their autonomy. Fortifications in this region seem to have been reoutfitted from the end of the fifteenth century, then during the middle decades of the sixteenth century and on into the seventeenth century. Thick masonry walls, backed with earth and rubble, were made wide enough to support defensive artillery. Higher parapets with openings for cannons, protected walkways to send troops to threatened positions, gun platforms, and lower outer walls to protect the major enclosure were constructed; ditches and moats were widened and deepened. The fortress of Bidar, roughly three hundred miles east-southeast of Mumbai, fronted on a river system and triple ditching. The upper fortress area was an ellipse about half a mile long; the city below was perhaps twice the area and encircled with a wall and bastions. Other cities such as Golkonda, Bijapur, Gulbarga, Naldurga, and Mudugal had fortifications with similarly formidable elements, sometimes reinforced by their siting on rivers and cliffs. Golkonda, a wealthy Shi'ia sultanate, was ruled by the Qutb Shahi dynasty from 1507 to 1687, when Emperor Aurangzeb finally absorbed the principality. By this date ten kilometers of wall enclosed four different forts. Engineers and artillery experts migrated from the Near East and Turkey. The forts had artillery, as did presumably the attackers. But moving the large cannon into position was not easy. As in Europe it took iron projectiles to do damage, and most forts in the south actually fell by bribery or negotiation.[47]

The Austrian Habsburg-Ottoman border still retained more the nature of an osmotic frontier zone than of the fixed boundary regime such as characterized Italian states and a French kingdom so jealous of very possible territorial acquisition. In eastern and rural Hungary, the fortifications that emerged were palankas or palisades, more akin to the wooden stockades that the United States would erect in the Great Plains in the nineteenth century. For all their expertise in siege techniques, the Turks did not fortify their European frontier—running for much of the sixteenth and seventeenth centuries through western Hungary—with fortifications as elaborate as marked either western Europe or India. Their own frontier was remote from the center of the empire, and into the seventeenth century the Turks were still advancing their lines forward. They relied on Tatars for protecting their rear and devastating the surrounding countryside; they assigned Janissary units for the duration of the siege to the ever more elaborately networked trenches. They raised earthen mounds to a height of the defenders' walls, and they were expert at underground mine attacks. Large armies up to 75,000 soldiers, 20,000 diggers, and 7,000 or so miners assailed Baghdad and about the same number were deployed against Vienna in 1683.[48] Where the Austrians still controlled the land—up to where the Danube curves south toward Buda (held by the Turks since the 1520s) and then beyond to where the river is joined by the Sava at Belgrade and resumes its eastward course—the Habsburgs erected far more imposing fortifications to control the strategic river passages. There, too, the up-to-date features of now highly elaborate fortress architecture—the casemate, demilune (or ravenel), and orillon—left their Italian traces.

More than two centuries later, American soldiers holding the western territories against the Indian tribes they had forced westward or into reservations garrisoned themselves in walled enclosures. Indeed the Indians had built their own fortified sites before the Europeans arrived. The rudimentary American forts were different in function from the European fortification of state space. As the historians and archeologists of the Iowa sites remind us, the white men's forts, continually constructed from the 1680s to the 1860s, were designed to dominate the zonal frontier of a de facto advancing imperial frontier: "to control and manipulate Indians and Indian economies to the advantage of European traders, governments, and settlers. . . . Forts were a primary tool through which Europeans wrested economic control of the Upper Midwest from Indians and the main tool the United States used to establish control and remove Indians from the Upper Midwest."[49] Traders built stockades that might be abandoned after a few seasons; however, when the Indian tribes allied with European powers, the forts became larger and took on such features as blockhouses and bastions.

Fortifications were critical to the claims of colonial territories, especially because fronting on an ocean frontier, colonies remained vulnerable to any rival power and not just an aggressive neighbor. In the Americas, the Spanish fortified Havana from 1558; to the north the French fortified Louisburg on Cape Breton Island, which they were compelled to surrender in 1745 and again in 1758. France had the vast possessions of French Canada, Pondicherry in India, and the Antilles. Vauban became an enthusiast for colonies; indeed, nowhere was he more utopian than his projections of colonial growth in his treatise of 1699, where he warned Louis that he was in danger of losing the colonial race with the Dutch and the British. Vauban looked in particular to Buenos Aires as the site for implantation of a French military settlement. And for French Canada he departed from his usual sobriety to project a steady growth in population from its 14,000 or so in 1700 to 100,000 by 1730, 200,000 by 1760, and 800,000 by 1820 (whereas in reality by 1811 it had grown only to 77,000).[50] In fact, the French would lose first Acadia in 1713, Louisburg twice, then Quebec in 1763; they would minimize their role in India in the 1750s, cede Louisiana to the Spanish, take it back, and then sell it to the Americans in 1803.

Over time, moreover, the coastal fortifications—which now borrowed from the merged doctrines of French, Flemish, and Spanish—became ambiguous assets. It was just as important to guard the great rivers that penetrated overseas possessions and drained the interior of its wealth, whether metals or furs or slaves: the Plata, Amazon, Orinoco, Mississippi, Hudson, and Saint Lawrence, and, on the other side of the Atlantic, the Niger and Congo.[51] The Qing analog was the upper Yangtze and Yellow Rivers. These huge streams drained a whole continent. They could be navigated so that explorations and settlements might be planted a thousand miles from a coast. By the nineteenth century, the British and French would ascend the Nile and the Mekong, respectively. Overseas imperial space was a huge quasi territory, with colliding peoples, exploitable ecology, and fuzzy boundaries. Advancing technology also pushed the elaborate fortifications toward obsolescence. Explosive shells could wreak havoc that solid cannonballs could not. This meant in effect that Vauban's careful designs for impregnability or plans for sieges became rather beside the point by the later eighteenth century: "The new military techniques threw Vauban's ideas into crisis. More than concrete points of fortification, it was the linkage of the territory that was of increasing interest, and in particular the routes that joined essential points of defense, as for example coastal cities and interior strongholds."[52] By the early nineteenth century, the economic and other resources of a territory displaced the focus on the fortress and siege with its "maxims" and geometric designs. The Napoleonic engineer Rogniat defended forts as rallying points for protecting armies and storehouses for supplies but admitted that in themselves they had become "dead bodies" that had no influence beyond the range of their own defensive artillery.[53] Cities in Central Europe demolished their walls as sieges ended and they required more space for their vigorous economic activities. Instead, after midcentury large cities, such as Paris and even New York, constructed barracks and armories for the authorities to guard against urban unrest and ultimately to signal the triumphant hold of the bourgeois militias that guaranteed social peace. Today the Parisian can ignore the great *casernes* of the Garde Républicaine, and the Manhattan resident can visit the armories on Park Avenue, converted through the twentieth century into sites for art exhibitions or musical events, just as the Italian tourist can stroll the walls of Lucca or the grounds of Florence's Belvedere. When sovereignty is contested in the urban context, as the conclusion describes, it is in the public square.

Territory and Sovereignty

The fortress manifested sovereignty, the key property of the territorial state. Sovereignty entails at least two criteria: the first is that one source of authority—whether the executive, the legislature, or the people as a whole—is supreme within the boundaries of the state, although different agencies can be allocated particular functions. The second is that no external authority can legitimately impose its will within the state unless sanctioned by treaty. Cumulative scholarly analysis in international law and political science has identified the modern concept of sovereignty with the Treaties of Westphalia, although the actual provisions of the treaties established important limits on the prerogatives of the signatory rulers.[54] The treaties have been credited as signifying the end of religious dispute as a cause of war and thus a free path to raison d'état, the complete decentralization of the empire, and the equality of states. In fact Westphalia and the related bilateral treaties sanctioned a supposedly Christian peace that preserved some form of imperial constitutionalism with the right of the estates (the territorial representatives within the empire) to vote on war and peace and the protection of minority Christian religious choices when exercised discreetly. Article 65 stipulated that "it shall be free perpetually to each of the States of the Empire, to make Alliances with Strangers for their Preservation and Safety; provided, nevertheless, such Alliances be not against the Emperor, and the Empire, nor against the Publick Peace, and this Treaty, and without prejudice to the Oath by which every one is bound to the Emperor and the Empire."[55] For all the acts of violence during the war, no matter how ferocious, there was to be a total amnesty.

Much of the long text supposedly re-created what had been the status quo but had not prevented the great religious conflicts of the 1540s and the self-immolation of 1618 to 1648. Many of the clauses dealt with rights of succession, transfer and divisions of territory, and the rights of the Swedes and French. It was hoped, the Treaties would inaugurate, or at least reassert, a fellowship of polities that shared important attributes of self-determination regardless of their size and faith. What the label "Westphalian" has come to mean in recent decades is a story of its own, as is the case for so many other political concepts such as republicanism, liberalism, federalism, and so on. Still, even at the time, the Treaties implied recognition of an international system that sanctioned territorial autonomy and sovereignty as well as ongoing reciprocal intercourse.

Modern Western notions of sovereignty began to find their way into international law, in fact, not in 1648, but with an admission of failure a century earlier: the weary emperor Charles V's peace of Augsburg in September 1555, negotiated by his brother, Ferdinand, king of Rome and presumptive successor to the imperial title. Despite all Charles's efforts—which meant efforts to make Catholic reform attractive enough to restore the loyalty of the Protestants—the frustrated emperor had not been able to end the religious civil wars of the empire. Consequently Lutheran princes (signatories of the earlier Confession of Augsburg in 1542) could keep their states Lutheran; princes adhering to "the old religion" could also remain undisturbed. (Calvinists were not given rights until Westphalia.) Subjects unwilling to accept the territorially decreed faith could emigrate elsewhere with their property and their "honor": no imputation of treason was implied.[56] Territory, the will of the prince, and innermost conviction were bundled together; the principle was known as *cuius regio eius religio:* "whosever the state, his the religion." Partition was the answer to unbridgeable differences, and emigration was the only license given to dissent. Complete sovereignty was not under discussion, but its most contested property, mandating religious observation, followed from territorial control.

Perhaps it was easier in the German lands to arrive at such a solution, even though it had taken more than thirty years from the Lutheran challenge to do so. The empire was understood as a federation; French commentators argued that, in contrast, their king in his kingdom had more rights than the emperor within the (elective) Empire.[57] Neither the Valois kings nor a significant number of French Catholic magnates would have been willing or able to concede such a settlement: there was no equivalent federal structure, although by 1590 Henry IV would concede to Huguenots the right of territorial defense in a limited number of cities, most significant being the port of La Rochelle. The preceding decades of religious civil war in France had not followed territorial jurisdiction, but had emerged from the assassinations and group murder between national factions in the 1560s and 1570s. Control of the territorial state as a whole became the stake for the magnates and their armies. Lutheran and Calvinist theories of resistance from midcentury raised the ante: resistance was justified when a ruler persecuted his subjects on grounds of religion. In the 1560s it still seemed possible to win the queen mother, Catherine de Médicis, for a policy of toleration; the party of moderates or *politiques,* and intellectuals such as Montaigne and even the defender of royal power Bodin, resisted the idea of religious compulsion even if they thought the Calvinists were themselves seeking political control. Catherine, however, feared the growing influence of the Huguenots and authorized the adherents of the Guise party to eliminate their leaders in the bloody purge of Saint Bartholomew's Night in 1572. Philip II's deputy, Alva, was simultaneously resorting to similar repression against the Calvinists in Flanders and the southern Netherlands.

With the failure of religious pluralism in France, Bodin modified his earlier belief that the estates of the realm should have a co-voice in government and argued instead for absolute, even despotic power of the monarch. Sovereignty could not be shared; neither was rebellion in any sense a latent right of subjects as Huguenot theorists had argued. "Majesty or sovereignty is the most high, absolute, and perpetual power over the citizens and subjects in a Commonwealth, which the Latins call *Majestas,*" Bodin argued. The monarch was supposedly subject to the fundamental dictates of natural law; there existed a normative order built on recognition of ancient rights of individuals and collective bodies that recognized property and liberties. Nonetheless, even were the estates to declare their monarch a tyrant, they could not take action or refuse obedience. "If the prince is an absolute sovereign, as are the true kings of France, Spain, England, Scotland, Ethiopia, Turkey, Persia and Muscovy, whose authority is unquestionably their own, and not shared with any of their subjects, then it is in no circumstances permissible either by any of their subjects in particular, or in general, to attempt anything against the life and honor of their king, either by process of law or force of arms, even though he has committed all the evil, impious and cruel deeds imaginable." The rather gossamer limitation on power that Bodin attributed to natural law, Hobbes would assign seventy-five years later to the contract among inhabitants that establishes civil, that is, political society. Since a sovereign is chosen to protect property and life, subjects have no obligation to surrender their lives; if the monarch can no longer provide protection in the case of military defeat, their obligation also ends. Hobbes is hardly softhearted when it comes to describing the ruler's authority, but he leaves his subjects with the recourse of disobedience and rebellion, whereas Bodin promises only a permanent state of exception.[58]

What remains perhaps most significant in Bodin are the justifications of obedience and legitimacy not chosen. There was no recourse to patriarchal analogues, as in Filmer (or in the Confucian tradition of East Asia), nor to God's endowing the monarch with the right to be obeyed, as James I and Charles I would claim. Sovereignty arose from the need to have a single source for legislation. It arose from necessity. In the Muslim world the moral force of the monarch, his fulfilling of ethical and religious obligations, and his personal lineage remained important.[59] Ottomans and later Timurids (Tamburlaine's line) and, through the Timurids, the Mughals claimed descent not merely from the dynastic founder but the great Chinggis Khan, ruler of Asia, a monster but a grand one. To which the Ottomans added after 1453 delegation from the last Roman emperor, ruling in Constantinople. Neither in Mughal nor Ottoman realms, however, did defense of religion mean the imposition of orthodoxy or the requirement of exile for minorities. Ever since the Arab conquests, the sultan recognized other non-Muslim communities in his domain, as did the Mughal emperor. Of course, the Mughal state expanded into a land that had had Hindus long before Muslims, whereas Charles V and Catherine de Médicis watched horrified as schism took root.

Renaissance political ideas, as Quentin Skinner has emphasized, were on their way to separating the idea of the state from the person of the monarch; and to separating the claims of authority from religious justification. "By the beginning of the seventeenth century, the concept of the State—its nature, its powers, its right to command obedience—had come to be regarded as the most important object of analysis in European political thought."[60] For Skinner, Bodin's analysis of sovereignty as an attribute of the state "constitutes a crucial transition in the development of absolutist political thought."[61] It arises from internal considerations, not from the Westphalian order, which it preceded in any case. Precisely in this self-generated necessity emerge the implications for the idea of territory. For if we are stripping away all claims to legislative capacity rooted in particular communities, then only the spatial scope of authority defines its limits. Inclusion within a boundary alone defines the power and the limits of sovereignty. This means that the well-defined Western state must be a spatial entity, separate from a religious organization that binds without reference to borders. Abu'l-Fazl in contrast followed the great monarch Akbar into his marvelous tent city as he moved his capital from sites connected too closely to Muslim practice. The emperor created the space of obedience virtually with his aura and the reach of his personal authority, as did the Timurids and Mongols before him. His Islamic empire had sacred sites, to be sure, but its spatial claims were elastic, if ambitious, indeed incidental in their own right to its mission and sovereignty.

The European state was increasingly defined within its borders. Still, it would be wrong to depict this process too uniformly. Bodin and Hobbes described the way states should be organized, not the way they were. Sovereignty is not easy to disengage. Even in emerging territorial states—so Peter Sahlins argues in his close study of boundary construction in the Pyrenees after the peace of 1659—the French and Spanish defined their respective rights for a long while in terms of jurisdiction over particular sectors of economic and legal life, even if these were based across the new frontier. Only a century later would state claims pervade all aspects of control on the respective sides of the border, and the actual site of the border still remains to be worked out.[62] Notions of sovereignty also remained intermingled with property rights. The agencies of empire such as the East India Company or the Dutch VOC were often private monopolies—not subversive states within states, and not proto-NGOs, but para-states authorized by state legislation to raise private funds, to use violence, and to punish.

––––––––––

This raises a larger issue: the entanglement of economic with political claims. Property rights and ownership are never totally separated from political rights and sovereignty. The acquisition of overseas empire makes this overlap starkly apparent, for it melds proprietorship with government. On the individual level, slavery had long fused chattel possession with the right to discipline short of inflicting death. But (as taken up in Chapter 5) territories as well as individuals could also be bought and sold and not just acquired by conquest. The establishing of colonies was raising immense questions about the relations of commerce to territorial control and about the limits of the authority that could be claimed over the tribes and states that came under European purview.

There is no scope here to examine the profound impulses that originated in the global economy: the flows of specie from the New World, via Europe to Asia; the growth of population and the disturbing impact of mendicants on the road; the opening of the long-distance grain trade from Eastern Europe and its incentives for imposing the so-called second serfdom; finally, leading into the eighteenth century, the Atlantic's emergence as a basin for exchanging sugar and its secondary products, European capital and African slaves. These trends, as much as warfare, had their own impact on territorialization. Dominican and Jesuit clerics construed the right to property as a fundamental principle of natural law, possessed by all men. To think about government, citizenship, power, and obligation, Annabel Brett argues, involved resuming a dialogue with Aristotle and with the idea of the polis via Scholasticism and natural law theory after many intervening centuries. This held for the Protestants, as well, whether Grotius or the early Lutheran jurist Melchior King, whom Brett cites as explaining that the law of nature commands mankind to divide things up: "peoples separatd [*sic*], kingdoms founded, dominia distinguished, boundaries put on fields."[63] Paradoxically the zeal for individual property can be justified by the command to use things in common, but the point is that only division can benefit the species as a whole. Getting places, controlling spaces, and establishing frontiers is crucial.

In the West the theory of statehood emerged to meet multiple challenges: It established the international parity of monarchies and in most respects the states with the emperor; it allowed the secular authority to claim power above or beyond religious convictions that tore the commonwealth apart. In his late lectures during the 1970s, Michel Foucault argued further that another key aspect of the early modern political order deserved historical attention. He suggested that the late medieval church had developed so intense a pastoral mission that it had an impact on the organization of the political world: "Governmentality," no less than sovereignty, he argued became the fundamental concern. As a key secular text, Foucault cited the 1555 treatise of Guillaume de la Perrière, *Le miroir politique,* which asked how a ruler should govern the economy, "to regulate individuals, property, wealth, as the good father had to do inside a family." Foucault contrasted this concern with the Machiavellian objective of sovereignty, which does not pertain to the welfare of the state's population, but to its territory: "Territory is the fundamental element of Machiavelli's principality and the juridical sovereignty of the sovereign."[64] But the institutions needed to demonstrate sovereignty, the military, fiscal, and legal apparatuses, were already long present. Now the state crossed another threshold. "With the 16th century, we enter into the age of behavior, into the age of instruction, into the age of governments,"[65] and, he added, "what's important, what has to be emphasized, what's a real historical phenomenon . . . is that this is the moment when that thing which is the state starts to enter and enter effectively into men's considered actions *(pratique réfléchi).*"[66] In fact, governmentality, or the state's adaptation of church pastoralism also depended on territorial circumscription, often on the basis of the jurisdictions developed by the church. Charles Cardinal Borromeo, archbishop of Milan, persecutor of heretics but also heroic model during the years of plague and famine in the 1570s, was the most active of the pastoral administrators. He zealously supervised execution of the Tridentine reforms and tirelessly set about reorganizing the parishes, monastic orders, and welfare institutions of the archdiocese, not without significant friction with the Spanish political administration, which was no less Catholic but intent on consolidating its own territorial power.[67] Territorial rationalization and territorial acquisition expressed and advanced the multiple activities that established early modernity: political domination, taking possession, and moral regulation. Sovereignty, ownership, and morality came with the territory literally and figuratively.

The Spaces of Early Modernity

The fantastically elaborated fortresses, which by 1700 had been emulated throughout Europe, were clearly prestige displays and occasions for architectural virtuosity. But, more fundamentally, they were instruments of war and domination. The fortification was the epitome of a claim on sovereignty. This was understood from the beginnings, perhaps since the

Hebrews and Greeks, for in contrast to battles in open territory, the fall of a fortified city implied the loss of sovereignty and exposed its inhabitants to a lapse of law; they could claim no restraint from their assailants. The medieval laws of war recognized that the siege had rules of its own. A siege started with a formal summons to surrender. If the demand was rejected, then hostilities began with a ritual salvo or trumpet call. If the siege ended with the overrunning of the city, civilians, aside from the servants of the church, no longer enjoyed the rights of noncombatants. When fortified cities resisted and fell, whether to Europeans or Turks, they were sacked, the males often killed, the women deemed objects of rape, and private property available for plunder. Non-Christians could be sold into slavery. Certainly, impatient soldiers, who had endured long and dangerous assaults, and often had not been paid in any timely manner, must be allowed to vent their frustrations and enjoy their victory. But the ravages demonstrate that power, control, and sovereignty had passed from vanquished to victor. The taking of a resisting city, from Constantinople in 1453, Rome in 1526, Magdeburg in 1631, to Nanjing in 1937, and countless others along the way and even since meant its reduction to a liminal space of lawlessness. Shakespeare's Henry V, in a brief but memorable scene, confirms the execution of Bardolph, his friend from carefree carousing days, because contrary to royal orders Bardolph had taken a silver pyx from a French church in the conquered Norman port of Harfleur. Harfleur, however, had meekly surrendered after Henry described the horrors that would result from defiance. Had the city resisted and been overrun, Bardolph might not have been punished at all. Shakespeare knew the rules.[68]

Fortifications did not bring about modern statehood, nor did the discovery of how to cast iron cannonballs around 1450 produce the European state system of 1700, nor did the fortress alone establish a prototype of modern territoriality. But they are connected to the territorial state as much as are confessional conflict, the two-century revival of Roman law along with the elaboration of "public law" on the European continent, and with political theory. Sovereign units defined by firm borders—with a center of authority recognized by subjects and foreigners alike—were encouraged by many trends. History is overdetermined, and the zealous historian can find that every significant development has drawn on (and in that sense is "caused") by any or all of its predecessors. The political scientist may call for parsimonious explanations, but the historical world, I believe, rarely lets us untangle causes (or isolate clean coefficients for multiple regressions).

Political space takes on clearer boundaries in these centuries, as state space intrudes on the space of empires. State space follows rules defined by *l'esprit mathématique* of the seventeenth century exemplified by Descartes's coordinates, Kepler's orbits, and later Newton's laws. (Foucault's "governmentality" was also to acquire its eventual mathematical foundations: the political "arithmetick" of William Petty, and the statistical methods of Blaise Pascal, the Bernoulli family, and other pioneers.) Whether seeking to inscribe the ideal arrangements of bastions into circles and pentagons, or trying to project the global meridians onto the flat spaces of navigators' maps and Mercator's projections by the ever-patient iteration of sines, tangents, and cosines, the mapmakers advanced the awareness of infinitesimals that Newton and Leibniz transformed into derivative and integral. The triumphs of baroque vertical spatiality, as worked out by Borromini and Bernini in Rome, with their vertiginous interchange between heavenly and earthly realms—modeled by the grand stairway, the concealed light, the depictions of ecstasy—still attract. But the ecstatic religious architecture stimulated by the Counter-Reformation would yield to a more terrestrially oriented splendor, whether for Bernini himself, as he depicted the great rivers of empire—Nile, Danube, Ganges, and Rio de la Plata—at the Piazza Navona in 1651, or by the next generations of architects who built the grand rectangular palaces of Versailles or Mafra, Caserta, or Wurzburg with Tiepolo's gorgeous evocations of the earth's continents.

Nineteenth-century authors would remember how important the lines of territorial sovereignty had become. Manzoni's beset betrothed can breathe again when they cross into Bergamo, a city just within the Venetian republic's terra firma, leaving Milan's abusive duke across the twisting border. Dumas's Musketeers have to cope with Cardinal Richelieu at the siege of La Rochelle, and their kangaroo court condemns Milady de Winter on the then frontier between France and the Spanish Netherlands. The Musketeers, recalled for their bonhomie, are anachronistic adventurers, violating the laws against dueling, executing women, and transgressing geographic and behavioral borders. The Japanese might see them as *ronin* or masterless samurai.

Indeed, far away the era of *ronin* was ending, too. The dramatic passage of power from an anarchic conflict of powerful lords to an emerging rationalizer of the state would culminate with the taking of Osaka Castle in 1614. The Tokugawa rulers of Japan, who fought their way to power between 1590 and 1630 and subordinated the welter of decentralized nobles, built their great pagodalike structures in key feudal cities. These strongholds do not come with the pedigree of Renaissance geometry, but they emerge from an era of artillery. They enclosed large citadels within thirty-foot slanting walls of stone and built within them intricate mazes and passages for defenders to move and fight and placed graceful pagodas atop. After relentless campaigns in the open fields, continual bargaining, frequent betrayals across the late Ashikaga era of civil breakdown, and three decades of strong-man consolidation, the feudal castles were taken by the new shogun, many destroyed and a few retained to signify sites of domination within. Island realms have an advantage in that their boundaries seem naturally given, but they still have to overcome the inner divisions, which Britain and Japan accomplished largely in the seventeenth century, admittedly with very different structures. By then, in so many states, with sovereignty established and territory enclosed, the agenda to which Foucault applied the term *governmentality* was to claim more attention. But it, too, would call for further territorial rationalization, now in the pursuit of production and revenue.

3

Contesting the Countryside

VAUBAN DID NOT DESIGN VERSAILLES. His king's palace was not a frontier fortress, but both fortresses and palace testified to the mastery of territory, to sovereign power, and to sovereign wealth. Developments of the sixteenth and seventeenth centuries—religious conflicts at home, protracted warfare, and the Europeans' claims to remote colonies—thrust the political rights that inhered in territory into the foreground of Western discourse. Within Europe politics had to be disengaged from religion and concepts of sovereignty refined in the fires of domestic rebellions and civil war; Machiavelli, Bodin, James I, and Hobbes among others, set the uncompromising tone of debate. The stakes of sovereignty, however, were already understood to be broader than power for its own sake. "If no force, no trade," James I's adviser was warned by his ambassador in the Indian Ocean at a moment that early economic writers at home were making clear the converse constraint: if no trade, no force. Maintaining authority whether at home or among rival nations required money.

The analysis of production and trade in the service of the state constituted a body of early economic thought subsequently labeled "mercantilism." Mercantilist writers disengaged economic activity and the logic of markets from general social description or pure political analysis. They did so, however, in the cause of politics. Early political economists, among them Antoine de Montchrestien, the Huguenot writer settled in London, identified national wealth as a dimension of state resources. The riches and production of the kingdom served national power. In effect, mercantilism was a prescription for the economic dimensions of international competitiveness. The idea of a trade-off between what later analysts stylized as "guns and butter," or civilian and military economic goods, was foreign to this mentality—there could be no butter without guns, fewer guns if there were less butter. Defense or acquisition of land would enhance power and plenty together.[1] Control of sea routes was certainly crucial.

Mercantilist policy advisers focused on the wealth of the state, not its individual subjects, but understood that the two were intertwined. A pauperized populace could not long sustain a strong state. Foucault used the term *governability* to describe the broader mission of ensuring the population's welfare. It supplemented, even displaced, the sixteenth-century stress on sovereignty defined, so he felt, by Machiavelli.[2] Pursuing governmentality entailed nurturing the demographic and economic resources of society to ensure its domestic vitality, whereas the concern with sovereignty arose from the needs of the state as a competitive unit among other states. The national territory remained the physical foundation of both dimensions of state viability. How should it be exploited? The Whig propagandist Daniel Defoe celebrated the bustle and the evident wealth created by trade in his economic and geographic survey of "the whole island of Great Britain,"[3] while other commentators on the continent or in colonies abroad lamented the persistent poverty of the countryside. The debates engaged agricultural proprietors, men of letters, officials, and clerics from Edinburgh to Naples, Buenos Aires, and Virginia to Versailles, Milan, Vienna, Berlin Stockholm, and Saint Petersburg, and all the other towns where a reading public existed. As a group, they debated each other's tracts, sponsored essays competitions, organized societies for agricultural improvement, and wrestled with difficult questions. Supremely aware of European civilizational attainment, men of letters asked how an organized society provided for the urban goods, the legal services, its religious establishment, military and administrative governance, as well as its writers, artists, and musicians. How was surplus to be created, how husbanded, how and by whom appropriated? Why were some societies so much better at generating wealth and surplus than others?

Tackling these questions meant thinking systemically about a national or regional economy, that is, analyzing not just the abstract working of markets, but of a territorial unit that continued through time and supported a political and cultural superstructure. To begin with how could states "see" clearly what productive resources their territories held and how could they decide what tax, property, and labor regimes allowed the maximum share of surplus to be moved to hard-pressed governments from hard-pressed peasantries? Today's theorists talk about the state's need for "legibility." The great eighteenth-century instrument for achieving it was the property map or cadaster, discussed later in this chapter as a fundamental instrument for administering territory. If land provided the underlying source of surplus, then the conclusion for fiscal policy might be to tax the yield of land and not people or consumption. For John Locke and others, including many who stressed the fecundity of agriculture, land yielded value only when humans transformed it—human labor was at least an equal factor of production; this theory justified the acquisition of co-lonial land from natives who allegedly did not transform it.[4] The tax con-sequences of these views had to be different. To tax agricultural products would not discourage the land from remaining fruitful; to tax the laborer might diminish growth. And capital—or "stock" as Adam Smith would call it—might remain the most elusive source of value; indeed, was it a source, or just the residue of prior "parsimony," or even, as Marx would suggest, originally the fruit of blatant conquest and subjection? Whether in the "plantations" or at home, how should one separate the value derived from acreage, whether appropriated by conquest or alleged purchase, from the income to be extracted by political control of those who labored? In theory economic rights had long been separated from sovereignty or political power, just as rights to usufruct or enjoyment of revenues had been separated from ownership of property, whether the owner was the sovereign or his subjects. But territory tended to tangle the political and the economic domains: it provided a common but contested ground.

Vauban Looks Inward

Close to seventy years old, the tireless Vauban turned his gaze from the French frontier he had spent thirty years fortifying to contemplate the economic state of the kingdom. Not that he abandoned his sieges and his ramparts, but the 1690s and first decade of the new century brought bleak years of hardship and misery. Louis's expansionism had prodded his enemies—Holland, the empire, Spain, and Savoy—to coalesce in 1686, and the king attacked preemptively in 1688. The Glorious Revolution of 1689 allowed the Dutch Stadholder and principal organizer of the anti-French coalition, William of Orange, to throw Britain into this war that would end only in 1697. The ensuing respite of peace would quickly end with Louis's ambition to establish his grandson as heir to the Spanish Habsburg line and led to a new major war from 1701 to 1713. Almost continual warfare only added to the miseries exacted by calamitous cold weather, wretched harvests, soaring grain prices, and local famines in the early 1690s. The revocation of the Edict of Nantes in 1695 provoked the exit of a talented and industrious religious minority. A population that had peaked at 22.45 million in 1690 dropped to 20.74 in 1695, a loss of about 7.5 percent. (These are today's estimates; Vauban believed that the population at the end of the century amounted to more than 19,094,000, but that the country might support 23 to 25 million.) Beggars and the wandering poor filled the roads and crowded the cities' shelters and public bakeries—the visible index of depression and despair.[5]

Paying for the war and helping a depleted country recover became as crucial as defending its borders. Feudal and seigneurial grants had diffused the economic resources of the kingdom—by some theories, contested to be sure, once the property of the king—to the locally powerful for almost a millennium. Not only in France but throughout Europe and in many of the states of Asia. The ancien régime did not yield its rents, tithes, and accumulated privileges easily. Indeed the contest between rulers and magnates led to crisis and revolution throughout much of the seventeenth century and again at the end of the eighteenth century, when the confrontations mobilized democratic spokesmen, as well.

In 1695 Vauban prepared a proposal for a 5 percent general tax *(capitation)* on the income from land, mills, and manufactures as well as royal offices and "rentes." He collected statistics and sketched out a social survey of his native district of Vézelay in Burgundy—underdeveloped and deforested with a peasantry ill nourished, meanly housed, and ill clad. Burgundy's woes prodded him to consider the larger canvas, and in 1700 he began sketching a project for fiscal reform. By 1707 Vauban presented his monarch, also worn down by more than a half century of rule and warfare, his long-worked-over *Projet pour une Dîme Royale,* his proposal for a Royal Tenth, which would overcome economic stagnation, fiscal inefficiency, and the injustices of privilege he felt afflicted his country. As with the idea of 1695, the plan was to replace multiple and uneven taxes—of which the major one, the taille, often exempted the nobility—with a single tax on combined sources of income with no exemptions but graded to spare the poorer classes of the country. The base rate would be levied at 10 percent of evaluated income, but for agriculture or artisans in times of peace it might be halved. The church would retain its tithing rights, and the notorious salt tax, the *gabelle,* would be moderated. (Not only was the latter tax a heavy burden and a major incentive to smugglers, perhaps most seriously it meant that country families who might have been expected to raise a pig to provide a long winter of pork and bacon could not afford the salt needed to preserve the meat and had to renounce what might have been an easy augmentation of their diet.) Underlying the proposal was a statistical estimate of national income and occupations. Though motivated by frustration at the country's poverty and an ardent reformist search for greater equity and prosperity, Vauban was no revolutionary. He believed in the role of an aristocracy, though one that would be bound closer to state service as in Prussia and Russia and would thus contribute to national efficiency.[6]

Vauban was not alone. His "Project" was sometimes attributed to the similar efforts of Pierre le Pesant, Sieur de Boisguillebert (or Boisguilbert), a Norman noble of the robe long ensconced in the parlament of Rouen who had also called for a 5 percent capitation in his own 1695 treatise, *Le détail de la France; la cause de la diminution de ses biens et la facilité du remède.* Two years later he wrote, "Since creation, it remains unprecedented that a rich nation should lose half its wealth within thirty or forty years without having suffered plagues or wars or any of the other disasters that usually bring countries to their ruin. . . . All landed property has sunk to half its former price." He dated the decline from 1660.[7] Vauban and Boisguillebert both pleaded for a rethinking of national wealth, in terms not just of specie, as favored by Colbert, the finance minister of the 1670s, but national resources more generally. "From all the research I have been able to carry out," Vauban estimated, "in recent times, close to a tenth of the people are reduced to begging; while of the nine other parts, five are unable to contribute to any charity for the first tenth because they themselves are almost as badly off; three tenths are quite strapped [*fort mal-aisées*] and laden with debts, and that among the remaining tenth, including the nobility of the sword and robe, churchmen, upper nobility, high nobility, wealthy merchants, the best-off bourgeois, there are only about 100,000 families . . . and only about 10,000 one might describe as really well-off. . . . The causes of the poverty of the people of this state are well known . . . it is important to seek a solid means to stop this disorder while we are enjoying a period of peace, which promises, so it seems, to be long-lasting."[8] The last phrase was probably a bit of indirect policy advice, and in any case soon proved to be wrong as Louis headed for war over the impending succession in Spain.

Vauban spelled out the economic and fiscal woes of the kingdom. The real wealth of a country did not consist of gold or silver, but "in the abundance of basic commodities" *(denrées):* wines, brandies, salt, grains, and textiles. France should be a wealthy country. It had a vigorous internal trade and demand for its products abroad; however, the land was yielding a third less than it did thirty or forty years earlier.[9] The working year for most of those employed—allowing for fifty-two Sundays and thirty religious holidays, a quotient of bad weather, perhaps three weeks of illness—was only 180 days, and when children and old people were subtracted, less than half the population was in the active labor force. The fiscal system was a major cause of the economic woes. The major taxes, the tailles, were irregularly assessed, either weighing too oppressively on the hardworking laborer or suspended for the wealthy.[10] Couple this with the abusiveness of uncontrolled tax collectors, the possibilities for evasion presented by the new and useless commerce in bonds—particularly bearer bonds that could not be traced—and the impoverishment of districts and families by years of warfare, and one could sense that the capacity for military exertions had reached its limit. Vauban took continuing and expensive warfare as a given. But with reform he believed that France would be wealthy enough to sustain it. Clear out the army of collectors, take away the greatest privileges, eliminate the pervasive venality and corruption—most interesting, perhaps, divide the territory into equal-size districts in which a sort of military fiscal police would visit families four times a year to ascertain wealth and assign tax burden—a system he believed the Chinese and Mughals followed—and a vast improvement would ensue. "The establishment of the royal tenth seems to me the only means capable for providing a real recuperation for the kingdom and that which can most add to the glory of the king and most easily augment his revolutions."[11] He indulged in a rosy conclusion: "Poverty will be banished from the kingdom; we will no longer see city streets and the major roads filled with beggars . . . commerce from province to province and city to city will be reinvigorated with no internal taxes or customs . . . commodities will be abundant and will facilitate international commerce, and since the people will cease to be in the impoverished state they are now it will be easier to find the necessary help for the fortifications of the frontier, the public works of the sea ports, the safety of the coasts . . . for the work needed to make rivers more navigable, to drain the swamps, to plant forests or clear them where they are overgrown, and finally to repair the great highways."[12]

Vauban thus went beyond the immediate fiscal emergency to raise perhaps the most perplexing inquiry of all: What quality inherent in resources or what activity imparted "value," whether the value arising out of a single transaction, or the value that increased over time? The economists on both sides of the Channel—in continual dialogue—and in all centers of learning, wrestled further with the distinction between value and price; these seemed intimately related but were not the same, so how did they differ? And the question of value was easily conflated with the issue of surplus, the economic product created that exceeded the subsistence needs of the population. Surplus could become "capital" to produce further surplus or it might be claimed by ecclesiastical or political authorities to cover the costs of war and administration—the latter of course including ostentatious display and the interest payments to those who might lend rulers the surplus they controlled. But no matter what its use, how was it generated? What was its source?

Did the devoted public servant believe that his elegant plan had a chance? In the event, court officials suppressed the tract (which did not impede its circulation) and rejected its proposals out of hand. Vauban died of pneumonia a month later. His reforms took for granted the existence of a stratified and largely agrarian society, but assumed it could be made more rational. Distinction and privilege, however, remained its very marrow. The grand monarch had reduced the corporate power of his nobles, but he remained entrenched in an institutional structure dependent on exemptions and tradition. At the same time across the Channel, the British were mobilizing their national wealth for the Whigs' and Orange war efforts with a different approach; they arrived at an oligarchic consensus that accepted self-taxation and created a national credit system through the through the Bank of England, which gathered the surplus from an expanding commerce by promising secure returns.[13] Vauban's plan distrusted bearer bonds as instruments for tax evasion and looked to the product of the land. Ultimately he put his faith in the massive fixity of the national space, its frontiers rendered inviolable, its interior the source of its wealth. The elements of this vision were to recur again and again as a fundamental territorial alternative.

Vauban's was a reform too far—a proto-Enlightenment tract for a society rife with extremes of wealth and poverty, replete with intellectual luster but institutional sclerosis. (France would impose a *dixième* in 1710, suspend it in 1717, reimpose it during wartime again in 1733, suspend it with peace, reintroduce it in 1740, and keep it in place, but based on outworn assessments and considered as an exceptional expedient for wartime. Still, it would remain the model for a single tax based on the value of land.) Vauban gave little thought to the conditions that enhanced agrarian output except insofar as they were impacted by taxes. More general approaches to increasing the output of the land would have to await later reformers, all of whom, however, saw an important relationship between government policies and agricultural output. Issues of agricultural productivity were critical for the councilors of the Kangxi and Qianlong emperors, for the Austrian cameralists, Tuscan and Neapolitan reformers, the Spanish Bourbon ministers of Charles III, the French reformers and *Économistes* who felt themselves part of Turgot's ministerial team in the mid-1770s, the ambitious samurai administering the outlying daimyo domains in Tokugawa Japan, and the British governors of Bengal.

Spatial knowledge (what Germans have termed *Raumwissen*) became the prerequisite for rationalizing state resources.[14] Ultimately within preindustrial societies—even those with an active commercial or manufacturing sector or those with access to bullion—state revenues had to be claimed from those who worked or controlled the land. The extraction of resources thus required imagining a new connection between the land and its peasantry. Reformist policy makers developed an implicit agrarian constitutionalism. By the mid to late century, they were to envision a class of peasant producers as well as landlords who would respond to market incentives—freer prices, labor mobility, and finally the removal of restrictions on acquisition and sale of land. Even when a significant share of their own states' wealth benefited from a robust offshore slave market, Western agrarian reformers came to decide that the productivity of their domestic peasantry would go hand in hand with their development as citizens. Political rights should correspond to economic responsibilities; civic capacities would mature with agrarian development.

A Century of Cold and Conflict

However, such a connection lay a century in the future. After a late sixteenth-century era of relative affluence, scarcity and the struggle over resources rapidly darkened politics across many global societies. Colder weather—the "little ice age"—seems to have characterized global climate for much of the seventeenth century. It arrived after a widespread period of affluence in the late sixteenth century. The historian Geoffrey Parker has magnificently followed its global ramifications in all their terrifying detail: crop failures; excess mortality; wars and insurrections in which civilians were routinely raped, plundered, and brutally murdered; massive population losses across the globe. Plague struck Spain in 1598–1599, Milan in 1600, again in southern Europe at midcentury and England a decade later; flooding and famine were endemic.[15] For Marx, looking back from the mid-nineteenth century, it was the nodes of commerce, the urban incubator of the bourgeoisie, that threw feudal society into crisis. But even without the generation of a new class motivated by the circle of commercial profits and investment, early modern agrarian states faced characteristic resource constraints and an abiding set of what Marxist analysts would call "contradictions."[16] Hard times stuck unevenly, of course, but the European evidence is of widespread misery. Falling grain prices meant not well-fed town workers but miserable peasants with higher real rents, taxes, and interest to pay; a depressed market for urban or rural products; and depopulation of the countryside. In France the average temperatures fell 1.3 degrees Celsius in the last fourteen years of the century relative to the previous decade, which meant a fortnight's delay in the harvests. The year 1692 was particularly cold, 1693 particularly wet.[17] Spain seems to have shared its neighbor's meteorological fortunes: It suffered famines in demographic crises in 1630–1632, 1647–1652, and 1684, followed by the tribulations of seventeenth century wars that prompted Vauban's reflections.

Developments in East Asia ran in sync. By around 1600 population had nearly tripled in Ming China while New World silver provided liquidity for a vibrant economy, characterized, as is the case with our contemporary era, with sometimes staggering inequality.[18] But this highly developed civilization was hardly immune to ecological and political catastrophe. In the upriver regions that drained into the Pearl River delta the economic and ecological balanced became more vulnerable by the middle third of the seventeenth century. Han Chinese peoples and the Ming state had pressed other, once predominant cultures to the margins. The new settlers farmed more intensively, cleared the forests, watched the silt wash downstream to fill in much of the delta, and led, in the judgment of Robert B. Marks's environmental history of South China, to "the shattering of the biological old regime." The Manchu invasions and the clamorous collapse of the Ming order culminated the misery: population in the south China region declined until the 1680s, and "the 40-year period beginning in 1644 was one wrought by crisis: civil war, banditry and piracy, peasant uprisings, trade dislocation, and declining harvest yields caused by colder temperatures all combined to make life in those years uncertain at best, unlike any that had preceded or followed."[19]

Historians have often been cautious about confirming a general crisis of the seventeenth century: the profession specializes in the careful chipping away at earlier generalizations.[20] Nonetheless, it is hard not to read the accounts of violence, impoverishment, hunger, and rebellion that afflicted so many regions without believing that systemic difficulties were involved. To be sure, some regions remained more exempt than others or experienced their hardship on a different time scale: seventeenth-century Japan was recovering from earlier civil war although brutally suppressing Christian inroads; the Mughal dynasty was continuing to construct an opulent state. Still, even where climatological shifts seemed minimal, the agrarian empires and monarchies faced institutional bottlenecks. Tax efforts in France had helped trigger the Fronde. Madrid's Minister Olivares's "Union of Arms"—an effort to extend the tax burdens from Castile to Aragon—provoked revolts in Catalonia, Sicily, and Naples, and royal tax decrees ran into the entrenched opposition of the wealthy local families in Peru and Mexico.[21]

The Ottoman Empire, so feared and successful through Süleyman's reign, faced military setbacks on the Hungarian frontier and against the Iranians, as well as a long-standing disintegration of the timar system of supporting its frontier armies. The timars were the smallest fiefs, each a collection of villages that could support a cavalryman (sipahi), his military equipment, and a couple of retainers. Originally at the disposal of the sultan, who in theory held ultimate ownership over the land, by the 1530s timar holders had become in effect a hereditary class.[22] As siege warfare and handguns spread, infantry became more crucial, cavalry more dispensable. The urban infantry, the Janissaries, played a larger role; the Ottoman cavalry played less of one, and the sultan had to find sources of income to pay for larger infantry forces. In general, armies based on assigned but revocable fiefs became harder to support—whether composed of soldiers who lived on their fief as did the sipahi, or were just assigned earmarked revenues, as provided by Mughal jaghirs. Peasants were fleeing the harsh burden of taxes and dues; commanders came with depleted units. Conservative reformers lamented the decline of an inherited caste; "the rational graded meritocracy constructed by the Ottomans was shaken from top to bottom. The pursuit of personal interest, vital to survival during the inflation episode, became endemic in Ottoman life thereafter."[23] "When it is a question of service on campaigns," wrote one reformer in a memorandum for Sultan Murad IV in the early 1630s, "not one man appears from ten timars, but at the time of tax-gathering, ten men dispute one timar."[24]

The decay of the timar system necessarily impacted the agrarian relationships on which it rested. The government absorbed many of the prebendal incomes and in return allowed its burgeoning officials, and not just landholders, to collect taxes and become quasi-private owners, a process to be completed after the land law of 1858. Officials and timar holders converted their holdings into *wakfs,* or fiscally privileged religious foundations, with themselves as trustees and beneficiaries. Whereas earlier the military class had, in effect, structured the agricultural relations of the countryside and mediated between state and peasantry, a new network of rent collectors now prevailed. The long Candian war with Venice to control Crete (1645–1669), disastrous for both sides, made the process even more relentless. Peasants in southeast Europe might flee to Hungary or Ukraine and the towns. There was both a shortage of agrarian labor and many men with no land; share tenancy *(métayage)* came to prevail, as did peonage. When peasants fled, those who remained behind remained co-responsible (along originally with the timar holder) for the tax deficiencies.[25] Collective responsibility and sharing remained also in India, certainly in Russia, and in Mesoamerica. It probably mitigated the catastrophes that could fall to individual family homesteads—the village had to provide subsistence—but it also limited the incentives for growth.

As with the other agrarian systems of the global old regime, the tug-of-war for revenue was endemic in the system even when states and empires were not at war. The great Emperor Akbar (ruling 1556–1605) sought to stabilize government levies in cash at one-third of the imputed revenue from village agriculture, although collectors were authorized to encourage agrarian development by reducing assessment rates on high-grade crops or extended cultivation of land. By the time the British took over the financial authority of Bengal with its power to tax—the *diwani*—from the Mughals a century later, the state quota had climbed to 50 percent. The actual annual levy was determined by a negotiation between the headman of the village (or villages grouped in parghana) and state officials or the proliferating local intermediaries, the zamindars—with all parties seeking to collect and retain as much as the system might bear. The results were harsh: if the initial monetary assessment decreed by royal collectors on reserve lands was contested by cultivators, the officials could impose direct levies of the crop, so-called sharing and measurement. Peasants agreed to a tax for one year at a time; wives and children of defaulters could be sold into slavery; a bountiful harvest in which prices plunged could mean not a boon but a hardship for the peasants, who had to settle rents and taxes in cash. The regime encouraged expansion of cultivation, but peasant labor was scarce, and abandonment of overburdened land became a serious problem. By the second half of the seventeenth century, so Colbert's emissary Francois Bernier reported, much of the Mughal territory was "badly cultivated and thinly populated and even a considerable portion of the good land remains untilled from want of cultivators.[26]

Aurangzeb (ruled 1658–1707), contemporary of Louis XIV and the last of the great Mughal emperors, dissipated his wealth in decades of warfare in the Deccan. New conquests that might be used for feudal assignments (jaghirs) became scarce at the same time as the lines of authority over the villages became muddled as centralized authority in the north broke down. The claims of ownership were often fragmented or parceled: village headman, tax farmers, zamindars, and others came to be known as holding dependencies. Under these conditions, it could become a burden for an official to receive an assignment of village revenues rather than an income paid directly. Inside the village collective obligation and rights might protect individuals, but they reduced incentives to expand the arable land.[27] As one of the most informed British experts summarized later, "The village as a unit stands [at the end of the eighteenth century] . . . exactly where it stood at the time of Aurangzeb, the revenue due from it being assessed, usually for the year, at a lump sum of money, fixed with reference to its productive capacity, and intended to represent ordinarily half the gross produce, but not distributed by the assessors over the individual peasants." Peasants sought to conceal their wealth, and the village was caught in a "barren struggle" to divide the rural product rather than a concerted effort to increase the annual produce of the country.[28]

India's "feudal" crisis grew more intense as the eighteenth century continued, but elsewhere after 1720 many societies seemed to ascend to a plateau of renewed prosperity and, if not peace, at least a diminished destructiveness of warfare—exception made for the African polities that bore the demand for increased slave labor. The populations of China and Europe increased as the climate seemed to warm after the mini–ice age of the previous century. More slaves could be transported to the colonies, more staples were shipped from the colonies to Europe, a vigorous sea trade obtained between Asia, the Americas, and Europe. The new calorific products of Africa and the Americas—yams, sweet potatoes, maize, potatoes—added to traditional grains, and rice quickly produced populations of much higher density.

International relations still exacted heavy demands on state and territorial capacities. Internal violence abated, but competition between states did not ease and neither did the fiscal pressure on them. Wars were less brutal but no less costly; they required larger armies and navies and more supplies. They surged anew in Eastern and Central Europe and in the distant colonial holdings. The Indian peninsula remained embroiled in continuing conflicts at the southern and eastern edges of the Mughal realms, now contested by Europeans as well as by ambitious local princes. The Manchu rulers of China were continually pushing west against the tribal kingdoms of north central Asia; the Ottomans faced Hungarian and Austrian pressure on the Danube and Russian expansion north of the Black Sea. Only Japan, battened down in its now pacified islands, enjoyed an environment free from the continual frictions of interstate competition, although the approximately 250 *han,* or feudal domains, with their *daimyo* lords engaged in stubborn mercantilist competition.[29]

No matter how much wealth was created, whether through improved agricultural yields, enhanced commerce and manufacturing, or the coerced output of slaves and serfs, the claims on the domestic product grew at least proportionally. States needed to capture as much revenue as possible, which meant a continuing conflict with civil society, whose diverse estates sought to retain whatever wealth they could. As always, states enjoyed limited options for covering expenses. They could sell offices and privileges to magnates, that is, exemptions from taxation or the rights to collect and retain ("farm") a share of the taxes owed by the nonexempt. They could appeal for "gifts" from their clergy or from nobles, who, generations earlier, had been granted tax exemptions. They could levy excises on traded goods; most significantly, they might try to tax peasant producers directly or through agents to whom they sold collection rights. Taxation, however, ran into the resistance of landlords, who hardly consented to share whatever surplus might be pressed out of their tenants in rents or labor services. Other societies continued to turn to their countryside resources as the basis for viability. As agrarian crises and periods of dearth followed the Seven Years' War, rebellion flared anew, as it had a century earlier—in central Russia under Pugachev and Stenka Razin, in Bohemia in the 1770s, and among the North American colonists resentful of London's new taxes or restrictions on their western settlement. How were the societies of the late eighteenth century going to resolve the worldwide upsurge of conflicting ambitions—aspirations that arose in some cases from the overburdened poor and in some cases from those ascending to new prosperity and consciousness of rights?

The Cadastral Struggle

The relationship of good government to productive agriculture was hardly a new insight. Today's visitor to the Siena town palace still beholds the great frescos that Ambrogio Lorenzetti painted in 1337–1338 to depict the effects of good and bad government on the prosperity of the republic— bountiful agriculture and humming commerce in the one case, devastation and discord in the other. Of course, the frescoes simplified cause and effect into a moral allegory, whereas economic outcomes in real life went awry even when rulers were not arbitrary and abusive. Indeed Lorenzetti's painted plaster had only had a decade to cure before the Black Death depopulated his thriving city and carried off the artist.

Lorenzetti's scenes are obviously not a map. They depict human activity oriented across occupational lines: dioramas of the rural economy. But maps and landscapes emerged from a surge of visual representation methods designed to serve different purposes with more specialized techniques, just as civilian and military architecture differentiated themselves in approximately the same era. Landscape painting was the cousin of the map. Slowly it emerged in the West as a theme in its own right—not just the background against which portraits or religious themes were placed, but an active arena of atmospheric effect, of distances, a way for subjects and viewers of paintings to immerse themselves in the representation of a landed milieu. And after a general absence of almost a millennium, there was an explosion of maps that depicted where landed properties bordered each other. After the Roman usage they are called cadasters (cadastres, catasti) in the West. The cadaster is a map, a visual depiction of properties from above, accompanied by a list of the proprietors and of the revenues they provide. Private owners often commissioned them—seigneurs or abbeys seeking to determine and establish their rights to rents and dues—but they soon served public rulers trying to rationalize and impose taxes. Mathematical sophistication enhanced the craft of each domain—studies in perspective and vanishing points for the painters, trigonometric applications for the mapmakers.

Along with the development of projection techniques, the major advance was to be that of triangulation—the determination of distances and locations by applying trigonometric functions to complex chains of multiple triangles. Triangular measurement of distances not only allows indirect computation of distances across rough terrain by sines, tangents, and cosines; it also ensures that the diverse segments of a large-scale map share common sides and thus serves to cross-check distances from one segment to another. It provides for mapping the same rigidity that triangles afford in construction. The large-scale map presents problems of projection that the cadaster does not usually raise, because the discrepancy of the earth's curvature and the painted two-dimensional surface can be left out of account for the property map. But the property map does depend on the refinement of surveying instruments that must themselves be based on trigonometric functions. The distance to the distant site is inferred from the angular properties of the right triangle not just by unfolding one length of chain after another.

The technique was known to the Greeks and the Chinese of the third century; the Dutch mathematician Gemma Frisius proposed it for mapmaking in 1533, following which English surveyors publicized it in Britain. The Dutch geographer Wilebrord Snell used it to map the distance from Alkmaar to Bergen Op Zoom in 1613, and the French Cassini family was to develop it first by measuring specific distances along a major meridian, and then, over three happily long-lived generations, by producing an accurately measured map of France. But this work moved slowly from the late seventeenth century; coastal and local maps were constructed, but linking together the whole was a daunting task. Mapping by triangulation also lagged behind the mathematical computation of logarithms and trigonometric functions because the refinement of instruments, needed to accurately record angles in the field, such as theodolites, lagged behind that of grinding out the functions on paper. Colbert authorized Domenico Cassini to map triangles south to north along the meridian of Paris in 1683, but the new patron minister of the Academy, Louvois (who had so supported Vauban's program of fortifications as minister of war), slowed down the commissions. The effort crawled north, to be suspended during the War of the Spanish Succession. Domenico died in 1712; his son Jacques reached Dunkerque by 1718. Perpendicular east-west lines of triangles were constructed in the mid-1730s along with other north-south meridians, such that Jacque's son César-François could complete the painstakingly overlapped triangular survey of France by 1745 in eighteen sheets. In fact, large areas of the interior were left untriangulated. The coasts and the eastern frontiers (not the Pyrenees) are covered with overlapping tangles, and seven chains of triangles run east to west perpendicular to the Paris meridian. Where Vauban had implanted fortifications, the Cassinis left their triangles. The folio was hardly issued when Cassini III undertook a second survey in 1750 to be completed in 1788 and comprising 180 sheets. The original stimulus was military—the desire to map the northeastern theater during the War of the Austrian Succession.[30]

The British put their efforts into solving the problem of determining longitude at sea and started a triangulation ordinance survey only in the

1780s, then went on to the challenge of a major survey of India from 1801, deigned to yield distances, locations, and the heights of the Himalayas.[31] Triangulation, the accurate determination of meridian (north to south) degree lengths, and the refinement of instruments in France and Britain were political projects designed to master national and eventually imperial space. Military applications were never far away, although scientific academies and their expertise need to be harnessed. The maps were beautiful, and their scientific value was complemented by the artistry of the cartouches that often accompanied them with their symbolism of power and fecundity. They were in effect sacramental, giving visible form to sovereign power. Arguably they allowed the visualization of the early modern state that objectified sovereignty (along with the person of the king).[32]

State cadasters depicted the productive side of these surveyed spaces. They had to factor in the boundaries that demarcate property claims, private as well as public. Property maps, public or private, emerged as analogs of the maps of political jurisdictions; as such they suggest parallels to the Western state system as it is theorized in the early modern era—the unit, jurisdiction, or property, as a black box, its internal human divisions subordinated to the fact of its being a unitary stake in a larger contention as a unit. When monarchs asked for land surveys to establish their tax claims, they also required indications of the land's productivity such that forest and farmland, often with statements of their value, were attached. The cadaster ideally codified the rights of sovereignty and the expectations of property. As a historian of the Savoy cadaster has written, "The cadaster occupies a strategic position in the social configuration. It unites and it separates, slips into the local dialogue, interferes in the relations between the individual and the collectivity, between tax payers and the state. On the one hand it protects, guarantees, envisages the risks of piece-by-piece seizures *(empiètement)*. On the other hand, it exposes bodies and properties to the blows of the tax collector and to the claims of others."[33]

Cadasters had existed since antiquity. The word derived from the Greek *katastichon* ("line by line"). In the Middle Ages there had been notable surveys, such William the Conqueror's Domesday Book and the French *compoix;* the Austrian territories recorded Urbare or tenancy records and contracts that stipulate rents and services. David Sabean has noted the important renovations of village property records and tax assignments in sixteenth-century Württemberg.[34] The Dutch were the first in the West after antiquity to develop careful mapping and related description of private rights. As they reclaimed their land from the sea, they assigned the polder rights collectively to associations and polder boards under the authority of the agents of the counts of Holland and of local representatives, which in turn commissioned the mapping of the emerging fields and allocated the taxes to maintain the dikes. In 1533 the count of Holland—aka the holy Roman emperor Charles V—commissioned a cadastral survey of North Holland to reform the dike tax, which he followed with a survey of the Rhine territories down to Rotterdam. As ruler in northern Italy, he also launched a tax survey of the duchy of Milan. Surveying itself in Italy might be assigned to peasants as an off-season job, but it also became professionalized with a degree program at Leiden, although service as a "sworn surveyor"—the oath was to designed to guarantee honest measurements—often remained a secondary activity.

The late seventeenth-century and eighteenth-century European states vigorously revived cadastral activity. The first step was surveying. Agricultural land was essential for productivity, but the land had to be measured and compartmentalized. Here was a key difference from the atlases and maps developed to serve the objectives of sovereignty. Then the bordering of states dominated the agenda; now the productivity of the interior claimed attention. By the mid-seventeenth century, rulers of the Baltic (Sweden and Finland as the core of the Vasa Empire, Denmark, including Norway, as its principal rival) would commission maps of their holdings. Gustavus Adolphus (1612–1632), who added territory from the Danes and Norwegians and the river mouths across the Baltic, had surveyors trained so that each year once the snow had melted they might begin "diligently to measure the land belonging to each village, both arable and pasture." His instructions to the chief surveyor in 1628 emphasized that he wanted "not only to protect his land and realm against the enemy but also to use every opportunity and means to improve their condition."[35] Both geographic or political maps, and geometric maps on a far larger scale, suitable for assigning taxes and calculating yields, were produced and bound as part of an imperial project. "The most striking developments in Nordic mapping are, first, the compilation in seventeenth-century Sweden-Finland of the Geometriska Jordebörckerna," initiated by Gustav II Adolf at the height of his reign as an expression of national power, reflection of the nation's glory and a symbol of its power; and second the mapping of the Swedish Baltic colonies to consolidate imperial power there. A national surveying agency—the Lantmäteri—would employ five hundred surveyors by the eighteenth century. By the conclusion of the reign, Swedish geometric mapping was the most comprehensive and best organized in Europe.[36] The impact of the surveys varied according to the vicissitudes of monarchical power. Charles XI imposed an absolutist policy over the resistance of the aristocracy, which included after 1692 producing a thousand-map cadaster of Swedish Pomerania across the Baltic, the first modern cadaster of territory within German-speaking lands. The string of Swedish reversals on the continent, including Charles XII's disastrous defeat by the Russians, set back the cause of expansion and of royal absolutism. The survey of the lands south of the Baltic would thus never serve as the basis for Swedish taxation, although the Prussian monarchs exploited the cadaster for the portion of Pomerania they captured and annexed in 1720. Within Sweden proper the aristocratic estates remained concerned that the royal survey would publicly reveal how much peasant land they had taken into their own hands and out of the fiscal reach of the monarchy. King Gustav IV Adolf was prepared to take the cadaster out of the drawer, so to speak, in 1800; however, rather than accept disclosure of noble holdings, the estates agreed to a hefty increase of their fiscal "contribution" by 56 percent.

As the Prussian finance minister Karl August von Struensee wrote in his major treatise on state financial policy in 1800: "Nothing serves better to instruct a statesman then a complete and reliable cadaster of his state. . . . Whoever seeks to govern a territory without this guiding thread will be tapping in the dark."[37] Details can be multiplied dozens of times. The cadaster was the tool of those seeking to systematize the revenue from land—whether for landlords or sovereigns. Norwegian evidence suggests, according to the historian of Nordic registers, that where subsistence agriculture prevailed, there was little impulse for enclosure or for mapping. "Enclosure appeared first and spread most rapidly where agriculture produced goods for market exchange and where desire to increase profit led to the need for absolute individual ownership of land."[38] Similarly, in Denmark the progress of maps went together with a change in the notion of ownership from use rights over arables, meadows, and forests to property that could be mapped.

Territorial precision emerged as both a condition for and result of rural capitalism. In Germany the surveys remained the activity of the territorial princes and were particularly important for projects of land reclamation, forestry management, and taxation. The most systematic Prussian project took place in Cleves in the west, where a royal cadaster was carried out in the 1730s as part of an effort to impose higher taxes on a province only recently acquired and where landownership was scattered and fragmented; until then only the earlier Swedish effort in Pomerania had been attempted. The royal bureaucracy, the Kriegs- und Domänenkammer, the managers of the crown lands, and a hard-pressed peasantry, supported the effort, whereas the nobility, which was slated to lose exemptions from the land tax (the Kontribution), opposed the project. The Cleves survey from 1731–1736 yielded maps of 66-by-105 centimeters as well as accompanying inventories, based on information from locals who pointed out property boundaries and buildings. Despite reliance on army officers to walk the village property lines with the surveying tools, the enterprise was costly, and when Frederick II came to the throne in 1740 and seized Silesia from the Habsburgs, he switched his efforts to that other end of his kingdoms. By and large the nobility threw sand in the wheels of cadastral projects, fearing they would lose tax privileges, and even the Prussian monarchs could make only limited progress. But the French invasions during the Revolutionary and Napoleonic Wars, entailing years of military exertions for armies on one side or the other, provided the impetus for a fundamental territorial reorganization in the German lands, including ruthless simplification of political and religious jurisdictions and cadastral mapping.

Rationalization of territory dominated high politics and internal administration. For the German states, where over 300 quasi sovereign units survived after the Treaties of Westphalia, the French conquests allowed a tremendous consolidation on behalf of the conqueror's mid-size allies. Between 1802 and 1806, Napoleon summoned their rulers to a great territorial banquet, prepared in Paris, that allowed thirty-nine rulers to absorb the often leopard-spot jurisdictions within their borders as well as the ecclesiastical principalities and ultimately to retain their gains in the

German Confederation after 1815. Territorial enlargement and administrative reform to overcome the fiscal demands of continued military exertions became twin objectives as the German princes' ambitions adapted to French power and the zest for spatial reorganization that had motivated the creation of French *départements* early in the Revolution. Internal administrative rationalization in some of the states was also unleashed. Under the leadership of the centralizing reformist prime minister, Maximilian von Montgelas, Bavaria, which faced major deficits but had also gained major territory as a result of Napoleon's favors, embarked on its own period of fiscal–teritorial rationalization. *Steuer-Rektifikation* or tax-rectification, suggested by one of the monarch's civil servants in 1799 became the slogan that overhauled the existing tax administration and transformed the realm's local assessments by agricultural use into uniform spatial units: "Since as long as the state remains a mere aggregation of diverse components," the monarch's constitution of 1808 declared, "it can never attain the full measure of strength that its potential might provide. . . . We are seeking to establish a uniform system."[39] From 1808 to 1867 the state was mapped and charted in twenty-two thousand maps on a scale of one to five thousand.[40]

Bavaria moved in the wake of its recent acquisitions and the need to exploit its resources to rationalize its territory. Having acquired Italian domains long before, their neighbors, the Habsburgs, began earlier and undertook one of the most exemplary cadastral projects in Europe. After Charles V acquired the duchy of Milan, he began a cadaster in the 1530s. Leopold I had sought to rationalize taxes and remove aristocratic exemptions after the Thirty Years' War; Charles VI, father of Maria Theresa, decreed the *censimento* of the duchy again in 1718, and the effort was carried on by his daughter. The province was rich and had no troublesome Diet to obstruct the effort; it was governed by a Giunta appointed from Vienna. The wars of the Polish and Austrian successions, with their invasion of Milan in 1733, interrupted the survey for sixteen years. The first supervisory Giunta, dominated by Gian Rinaldo Carli, carried out most of the surveying from 1718 to 1733; the second, led by Pompeo Neri, completed the registers during 1749 and 1750. The new, reformed tax assessment followed only in 1760. Neri, who brought the effort to a delayed but serious conclusion, allowed that "this magnificent Project was executed with the most happy success," producing a topographic map for every one of the communities in which would distinctly appear the shape and situation of every piece of land with its measurements and the most minute distinctions.[41] Adam Smith praised it as "one of the most accurate that has yet been made."[42]

The novelty lay in the mapping and the classification. Standard scales (one to two thousand) yielded 2,387 maps covering an area of about 12,600 square kilometers (about five thousand square miles). Earlier surveys had taxed the landowner in the province where he lived, but supposedly on the totality of his holdings and it had depended on the landowners' honest reporting of their dispersed properties. The new cadaster was to provide the basis for assigning the tax to the land where it was located and surveyed. Rather than try, moreover, to estimate what individual holdings might yield, value was imputed per hectare according to the average yields for diverse uses of the land throughout the province, that is, depending, on whether it was allocated for pasture or planted for grain or olives, vineyard or mulberries (for silkworms), and so on.[43] As the Risorgimento political economist Carlo Cattaneo noted, the virtue of the assessment method encouraged industrious landlords to produce more than the imputed average since the surplus would escape taxation.

Landowners, however, complained that the new assessments were three to four times the previous ones and faulted the first Giunta for not having counted the costs of irrigation water as a major deduction and thus raising the value of the underlying land from 30 to 50 percent.[44] Mulberry cultivators (for silkworms) raised tearful protests that particularly provoked the official. Although most communes were very happy with the assessment results, Neri claimed, the lawyers for the silk farmers protested loudly and selfishly for their own narrow, special interests. "It would have been wiser, when appealing on behalf of the public, to speak on behalf of the funds for the woods, meadows, gardens rather than just the mulberry growers." In fact, "they have taken their stubborn search for tax breaks to the court of Vienna together with all the other contemporary machinations that are played out to escape reform and perhaps unwittingly have sought to harm their own country." Neri's report revealed how important the cadaster was for eighteenth-century territorial wealth and power, even as it was contested piece by piece by the local "optimati." Although organized by royal commission, much of the work of individual valuation and assessment had to be delegated to local officials and councils (three of whose elected representatives sat on the Giunta).[45] Cameralist reformers, the foot soldiers, so to speak, of so-called enlightened despotism, ultimately had to work through and with the ruling classes that so resisted their aspirations.

Neri spoke for an enlightened absolutism that was hardly absolute. Like his contemporary Turgot in France and the reformers under Philip V, Ferdinand VI, and Charles III of Spain, he advocated a single tax on the value of land. It accorded with the idea that land was the source of surplus and a tax on it would be easy to collect. It would eliminate the constant contestation with local magnates, jealous of their age-old tax concessions and could be imposed on extensive church holdings as well as secular land. But the monarchs often had to yield. Maria Theresa compromised with the church in the Concordat of 1754, which protected church properties until Joseph II voided the treaty in 1784. Joseph's successor Leopold (1790–1792), alarmed by the upheavals in France, was to yield again.

Milanese cadastral procedures influenced neighboring Savoy and Habsburg Tuscany. Savoy (unofficially Piedmont, or officially the kingdom of Sardinia, so named from the island it acquired in 1720) long faced tenacious tax resistance from a nobility that enjoyed hilly redoubts in their Alpine hills. The goal of a land tax announced in 1564 was reaffirmed in 1600 along with a property survey that was decreed in 1601 but that remained a dead letter for a century. After many false starts, including new royal decrees in 1697, Victor Amadeus I decreed a general cadastral survey in 1728—one of the first to include a mapping of private parcels "with specific distinction of their quality and nature, by location, by owner, and by owners' cumulative holdings [mas]." The resulting *perequazione* (reproportioning), published in 1731, assigned taxes by commune; local officials were to distribute the burden by property owner. In Savoy as elsewhere the surveying teams encountered the hostility and suspicion of local peasants and officials along with disagreement over the instruments that should be applied in such a hilly terrain. Surveyors swore an oath on the gospel that they would honestly measure and record the quality and revenues of the land.[46]

The result was a meticulous and beautifully executed effort to depict the landholdings of the principality. Was it accurate? Surveyors often had to rely on the data furnished by landowners themselves. The nobility distrusted the centralizing state and protested the new surveys: "We are attacked on all sides. God, what a century!" the estate agent of the Marquis de la Roche wrote his master. The nobles' delegation self-righteously lamented, "It seems beyond doubt that the king intends to impose the *taille* on the Savoyard nobility. At the same time it's being made clear to the nobility that their loyalty is viewed as so equivocal that imposing the *taille* will appear as a consequence and a sort of punishment for the lack of zeal for royal service attributed to us. The Savoyard gentry may be unhappy but their loyalty is beyond reproach. All of us would accept uncomplainingly if our lands, of so little value as they are, passed to the crown—but the imputations of disloyalty are really depressing."[47] At the end the tax assessments were adjusted by arbitrary estimates: the abbot of Mellarède claimed that the allocation of taxes, theoretically based on the cadaster, was "almost independent of its estimates." Indeed the inventories were sometimes adjusted to justify the assessment. When the survey was finally published in the fall of 1738, government officials praised the "laws of an equal society" where every subject would pay his fair share while the nobility, according to the Count of Menthon, "talks only of the desolation and poverty caused by the new cadaster."[48] It took another thirty-three years but in 1771 the court in Turin moved to suppress seigneurial dues.

Spanish Bourbon reformers had also mooted a *única contribución* on income from land—noble as well as common—and on professions and trade. They succeeded in Aragon and Catalonia, imposing a tax called the *catastro,* and extending it to church properties in 1753. The Milanese effort was one of the inspirations for Ferdinand VI's finance minister, the marqués de la Ensenada, to survey provinces of Castile along the lines of the Catalan catastro from 1749 on. The new intendants' calculations suggested that a four percent tax on all properties would cover the hodgepodge of unequal returns. But Ensenada was dismissed in 1754, and the single tax decreed in 1757 remained a dead letter in the transition to Carlos III.[49]

Meanwhile Maria Theresa and Count von Haugwitz tried to rationalize fiscal reform for Austrian and Bohemian lands. But what the Habsburgs could push through in their Italian possessions they could not impose against their own nobility at home. The resulting Theresian cadaster rested on new surveys only in the Tyrol; elsewhere it depended on declarations by the nobility—a procedure that actually yielded results since the penalty for false declarations could be confiscation of property and the government had informers in the field. The empress's son and co-ruler, Joseph II, sought a general land tax to be paid by every subject. Plans for a general cadaster were announced in early 1785 and fixed into legislation by the patent of April 20: "We can pay no attention to the customs and prejudices which have become established over the centuries. The land, the soil, gifts of Nature to Mankind, are the source of all value. From this comes the undeniable truth that the state's need for money must be met from the land alone and that there can be no differences amongst the possessions of men, no matter what their estate."[50] The reform used peasants as surveyors; they were given rudimentary training and supposed to finish their survey by the fall. The tax was based on income adjusted according to nine classifications of land use—arable, wastes, ponds, meadows, gardens, pastures, bushes, vineyards, woods—and the proprietors' declarations of income they had received from 1774 through 1782. The surveyors required four years, and they produced no maps.

Noble opposition was vigorous, and even some peasant communities and headmen resisted. The emperor dismissed Karl von Zinzendorf, head of the *robot* abolition commission at the end of February 1788, after his minister lamented that the cadaster "was rushed, filled with contradictions and altogether a failure," and threatened to dismantle it after Joseph's death. Three months later Joseph had to scold Vice-Chancellor Kolowrat: "All this [complaining] is empty blabber and a superfluous waste of time. . . . My principles are unshaken: everyone must pay according to his income." The Austro-Bohemian chancellery decried the impending impoverishment of the nobility: "A stroke of the pen is wiping out the right of property which ought to be sacred to the ruler."[51] Five days before the decree was to be officially announced in February 1789 a second chancellor resigned, provoking Joseph to complain of his "obstinacy and quixotic stance," but the decree was announced on February 10, 1789. The new taxes moreover imposed a ceiling on peasant rents to the landlord as well as on their church tithes and taxes to the state. The peasant was to owe the state about 12 percent and would pay the lord and church together about 17.5 percent of his gross income—a total burden of about 30 percent. Most of the estates protested; the nobility of Styria said they would face terrible poverty and expropriation. All very well—the cadaster was introduced in Austria and Bohemia, though not Hungary—but the emperor died in 1790 and his brother Leopold II, taking power for two years as the French Revolution broke out, canceled the new tax ordinances. Systematically mapped cadasters would wait until after the Congress of Vienna when the emperor Francis undertook to impose his *"stabile"* from 1817—a mapping based on triangulation.

Unsurprisingly, French cadastral efforts remained hostage to the stalemate between king and aristocracy that characterized the years between Louis XIV and the Revolution. The splendid Cassini atlas of the kingdom was a royal project and collided with no class privileges; not so a national cadastral effort. Villages and estates, noble lands, parishes, and forests were mapped throughout the ancient regime; monarchs had done partial surveys from the Middle Ages on—but no systematic state cadasters were introduced until 1807, when the Napoleonic regime initiated what would become known as the *ancien cadastre.*[52] The resulting survey became seen as a signal achievement of the French state—but it required the revolution and the empire to get it under way—an irony that Tocqueville would certainly appreciate.

The cadaster was thus the preeminent technology for centralizing rule, and its fate was subject to the balance of social and political forces. Who controlled the national territory? When surveying remained a market tool, it could proceed without public conflict. In Britain authorities and local landowners provided their own plats, that is, surveys of individual estates with maps and written descriptions. Since cadastral projects in Europe responded to state fiscal needs, the centuries-long British movement to enclose lands on behalf of local gentry and prosperous farmers did not produce national surveys until the eighteenth century. After 1750, however, mapping was a requirement for registering enclosures. Where the British state ruled by conquest, it could impose a national survey. Once Britain confiscated major portions of Irish land after Cromwell suppressed the rebellion of 1641, it charged William Petty—encountered in the previous chapter as the pioneer of "politickal arithmetic" with carrying out the so-called Down Survey. The histories of the war recorded devastation, violence, starvation, and expropriation; the maps recorded confiscated town lands as well as the quality of the land—whether arable, bog, forest, or mountain.

Colonial North America presented a mixed picture. Land surveys did not have to untangle centuries of overlapping rights and claims, but were needed to allocate vacant land as settlements moved inland. Access to river frontage was stipulated early on, and a few vast proprietorships, envisaged as manorial, marked Maryland and Carolina. In the southern tidewater region, maps recorded the plantations awarded by colonial proprietors. As settlement proceeded inland, the granting of "headrights" or individual properties if they were "seated and settled" led to a vigorous development of individual surveys. Initial village settlements in New England distributed small tracts but, by the eighteenth century, the move into the interior stimulated a vigorous commercial land market with large properties carved out and accumulated in frontier regions, such as Maine. The revocation of New England charters in 1690 as part of the effort of the new British regime after the Glorious Revolution to consolidate a dominion of New England also allowed large-scale acquisition to intrude on the early communal impulses. Geodesy or surveying became a widespread branch of expertise.[53] The cadasters served owners and speculators and eventually local governments but not a central state.

The map in short was the uncontested project of expanding empire and ambitious state wedded to the scientific curiosity that impelled European expansion. The cadaster represented the triumph of the centralizing forces in the long battle between monarch and landed elites. Maps and cadasters alike affirmed the integral connection of public power to the resources of territory. Recall William Petty, surveying Ireland: a mapmaker in the service of a conqueror, but also an early estimator of national income and a theorist of economic surplus. In his 1662 *Treatise of Taxes and Contributions,* Petty broke down the yield of the land. Once an individual farmer had taken the seed needed for planting and paying others for his clothes and necessities, "the remainder of Corn is the natural and true rent of the Land in that year; and the medium [mean] of seven years, or rather of so many years as make up the Cycle, with which Dearths and Plenties make their revolution, doth give the ordinary Rent of the Land in Corn."[54] Sow and ye shall reap; crucial to the emerging economic mind was that ye shall reap more than what you sow.

Physiocracy Goes Global

From land to grain—from the surface of the globe to the resources it yields: Petty's work prompted the reflections of Richard Cantillon, A wealthy banker of Anglo-Irish stock, longtime resident in Paris with his beautiful daughter, he was apparently murdered in London in 1734 by his French chef, who torched the house and most of his papers, then escaped to Holland. For Cantillon, whose *Essay on the Nature of Trade in General* had fortunately been published before his cook's rampage, "all the classes and inhabitants of a state live at the expense of the Proprietors of the Land." As Schumpeter expounds Cantillon's analysis, "Whereas every other income item is being balanced by a cost item, the landowners' rent is the only one that is not so balanced because, to use a later phrase, it is a return to a 'costless,' that is, non-produced, natural factor."[55] Land is a free and productive good, God's gift of capital, so to speak, to man.

Cantillon envisages that the return from a property is divided into thirds. A third will cover the farmers' yearly outlays aside from rent—in British usage farmers are construed as substantial long-term leaseholders; another third will be retained by the farmers as profit; the final third goes to the proprietors or landowners. They in turn spend half of these receipts in towns, which is augmented by the half of the farmers' combined two-thirds (outlays and profit) that is spent on urban goods and services—such that half the profit of land goes into urban production: a model of economic circulation that anticipates Quesnay's *Tableau économique* of the 1760s. As one of Quesnay's fans, the elder Marquis de Mirabeau, summarized the circular flow a generation later, "God alone is the donor and the remunerator: everyone else is only, can only be a distributor. . . . But [agriculture] is a type of work that God recompenses by the instrument of nature, whose effect he doubles and makes a pure gift, indeed can triple and multiply the closer we come to his order and laws. . . . It's the art by which man . . . makes himself into a sort of substitute for the Creator, it is *agriculture*."[56] Formalized as economic theory by the circle of French analysts who took the name "economists," these ideas became known as Physiocracy—a corpus of teachings often dismissed as fixated with agriculture, but one that if shorn of the Quesnay coterie's enthusiasm, offered a cogent program for development.

Starting analysis with a focus on the countryside has certain implications. In several respects it is progressive. Taxation can be simplified
and fairer: since wealth originates with nature's bounty, the ruler should
base taxes on land ownership and not on the toil of those who don't
profit from it. Second, there is a concern with development, not just fiscal
returns. The new ideas look at the kingdom with respect to society as
well as to the state. Thus they differ from seventeenth-century mercantilism. Mercantilism had focused on fiscal health: the revenues of the state,
its mobilization of resources to compete in a zero-sum world of imperial
competition. Mercantilist doctrines had also focused on trade and exchange as the source of wealth, measured success by bullion and trade
surpluses, and by keeping industry at home. States were competitive entities; empires were the most competitive of all. Mercantilism showed how
to mobilize wealth for the state in a world where the total above ground
was likely to be fixed and profit could derive only from redistribution.
Extraction of metals alone might add to the global total. The early mercantile writers, Thomas Mun and the Huguenot in London, Antoine de
Montchrestien, confronted the collapse of British cloth exports caused
by the reopening of the Spanish-Dutch conflict in 1618 along with the
Thirty Years' War.[57] For Mun foreign commerce determined the domestic supply of money and the rate of interest. Mun had no obsession
with amassing bullion as such; however, he still believed that only foreign and not domestic demand contributed to the net wealth of the
kingdom. Savings and production at home served rather as the prerequisite for profitable trade. "Industry to encrease, and frugalitie to maintain
are the true watchmen of a kingdoms treasury."[58]

The mercantilists stressed commerce and what today's economists
call a surplus on current account—which rests in part on hard work and
restraint of consumption. But something must be traded. For countries
endowed with minerals, wealth can be extracted from mines; for coastal
lands it can be drawn from the oceans. Wealth as an underlying resource
can come from the agricultural capacities of the soil itself—the Physiocrats'
answer. And thus we return to territory, now as the land over which exclusive proprietary rights can be claimed. It produces value, but squatters'
rights aside, the claims must ultimately be guaranteed by politics.

Writers on political economy often accepted parts of the Physiocratic
doctrine, which were propagated tirelessly by a small circle of intellec-

tuals, but not others. Few thinkers accepted that agriculture was the only source of surplus in the economic cycle, and not all fiscal reformers ratified the idea that a single tax on agricultural land should be the major source of state revenue. But what attracted almost every economics writer was the notion that restrictions on prices and the export and import of grains should be lifted. So, too, prohibitions on the purchase and sale of land—whether deriving from entailed estates, the church's privileged holdings, the traditional village common lands, or from the customary "wastes" set aside for pastures or squatters—must be eliminated. Only when land became a commodity could the productive potential of territory be realized.

Land, of course, even arable land, is not a homogenous resource. There are woods and "waste" and commons as well as the acreage that is sowed, and the quality of the soil will vary widely. Population pressure also has an impact over the exchange value of land and its product. By the early nineteenth century, David Ricardo suggested that the rising price of corn (that is, wheat) was a consequence of the need to bring ever-less-fertile land under the plough. The price of wheat depends on the price and productivity of the last units planted, and society puts into service the least productive or more marginal lands last. But wheat prices rise as a whole. As a growing population requires pressing more marginal land into service, landlords who have older and more productive land are made wealthy without effort. Scarcity cannot increase overall wealth, but it can shift wealth from one class to another.

It is worth bearing this later analysis in mind because it reveals some of the implications of eighteenth-century theory. For Turgot and the Physiocrats and for Pompeo Neri, the director of the Habsburg cadastral effort resumed in Milan after the war of 1740–1748, land should be the factor of production that is taxed because of its inherent fruitfulness. The Milan Giunta understood that land can be graded according to its productivity, and the cadastral survey was to classify each piece according to possible yield. The surplus above what society required merely to subsist—which landlords and nobles often took for themselves, which supported the church, and which ultimately must support government and its projects—could be paid for from nature's bounty. In response to a questionnaire from the Contrôleur-Général Bertin, Turgot set out an outline of tax policy in 1763, maintaining that consumption taxes were unfair both to the poor and to the proprietors of poor lands who had to work harder for their product: "Who is liable to taxation? Proof that only the proprietor of the soil [should be] liable. . . . Only the owner of landed property has a true revenue."[59] Tax land according to its productivity and in effect one taxes only God.

The French understanding of surplus was not that of Smith and the British theorists nor that of the important late eighteenth-century Milanese political economist Pietro Verri, whose 1771 *Meditations on Political Economy* prompted Voltaire to write him that he had never read anything "truer, wiser, or clearer."[60] Verri sharply rejected the Physiocrats' dismissal of nonagricultural activity as "sterile." As the Abbé de Condillac would repeat a decade later, no economic activity—indeed no phenomenon in the universe—was pure creation; it was always a *modificazione,* a transformation, hence to be thought of, as today's language would have it, as value added.[61] For that reason, like the Physiocrats and Condorcet, Verri chose the term "reproduction" (defined as "renewal") for what we would call production. For the French, surplus was merely the yield on agriculture that could pay for the manufactures and services produced by those not in agriculture, including those of the legal, notarial, and ultimately military professions. François Quesnay brutally labeled all these components of national output as the work of *"les stériles."*[62] It was the fruitfulness of the soil that supported their labor and their contributions.

The great innovation of his "Tableau" was the diagrammatic representation of sectoral output that was self-reproducing and went from one cycle of activity to the next, using agriculture to pay for all the non-agrarian enterprises including government. The third version of Quesnay's Tableau in 1766 revealed how the table or "zic-zac" worked. It essentially elaborated Cantillon's scheme. At any given time, proprietors or landowners have collected, say, a billion of product that will be the input for the year ahead. Spending half in the city (500m), they also advance half to the farmers who rent from them and who double, say, their value through the land. The farmers then return half of this amount for their rent (500), then spend one quarter (250m) for their own sustenance and another quarter (250m) in towns for the manufactures produced by the sterile class. The *stériles* spend 250m of the combined 750m they have received on their own and on their workmen's food, and 500m to reproduce the goods they have sold to landlords and farmers. The system does not depict growth, merely reproduction.[63]

For Verri and then Smith, however, surplus represented an excess of production over consumption; its significance lay in the fact that it could be carried forward to an expanded level of activity; that is, it represented capital. One needs to observe two objects above all, Verri insists, and they are annual reproduction and annual consumption. If they are equal, the nation preserves its wealth; if consumption is greater, the nation grows poorer. If production exceeds consumption, it grows wealthier. What is more, agricultural output can always be improved—it never reaches an absolute limit, although the limits of demand may be reached.[64] Smith wrote a few years later, probably having read Verri: "There exists another balance, quite different from the commercial balance (i.e., the balance of exports and imports), which necessarily determines the prosperity or the decadence of a nation. This is the balance of annual production and consumption."[65] It is this growth or what Smith calls the "natural progress of opulence,"[66] and not any given level of wealth, that becomes the implicit object of economic scrutiny. Smith's problem is not merely the wealth of nations (a phrase he may have gotten from the French), but the growing wealth of nations. If surplus is not consumed in vain display, but accumulated by virtue of parsimony, it can generate greater output.[67]

Rather than identify a single source that could be safely taxed, Smith advised his readers to avoid those that would impede the generation of society's growth, of which protective tariffs were the worst since they impeded the international division of labor and its spurs to growth. He paid great attention to the Physiocrats but rejected their idea that only the land could generate an economic surplus: "The capital error of this system, however, seems to lie in its representing the class of artificers, manufacturers and merchants, as altogether barren and unproductive."[68] Smith's critique of his French contemporaries hardly meant that he scorned agriculture. On the contrary, he praised the steady returns and quality of life it offered:

> The man who employs his capital in land, has it more under
> his view and command, and his fortune is much less liable to

accidents, than that of the trade, who is obliged frequently to commit it, not only to the winds and the waves, but to the more uncertain elements of human folly and injustice, by giving great credits in distant countries to men, with whose character and situation he can seldom be thoroughly acquainted. The capital of the landlord, on the contrary, which is fixed in the improvement of his land, seems to be as well secured as the nature of human affair can admit of. The beauty of the country besides, the pleasures of a country life, the tranquility of mind which it promises . . . have charms that more or less attract everybody; and as to cultivate the ground was the original destination of man, so in every stage of existence he seems to retain a predilection for this primitive employment.[69]

To be sure, this Virgilian passage was intended to bolster the argument that town and country benefited from each other; ultimately without the town, the country remained sunk in primitive poverty, Smith might have protested Quesnay's attributing economic surplus to the land alone, but he admitted that the capital acquired by commerce and manufactures "is all a very precarious and uncertain possession, till some part of it has been secured and realized in the cultivation and improvement of its lands. . . . The ordinary revolutions of war and government easily dry up the sources of that wealth which arises from commerce only."[70]

The notion that the land was the sole source of surplus even in agriculture, not surprisingly, was heavily contested. In his widely admired tract written in 1766, *Reflexions sur la formation et la distribution des richesses,* when he was serving as Intendant of Limoges, eight years before being called by Louis XVI for his brief career as comptroller general, Anne-Robert Turgot called the surplus the *produit net* and, although he separated himself from the "sect" of the economists or Physiocrats, he began his analysis with agriculture. Specialization of labor was required to meet even the most basic human needs, but the worker of the land retained "the same primacy, the same pre-eminence as, when he lived alone" [although Turgot has written that he could not have lived alone] and had to provide just his own food. The fabric of reciprocal needs "binds society together, but it is labour on land which is the prime mover" (§5).

The land, as worked by men (so Locke had already taught) was the basis of wealth: "What Nature gives . . . is a purely physical result of the fertility of the soil, and the appropriateness, much more than the difficulty, of the means [the primary producer] has employed to make it fruitful." "As soon as the primary producer's labour provides more than is enough to meet his needs, he has a surplus which nature gives him as a pure gift, over and above the wage of his labour" (§5).[71] Land and labor both contributed to society's production function.

Society was thus divided into three orders: those who worked the land, artisans who produced other goods, and the landowners, "the only order who not being bound to any particular work by their need for a livelihood, are independent and therefore available for employment in meeting the needs of the community as a whole, such as war, and the administration of justice" (§15). Still, for all the search for a prime mover, Turgot had a highly modern sense of the economic cycle—capital, "accumulated moveable wealth," was as necessary as labor and skill. If there is a "disturbance of any kind in the pattern of expenditure or the different orders of society," capitalists would cut back their enterprises (that is, investment), production would fall, and "ordinary labourers, no longer able to find work, will sink into the deepest distress and destitution" (§68). Like Smith, with whom he conversed in the year before writing his *Réflexions,* Turgot praised thrift and criticized extravagance (§80), since "it is the abundance of capital which brings enterprises to life, and a low rate of interest is both the effect, and the indicator, of abundant capital" (§88). But unlike Smith, Turgot was unwilling to abandon the primary role of land. Capital was available because of thrift, not the inherent potential of technology or organization; land alone offered an inherent fruitfulness. "There is no revenue other than the net product of land. All other annual profit is either paid from this revenue or is part of the cost which serve to produce it."

Ten years later, and after the first rejection of Turgot's program, the Abbé de Condillac was emphatic about rejecting the exclusive role of land as a source of surplus. Labor was always involved, whether in agriculture or in manufacturing, in creating goods that had value, and the value added or net product arose from the change of form of any raw material or prior product.[72] Condillac anticipated Marx's sharp critique of the doctrines. The theoretician of socialism was a sharp reader of earlier theory, if often abusive and determined to impose his own problematic concepts of use and exchange value, surplus, and exploitation. He appreciated the Physiocrats and Turgot since, in contrast to the Mercantilists, who identified profit with the redistribution of already existing value from one country to another, they sought the sources that increased wealth as such. But they erred in attributing the surplus to land: although "it is the great and specific contribution of the Physiocrats that they derive value and surplus-value not from circulation but from production," as Verri had understood, they mistakenly attributed it to the properties of land and not to the social conditions in which agricultural labor was extracted. Physiocracy, Marx concluded, was a bourgeois doctrine built on feudal premises.[73]

Given that land and not agricultural labor was the ultimate source of surplus under Physiocratic precepts, what policies were advisable? The program of the Physiocrats, and their intellectual kin Turgot, was supply-side economics applied to agriculture and simple in theory: liberate grain prices; liberate the land from "feudal" or aristocratic entail and the "dead hand" of the church; move unused common lands into the market; and, ultimately (as Vauban and Boisguilbert had urged), rely on a single land tax since land was the source of surplus. Reforms on paper, however, were hard to translate into practice. Freeing prices threatened domestic unrest; the numerous clergy and religious houses apparently exerted a deadweight on the economy, while a profusion of notaries lived parasitically on all legal transactions. Reforms decreed at the center could be blocked on the local level. The common lands of Savoy, for example, so the cadaster of 1728–1738 revealed, produced little revenue. In the Tarentaise 70 percent of the land was communal but produced only 20 percent of the revenue. The conclusion was to sell the excess, but despite the orders of a new "economic hierarchy" in 1739, village councils blocked action, and even by the time of the Napoleonic invasion, the land situation had changed little from a century earlier.[74]

It was particularly hard to impose the policy conclusions in France— that is, to tax the landlords but not the cultivators—and despite their close connections at the court of Louis XV, where Quesnay was a favorite of Mme. de Pompadour, the Physiocrats could not carry their policy recommendations. A flurry of reforming edicts had to be defended in the regional parlements across the kingdom. As controller general in 1774,

Turgot decreed the end of the *corvée,* which he criticized for conscripting peasants for work on the public roads while the landlords were the ones who benefited from the improved access of grain to markets. "How can it be just to force those who have nothing to donate their time and un-paid labor, to take away their only resource against poverty and hunger to make them work for the profit of citizens wealthier than they are!"[75] (Turgot's reform, however, was rolled back piecemeal, until more successfully managed by his later successor, Necker.) He urged removal of the taxes on leather and cattle, wanted to lift the restrictions on selling wood outside the city of Paris that its officials imposed on the owners of local forests—it is "contrary to the first principles of *property and liberty.*" Complete the abolition of all river and canal tolls within the kingdom, he appealed, and begin a national road and canal transport service: communications are part of the "the protection that we owe to agriculture which is the true base of public prosperity and abundance and the favor that we want to grant commerce as the most certain encouragement for agriculture."[76] Most radically he argued that if price controls on bread were abolished, suppliers would respond to the incentives; expanded production would follow, and the new equilibrium price would be no higher than the earlier controlled price. Likewise let grain travel freely out of district and even out of the country. Decree followed upon decree liberating commerce in 1774–1775. But what would happen in the transition as milling and bread prices soared in a country where bread was an urban staple and could claim half of a family's budget?

The new monarch Louis XVI initially accepted Turgot's policy, but faced with a wave of aristocratic protest as well as urban demonstrations—the so-called flour wars of 1775—he abandoned the experiment. (In Tuscany the reform as carried through, as it would be in Spain—years later.) As for the tax reforms, they were quashed at the outset. The preliminary requisite for the single tax had to be a national property register. At Versailles on September 1, 1775, when Louis XVI expressed his enthusiasm for Turgot's idea of a national cadaster and an equal tax burden, "all the ministers remained silent until one ventured, 'Sire, the astonishment that your Majesty sees among the council is justified: M. Turgot can't be ig-norant of the fact that for two hundred years there has been a cadaster planned but it has been understood to be impossible to carry out. . . . Besides the immense cost of the operation it would turn the state upside

down without bringing any prompt or real relief for the people.'"
Everyone agreed. "And the king decided to keep his conviction *in petto*."[77]
Turgot was soon out of office with his reformist program in shambles.

Elsewhere Physiocratic policies made headway in some places but
not others. Despite the cadaster's success in Lombardy by midcentury, the
Verri brothers, Pietro and Alessandro, who edited the Milanese reformist
journal *Il Caffe* in the 1760s, could not convince the new economic
council to follow the Tuscan example and allow free trade in grains (including the right to export them out of the province). Vienna ruled the
province but despite his own Physiocratic preferences, Chancellor Kaunitz
was not willing to intervene with a heavy hand.[78] The reformist Cardinal Boncompagni advanced reformist ideas against resistance in the papacy's province of Bologna. The prescriptions were echoed in southern
Italy, absorbed throughout the Iberian world, admired by Thomas Jefferson, whose friend Dupont de Nemours was a leading Physiocrat, and
exerted an impact even on the British fiscal administration in Bengal.

Confronting a society of entrenched exemptions for landlord elites
throughout continental Europe, the reformers began with the conviction
that taxes should be switched from persons or families, overwhelmingly
living near subsistence, to the underlying productive asset that was distributed so unequally. The Physiocrats separated the *taille personnelle* from
the *taille réelle,* the tax on land. Even when other reformers criticized the
idea that land was the source of all wealth, they often concurred that that
land could be measured and evaluated and the burden assigned to landowners rather than poor tenants, whereas the effort to estimate the non-
landed wealth of an absentee proprietor yielded derisory results. Still, there
were important dissenters. Pietro Verri argued that taxing land alone
would reduce capital and spare a genuine source of wealth: "I can't associate myself with either the [French Physiocrats'] views on taxes . . . or
on the supposed sterile class."[79] "Reproduction" or surplus could be attributed equally to manufacture as to the labor of the fields, and even a civil
servant sympathetic to the program of throwing land on the market, such
as the Tuscan economist Francesco Maria Gianni, argued vehemently that
a single tax on land "will always be absurd, and pernicious," and that cadasters can never provide a valid basis for assessing income from agriculture.[80] Other compromises also made sense. Aware that landlords and
their tenants put effort and savings into improving their lands by fencing,

buildings, and irrigation, policy makers did not want to penalize or discourage such investment. In the case of the Lombard reforms, the idea was to tax what the land could be expected to yield before landlords had improved it—that is, on its "bare income," *nuda rendita*. Investments and improvements were to be deducted from the value of the property, itself determined by capitalizing the rental that a given category of land was yielding.[81] Finally, there was just plain resistance that prevailed. Nobles fought for their exemptions, and the Giuntas that ruled the province for the monarch in Vienna found it hard to resist their pleas. For all the success of mapping property, taxation did not increase.

For over a generation Spanish developments revealed the tug-of-war as starkly as events in France. Until the Revolution came to the French countryside after 1789, French reformers were weaker politically, although productively Spain had remained poorer for over a century. Charles III of the Neapolitan Bourbon line, who succeeded to the Spanish throne in 1759 after reigning in Naples, faced a decade of drought and poor harvests, which compelled the abandonment of early reforms. The effort to free the grain market in 1765 by eliminating price controls and allowing grain to be shipped outside the local provinces led to riots by the next spring, which led the king to sacrifice the reforming minister, the Marquis of Esquilache, whom he had brought with him from Italy. Charles remained favorable to reform proposals and by dint of a long reign could impose some of them, even though he confronted elites powerfully entrenched in local governments. Colonization schemes in the south produced some marked successes, as Minister Pablo de Olavide allocated the uncultivated and primitive Sierra Morena and the Cordoba area into land for grain, flax, silk, and hemp cultivation. Imposing reform where the land was settled and powerful landowners controlled the town councils was harder. In an effort to redress the local political balance, Esquilache's collaborator Pedro Rodríguez de Campomanes introduced election of commoners in the towns of Castile to represent the smaller tax payers and to rent out common lands to smaller holders although most of the leases would be distributed to the local elites. Between 1766 and 1768, the monarchy decreed distribution of common lands to day laborers and small farmers. Common lands had long been arrogated in Britain, and church lands had been taken in the Reformation. In Spain the tracts of vacant lands, the baldios, remained extensive, nominally belonging to the king but controlled often by town councils and thus by their wealthy landowners.

The church, of course, remained a major landholder, although the Jesuit order, caught up in politics and resented for its defense of indigenous communities in the Argentine interior, was expelled and its properties confiscated in 1768. The Spanish Gracchi—in this case Campomanes and his new recruit Joseph Moñino, Count of Floridablanca—had come to power . . . briefly. By the early 1770s the reformist initiative abated as officials quarreled and were reassigned. No ideologically driven disposal of Jesuit properties ensued—many were recycled for hospitals or municipal purposes.[82] But the reformist ferment continued. The Royal Basque Society of Friends of the Fatherland inspired Campomanes in 1765 to create the Royal Economic Society of Madrid in 1775, to which the Council of Castile sent a mass of files on economic conditions with the request that it produce a comprehensive plan for reform. The task languished for six years then was assigned to a twelve-man Special Junta for an Agrarian Law, headed by the up-and-coming young Gaspar Melchior de Jovellanos, who by the mid-1780s had become a convinced Smithian. The new Junta published the material collected on the countryside and began discussion of legislation in 1787. Unease at the revolutionary events beginning north of the Pyrenees led Floridablanca to back away from reform and reassign Jovellanos to his native Asturias as well as to dismiss Campomanes. But political winds shifted once again: Manuel Godoy, a progressive, succeeded Floridablanca while Jovellanos produced the major statement of Spanish agrarian reform, the Informe de la Sociedad Economica en el expediente de ley agraria.[83]

For Jovellanos as for Campomanes, the retarded agrarian structure followed from outworn social and political privileges, preeminently the monopoly rights over land held by the sheep owners grouped in the Mesta, and the laws of entail that impeded the formation of a robust farmer class. Agrarian legislation, argued Jovellanos, should be designed to prevent obstacles (estorbos) to production—assuming that "man was naturally active"[84] (§24, p. 8), but they had to be changed all of a piece if they were to succeed. The sale of the common lands would have little effect if the laws of entail allowed wealthy families and religious bodies to remove land from the market and thereby maintain it at a "scandalous price." Because it lacked entail and other protective legislation, Jovellanos argued, the fledgling United States with only four million inhabitants had already managed to export large amounts of agricultural goods (§§154–156). Establish, therefore, a nation of yeoman farmers, and our "settlers will possess the social and domestic virtues that constitute the happiness of families and the true glories of state." But there were other intertwined obstacles. Any limitation of entail would avail little if the privileges of livestock grazing were preserved. The grazing rights enjoyed by the Mesta were exorbitant; Spain sacrificed its grain and its people to its sheep. Declare "the dissolution of this overmighty brotherhood, the abolition of its exorbitant privileges. . . . Let the seasonal migration of livestock enjoy [only] that just measure of protection that the laws owe to all branches of industry. If wool remains high in price, the grasslands will yield a high price without requiring odious privileges, while if farming promises a better profit, transhumancy [the seasonal grazing migration across the countryside] will also be reduced, and an equilibrium will be established" (§§139–140). "What purpose would enclosure serve if the system of protecting parcels and the privileges of livestock grazing persisted? What use would be irrigation if enclosure were not allowed? . . . The greater the evil, the more urgent the remedy . . . the issue is no less than one of opening up the prime and most abundant source of public and private wealth: of raising the nation to the highest summit of splendor and power and of leading the people confided to the care of Your Highness to the ultimate point of human felicity . . . it is a question of . . . restoring landed property and labor to its legitimate rights and of reestablishing the rule of justice" (§§422–423). Correct the abuses, aid in the repopulation of the deserted settlements of the South and Spain would become a land of virtuous smallholders: "Living with his family at the site of his labor," so Jovellanos indulged his idyll, the small proprietor, "can devote himself without distraction to his livelihood . . . husbandmen may exhibit dedication and thrift and produce the abundance that these qualities generate; then conjugal, paternal, filial and fraternal live will reign in their families; peace, charity, and hospitality will prevail; and our farmers *(colonos)* will possess the social and domestic virtues that constitute the happiness of families and the true glory of states."[85]

Small bits of the countryside were actually redeemed for agriculture and settled. It was easier, of course, to spin Physiocratic reveries in Jefferson's Virginia, where land was plentiful and monopolies not yet established. What made partial reform at all possible in old Europe was the availability of Jesuit and Catholic lands that might go on the markets, but in some pockets secular landlords could still resist tenaciously. Certainly the viceroy of the kingdom of Sicily, Domenico Caracciolo (1780–1789), was as intelligent as the other reformers, but he could not succeed in his project of a cadaster and tax reform. "When I was relegated to this most remote corner of Christendom," Caracciolo wrote later, "my first thought from earliest arrival was to attack the radical vice that produced the people's misery, that is the unjust and tyrannical distribution of the taxes."[86] Sicily and Naples remained one kingdom, but with two different political systems, joined in a personal union by Charles of Bourbon, the same monarch who later reigned as the reformist Charles III of Spain. Mainland Naples bore the stamp of Spanish absolutism, and until the mid-1770s it had benefited from a skilled reformist prime minister, Bernardo Tanucci. The Francophile Caracciolo, who had thrived as ambassador in Parisian social and intellectual circles, was summoned to rule as viceroy in Palermo after 1780, but enjoyed decisive power only for the last three years of his life (1786–1789) as prime minister of the whole kingdom. A Neapolitan by birth, virtually exiled to the island capital dominated by a fossilized nobility, he had to confront his conservative predecessor as prime minister, Sicilian by birth, and a queen who, although a daughter of Maria Theresa, had no resolve to emulate the Austrian empress's reformism. The viceroy might govern Sicily in theory, but his policies required the assent of the king who would consult the "Giunta" of three leading island nobles and three Neapolitans.

Administration in Sicily lay largely in the hands of its great nobles whose unruly delegates convened every third year or so in an unreformed parliament of three "arms" or houses—the "military" estate, where 228 hereditary peers represented the 885 princes, counts, marquises, and barons; the ecclesiastic chamber; and the domainal arm, representing principally the cities, including Palermo, where many of the fractious nobles lived and indeed had indulged in a revolt in 1784. The normal budgetary procedure involved parliament voting a three-year gift on the proposal of the king and then splitting up the bill among the diverse estates. About 16 to 18 percent was assigned to the clergy and the nobility each, 10 percent to foreigners, 10 percent to the city of Palermo, and

46 percent or so to the domainal arm. It was estimated that the great feudatories paid approximately 7 percent of their revenues in taxes, while a household capitation and consumer excises threw the main burden on an immiserated peasantry and town commoners. The universities had decayed; the courts needed reform. Once Tanucci retired in his seventies from the Neapolitan cabinet, reformist spirit waned and the king grew passive; the influence of the queen, of her British lover and naval minister, Admiral Acton, and that of her mother's court in Vienna grew larger. From any reformer's viewpoint, Sicily was a territory from hell.

The freethinker intellectual Caracciolo, who, like his contemporary Thomas Jefferson, was truly at home in Paris, was named primarily to restore order to the fractious island whose intellectual currents reflected a British distrust of abstract intellectuals but lacked the stimulus of Britain's commercial society and scientific curiosity. Caracciolo had been ambassador while Turgot's ministry was in power; he consulted with Pompeo Neri, who had completed the catasto in Milan; as he later wrote to Acton, he believed that "the tax on land is the queen of taxes, the most just, and the most advantageous for the king and the least onerous for the state. There are big things to do in Sicily."[87] He developed a plan for a cadastral reform akin to that pushed through in Milan. But he would have needed a monarch who gave him the same power that Maria Theresa had reposed in Neri. This was the lesson that Pietro Verri had drawn: the tax reform in Lombardy could never have been accomplished had there been a senate of local notables; reform required legal despotism to establish the felicity of the people.[88]

The new viceroy had some remarkable successes. He suppressed the Inquisition, taking its properties and burning its records; he dissolved the seventy-four gilds that were a source of recurrent demonstrations and rebellions, but he had his plans to shorten Palermo's raucous and costly Saint Rosalia holiday from five to three days reversed by Naples. His grand plans for tax reform were slowly paralyzed. Caracciolo personally appeared before the 118th Sicilian parliament in May 1782, asking for a new census (the last count dated from 1748), a fresh assessment of properties, and a different distribution of taxes. There followed a week of debate; the tax was approved, but the idea of shifting the burden or initiating a new census and assessment was accepted only by the towns of the domainal arm that bore almost half their burden while it was rejected by the military and ecclesiastical "arms." Their parliamentary votes, however, were nonbinding, and Caracciolo recommended to the king that he proceed with a cadaster on the basis of the third estate's positive vote. The monarch instructed him to propose the modalities of the land survey but postponed a final decision. Caracciolo's political sense failed him, and he transmitted further requests via Acton, who essentially delayed and buried them under the excuse that officially they had to come from the Giunta of Sicily. The viceroy persisted in urging the proposed cadaster as a panacea for the island's ills: "This is the epic of regeneration for Sicily, the greatest cause and perhaps the most serious in the happy reign of Ferdinand IV. What is needed now is a sovereign act of supreme political economy *(alta economia di stato)* and a grand remedy for Sicily's public welfare."[89]

But the viceroy in Palermo remained remote from the court in Naples, vulnerable to the machinations of the intervening officials, and opposed by the barons entrenched in the constitutional delegations and Giunta. The catastrophic earthquake of February 5, 1783, in Messina just across the straits in Calabria, which left 30,000 dead in a zone of 400,000 inhabitants, allowed the island's Giunta to propose a special parliamentary session that would offer a "free gift" of 400,000 scudi (less exemptions) if the plans for the land survey were dropped. As Caracciolo himself had to recognize, the offer seemed like an extraordinarily generous public response; however, it was a gift that spelled disaster for his hopes of a new cadaster. The domainal chamber, supported by the viceroy's public statement, demanded that the 400,000 scudi gift be collected equally from the three estates, a demand supported by town delegations across the island. But the parliamentary delegation that spoke for the chambers between sessions denounced the move, and on July 3 the king wrote to say that he accepted the donation, but that the domainal arm's effort to lower its share was "irregular and capricious," and the gift must be allocated as the two upper chambers demanded. Caracciolo recognized that this spelled the end of plans for tax reform: "a million and a half souls remain condemned by the cupidity and ambition of about 70 baronial families."[90]

The earthquake had further social ramifications. Faced with heavy expenses for aid and rebuilding, the Naples court established a special institution in 1784, the Cassa Sacra, to raise funds for relief and reconstruction by administering and selling off the ecclesiastical properties of Catanzaro and Reggio in Calabria. The baronial and wealthy classes of Calabria seized the chance to buy these properties before the Cassa, managed inefficiently and in debt, was dissolved on the eve of the Neapolitan revolution of 1798. The result was to consolidate the holdings of a new landlord elite (what counted for a southern *borghesia*) freed from many of the common customs that had softened the old property relationships and to confirm an even more dependent status for peasants and tenants,[91] As a critic wrote acutely in 1789 about the reasons for the degradation of the province since the earthquake: despite the government's significant aid, "instead of reviving from its misery Calabria becomes poorer and more desolate every day." The major part of the territory remains in the hands of a few citizens "who oppress the rest of the nation who must become their servants and their hired hands to survive." Or, as another critic wrote, the Cassa Sacra was not an agent for Calabria's recovery but rather its further ruin.[92] Its impact, wrote Vicenzo Cuoco, the historian of the Neapolitan revolution of 1798, was worse than the earthquake, or as even the confessor of the king publicly recognized, it was thought of as "the *second calamity* of Calabria and perhaps worse than the first."[93] Nor were the sales of land finished. From 1806 to 1815 the French rule of the Neapolitan mainland brought the auction of convents and monasteries throughout the kingdom. On the one hand, the transfers fulfilled Enlightenment precepts and helped consolidate the commodification of the Catholic countryside; on the other, the new market order meant further exclusion of the marginalized rural classes.

Looking at France, Spain, and Italy, it is tempting to conclude that the vision of a market-oriented agrarian order was attractive in lands where the Catholic Church and an entrenched nobility had accumulated privileges; where industry and commerce played less of a role than agriculture; and where political concepts, often of Roman inspiration, remained more utopian than in commercial and Protestant realms, where land had long been on the market and the advance of trade motivated political and economic analysis. In fact the persuasiveness of agrarian doctrines, if not the Physiocratic analysis strictly speaking, was more general. In the United States, the program appealed to the emerging Jeffersonian party. Even earlier, agrarian preferences fit in with the colonists' growing distrust of England and their reaction to its mercantile legislation that tried to restrict independent trade. Benjamin Franklin, for instance, had fallen under French Physiocratic influence during his stays in Europe in the 1760s, and as conflict grew with London after 1763, he became sharply critical of Britain's manufacturing vocation, which he thought responsible for much of the poverty of its workers. He wrote to Lord Kames in 1769 that nations could acquire wealth by war and plunder, by commerce, "which is generally Cheating," or "by *Agriculture* the only *honest Way;* wherein Man receives a real Increase of the Seed thrown into the Ground, in a kind of continual Miracle wrote by the Hand of God in his Favour, as a Reward for his innocent Life, and virtuous Industry."[94]

Certainly North American opinion did not unanimously reject commerce. John Adams did not believe that his countrymen would resist the charms of luxury and fashion; every man aspired toward distinction.[95] The American republic would be an active commercial power, Ezra Stiles enthused. "Navigation will carry the American flag around the globe itself; and display the thirteen stripes and new constellation at *bengal* and *canton,* on the *indus* and *ganges,* on the *whang-ho* [Huangho or Yellow River] and the *yang-tse-kiang* [Yangtze]," bringing knowledge of the world back home.[96] Commerce would allow Americans to export their agrarian surpluses. The difficulty, however, of penetrating foreign markets in the mid-1780s after independence produced a debate on trade, and the reassertion by some of the need for a Spartan agrarian simplicity. For New Englanders and merchant spokesmen elsewhere, rude and virtuous isolation seemed an unrealistic and unappealing vocation—the realization came with the growing sense, too, that the new republic needed a cohesive state able to compete in a world of contending empires.[97]

Still, in the first decade of the fledgling federal republic, James Madison and Alexander Hamilton drew competing conclusions for economic orientation. For Madison and like-minded Americans, manufacturing was associated with the production, not of the necessities that every household might need, but of luxuries. Precisely the conditions that the Physiocrats yearned for in Europe but existed in the new United States—the abolition of privilege, the opening up of land—made an agrarian alternative easy to contemplate. But American agriculture, efficient and vigorous, still needed export markets, and Britain closed its markets and those of the nearby West Indies. Madison argued that it was practical to pry open British trade because her economy supposedly required American commodities more than the United States required British luxuries. Hamilton believed the program misconceived: the manufacturing nation had the greater leverage, and he wanted British capital as an essential component of a national financial system that through the instrumentality of a sound national debt would weave together public and private interests. Madison in short wanted to reject the British model; Hamilton wanted to reproduce it. Early financial developments hardly confirmed the wisdom of either side in the debate, Hamilton established his new Bank of the United States in 1791, but a panic in March 1792 seemed to discredit the initiative. Hamilton, though, prevailed in 1794: Madison's program of discriminatory tariffs against Britain was rejected and Jay's Treaty precluded such tariffs for a decade. On the other hand, the early venture-capital establishment, the Society for Establishing Universal Manufactures, with which the treasury secretary was associated, clamorously collapsed in 1795, and with it Hamilton's aspirations for state-funded industrial development were also set back. This did not foreclose an era of capital and commerce; American exports and American shipping thrived in the next eight years before the British-French wars began to squeeze neutral goods and crews.[98]

Hamilton had little motivation to encourage westward expansion: the East Coast was where the labor supplies were and manufacturing would be sited, not the plentiful land of the interior. Madison and Jefferson, however, contemplated a national territory that might reach continental proportions. The Democratic-Republican agrarian strategy also rested on Jeffersonian partiality toward the French republic in the Anglo-French global rivalry (tested though it would be by the XYZ Affair and the clumsy diplomacy of Citizen Genêt). The British sought to slow down the Americans' control over their vast hinterland—an effort temporarily crowned by the concessions they extracted in Jay's Treaty in 1794, but one ultimately nullified by Jefferson's Louisiana Purchase of 1803, in which France in effect provided the territorial rights needed to make the agrarian program plausible in the Americas. America's capacious territory would form the basis for what Jefferson contemplated as an "empire of liberty"; as Franklin and the French economists had argued fifty years earlier, the land remained the underlying source of national wealth. Territorial expansion, advocates claimed, could forestall political degeneration, averting

Britain's social divisions and impoverishment of labor.[99] Although the future peril of an emerging urban proletariat remained vivid, the two peoples who would actually pay the cost of expansion—Native Americans and slaves—were not reckoned as part of the human calculus. It was critical that the land and sovereignty—territory as a political and economic resource—remained in the control of the new country's own political classes.

Although Britain progressively lost the colonies between the West Indies and Canada after the 1760s, it simultaneously acquired an Indian empire—hardly vacant land but nonetheless a realm where Physiocratic precepts seemed to provide policy guidelines as they did on the crowded and stratified European continent. As Smith's skepticism revealed and subsequent commentators have pointed out, it was hard to countenance the Physiocratic argument in bustling Britain.[100] Thus it seems initially surprising that the ideas had so much appeal in British-controlled Bengal, where they motivated the governor general, then George Lord Cornwallis, responsible for the military debacle at Yorktown twelve years earlier, to decree a tax freeze—"the permanent settlement" on behalf of the proprietors of land and their tax-farming intermediaries, the zamindars as of 1793: "They and their heirs and lawful successors will be allowed to hold their estates at such assessment for ever."[101]

The intent was to stabilize a class of gentry willing to invest in a productive agriculture, but the result was to entrench a system of grinding down peasant tenants. How did the policy go so awry? The founding historian of "subaltern studies," Ranajit Guha brilliantly analyzed the unlikely and perhaps disastrous influence of Physiocratic or market-based tenets on British India fifty years ago. Following Clive's victory at Plassey, the East India Company acquired the Mughal right of *diwani* or financial administration in 1765 and had to make sense of the complex Mughal Indian land systems. The first British expedient of selling five-year leases (the so-called farming system) proved disastrous; there was no check on the demands of the zamindari vis-à-vis their cultivators or *ryots,* and no incentive for long-term improvement. Impoverishment of the villages seemed to follow quickly to be culminated by a devastating famine in 1770. Short-term revenue farming seemed at the root of the catastrophe: the new colonial regime, junior British officials who had to deal with the famine-devastated districts suggested, had surrendered too many of the Mughals' rights of proprietorship to the landlords who leased from the British and collected oppressive rent from the villages they were granted. They advocated permanent rental of small holdings to the principal cultivators of the villages, thereby encouraging a class of midsize landholders. Such a plan did not suit the interests of the British and Indian speculators of Calcutta nor the clique around the governor general, Warren Hastings.[102] The alternative reform foresaw transforming the zamindari from a decaying class of rent collectors into agricultural investors. Motivated by such a vision, Philip Francis, a member of the Supreme Council of Bengal and an enthusiast for French economic ideas, proposed a plan of "permanent settlement" in 1776 that would confirm the zamindari as outright owners and encourage their investments by letting the new proprietors know "once and for all" how much they were to pay the British government.[103] Oversimplified analogies with Britain played a role in this policy vision. The retention of ownership by the political sovereign, it was argued, was the essence of feudalism and associated with the backwardness of France and Scotland before the union of 1703. Conversely, the robust agrarian constitution of eighteenth-century England supposedly rested on the fact that the narrow class of ultimate proprietors leased lands for life or long-term to a class of gentry farmers who had invested in the improvement of properties they saw in effect as their own. The rulers of British India must build on zamindari tenure in an analogous manner.

No scheme of agrarian democracy was at stake. Although Francis was an enthusiast for the Physiocrats' emphasis on generating surplus in the countryside, he was unwilling for the state to intervene in the way that the Habsburg officials sought to do in Milan. Whether Neri in Italy or Turgot in France, state reformers felt they must eliminate the differential privileges of status when it came to taxes. The premise of their reforms was determining the potential value of the land. Francis drew the opposite conclusion from the Habsburgs or continental tax reformers: there must be no systematic cadastral survey—the British had the right to tax only what they needed, not to determine what the land might pay. The ryots or cultivators were not a class that the empire was to deal with directly; the zamindari would come to their own terms with them.[104]

European rulers on the continent understood that they must protect their tenants from their powerful aristocratic landlords if only not to lose control of their own revenues. London and the East India Company were running a distant empire that was supposed to yield a profit. Francis believed that in India the rulers had to enhance the power of the magnates—providing them economic incentives to improve their holdings. What resulted, however, was hardly the formation of an English gentry or even the growing surplus and "net product" described by the reforming economists whom Francis read, but rather the reduction of peasant cultivators to chronic debtors and agricultural laborers—the rank exploitation that characterized such districts as Mecklenburg and east Central Europe. Other British or East India Company officials distrusted the idea of entrusting the zamindari with the prosperity and happiness of India; many of the smaller agrarian entrepreneurs who had taken leases after 1765 deserved to be confirmed in their tenure. But how should one sort out the virtuous farmers from the interests that Warren Hastings's corrupt interval had fostered? And an empire, especially an empire that was not to be settled by British colonists, demanded an interlocutory class of magnates.

Although Francis's ideas were rebuffed after 1776, they made a comeback. Thomas Law, the officer in charge of Bihar, argued in 1789, "The basis of prosperity is laid by fixing the land tax." Take away the zamindars' judicial prerogatives—which were an example of "feudalism," but confirm that the "Zamindar is indisputable proprietor of the soil and [the] Ryot but a vassal or peasant."[105] When Lord Cornwallis arrived, a few years after his defeat in America, he reintroduced the idea of the generous permanent settlement, that is, the freeze on taxes. He, too, saw the justification of wagering on an aristocratic zamindar class in the stimulus to agriculture. "The grant of these lands at a fixed assessment will stamp a value upon them hitherto unknown. . . . There is every ground to expect that the large capitals possessed by the natives . . . will be applied to the purchase of landed property as soon as the tenure is declared to be secure, and they are capable of estimating what profit they will be certain of deriving from it, by the public tax upon it being unalterably fixed."[106] The new owners would invest in wells and aqueducts and the manufacture of raw materials, such as cotton, to be exported to Britain for textile production that might then find an Indian market.

The result, of course, was not what had been so rosily predicted. No reform of the countryside followed. Nor did commerce benefit. Unlike Quesnay, Francis did not believe that manufactures were economically "sterile"; nevertheless, land was the basis of wealth and commerce, and industry prospered in the shadow of agriculture. Moreover, the burgeoning British cotton industry did not want competition from Indian calicoes. What really mattered was the management of India's agriculture and manufacture for an imperial establishment.

But the rural desolation that resulted from misplaced emphasis on market incentives had more general causes. Physiocratic concepts and market based reforms in the eighteenth century addressed the problems of bequeathed by archaic taxes and "feudal" restrictions on entrepreneurship, but they had little to say about dependent labor as such. Instead, two policy visions worked to distort the actual impact of reforms on those who labored on the land. For Quesnay and the British administrators of Bengal, the agrarian investor—the leaseholder or owner and the employer or landlord of the rural laborer—was the crucial protagonist. This class of agricultural entrepreneurs, whether a reformed zamindari or the British gentry, were the "change agents" of the countryside. For agrarian enthusiasts such as Jovellanos and Jefferson, the cultivator himself was the critical agent. In achieving his destiny as a yeoman peasant, living with his family in domestic bliss, enjoying the salubrious influence of the countryside, the cultivator would be the molecular unit of prosperity.

In different ways, Jovellanos and Jefferson counted on vastly expanded access to land. For Jefferson the vast size of the American "empire of liberty" guaranteed plentiful land. For Jovellanos and other reformers the removal of encrusted monopolies, antique collective privileges, and since the late 1760s access to church properties provided the land that allowed the farmer to prosper. Neither France nor Bengal had such reservoirs of territory, and as a result the emphasis had to be on the fiscal policies and the opening of the market that would permit progress. Capitalist incentives, not territorial abundance, were crucial, whereas Jefferson and Jovellanos retained a precapitalist faith. Their market thinking remained more partial. With lands in the New World—and a population of slaves or Indians—the transformative impulse did not have to focus on the role of the agrarian bourgeoisie as such. In effect, the need was to liberate land, and the liberation of labor would follow eventually and bloodlessly by itself. This expectation proved as illusory as the belief that total marketization would bring painless growth, which characterized the other strand. We come to the underlying deficiency that Marx emphasized in his respectful but critical reading of the Physiocrats. We need not agree with Marx that labor was the sole source of surplus any more than with the Physiocrats, who believed that the bounty of land provided its exclusive source. But Marx did point out that it was utopian to believe that territory, no matter how fertile or extensive, was the only motor of growth. Labor alone (as Locke had already pointed out) unlocked the potential of the land. However, the capacity to harness labor to the land—call it the social constitution of the countryside—fell into crisis at the end of the eighteenth century. Governing within borders, farming within boundaries produced the surplus of the countryside only when labor remained within borders. Understanding these problems as contemporaries confronted them requires closer examination of the labor conditions that persisted and plagued the agrarian world from the late eighteenth century to the mid-nineteenth century.

Portolan or Compass Rose charts originating in the late Middle Ages and Renaissance allowed a ship to align itself according to thirty-two "wind rose" lines radiating according to the compass directions drawn from each of the many points established on the map. They served best for close-in coastal sailing. But the farther from any vertex, the more the map's lines diverged from the local compass or celestial orientations. The cylindrical Mercator projection of the mid-sixteenth century allowed so-called rhumb lines, or loxodromes, to be drawn by straightedge across the meridians of longitude at constant angles, thus enabling a navigator to plot a course from point to point with a uniform bearing.

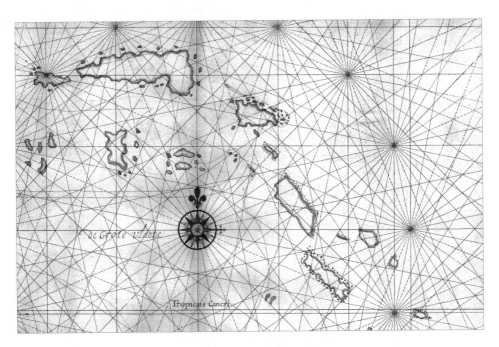

Joan Vinckeboons' portolan chart of the Bahamas Channel north of Cuba, circa 1650. Library of Congress. www.loc.gov/item/00560610.

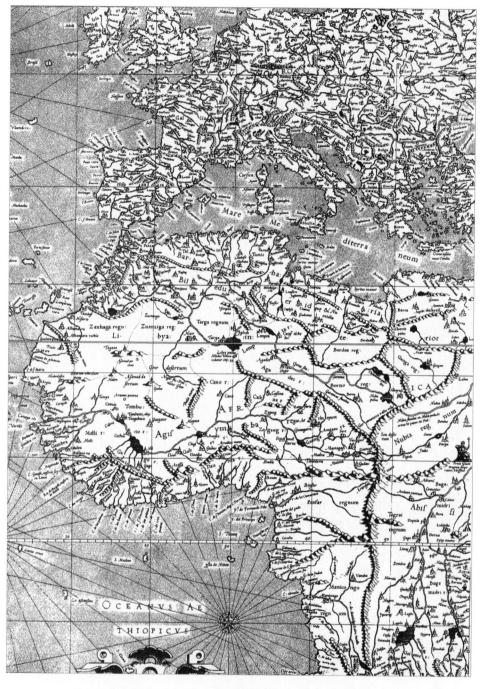

Section of Gerardus Mercator's 1569 world map. This map still incorporates portolans but is distinguished by its rectangular parallels of longitude and latitude, which vastly enlarge areas toward the poles. Basel copy, photographed and reproduced by Wilhelm Kruecken. Wikimedia. https://upload.wikimedia.org/wikipedia /commons/4/4a/Mercator_1569_world_map_sheet_10.PNG.

La Rocca di San Leo (Marche, Italy), circa 1480. Francesco Maurizio di Giorgio Martini, painter and architect, a native of Siena, designed important fortifications in the Marches and the Italian south, and published a treatise on the new military architecture. The elegant fortress of San Leo, however, relied more on its hilltop site to protect its walls than on the hexagonal bastions added later. Photograph by V. Virgola, 2006. Wikipedia Commons. https://commons.wikimedia.org/wiki/File:La_rocca_di_San_Leo.JPG.

"Fortified Hexagon with diverse ramparts and bastions." This engraving illustrates the elements of fortress architecture as they had evolved by the end of the seventeenth century. From Nicolas de Fer, *Les forces de l'Europe, ou Description des principales villes; avec leurs fortifications . . . pour l'usage de Monseigneur le Duc de Bourgogne* (Paris: chez l'auteur, 1695). Reproduced courtesy of Pusey Map Collection, Harvard College Library.

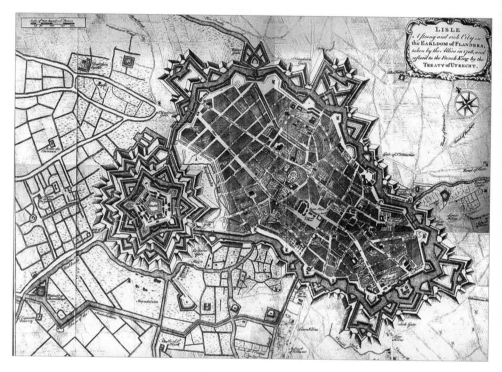

Lisle (now Lille), the fortified northeast anchor of Louis XIV's expanding domain. Vauban added the citadel at the left of the city fortifications, which had been constructed before Vauban's extensive program of frontier fortresses. The citadel protected the city's garrisons from popular uprisings as well as foreign invasions. From de Fer, *Les forces de l'Europe, ou Description des principales villes.* Reproduced courtesy of Pusey Map Collection, Harvard College Library.

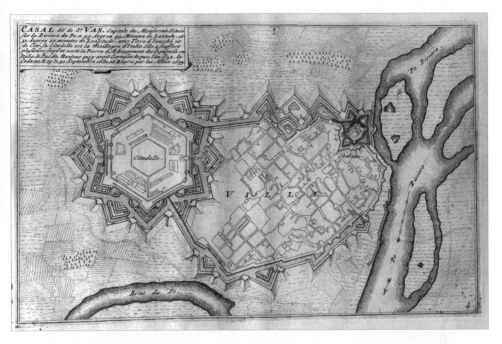

Plan of the fortress of Casal (St. Vas) on the river Po, described here as "the best citadel of Italy." Note the citadel within the fortified city on the left of the image (which is laterally reversed, hence to the east of the river). From de Fer, *Les forces de l'Europe, ou Description des principales villes*. Reproduced courtesy of Pusey Map Collection, Harvard College Library.

Detail of property holdings from the 1728–1732 Cadastre of the Duchy of Savoy, at that time a part of territory straddling the Alps in the kingdom of Sardinia, but ceded in 1860 to France. Each numbered property (inverted with respect to the lettering) was associated with an inventory listing and valuation for taxes. Coloring of the 1.5-meter-wide map sheets indicated land uses, such as forest, pasture, vineyards, wheat, and so on. Reproduced from *Le cadastre sarde de 1730 en Savoie* (Chambéry: Musée Savoisien, 1980). Courtesy of the Département de la Savoie, Archives départementales [C 2617].

American Progress, painted by John Gast in 1872 and widely reproduced. The symbolic figure of Columbia strings telegraph cables and leads the transcontinental railroad across the Great Plains as daylight advances from the east and Indians fade into the still-darkened west. Library of Congress Prints and Photographs Division. http://www.loc.gov/pictures/item/97507547/.

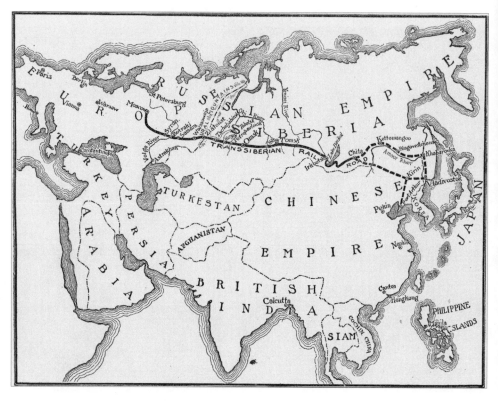

The Trans-Siberian Railway, constructed in the 1890s, extended from Moscow to Vladivostok and made vivid for many Russians the power of their continental domain. From John W. Bookwalter's "The Trans-Siberian Railroad" in *Ainslee's Magazine* 3, no. 1 (Feb. 1899): 397.

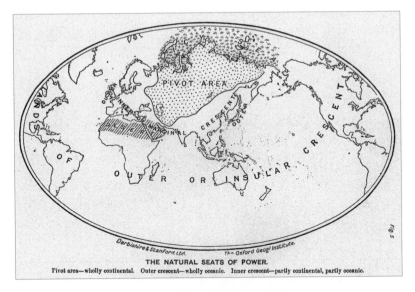

Halford Mackinder's original 1904 version of his theory of Eurasian domination (here identified as the Pivot Area). Mackinder later summarized: "Who controls eastern Europe rules the Heartland; Who controls the Heartland rules the World Island; and Who rules the World Island rules the World." From Halford J. Mackinder's "The Geographical Pivot of History," *Geographical Journal* 23, no. 4 (Apr. 1904): 435.

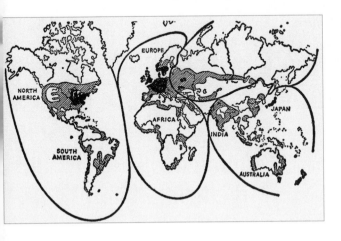

Karl Haushofer's map of Pan-Regions divided the world into four imperial domains. The British Empire would fall apart and yield to Americas dominated by the United States and a Eurafrica ruled by Germany. From "Facts in Review," German Library of Information (New York: 1941), reproduced by John O'Loughlin and Herman van der Wusten in "Political Geography of Panregions," *Geographical Review* 8, no. 1 (Jan. 1990): 1–20.

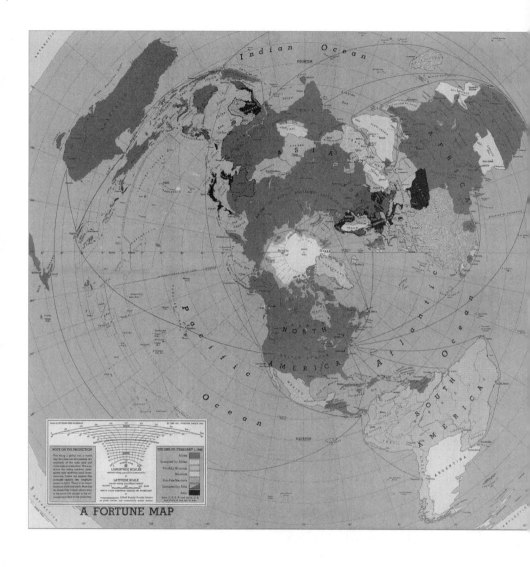

A FORTUNE MAP

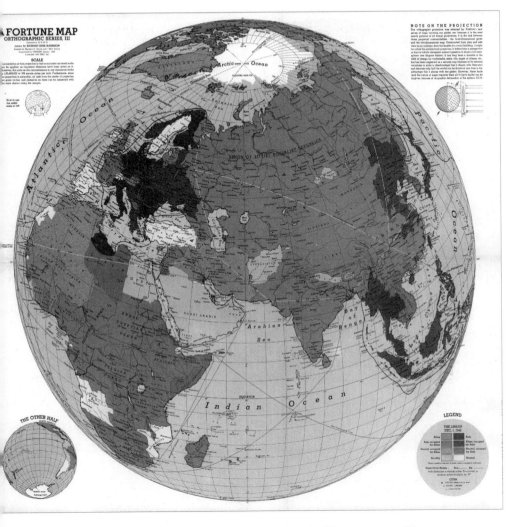

Two maps published for *Fortune Magazine* by their brilliant cartographic illustrator, Richard Edes Harrison: "One World, One War," from 1942, and "World Island," from 1943. Harrison used orthographic projections, declaring that "the Mercator projection is a mental hazard" in a time of global war. The maps were later collected in *Look at the World: The Fortune Atlas for World Strategy* (New York: Knopf, 1944), and they reflected the American adaptation of geopolitical concepts that came with its new global preponderance. These sheets are available from the Pusey Map Room Collection and reproduced courtesy of the Harvard College Library. On Harrison, see Susan Schulten, "Richard Edes Harrison and the Challenge to American Cartography," *Imago Mundi* 50 (1998): 174–188.

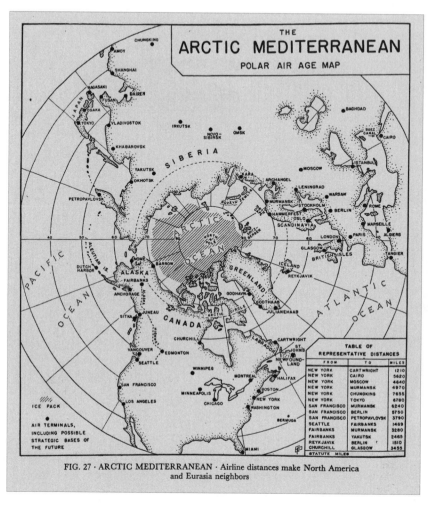

FIG. 27 · ARCTIC MEDITERRANEAN · Airline distances make North America
and Eurasia neighbors

The Artic was conceived as an inland sea analogous to the Mediterranean for
the "air age" in this wartime map. From Russell H. Fifield and G. Etzel Pearcy,
Geopolitics in Principle and Practice (Boston: Ginn and Co., 1944), 182. Accessed at https://
archive.org/details/GeopoliticsInPrincipleAndInPractice212PagesByRusselH.FifieldAnd.

Does satellite imagery transcend boundaries? Google Earth still pays homage to territorial divisions in its dizzying surveys of the global surface. Map data: Google, DigitalGlobe.

But "Europe at Night," as recorded by the NASA-NOAA Suomi National Polar-Orbiting Partnership satellite in 2012, shows that spreading metropolitan conurbations, sometimes described as Megalopolis, may increasingly shape modern territoriality. Credit: NASA Earth Observatory/NOAA NGDC.

4

Projects for an Agrarian Regime
(1770–1890)

PHYSIOCRATIC POLICIES, including cadastral reform, taxing productive land, opening markets, and eliminating monopolies, addressed problems of global agricultural output and surplus for the state, but they prescribed little with respect to the treatment and status of agricultural labor, which might be bound or free. Major societies across the globe in 1775 enjoyed better weather, were wealthier, and were more conscious of their civility and progress than a century earlier. But in many regions of the global countryside, the great backdrop of the population was entering a phase of frightening turbulence.

"High" politics was part of the unrest: Russia, Prussia, and Austria had amputated a large area of the Polish kingdom, and Russia and Turkey had gone to war over the territories north of the Black Sea and Greece, while the Balkans simmered as Venetian control ebbed. Political confrontations in Britain's North American colonies were heading toward military confrontation even as the British were decisively consolidating their control in the east of India. But the unrest that threatened did not derive from imperial rivalries alone. It arose from society, peoples sometimes rising, often moving.

Emancipating the Serf, Settling the Peasant

Lurking behind the competition that preoccupied rulers and chancelleries were the dark discontents of an agricultural population whose poverty kept them outside the circle of civic participation. Liberating land for the market seemed less fraught with risk than did liberating agricultural labor. Agrarian reformers envisaged productive working settlers in the countryside, yeomen in the old English sense, farmers in the North American—picturesque designations that obscured continuing ties of dependency. Even for democrats and revolutionaries, it was implicit that the rural laboring class must remain in place. Vagrancy and migration undermined the productive system. For men simply to follow animals, whether sheep or cattle, would destabilize the countryside. Even if one legally emancipated serfs or slaves the agrarian economy needed them as tenants and cultivators. The unspoken requirement for the happy cultivator was that he and his family be anchored to his hearth. Transform the nomad, discipline the tribe. Shepherds, cowboys, and indigenous and seasonal migrants were regarded with mistrust. Cadasters and boundaries played a role not only in demarcating property but in ensuring the geographical stability of countryside workers. So the agrarian world of the Enlightenment faced contradictory aspirations: personal freedom, at least for white cultivators, seemed necessary both for productivity and human dignity. But loyal and permanent service, except for the settlement of colonial lands, should accompany freedom.

The empress Catherine flirted with agricultural reforms even as a great and frightening peasant revolts racked Russia. Peasant upheaval seemed to endanger her regime before it was suppressed with great harshness. Heartland provinces of the Austrian Empire were about to erupt in angry peasant demonstrations that would also have to be quelled by soldiery. Reformist rulers and intellectuals in France, Spain, and Naples, as discussed in Chapter 3, had to contend with privileged and powerful landlord classes and vested corporate privileges, whether of the church or gilds, and in Spain the sheep ranchers. The reforms of church and trade these statesmen introduced in their colonies would foment the ambitions of the creole elites for home rule. And in turn their peasantries and indigenous subjects could be pushed to revolt. An Inca leader, taking the name of his great ancestor rebel of the sixteenth century, Túpac Amaru, would soon threaten the Spanish administration of the Andes. Faced with protest at home, rulers could become alarmed by the circulation of liberal projects; a cycle of reform could be followed by an interval of repression. Ideas bubbled everywhere while books were prohibited from Madrid to Saint Petersburg and authors were jailed.[1]

For many reform-minded statesmen, solving the fiscal problem seemed the most urgent task. But it was not necessarily the most fundamental. Underlying the accumulated privileges and abuses was the inequality of the countryside defended so tenaciously by aristocrats and estates. This was evident throughout the societies under consideration. Start with the Habsburgs, with their congeries of peasant lands, who could push through the cadaster in Lombardy, a fundamental achievement of enlightened despotism, even as the monarchy faced rebellion in its Bohemian heartland. In Central and Eastern Europe the most serious affliction at the root of peasant poverty and periodic unrest was serfdom. Serfdom was a status of inherited legal dependence to a landlord or manorial unit that entailed a host of petty obligations and restrictions transmitted legally across the generations. Most centrally it imposed the duty of *robot* as it was known in east Central Europe. Robot was the labor, measured in days per week, sometimes up to five or six, that peasants had to provide on the lands that landlords held and cultivated directly without leasing them out—a system called *Gutwirtschaft*. Such an obligation obviously limited the work that peasants could put in on the lands they rented as tenants for their own production and from which they had to pay rents to the landlords, taxes to the state, and tithes to the church. As in France and northern Italy, peasant lands were taxable; noble lands were usually exempt. The serf was subject also to the local courts of his feudal lords. Obligations were fixed in *Urbare* or contracts, some dating back to the Middle Ages, but renegotiated after severe peasant unrest in the 1680s. Noble landowners sought to evade the limits the contracts set on peasant dues, while the monarchs tried less successfully to prevent landlord abuses. Under Maria Theresa the monarchy pressed harder to protect its peasantry and encouraged thorough reform on the royal estates that the crown administered as their own—augmented since 1767 by the nationalization of Jesuit properties. But the effort was supremely difficult in a countryside where landlords kept order, comprised the administrative elite, and were organized in regional estates.

Increasingly the problem of low agrarian productivity was identified as a result of a servile peasantry. The idea of increasing peasant productivity and industry was in the air, and it implied removing the yoke of personal servitude. The reformers included Anton von Blanc, who spoke the language of natural rights, and one of the outstanding statesmen of Enlightenment Europe, Count Anton Wenzel Kaunitz, who aspired like the Physiocrats to nurture a class of yeoman peasants. In 1767 Kaunitz presented a six-point program to the empress, Maria Theresa (having already written to her son and coregent, the future Joseph II), which recommended the abolition of serfdom, the commutation of labor services into cash payments, the breaking up of large estates into peasant freeholds, the abolition of the village commons, and the better collection of statistics.[2]

Legislation of March 1770 allowed peasants who used the common to receive a part of the pasture for their own use and, after hedging or enclosing it, to register it as their own, although without the right to sell it.[3] The need for action became more urgent given peasant flight from the estates in Galicia, newly acquired with the first partition of Poland in 1772, and the angry discontent and despair percolating among the Bohemian peasants. Since Galicia's landlords were not entrenched within the complex Habsburg estatist structure, Vienna could act with a freer hand and instituted a cadastral survey, decreed that all land was taxable, and moved to reform the seigneurial courts.

Bohemia remained the most contested region. Peasant obligations were as severe as anywhere in Europe, and the landlords, many who had established themselves as a victorious military class after the Protestant rout at the White Mountain in 1620, had tightened personal dues and services in the preceding century. Blanc wanted a three-day limit on peasant labor services, conservatives wanted more deference to the lords' rights, and the estates resisted any formal limitation on labor services. The opponents of reform were led by Aegid Borié and at this stage by Joseph (surprisingly in light of his later record, but perhaps motivated by his conflicts with his mother), who worried about subverting the social order of the monarchy. Debate was made urgent by the revolt that broke out in early 1775. Now Joseph decided that reform must be rushed, and Kaunitz and Blanc worked out a robot decree in August. This limited peasant labor obligations, and envisaged future action on converting tenancies into freeholds (which could be accomplished on royal lands), although as often with Austrian reform postponed. The underlying issue was how to abolish serfdom itself; Kaunitz went ahead with enfranchisement and distribution of lands on two of his own estates. The court did the same for the Jesuit estates that had become royal property a few years earlier. But piecemeal emancipation seemed insufficient in light of the peasant unrest, and while Joseph resisted, he recognized that his mother the empress "wanted to abolish serfdom and . . . to change the whole rural economy and system of ownership . . . to alleviate the debts and obligations of the serfs without having the slightest regard for the lords."[4] Kaunitz may have shared Maria Theresa's preferences, but he sided with Joseph, fearing that conditions were too precarious for a wholesale emancipation. The 1777 patent urged a blanket reform but did not compel it; still some important nobles carried out their own reform, and by 1789 Joseph (having ruled for nine years without contending with the presence of his powerful mother) decreed an end to robot in general. As noted above, in February 1785 the emperor announced a new cadaster for all lands to be followed by a uniform tax and peasant payment to replace their tithes and various servile dues. The revolution in neighboring France and the death of Joseph in 1790 quickly led to postponement and repeal. What remained of serfdom would be abolished only in the revolution of 1848.[5]

How profound was the impulse to emancipate the peasantry? The Empire, after all, depended on its estates in its hodgepodge of provinces— overwhelmingly landlord elites who had to provide the grants needed for war and diplomacy. But the governing officials understood that ultimately wealth was created by the peasantry and that this most numerous class by far was subject to arbitrary and often miserable conditions. At midcentury the government had sought to inculcate a bit of discipline: to curb the "gaiety" and license of church holidays and festivals, and to encourage marriage and a robust population. Outside Vienna and Prague—some exception made for the theater tradition that the Jesuit education had encouraged and that constituted the most prestigious manifestation of culture—the clerical provincialism of rosary and confessions dominated. Maria Theresa was the least dramatic of the enlightened monarchs, but in her maternal way, probably the most effective and most concerned for "her" peasantry. Her own children had married into courts from Versailles to northern Italy and Naples and, even when caught up in personal intrigue, were aware of the reform currents discussed everywhere. Joseph was a more decisive intellectual, famous for his effort to shed clerical influence in his realms, and more open to the agrarian doctrines emerging from France. He mouthed the homilies of agrarian development but refused adherence to the doctrines. Austrian cameralism, as exemplified by Joseph Sonnenfels, did not celebrate the development of individuality as did the different doctrines of French Enlightenment thinkers or, later, Kant and Wilhelm von Humboldt in Germany. But cameralism was not just a doctrine of social control; it shared in the pervasive eighteenth-century aspiration of felicity or happiness. Sonnenfels wanted the Austrian subject to be a productive citizen of the state without the suffocating corporations that formed the texture of the old regime. Johann von Justi, the leading lecturer at the Theresianum, gave a somewhat greater emphasis to natural rights, but he again stressed the societal framework. Kaunitz believed, according to the splendid biography by Szabo, that the land had to be peopled by productive citizens. Still, the peasantry remained a class apart who had to be moralized—given "a horror of theft, lying, drunkenness, ingratitude, and all the vices that the laws do not punish. One must inspire them with a love of the Prince, as their common father and of their country as the mother who nurses them, with submission to their station in society, with fidelity and obedience."[6]

What the reformers sought was a circumscribed citizenship: a sort of civic participation through productive labor, freed from abusive obligations and allowing access to public courts in cases of disputes. At the same time their underlying paternalist stance extended to the bureaucracy and other classes of the monarchy, all of which were defined in terms of service rather than self-fulfillment. Under Joseph a series of legislative decrees sought to impose this view of a liberalized service ethos. The Untertanspatent and Strafpatent of September 1781 sought to restrict the role of domain courts. A peasant could bring a suit against his lord and could claim the service of a public attorney. A decree of November 1781 gave peasants the right to buy land, but forbade cash-strapped nobles from compelling them to do so or from evicting peasants who had gone into debt. By legislation of 1787, lands were to pass to the eldest son, and the farmstead could be sold as a unit. Some historians have defined this effort as one aiming solely at efficient administrative and social control.[7] It might be more accurate to say that the distinction between social engineering and advancing an active citizenship, between *Polizey* and emancipation did not play a real role for the cameralists. It was personal and religious subjection that allegedly held men back, not a properly adjusted political framework. The French critic and later revolutionary Brissot de Warville, critiqued the paternalism: "Prince! A good state is one where the government does little, and the people do much. . . . You want to enchain them because you believe they are happy."[8]

The underlying contradiction of agrarian reformism was that it presupposed social conditions that were hard to find. The formulae for agricultural productivity envisaged strengthening the viability of a rural middle class or gentry—either landlords or substantial tenants who would invest in their land and realize its potential for surplus. But this set of conditions rarely prevailed—outside Britain and Holland, perhaps in the uplands of northern Italy, Danubian Central Europe, and in the territories settled by British colonists in the New World. It did not follow when British soldiers took over densely populated India; neither did it occur when Spanish soldiers and traders colonized the sparsely settled areas of South America. Not that the Enlightenment elite did not believe in the agrarian virtues. Reformers waxed eloquent about the idylls of the farm family. Just as Jovellanos evoked the eclogues of antiquity, the Argentine statesman Manuel Belgrano, a talented student of European Physiocrats born in Buenos Aires in 1770 and named by Madrid to the Consulado as early as 1793, unleashed his rhetorical gifts in his official reports and in his newsletter, the *Correo de Comercio de Buenos Aires* (1810–1811):

> Agriculture is the true destiny of man. In the beginning of
> all the world's peoples every individual cultivated a portion
> of the earth, and they were powerful, healthy, rich, wise and
> happy while keeping the noble simplicity of the customs. . . .
> Everything depends and results from the cultivation of the
> land; without it there are no raw materials for the arts,
> industry therefore cannot develop, no material can be
> supplied for commerce. . . . Every form of prosperity that is
> not founded on agriculture is precarious, every form of
> wealth that does not originate in the soil is uncertain, every
> people that renounces the benefits of agriculture and which,
> misled by the flattering benefits of arts and commerce, does
> not let itself be guided by what its terrain can supply, is
> comparable—a wise political leader has said—to a miser who
> to earn a higher chancy profit postpones placing his money
> with a wealthy man's accounts in order to give it a family son
> who will squander it in a moment and return neither principal nor interest.[9]

Although it possessed an immense and uncrowded hinterland radiating from the Rio de la Plata estuary, Belgrano's Argentina seemed to demand the same agrarian remedies as the densely settled states of Europe. Cultivators needed land; land required proprietors. Belgrano championed agriculture, not only as an alternative to industry but also to the cattle ranching that had metastasized in the pampas surrounding Buenos Aires and was leading to an impoverishment of those who did not belong to the elite of landlord *hacendados:* "We see most of our agricultural workers afflicted by poverty and unhappiness, with only their sad huts in which fathers and sons dwell together to find some shelter from the elements." The underlying cause was the failure to own the land they worked: "The lack of property is the great evil from which originate all the unhappiness and misery . . . with it the abandonment, the aversion to labor." In Argentina, as in Europe, not to speak of British Bengal, the underlying impediment to progress lay in the fundamentally unequal distribution of land, and this despite the fact that the land had been virtually empty, not crowded. Belgrano attributed the inequality to Spanish colonial policies and the original distribution of crown-claimed lands *(realengos)* and believed the remedy was for the new government to redistribute the holdings in long term leases *(enfiteusis)* and auction off the unused tracts, unless they were cultivated.[10] Settling the empty lands was a goal worthy of an enlightened government.[11] This did not mean encouraging equality: different talents for agriculture led to property differentials, he believed, along with Turgot decades earlier, and should be respected. Education and state provision of infrastructure were also crucial.

Recent Argentine historiography has revised earlier claims that a late colonial ranching elite dominated political and economic development. This narrative reflected the classical nineteenth-century analysis, proffered by Domingo Faustino Sarmiento, that Buenos Aires liberals had had to overcome the "barbaric" legacy of gauchos and caudillos. Analysis of landholdings in diverse provinces and the capital suggests a greater diversity of activities in the late eighteenth century.[12] Nonetheless, whether or not *hacendados* functioned as an effective ruling elite, landownership in the colony was highly unequal, and wealth grew more unequal. The restoration of peace between Spain and Portuguese Brazil in 1777 led Madrid to remove the mercantilist restrictions that had limited exports to Spain. The result was a rapid growth of trade from Buenos Aires first to Spain, then to Britain, and the proliferation no longer of bullion shipments, but of leather exports from 150,000 hides per year to almost a million. When in 1794 the *porteños* petitioned for an end to the duties that remained, they could proudly claim that the cattle industry could provide more wealth than all the mines of Peru.[13] The viceroyalty would become dominated by the powerfully organized *hacendado* landlords and *porteño* elites, soon to divide bitterly but together resisting the British effort to occupy Buenos Aires in 1806, and declaring self-government, if not formal independence from Spain on May 5, 1810. As the chief economic spokesman of the colony, Belgrano was named one of the four officials of the junta and tirelessly advocated agrarian development rather than just a ranching monoculture. "There is no doubt . . . that agriculture, that vital art for sustaining the happiness of a people, must be favored preferentially. Until the land has been completely populated with useful plants [vegetables] and until men have established a firm and sustained method of agriculture and labor, they must not think about protection for any other sector."[14]

But the people had to be settled and civilized. Agrarianism and Physiocratic approaches required fixity of settlement and an end to nomadism. Belgrano's agrarian vision focused on the pampas, the vast hinterland radiating around Buenos Aires province and the Banda Oriental, the strip to the northeast of the Plata estuary that would become Uruguay. But during the century stretching from the dissolution of the Jesuits and their expulsion in 1768 from the "Jesuit province" of Paraguay, until the 1860s when the devastating war of the Triple Alliance reduced that country to about half its territory and half its population, upriver Argentina with its state of Misiones and its northern lands stretching to the Andes and the Chilean border was disputed territory. It was contested between the Iberian colonial powers, then between the new national governments, between state authorities and Guarani Indian communities, between settled towns and cities and autonomous ranches. If the Spanish and Portuguese could agree on anything, it was the subjection of the indigenous folk and the elimination of their evasive status across borders. In all respects the region of Misiones was a zone of ambiguity with incomplete territoriality. Settling the peoples who populated the critical border lands into fixed locations seemed a crucial task. In Argentina the state builders distrusted the dispersed population and sought to concentrate them in villages, especially on the Paraguayan frontier. The Spanish missionaries—from the Jesuits in Paraguay to Franciscans three thousand miles to the northwest in California—had pursued a similar policy of redeeming the Indians through religion, labor, and military discipline. Gonzalos de Doblas had proposed between 1803 and 1805 that the Indians be grouped into villages and compelled to work: "We cannot let any territory remain uncultivated if there are hands who can and want to work it, even if it is necessary to oppose the will of those who possess it." The governor of Misiones, Bernardo de Velazco, wanted to create frontier militia men, set up presidios, and criminalize the idle.[15] The vagueness of nonregulated settlements or *agregados,* the disquieting presence of uncultivated land, and a "wandering" population seemed of a piece as did the vagueness of contested borders.

Belgrano himself was ordered by the Junta of Buenos Aires in mid-September 1810 to secure the upriver province of Misiones from Paraguay, whose authorities were allegedly plotting with the counterrevolutionaries of Buenos Aires. He headed north, asking for a band of clarinet and trumpet players "so that we can take advantage of the Jesuit maxims and win the Indians' hearts with music." Music did not help against Bernardo de Velazco's army, now fighting for Paraguayan independence from the Argentine, and he was defeated in January 1811.[16] Belgrano returned to the capital—an ardent spokesman for farmstead agrarian development but unable to make the headway he wanted against the indigenous population and having to come to terms with the slave population that Madrid had authorized, and finally compelled to watch a republic of cattle barons derail his commitment to productive agriculture.

The agrarians' vision was one of settlement. The cultivator was to be stabilized, not by the arbitrary authority of a landlord but the demands and rewards of the land directly. Sheep and cattle, who wandered with shepherds and cowboys in their wake, undermined the utopia, both by militating against enclosure and farming and by dragging a migrant and roustabout population behind them. Peasant emancipation had to yield an orderly landscape, and as territory was ultimately a resource that yielded its surplus for bordered nations, so it required bordered villages and farmers. Unfortunately, the policies envisaged led to perverse results. Emancipated serfs in Prussia became landless laborers; emancipated slaves in the American South became indebted sharecroppers. Emancipated serfs in Russia often remained enclosed for another fifty years in village property. In Bengal the British decision to fix the tax rates on land, the so-called permanent settlement, contributed not to the strengthening of a benevolent gentry but to the further impoverishment of the ryot, or laboring class. Where cultivators had effectively achieved control of their land before the great reforms, they could sustain their independence and fulfill the agrarians' dream. The economic resources of territory demanded the discipline of settlement. Just as the world of contending sovereignties, transformed by military transformation at home and the promise of transoceanic empire, reinforced the frontier, so the economic promise of the land reinforced the need for boundaries.

Let us remain for a moment at the edge of the Euro-American world, in the hinterland of Buenos Aires. Even as Manuel Belgrano had been celebrating the virtues of agricultural development for his emerging nation, Pedro Andres Garcia, an Argentine civil servant assigned to survey the thinly populated landscapes around the port city, advised the Junta that proclaimed autonomy in 1810 on how best to develop their vast territory:

> The most expert laws, the most rigorous police measures can never be effective for a population dispersed across immense spaces and for families who can move their homes with the same facility as Arabs. . . . It is indispensable therefore to transform these men into virtuous citizens, diligent and productive. I have the satisfaction of speaking with a government that fully understands that policy can often produce such an impact; and for that reason, without losing time, I am going to propose the means that seem to me most urgent and necessary. They can be reduced to four: First, precise surveys of the land. Second, its division and allocation. Third settlement of small villages. Fourth, security of the frontiers and of the lines where these are to be fixed.[17]

Andres Garcia's recommendations for the perimeters of white settlement concisely summarized two centuries of European territorial theory and practices. Rationalization of the countryside was an enterprise that encompassed territorial boundaries, greater tax equality, a freer market for land, and productive citizenship in one sociopolitical agenda. Wandering peoples were conceived of as savage and inimical to development. Villages had to be planted in the interior as fortresses once were at the frontiers. Fixing territorial frontiers seemed particularly urgent for the contested sovereignties of the plains and upriver lands of southeastern Latin America as it did in western North America (and the grasslands of southern Russia). "Security of the frontiers" restated the continuing preoccupation with borders of both states and empires. At the edges of Iberian-American settlements in the Western Hemisphere rival state claims remained—just as three quarters of a century later drawing clear borders would become critical for the colonial enterprise in Africa, as well as Central and Southeast Asia.

There was, of course, a major difference between European and American agendas and those for overseas empires. The agrarian theorists of the eighteenth century wanted to make citizens of their own peasantry, as well as increase their agricultural output. For most of them, these dual achievements went together. Overseas empire (along with the North and South American frontier regions that had to be cleared of Indians) admittedly had a more instrumental set of objectives, as planners in the East India Company revealed, and they increasingly presupposed racial inferiority in Africa and Asia. When the colonial powers drew their lines in the colonies three generations later, they did not conceive of citizenship as a goal, unless for their own settlers. They thought in terms of reinforcing their own control, domination of the remote colonial power, and the subject status of the locals.

Governing at home was different, even for composite states in Europe such as the Austrian Empire. Advanced opinion paid attention to the countryside and agricultural society, sharing a conviction that the land was a source (if not the only source) of economic surplus and development. The task of wise policy must be to eliminate the obstacles to that benevolent source of growth. The obstacles might derive from an entrenched feudal elite with its corporate privileges and tax immunities. But impediments also arose from the vast lands removed from cultivation and improvement, whether by virtue of aristocratic entail, religious donations, ancient provisions for pasturage, or outworn village rights over common lands. Advocates of agrarian productivity were impatient with these remainders of the old regime, which they anticipated removing with comprehensive legislation.

The obstacles they beheld were not technological, but societal; they originated less at the perimeters than within, and they derived from the stubbornness with which indigenous inhabitants or peasants or nobles clung to their collective usages and customs. But this pointed to the limits of the remedies. A territorial survey did not eliminate class in the countryside; it did not simply aggregate all residents as virtuous citizens. Neither could the generous land provide its bounty without hard labor. Indeed the cadasters that proliferated throughout the eighteenth and nineteenth centuries were distinguished not only by the attention they paid to property boundaries but the type and value of the land they enclosed: Did it produce, for example, high-value-added olive oil (or mulberries), first-class wheat, less desirable rye? Did the land have to lie fallow for a year, or perhaps two years? The cadaster offered a geography of differential opportunity and success. And on top of the inherent differences in the soil came, as most reformers did understand, differences in personal talent and industry. Territory reformed with respect to production proved no more a source of wealth for all than new state frontiers were a guarantee of peace for all.

Territory as such, even if rationally charted and cultivated, thus overcame poverty no better than it overcame war. It was a spatial and a legal utopia. The prescriptions of the eighteenth century that emphasized the value of land and commodity markets and economic individualism suggested that the idea of territorial reform was a bourgeois utopia in particular although it correlated with a mentality and not a given class. The idea served the interests of reformist monarchs and aristocrats, entrepreneurial peasants and ambitious gentry; it accepted differential rewards on the basis of individual talent and industry but sought to curb the abuses left by "feudalism" or crass force. Territory appeared as the source of wealth as it had of power; it was in fact its instrument and objectification, the form in which socioeconomic relationships of subordination and control played themselves out. Not that its physical attributes—whether its spatial extent and geographical features, or the crops that it supported—were beside the point, not at all. Land as such was bountiful, a gift continually renewing itself. But only when enclosed did the land yield up its assets. And only as territory might it stabilize the population needed to extract its riches. Territory entailed appropriation and control, unequal access, the capacity to create inequality, to accumulate, and to prolong mastery and enable markets. Here and there, however, some communities resisted. They defended counter-spaces, enclaves devoted to the collective, or unbounded spaces in which they migrated, hearkening to a utopia different from the farm and the market. Before following their defense, however, we must see the inexorable pressure to put land on the market.

Reappropriating the Land

E. P. Thompson made famous the notion of the "moral economy," in which communal concern for living standards tempered the search for profit. Coexisting with the moral economy on a global level was what we might call the immoral economy—the condition of slavery, the coerced labor of serfdom, and, even today, the persistence of trafficking or harsh child labor. Both the moral economy and the immoral economy demonstrated the persistent role of nonmarket forces in economic outcomes, whether those of human sympathy or those of coercion. Among the many other meanings assigned to it, modernity has meant the limitation of both moral and immoral economies and the growing role of a market economy, above all with respect to land and labor. Champions of the market economy in land, however, hardly conceived of it as morally neutral. Whether Physiocrats or twentieth-century development economists, they envisaged it as a moral as well as an economic step forward: it endowed societies with greater wealth and ultimately greater liberty.

Writing about the British possessions on the eve of decolonization, the colonial administrator G. K. Meek recognized that "land has something of a sacred character and rights over land are more jealously treasured than any other forms of rights." But these attitudes accompanied subsistence agriculture and low standards of living. "If these are to be raised, as raised they must be, then commercial crops must be grown for export, and self-subsistence economies replaced by those of a wider kind." Focusing on African colonies, he argued that the transformation was already under way with beneficial and adverse consequences: "Land is being commercialized; the basis of holding land is changing from one of community and custom to one of individualism and contract; wealthy native capitalists are appearing; agricultural debt is already in full swing, and many peasants are becoming labourers on lands which were once their own." Until recently, he continued, pastoral lands, ill-defined rights, and often the communal redistribution of land had been the rule. But with marketable crops, individual ownership would advance: "Boundaries become more clearly recognized; the units occupying the land tend to be narrowed down to the small family or individual; the conception of ownership gradually begins to replace that of usufruct."[18] In short, some of the same changes were overtaking Britain's dominions that centuries before had taken place in England and then continental Europe and the Western Hemisphere.

Critics on the right and left understood the social and political disruption this transition caused. In the same years as Meek was commending the African transition, Karl Polanyi suggested that nineteenth-century civilization—pacific, commercial, and liberal—had collapsed. It had rested on four institutions: the balance of power, the gold standard, the self-regulating market, and the liberal state. "But the fount and matrix of the system was the self-regulating market. It was this innovation which gave rise to a specific civilization." And it collapsed because the idea of a self-adjusting market implied a stark utopia. "Such an institution could not exist for any length of time without annihilating the human and natural substance of society; it would have physically destroyed man and transformed his surroundings into a wilderness."[19] Polanyi did not live to see market liberalism resurrected as the foundation of global economics and politics toward the end of the twentieth century. And the theorists of the eighteenth century, as well as the development experts of the twentieth, would certainly have contested the critics' diagnosis. For them the market and the liberal system guaranteed and did not undermine peace and certainly not progress.

But Polanyi was right to understand the advent of liberal markets as a tremendously destabilizing force. Markets—the exchange of goods and services, often by means of general monetary claims on these products and efforts—developed alongside liberal politics in Europe, although markets also existed in societies that lived under greatly different political arrangements, whether tribal or patrimonial. Markets could strengthen the thirst for liberal government, because both markets and liberalism acknowledged the pursuit of perceived personal and family advantage as valid and constructive impulses for living in society. But markets simultaneously undermined the bonds of liberal society, as well as other community forces. Markets substituted reciprocal interests for emotional sympathies, religious prescription, and legislative authority. However, it was not just markets in general that proved so corrosive—after all, did not they correspond to what Adam Smith had seen as the great human propensity to truck and barter, rather than just annihilating, as Polanyi argued, the "human substance of society"? In particular it was the market for labor and the market for land that destabilized society.

The market for labor—rural, urban, or often mixed—is not our primary concern. There were in fact at least two different labor markets, although they overlapped and laborers might pass from one to the other. In the one, agricultural workers offered their work in exchange for access to land they might cultivate for themselves, or for wages and perhaps housing. In these cases labor retained personal freedom although their cumulative debts to landlords or moneylenders might severely limit their de facto liberty. The other market was one in which workers were bought and sold by others as slaves or, under milder circumstances, were bound, whether by their own choice or that of parents or civil authorities, as indentured labor for a certain term of years. The market for free labor or indenture effectively wiped out the market for unfree labor during the nineteenth century, although it took a major war in North America and rebellions elsewhere (Haiti, Cuba) to advance this work. As Polanyi argued, however, the growth of a rural labor market also meant the simultaneous erosion of traditional forms of poor relief and the patriarchal relations that might protect country families from eviction in hard times.

This chapter focuses not on the "freeing" of labor but of real estate—the prolonged process of liberating land from restrictions on purchase and sale, the commodification of the countryside.[20] Making land marketable was not a one-off transformation. Land could rarely be placed on the market with total rights. In some states, the monarch was deemed to retain ultimate ownership even as use rights were bought and sold as property; a ruler might retain land-tax rights or quit-rents as an acknowledgment of sovereignty, as well as his own properties and large royal forest domains. Some lands could be sold only to aristocratic landowners, those with an inherited title; other lands conferred titles. For the

European countryside, the term *entail* applies. Entailed property, including religious and communal holdings, could not be bought or sold without political or judicial approval. Many estates and holdings were to be held only by titled holders; many could not be divided but had to pass as a whole. The right to entail land was strengthened by legislative action in some European societies into the nineteenth century (German estates could be registered as *Fideikommisse*, regardless of owners' status in Prussia, but restricted to nobility in Bavaria). But what seemed a protection at first often became a burden when the owners could not mortgage their holdings or sell off partial tracts. Some landholdings and homes in the Anglo-Saxon world were held in the more general pattern of a "trust," where the property remained intact, followed publicly legislated lines of inheritance—and in effect was passed down from one custodial owner to the other. Even today landownership comes with various rights or restrictions and burdens: claims of local and national governments to woods or seashore, and accumulated arrangements that restrict partition, particular uses, or even the sale to owners of different classes and (by private understanding) to minority religions or races.[21]

Aristocratic entail was only one form of insulation from a market in land; communal or village holding of farm land, as in the Russian village *(mir, obshchina)* or the Mexican *ejido* were others. As Meek generalized from a long list of African, Middle Eastern, and Central Asian usages, "The annual or periodic allocation, or re-allocation, of village lands is a common technique of native systems for ensuring a fair distribution of land."[22] Even when tracts and villages were bought and sold, residual common rights remained held in custom by village collectivities. Grazing rights and woodland access were often not marketable even when land was. In most societies a range of rights for use of the land existed, often held by different people. In Britain land was marketable often from medieval times, but the forms of tenure—freehold, copyhold, sometimes knights' tenancy—differed, and they complicated the land market. In the Americas and Australasia, European sovereigns might arbitrarily assign or sell land grants, including in Spanish America (as discussed above) the rights to control local indigenous labor, a prerogative similar to that which Mughals and Ottomans assigned to their military captains and that Russian and Habsburg monarchs had granted their state servants. Such lands were often confined in ownership to the hereditary governing elite, although various rights might be further sold, and transfers at the will of the local feudatory could be easily ratified.[23]

But the logic of reform tended toward ever-greater inroads of market relations and indeed despoliation, first of church lands, and even, in revolutionary circumstances, of large aristocratic estates. In Europe, Roman Catholic Church lands presented an easy target. Once estates were bequeathed to the "dead hand" of the church, an ongoing institution, they would never be released short of seizure—the process of secularization and sale that the Spanish appropriately called *desamortización* and that is often translated as "disentail." The French National Assembly nationalized church land in November 1789 and began sales in 1791. Joseph II of Austria in the 1780s sold monasteries and convents and gave the proceeds to the secular clergy and parishes. In fiscally strapped Spain, hapless royal ministers had sought to impose a *única contribución* in Castile to replace the hodgepodge of levies and immunities, but they met stubborn resistance from local authorities and nobles and finally abandoned the project in 1770 (although it would be enacted in 1845). The papacy finally consented to taxation of Spanish church properties in 1753.[24] More successful would be the seizure of Jesuit lands in 1768 and other church properties in the 1790s. The voracious market beckoned—a market for land and for the labor that worked the land—as the solution to a socioeconomic order originally founded on nonmarket hierarchies. The post-Napoleonic reaction would slow down the process, but when the Spanish liberals came to power in the 1835, disentail resumed as a national program under Minister Juan Alvárez Mendizábal. Conservative governments interrupted the process in 1844, only to have it resume from 1855 to 1859 under Joaquín Baldomero Espartero. State power, agrarian productivity, conflicting programs for agricultural labor—whether through plantation slavery or the citizen producer—and finally the incentives of purchase and sale form the great trajectory that we follow in this section.

Analyzing the cadastral records, Richard Herr's monumental study of Spanish land use follows in great detail the mechanics of disentail in the region of Salamanca and Jaen after 1798. Such close study reveals great variety among those who took advantage of the land sales: sometimes landowners from neighboring villages, often commoners, in some places the local officials and church administrators who bought the rights to tithes, and finally peasants who combined their resources to acquire the lands they worked. Contesting a narrative of immiseration through the sale of common or church lands, Herr insists that disentail meant development. Before the lands had come on the market, peasant income declined to the level of bare subsistence. If they had once prospered the pressure of population had increased, even as landlords raised rents across the board—Herr refers to Malthusian and Ricardian pressures that led to the depopulation of regions that Spanish reformers saw as the major cause of rural poverty.[25] "Freeing a major factor of production through disentail had the opposite effect on the societies. It improved the lot of the higher socioeconomic levels, and within those the levels of the most venturesome individuals. By putting property in the hands of the enterprising men and women, disentail fostered economic growth. "On the other hand it aggravated divisions within the communities between those who bought land and those who didn't. Later critics would denounce *desamortización* and the reformers who conceived it, in large measure because of its effects on rural social structure, overlooking the economic growth it inspired at the national level and frequently at the community level as well. . . . The challenge facing them was to find a way to get into the market economy that would provide an escape from the dual trap of Malthus and Ricardo."[26]

Aggregate estimations have been attempted recently by Rueda Hernanz—who, making use of Herr's findings, has attributed to the process a vast transformation of landholding and a liberal/market process, if not a "bourgeois" revolution. Total land sold at auction through 1924 amounted to perhaps 13.1m hectares (equal to 130,100 square kilometers or 50,580 square miles), but accompanied by other modalities of redistribution, such as allowing the cultivation of vacant land, the total reached 19m hectares, or 38 percent of the national territory and 50 percent of the arable. In the period from the Jesuit confiscations through the French wars, perhaps 8.8m hectares went on the bloc and were acquired perhaps by close to half a million purchasers (we know only the purchases and assume many bought multiple tracts); the midcentury liberal wave distributed 4.4m hectares to a far smaller cohort, while from 1855 to 1924, 6.7m hectares went to half a million beneficiaries.[27]

Other recent works extend the analysis to urban Spain over the remainder of the nineteenth century. Examining the disentail of urban properties in the province of Cáceres—which included properties owned by the government as well as by church authorities, Roso Díaz has demonstrated a clearly "bourgeois" profile. Although two-thirds of the purchasers bought small or median-valued houses, 90 percent of the auction yields went to acquire half the properties. Attempting a breakdown by professional affiliation, the researcher found that businessmen *(comerciantes),* the liberal professionals, and the holders of public office (including the ubiquitous notaries) were the most numerous purchasers.[28] Of course, there was a different motivation in the town: rural property was bought to increase landed holdings; urban houses were bought often to demonstrate or enhance a bourgeois lifestyle. They affirmed a new political elite but could hardly galvanize a more productive rural economy.

In Mexico and Latin America, the original Jesuit confiscations from the late 1760s made little difference in the distribution of property. They were laden with debt, found few buyers, and the receipts went to defray the royal budget. In 1804 as war resumed with England, Charles IV extended to the colonies secularization of other church properties that had been spared in Spain, including family chaplaincies. In Mexico, the properties of monastic orders and churches—endowments, buildings, contents—amounted to perhaps a fifth or quarter of national wealth.[29] While perhaps 15 percent of church properties were secularized in the decade from 1798 to 1808, in New Spain the total reached 25 percent.[30] In the immense arc of the Andean territories—Venezuela, Columbia, Ecuador, Peru, and Bolivia—Simón Bolívar decreed the privatization of communal lands. Villages had lived with considerable degrees of inequality so long as local notables had preserved religious rites, but with privatization came the right to sell allotments and the erosion of communal life. Some villages agreed to pay a new "national Contribution" (replacing the colonial taxes Bolivar had abolished) to preserve their collective rights.[31]

Mexican secularization reached its dramatic climax when the liberals came to power in the 1850s. Following their suppression of a revolt in the wealthy mill city of Puebla in early 1856, the government decreed the "intervention" or sequestration of church properties, including the mortgages that the religious corporations had extended with the idea of collecting rents and loans, and it then sold them for down-payments of cash or government bonds. The Lerdo law (Ley Lerdo) of June 25, 1856, was national in scope and stipulated that tenants of church-owned houses were to be offered ownership for a capitalized multiple of their rent, and if they declined, the properties would be auctioned. In either case, the church would hold the mortgage but no longer have title.[32] Analysis of the auction of church lands reveals, probably unsurprisingly, that they were purchased by a bourgeois elite; only the tax had to be paid in cash and the price was set below their assessed value. A massive transfer of property titles ensued through 1857, although the counterrevolutionary government that followed in 1859–1860 ordered the return of titles to the earlier owners, allowing tenants to remain and promising to recompense the transfer tax that had served as down payment. But there were limits to the rollback: where the conservatives prevailed, the church often hastened to sell its properties on voluntary terms; where liberals controlled territory during the ensuing civil war, as in Veracruz, the surrender of newly acquired titles was also limited, and those who had returned titles to church institutions had their de facto rights confiscated.

By the "Laws of Reform" in July 1859, the Juárez government simply decreed the nationalization of church real estate and capital and suppressed the monasteries (though not the nunneries), declaring that the monks would join the secular clergy. Church property was to be sold at two-thirds its assessed value, only half of which was to be paid in currency, the rest in state bonds, and even the cash required would be lent by the government. The liberal victory at the end of 1860 left diverse claims between old "denouncers," those who had originally stepped forward to purchase properties that tenants had not claimed, and new "adjudicators," those who had bought at auction—or those in either case who had purchased property during the liberals' earlier dominance versus those who had purchased from church authorities by agreement and who were allowed, by the triumphant liberals' law of February 5, 1861, to confirm their purchases from the state for an extra 20 percent. Contesting interpretations that credit disentailment with providing a great spur to industrial modernization, the most meticulous historian of these confused transfers concludes that they enlarged middle-class ownership of urban housing, and consolidated a new rural elite. The continuing urgent need for financing the contending regimes meant church properties tended to go to the wealthy purchasers or those who might provide substantial credits.[33]

Still, disentailment meant disentailment—that is, the passage of land from a noncommercial, special, and safeguarded property into the flux of commercial relations. "All that is solid melts into air," wrote Marx about the bourgeois ascendancy. Certainly disentailed land did not melt into air, but it became a commodity; mortgagers replaced old owners. Renters could transfer property—land was demystified, territory stripped of the aristocratic or church refulgence that surrounded it in the eighteenth century. Nor did it require anticlerical legislation: large properties that included tenant families of long standing, the *mayorazagos* of Mexico could be split up as debts accumulated. The great domains of General Rincón Gallardo between Jalisco and Zacatecas were divided both into large haciendas for his sons and ranches sold to tenants, creating about 260 new properties both on the former entailed domain and the wider holdings.[34] The boundaries of territory were translatable into a universal medium, money or wealth. Sovereignty and property overlapped in a space of bourgeois fungibility.

Revealing, too, was the opposed situation, as in China, where the state did not create property as such although private ownership remained compatible with its penetration of economic relations. As a legal historian of Chinese patterns of contract and property has argued, there was no general term for property with respect to uses of land. There were ideas of justice or injustice in terms of distribution though no word for rights. "The reason property never became a root metaphor, never became a way of imagining the nature of political power or of the relationship between state and individual is that until the twentieth century the root metaphor of 'family' had such power that there was no room for others." The state manifested itself as an extension of family but occupied a space beyond. "State paternalism was the traditional Chinese understanding of the relationship between state and people. Political discourse occurred within this framework. The emperors were the sons of heaven but parents of the nation. . . . A family was a bounded space into which the state would not intrude and the head of family had standing in the community if he acted as a father ought to act, not simply because he held property."[35]

If in China landed property was maintained in a culture with a relatively low level of legal formalism, in the West, the opposite was case. But the historian has to remember that a highly developed legal culture does not necessarily determine actual practices. Stubborn communities, on one side, powerful and abusive landlords, on the other, can work around the stipulations of even a highly legalistic culture, indeed often within courtroom confrontations. As in Spain and elsewhere, Latin American liberals believed in the virtues of private holdings. Conservatives might stress indigenous laziness and drinking as causes of low agricultural productivity; liberals blamed communal holdings.[36] In Mexico, the Lerdo Law was targeted in the first instance at church properties, but it decreed that *all* corporations must divest their lands, which meant that village common properties and rights were rendered precarious.

Impact of the law could be attenuated, however. Even before the Ley Lerdo, Mexican states had sought to wrest land from Indian communal control (often organized as *repúblicas de indios* in the colonial period) but had often been frustrated. Indian communities claimed that they retained *tierras de repartimiento,* in which Indian families passed down usufruct rights to farm lots, which had often become quite unequal; but they also established common tracts or *ejidos.* The Lerdo Law specifically exempted Indian common lands *(ejidos)* from privatization, but it often also failed to privatize the other categories of communal land. Peasant influence remained strong for a couple of decades after the civil war and French incursions (1856–1867). After 1856 some communities converted the vulnerable tracts to cooperative ownership *(condueñazagos)* and searched out titles granted during the communal period. As they had in various states, Indian communities went to court to protest and postpone the inroads on village land rights. Peasants could invade lands and then offer to buy them. Maximilian's brief and partial conquest from 1863 to 1867 saw an imperial effort to reestablish Indian rights and an Indian voice in government. But the liberals who won the conflicts with the conservatives and then defeated the French party governed a countryside that rested on a contested coexistence with indigenous communities.[37]

The greater threat to Indian property arose not from doctrinal pursuit of individual property, but the accommodation of foreign and domestic corporate investors as this emerged under the administration of Porfirio Díaz after 1878. Decrees of 1883 and 1894 would bring a relentless drive to survey vacant and undeveloped land and to cede large portions of it to the surveying companies, often in foreign hands. Way beyond the beneficiaries of the 1850s and 1860s, a new elite of large landowners and foreign investors were given license to appropriate vast areas of the national territory. The tools of scientific surveying—again the cadastral premise for enforcing ownership and control—served a transnational elite that accelerated acquisition. Indigenous villagers were not totally expropriated, but, just as occurred in so many other areas, many became landless laborers.[38]

As the Italian writers to be discussed in the next section understood, cooperative effort to establish joint property that conformed to laws of incorporation offered a solution, but it was hard and laborious to organize. Continuing litigation and sometimes collective protest also slowed the fate of indigenous villages, but it would take a prolonged revolution to halt the slide into dependency. The fate of Indians on United States soil was perhaps even more dismal. Even as their tribal land grants were continually reduced in size, reformers who believed that freeing them from an infantilizing tribal authority and giving them individual legal ownership urged the Dawes Act of 1887, which allowed individual families to withdraw their own plots. But few alternative solidarities were available to help Native Americans survive as small proprietors.[39]

Catholic countries in Europe, of course, had provided the model for Mexico's liberal reformers. Monarchs had begun the expropriation of hapless and occasionally vast properties in Iberia and the Austrian lands, and the French occupation between 1794 and 1815 empowered local reformers to import and administer similar measures. The West Bank of the Rhine, annexed to France between 1795 and 1797 saw monastic and church properties put up for auction; northern Italy did, as well. When Napoleon summoned the princes of the Holy Roman Empire between 1803 and 1805 to effectively dissolve their ancient confederal structure, he encouraged the medium-size states—Bavaria, Baden, Württemberg, and many other smaller ones—to swallow up the three-hundred-odd tiny principalities, imperial knighthoods, and church properties that had survived the Treaty of Westphalia. (The church territories included the major archbishoprics, among them four Electors of the Empire, as well as many monasteries.) Thirty-eight states emerged from this territorial banquet, some of which threw their new lands into the property market. The new elites in charge of northern Italy (and even papal Bologna) moved to dissolve religious properties and put them in the hands of those who would support a new secular elite. When the French were defeated, the process slowed: the kingdom of Sardinia (Piedmont) reverted to an absolute monarchy respectful of church holdings. Nonetheless after the revolution of 1848, the government of the liberal Right under Cavour decisively moved against monasteries and convents. When Piedmont (Sardinia), now the core of the kingdom of Italy, annexed the papal territories of Bologna and the Marches in 1860 it would resume its work—proceeding, as elsewhere, not only against church estates, but against the collective and village rights, the so-called *usi civici* that impeded full private disposition of the land. Wherever accumulated law had granted the sovereign or the community protection of its hold on the land—whether Roman law with respect to residual sovereign rights that had been devolved on to local authorities, or German law that had privileged communal control—the spokesmen for market progress moved to loosen and dissolve the remaining restrictions over purchase and sale. Those in a position to acquire land remained convinced that market incentives were the key to quickening the economic vitality of the countryside.

Even outside Catholic Europe and its former colonies in the Americas, the pressures of the market continued. As bureaucrats of the Ottoman Empire embarked on the Tanzimat era of secularizing reform, they endeavored to rationalize the land regime, especially in the southern provinces of Syria and Transjordan, which had become the site of more vigorous colonization. The land code of 1858 sought to register all land under individual, not corporate title, and to establish title for tax purposes.[40] Scribes arrived and took sworn statements in public meetings; increasingly the land was specified in terms of area. The new code allowed more extensive sorts of inheritance but provided for escheat of the land to the state if left uncultivated for more than three years. The threat of colonization schemes in Transjordan led Bedouin landowners to register property, as did incentives in the form of reduced registration fees and lower tax burdens. As cultivation replaced pasturage, the new regime of registration provided a more welcome security of tenure. The capacity to mortgage land still lagged, with Muslim clerics opposing legislation proposed after 1908 by the Young Turk revolutionaries, who resorted finally in 1912–1913 to decrees that provided for a new cadaster and the right of hypothecating land. The legislation came too late to be implemented in the Arab provinces, but by this time Ottoman land law had converged with the European concepts that the Mandatory powers, France and Britain, would legislate in their new imperial possessions.[41]

The most recent historians of Ottoman land tenure have compared the Ottoman evolution with the Russian policies for the mir and British practices in North India. Personal freedom of movement and individual claims on land came a century earlier than in Russia but reformers left it to villages, more than did the Raj, to work out what rights might be claimed, whether to plots or shares in a community of cultivators. The cadaster was intended as the culminating step of "building an increasingly unified status of property-owning subject, wherein neither gender nor religion was relevant to accession or devolution."[42] Within the village, however, peasants in the interwar era still held scattered plots designed to provide equity in the quality of land and requiring collective coordination in cultivation. Lowland towns became more oriented toward commercial agriculture; highland villages retained cooperative farming, but even in the more commercially oriented settlements, property holdings were defined not in terms of individual fields held but by shares in the whole— as in a cooperative apartment building distinguished from a condominium. Agriculture remained poised between traditional practices and modernized property law.

Thus the rural world, including the towns that serviced its agricultural enterprises, was evolving in spurts from a society of customary dues and deference based on seigneurial and ecclesiastical legacies to one where bourgeois proprietors, certainly, and country folk, hopefully, responded to market rationality and opportunity. Continuity existed: city dwellers might still find the signs of a "timeless" countryside.[43] Precommercial custom could coexist with market activity. Having a market for land did not necessarily erode the sense of rural hierarchy; indeed, it often gave old elites new sources of social supremacy. Still, subjecting land hitherto tied up in empty holdings, sparsely settled and decrepit monasteries, or wastefully planted low-value crops quickened the pulse of rural commerce, drew rural inhabitants into a new sphere of calculation, made some rich, and made others' lives more precarious even as it raised aggregate social income. Shifting fortunes was one of the great literary themes of the contemporary novelists—Dickens, Balzac, Galdós in Spain, and Fontane in Prussia, later Howells and Samuel Butler—who created the art form par excellence of market society even as they often lamented its crude triumphs. Family and property merged into imagined narratives where once rank and honor had prevailed. *Downton Abbey* provides all the pleasures of the art form for a generation that may have shortchanged these achievements of print culture.

The extensive lands of Russia remained the most resistant—but certainly not immune—to the general trends of the century. Personal bondage was ended by the emancipation decrees of 1861, which simultaneously sought to codify the tangled structure of village communes settled on noble estates. Along with personal emancipation, up to half the lord's land—to simplify the variety of arrangements mandated or allowed—went to the village, and he was compensated with state bonds, serviced by the peasants. These redemption payments significantly exceeded the market value of the lands ceded in the less fertile regions; in the black earth districts they were roughly on a par, but nobles had to cede less land. Peasants had lived in communes that either allowed hereditary household tenure of village land or periodically redistributed fields among families. Even in the first system it was hard enough to disentangle a family's property (and within the family the claims of individuals were also unclear). In the second system it was still less possible without renouncing rights to the strip lands, and even then the peasant was still liable for his share of the redemption payments the commune owed to the former landlord. Courtyard serfs (what Americans might have called house slaves) were left without land and would become hired hands or industrial workers.[44]

Nonetheless, peasants were buying land outside the communes, presumably from a nobility, as depicted by Chekov, that was slowly losing the capacity or the will to run the properties it did not have to cede. Indeed the reader confronts two contrasting pictures: recent statistical work assimilates the Russian peasant much more closely to the Western European model.[45] Agricultural yields and peasant income were allegedly rising as fast as in Western Europe. Smallholdings—some involved in market gardening and dairy farming for the growing cities—were sources of growth: recent statistical work suggests that the *obshschina* and its *mir* hardly imposed the stagnation that earlier commentators had observed: "Whatever the cause, whatever the result," so Geroid Robinson concluded after years of close study in situ, "the commune was; for history, that is the outstanding fact."[46] How restrictive it was, though, remains a question.

Without any pretense of reconciling these divergent assessments of agrarian vitality, we can pause for a moment to contrast Russia and the United States during their respective great reforms, two giant countries with vast landed reserves: on one continent an industrially laggard, bureaucratically ruled state of eighty million that despite its having granted personal freedom to the mass of its population, preserved a structure of hereditary privilege for its landlord class and kept its peasantry entangled in dependent peasant collectives. On another continent, the United States, having by dint of a great war legally emancipated its black slaves, still unwilling to rescue them from debt servitude; rather opening its huge grasslands to individual white families willing to farm once the aboriginal populations were relentlessly swept into tribal allotments. A white democracy in America reveling in individual allotments and the middle-class main chance. A self-questioning elite in Russia believing that it sat atop a human coral of intimately interwoven existences.

Given such different organization of the rural world, in what sense did territorial vastness exert any formative role? Size, it is plausible to conclude, did not determine one pattern of settlement or another, but it confirmed and strengthened earlier societal choices. Path dependency might perhaps be overcome, but not easily and only after decades of hysteresis. Tsarist Russia had originally confronted not sparse and scattered tribes but the formidable military powers of Mongols and Tatars and, to its west, ambitious Poles and Baltic German knights. Maintaining the state meant planting a military class and giving them harsh power over a subject peasantry. As the land was conquered the pattern served expansion. America brought its patterns of settlement from Europe and could largely replicate them as its peoples spread easily into its trans-Appalachian, then trans-Mississippi west. Russian landed space and its borders made the village and its servile labor force and pool of twenty-year soldiers necessary; American landed space made its restless atomistic homesteading possible. Territory's size allowed exaggerated forms of societal and political organization in both cases.

Territory had earlier manifested itself as a bordered and fortified space, to be claimed and expanded against others; it was the precondition of rival sovereignties. By the eighteenth century it appeared as a source of wealth for states and societies. Bourgeois political economy, however, subtly altered the phenomenology of bounded space. Policy makers, landowners, and political economists had moved from the claim of its felicitous fecundity to the analysis of differential potentials. Even as the Physiocrats and reform-minded administrators had celebrated agrarian wealth, they classified its sources so they might determine how to extract its surplus with the least possible impact on its productivity. Through the eighteenth century, they celebrated its wealth as the product of inherent fertility and the efforts of the stable cultivator. But the successor economists soon recognized that the land's differing fertility or even its location granted inherent advantages and returns not to those who worked harder, but to those situated strategically.

In one respect, the phenomenology of agrarian territory was similar to that of fortified territory in the Renaissance. Advantage depended on possession of particular locations that broke up an undifferentiated landmass. Fortification marked the emerging Cartesian space of the early modern era; markets dotted the economic space of the eighteenth and nineteenth centuries. The nonhomogeneity of landed space (along with the capacity to enclose it) helped establish hierarchies, first of power, then of income. These respective assets rewarded virtue—whether military and strategic, or entrepreneurial and technological—but they also precluded equality. And insofar as possession, whether of defensible centers or favorably sited agrarian enterprise, conferred differential advantage, good fortune retained an irreducible element of arbitrary reward.

The economists would label this premium that flowed to prior possession "rent"—not the payment that tenants paid to landlords, but the reward flowing from location. Its beneficiaries envisaged it as a bonus for foresight; its critics saw a payoff for monopoly control. In either case it implied a perception of striated territoriality. Ricardan space posited an old core of cultivation with the best lands and growing additions of less fertile land. In other words, a gradation of more fertile to less fertile land and more developed to more sparsely developed land. Johann Heinrich von Thünen—the remarkable Prussian landlord and economic autodidact—modified Ricardo's gradations of land to allow for the costs of bringing grain to a market center. Thünen was born in Oldenburg in northwest Germany and purchased an estate in Teltow about thirty miles south of Rostock in Mecklenburg, whose returns, investments, laborers' wages, and mortgage interests he diligently recorded in detail; driven, as he said, "to arrive at a clear idea of the laws that determine the price of grain and its influence on investment in the agricultural enterprise."[47] He carefully read through the French and British economists, humbly correcting what he believed was Adam Smith's error in isolating the pure concept of rent on land. Underlying the meticulous record keeping, however, was a thought experiment that became the basis for what economists would develop as location theory. "Think about a very large city in the center of fertile plain untraversed by any navigable river or canal," Thünen's tract began—and out of that model he went on to derive concepts of economic rent and indeed fundamental insights into the marginal theories of wage and price determination.[48] The land itself was presumed to be of equal fertility throughout; however, the profit one derived from wheat sales depended not only on the price of wheat and the myriad costs of cultivation and harvest—into which he factored the entire maintenance of personnel and estate costs—but thereafter on the costs of transport to the urban market. The Teltow estate itself that he so lovingly documented did, however, produce differing results on differing fields; manuring also varied, and the yield from forests also had to be calculated differently—in sum a mass of detail was presented, all then to be integrated into his isolated state. Real states, he admitted, had many towns and enjoyed access to water transport and had lands of differing quality; tariffs worked negatively on wealthy as well as poor states. The individual might have been following his own interest, but (in a German version of the invisible hand) acted as the instrument of a higher power and worked, often unconsciously, toward the great and artful construction of the state and civil society.

What these economic reflections implied was that landed property, land with boundaries with differing degrees of exclusive rights, generated inherently unequal profits depending on the distance from consumers. From a Physiocratic notion that emphasized the surplus generated by territory as a general category within a national territory (although the writers recognized the differing value of terrains), nineteenth-century analysis, whether Ricardo's or Thünen's, emphasized the way factors created differing interests for property holders. Thünen in his solitary brilliance derived the bases for marginal analysis: apologizing for his algebraic formulae, but insisting on the utility of mathematics, Thünen demonstrated that the interest rate was equal to the rate charged for the last bit of capital invested, and the worker's wage would be equal to the value produced by the last worker hired in a large enterprise (or employed at the very edge of cultivated territory, where it bordered on free land), from which followed the law for the division between capitalists and workers.[49] The land generated wealth, but it also necessarily generated classes. For Ricardo it was the quality of the land; for Thünen it was the location of the land with respect to centers of settlement that provided the distinctions. Differing outcomes and bourgeois stratification were inherent in rural property for the major theorists of spatial assets in the early nineteenth century, a significant reemphasis from a century earlier where land had been conceived of as a stake between the state or monarchs and the classes of owners. Territory conferred wealth, but often without respect to merit. Even more dramatically urban agglomerations, growing rapidly in the industrial era, generated fortunes in real estate because of the scarcity of property. Disproportionate profits arose from possession of tracts that were absorbed into expanding cities. For the American reformer Henry George, writing later in the nineteenth century, the policy that should follow was clear: impose a tax on land and rents since the gains from them were unmerited. His single tax would be large enough to remove the need for other levies as well as diminishing inequality. The idea caught on; single-tax leagues were formed across the globe.[50]

Bourgeois society brought with it wealth, unequal advantage, and a concept of natural endowments that accorded with this inequality. Territory as wealth came in patterns of radial (or striated) landscape. It was not only divided and bounded, but contoured into zones of greater and lesser yield, just as maps depicted differing elevations. The political economists and the reformers could live with that landscape, indeed devised schemes to transfer the wealth from the beneficiaries to society. By suitable taxation and enhancing market access, wise policy could supposedly remove the encrusted legal monopolies that aggravated the inevitable inequalities that striated land brought with it.

But other advocates came to more radical analyses—and often more ancient. Ownership of land, they believed, no matter how taxed, was key to inequality. Some, as we shall see, believed that these inequalities must yield peacefully in the course of social progress. Others sought to restore collective practices that had withered in the modern era. Still others by the twentieth century would demand forced collectivization. The career of the revolutionaries is well known, but the contributions of nineteenth-century agrarian collectivists—theorists and legislators—remain largely forgotten although they generated bitter disputes. As with so many utopian projects their projects were advocated or contested on the basis of supposed evidence drawn from practices outside Europe or from a murky past.

Myths of the Collective

After all, if land had once been owned collectively, what Marx termed primitive communism, might not communal property be achieved once again? This raised the stakes for history and anthropology especially for the positivist thinkers of the middle third of the century, whose massive tracts focused less on appeals to rights than on alleged laws of development. Nor, they claimed, had all the data vanished into historical mist. South Asian tenancy, Mexican villages, and, on the margins of Europe, the Russian communes all could be marshaled in evidence. But did these sites confirm a hallowed and historically legitimated forms of collectivism (a controversy bitterly dividing historians); or might they provide a rural path to socialism (a controversy that would divide Marxists)? Were even the remaining collective rights to pasturage or woodland a genuine alternative for development in an era of industrial capitalism, or just an unproductive impediment to progress that should be dissolved and superseded, as Mexican and often European liberals so staunchly believed? How curious that the history and future of the agricultural domain, the domain of productive territory, should become so major a stake precisely in an era when industrialism seemed to carry all before it! However, the same decades that brought the advances of steam and steel, also saw the surge of populations into the frontier territories of the Western Hemisphere and Australia. Perhaps only with the realization that the resources of territory were becoming depleted did its economic properties become so heated a stake.

Scholarly controversies, no matter how determined by the internal dialogue of a discipline, often are responsive to larger social and political developments. They follow an intrinsic logic, which must be mastered in its own, often technical, terms, but they also internalize the influence of broader controversies. The social-science question that raged back and forth centered on the origin of landed property—individual or collective. It evoked a broad clash of scholarly opinion during the later nineteenth century, some couched as economic theory, some as anthropological generalization, some as research into antiquity. With respect to the issue of land, it is opportune to tune in not at the beginning of debate, but with the extreme defense of individualism, the 1889 essay on the origins of property in land by Fustel de Coulanges, the fiercely conservative and positivist scholar who straddled the disciplines of sociology and history ("History is the science of social facts; that is to say, it sociology itself")[51] in the years after France's defeat by Prussia. He had made his mark with his essay a quarter century earlier, *La Cité Antique,* which emphasized the role of family religion (and paternal structure) in allegedly creating the nuclear units of antiquity, the family, and the polis. Denouncing German scholarship for half a century of anti-French bias as the catastrophe of 1870 overtook his country—"They invented the unsustainable theory of the Latin races to buttress their dynastic ambition with the false façade of racial conflict"[52]—Fustel continued to combat the allegedly tendentious errors of academics across the Rhine: The Roman Empire had not been decadent; together with the early Frankish monarchy, it had always remained hierarchical. Frankish institutions had never been elective. The early Germans were not a separate race, and most emphatically they had never practiced redistribution of land nor held property in common.

The latter theory became his particular bête noire: after a study of the Frankish monarchy came a monograph on "The Allod and the rural domain in the Merovingian Era," followed by other contributions, all denouncing Germanophiles who believed in a stage of primitive landed communism. In his article of 1880 in the right-wing *Revue des Questions Historiques,* he attacked head on the theory—by then, he asserted, forty years old—that cultivation of land was originally communal. "'All land in the beginning was common land,' so Fustel disapprovingly cited Georg L. von Maurer, 'and belonged to all; that is to say the people.' . . . In a word, the system of agriculture was, in the beginning, an agrarian communism."[53] Fustel's clear rejection of this allegedly Germanic theory rallied Anglo-Saxon as well as French conservatives. As the Toronto-based scholar who published his tract in translation was happy to report (along with his own observation that "there is absolutely no clear documentary evidence for the free village community in England"), Fustel denied altogether the existence of that free, self-governing village community with common ownership of the village lands, which Maurer had made familiar as the *mark*. And as the translator was further satisfied to insist about other examples of common lands, such as Indian villages and Russian mir, "all that can be said at this stage is that most of them prove only a joint-cultivation and not a joint-ownership."[54]

The word *mark*, according to Fustel, referred to the boundary of a territory, usually the boundary of a private property; it was not a communal territory. Furthermore, early German law was based on the assumption of private property in land and never on common ownership, whether by a whole people or by a village group; neither was there any evidence of periodic redivision of communal lands. Customary rights to exploit a common were rights of use over property belong to a landowner, not a claim to ownership on their own. Over and over Fustel pounded home his own version of what today's American judicial conservatives call original intent: that historians might want to hold pleasing imaginary theories was not new, but to pretend they were historically grounded was. The task was not to judge whether a theory was attractive, but whether it was supported by the documents: "The basic task of critical judgment when it comes to the history of the past is to believe the ancients."[55]

Fustel's was perhaps the most strident voice of a tradition that fused morality with ownership. Curiously enough his insistence on individual ownership accompanied a belief in family solidarity that precluded any wider commitment to village communalism. Religion and property together emerged and reinforced the family. "Household religion taught the man to make himself patron of the land and assured his power over it: religion and property have been born together in the soul and have formed together with the family an ensemble indivisible and indistinct."[56] In this conviction he reflected the premises of the Napoleonic Civil Code, which also combined a clear defense of property with a consolidation of marriage and family. Innumerable commentaries on Roman law in France and Italy made the same point.

There was a countercurrent, based on German scholars, but also present in Britain, and defended by those with more anthropological sentiments. In his celebrated 1861 treatise on ancient law, Henry Sumner Maine argued that "it is more than likely that joint-ownership, and not separate ownership, is the really archaic constitution, and that the forms of property which will afford us instruction will be those which are associated with the rights of family and of groups of kindred."[57] But Maine was not to draw democratic conclusions from his observations. Reviewing his earlier work a generation later, he agreed that "the land tends to become the true basis of the group; it is recognized as of preeminent importance to its vitality, and it remains common property, while private ownership is allowed to show itself in moveables and cattle." Such common property, however, was to disappear, but not, ironically, by virtue of an ancient aristocratic assault on common holdings but rather "by the successful assault of a democracy on an autocracy."[58] Ten years later in his remarkable comparison of Indian and English village organization, *Village Communities,* Maine argued that the autocratic manor, introduced under British feudalism, was far more favorable for agricultural development, than a land free from feudal services.[59] The Belgian Christian socialist Émile de Laveleye, a founding member of the Institut de Droit International in 1873, turned to Maine for evidence that property had once been communal—but failed to cite that Maine had concluded that the cost of communal organization was stagnation. Somewhat wistfully, Maine argued that modern market relations and loans at interest required an arm's-length relationship. Intimates did not readily indulge in such practices: "The rule [of the market] only triumphs when the primitive community is in ruins."[60]

Where Maine reconstructed a democratic trend that undermined collective property, Fustel insisted that collective property had never really existed. For Maine family rights had provided for a primitive collectivism; for Fustel, they were instantiated in the supremacy of the male head of household and his individual possession of land. Behind the idea of property held in common Fustel saw the specter of the commune and indeed the Prussian march into Paris. His adversaries, Maurer and then the Belgian Laveleye, offered a pernicious and careless collectivist narrative that had to be scotched. Indeed, Baron Laveleye was a consistent adversary; the Institut de Droit International united a cohort of emerging international lawyers who regarded law less as a sovereign code than as an instrument of enlightened society in its own right. As international lawyers, many Protestant, they espoused international arbitration and envisioned themselves as representatives of Europe's claim to civilization.[61] Laveleye was more a collectivist than his fellow meliorists. He envisioned modern society as torn between the haves and have-nots. The advent of political equality no longer allowed simple suppression of the laboring slave as in antiquity: "Today the slave has become a citizen and as a free laborer he is recognized as the equal of the richest citizens."[62] That meant that the constitution of the countryside would have to change. In antiquity hierarchic class relations and the entire organization of the state rested on possession of land. In all primitive societies, and still today in Russia and Java, the earth, collective property of the tribe, was periodically redistributed among families. "Citizens of America and Australia," he appealed, "do not adopt the harsh and narrow law that we have borrowed from Rome and which leads us to social war. Return to the primitive tradition of your ancestors."[63] Laveleye argued that Fustel was wrong to consider the section of land that was attributed annually to families by the village as private property.[64] The bulk of the Belgian's volume traced the residues of primitive collective property in Europe and Asia. It had disappeared earliest in England, thus allowing an aristocracy to live on and prevent the constitution of a rural democracy as in France. Agricultural cooperatives could reconstitute these ancient customs under new conditions.[65]

Maurer, Morgan, Maine, and Laveleye formed a formidable cohort of social and legal historical anthropologists. The German social historian Karl Lamprecht would later maintain a related line, although his German colleagues vociferously sought to discredit him, not for finding communal property, but for suggesting that society might in effect organize itself without the state and in particular the Prussian state. But the adversaries of the "collectivists" were also widespread and tenacious. As far as the Russian mir was concerned—Fustel disdainfully responded—it was only a small village, no more than two hundred inhabitants, not a tribal community, and certainly not a national or ethnic community. Science could hardly confirm the notion the Russians practiced collective property from these impoverished backward islets.[66] Fustel had his English and American admirers, above all the Bostonian Denman Waldo Ross, who before devoting himself to art collecting after the death of his father, produced a major tract on *The Early History of Landholding among the Germans,* which supported the acerbic Frenchman.[67] The dispute was taken up by Émile Belot, who researched the early history of white settlement in Nantucket Island and found three forms of property— individual, communal, and mixed. For Belot, who taught at Strasbourg and Lyon, Nantucket was an exemplary laboratory—a colony that recapitulated the history of primitive man (even if its settlers arrived in 1671 imbued with the ideas of seventeenth-century Puritans). He envisaged them as carrying the customs of the primeval Scottish villages from which their ancestors had allegedly derived, and their little community supposedly demonstrated not that collective property had never existed, but that it had been quickly suppressed as a random and contingent experiment destined to be superseded in the course of civilization.[68]

This was indeed a marvelous, if somewhat obscure, debate in which the sparse settlement of a small island off the shore of Cape Cod and the impoverished villages of Russia might prove universal laws of social development! But it is necessary to recover the "moment" of the 1880s, in which the post-commune embers of socialism were suppressed, whether under Bismarck's antisocialist laws, the trial of the Haymarket bombers, or the earlier schisms of the earlier socialist and labor movements who split between anarchists and Marxist adherents. The 1880s was a decade for reaffirming positivism and property, but also a moment to mobilize antiquity to defend ideological preferences. Fustel relied on discrediting his adversaries; Marx and Engels turned to an enthusiastic reading of primitive society based on Lewis Morgan, Johann Jakob Bachofen, and other heterodox theorists. Marx and Engels could not remain aloof from these debates, above all since Marx had placed the expropriation of aboriginals' soil at the origin of private accumulation. Both theorists found Lewis Morgan's *Ancient Society* "one of the few epoch-making works of our time."[69] Engels, writing a year after his collaborator's death in 1883, produced an exuberant tract that gave primitive sexual promiscuity as much credit for founding human society as primitive communism. He described a trajectory from primeval promiscuous communities and Bachofen's *Mutterrecht* to patriarchal family collectives such as the south Slav *zadruga,* Russian extended families "who all live together in one household, till their fields in common, feed and clothe themselves from the common store and communally own all surplus products" and who then coalesced into the *obshchina* or village community.[70] Into this pastoral picture, Fustel's

Greeks had intruded almost as bourgeois disciplinarians. They established monogamy (intended to bind women but not men, as it was accustomed by prostitution): "It was the first form of the family based not on natural but on economic conditions, namely on the victory of private property over original, naturally developed, common ownership." Class conflict and sexual conflict emerged together.[71]

The Russian sociologist Maksim Kovalevsky had supposedly demonstrated that the patriarchal household community was the connecting link between the mother-right community and the modern isolated family: "The question is no longer whether the land was common or private property, as was still discussed between Maurer and Waitz, but what *form* common property assumed."[72] Tacitus had left no doubt that in Caesar's time the Suevi owned and tilled their land in common; the issue was when they went into the village community. But collective ownership was an attribute of gentile (that is, based on the *gens*) or tribal society: as soon as society passed beyond the limits in which this constitution (tribal councils) could prevail, "the gentile order was finished. It burst asunder and the state took its place." And with the state, the division of labor, private property, and eventually commodity production. "In contradistinction to the old gentile organization, the state, first, divides its subjects *according to territory*," not by blood.[73] "The highest form of the state, the democratic republic," Engels continued, "which under our modern conditions of society is more and more becoming an inevitable necessity and is the form of state in which alone the last decisive struggle between proletariat and bourgeois can be fought out—the democratic republic officially knows nothing any more of property distinctions. In it wealth exercises its power indirectly but all the more surely . . . the possessing class rules directly through the medium of universal suffrage."[74] The state was a necessity because of class cleavages; when those were overcome it would be placed "into the Museum of Antiquities, by the side of the spinning wheel and the bronze axe." Morgan, to his credit, had recognized this: although property had become an unmanageable power, it would be superseded by "democracy in government, brotherhood in society, equality in rights and privileges, and universal education . . . a revival in a higher form, of the liberty, equality and fraternity of the ancient gentes."[75]

The difficult question for Marx and Engels was whether the Russian mir might serve as a particular Russian route to socialism without the long traversal through bourgeois property conditions. A generation earlier Herzen had explained the revolutionary potential of the Russian peasant and his village to Michelet: "As the first step towards social revolution Europe encounters a people which offers a system, though half-savage and unorganized, but still a system—of perpetual redivision of the land among its tillers. Note that this great example is set not by educated Russia, but by the people at large. . . . In Russia the future belongs to the peasant, just as in France it belongs to the workman."[76] This was hardly what Marx and Engels had believed. As late as 1874–1875 Engels had deprecated the mir's communal potential for revolution. The peasant commune might help to mobilize a momentary radicalism, which the socialist organizers associated with Bakunin, but which would then lapse into reaction. Communal forms existed everywhere, noted Engels in the mid-1870s, but to what avail? Anarchist (Bakunist) revolution had just failed miserably in Spain in 1873, and while revolution was certainly coming to Russia (unless the impending war with Turkey would postpone it), and although peasant participation would be needed to make it successful, premature revolution would fail.[77] Still, Engels noted, "The possibility exists of transforming this communal form into a higher one, if only it is reserved until such time as the conditions are ripe"—and if the Russian peasantry would not insist on family landholdings but proved willing to embrace directly the collective organization of agriculture. All this could happen only if a socialist revolution in the West prepared the way.[78] A Russia in which capitalism had not fully matured might be swept into socialist revolution if Germany and Western Europe were already caught up in the process. The remote future might be certain. The near and mid-term prospects were discouraging; the answer took refuge in ambiguity.

Even such a partial concession to special Russian conditions, however, was not what the young Marxist revolutionaries who split with the Populists wanted to hear: Vera Zasulich wrote the guru asking him to clarify. He fudged and attempted an unsent evasive answer. But in 1882 Marx and Engels included a preface to a new Russian translation of *The Communist Manifesto,* finally conceding that if a Russian revolution helped spark a proletarian revolution in the West "so that the two complement each other, then contemporary Russian land tenure may be a starting point for communist development."[79] Was this a consolation prize for the *Narodniki* or Populists currently being harassed in Russia? Georgi

Plekhanov, Zasulich's party comrade, insisted the commune was an archaic and degenerate form—the Russian revolution must triumph as a proletarian revolution or not at all. After Marx passed away the next year, Engels, too, abandoned any concession to a Russian peasant route to socialism—Russia must pass through capitalism and the triumph of bourgeois property relations, in the countryside as well as the city: "History is the most cruel of all goddesses. She drives her triumphal chariot over heaps of corpses, only in war, but also in times of 'peaceful' economic development."[80] On the other hand, he realized that the peasant in Germany and France would never easily accept collectivism; the class could be won over only by promises of mortgage forgiveness and ownership of their plots. Only the large-scale estates could serve as a basis for socialism in the countryside.[81]

It was one of the historical ironies of the era that in the very moment Fustel was seeking to stamp out collectivist mirages the American real estate magnate (and Harvard dropout) Henry Wilshire, after whom Los Angeles' famous boulevard would be named, was helping to develop what would become the Marxist theory of imperialism. Likewise, Henry George would take Ricardan theories of rent and apply them to urban property. Population increase and urban development rapidly increased the value of real property in the city and country without any additional effort expended by landlords and owners. Their "rent" or surplus, accumulating through no merit of their own, was the logical source for taxation—it was unearned and allegedly the owners would not abandon their property if some profits were taxed away (of course, the problem of adequate investment in urban capital was ignored)—and Henry George became the major figure in an international movement to institute the single tax—an echo of the debates between Pietro Verri and Turgot a century earlier.[82]

The debates on collective rights continued to simmer in Italy—less in terms of land cultivation than of the residual rights to woods and commons that had largely disappeared in France and Britain but were still significant locally in Italy. As in France, Italian legal scholars in the late nineteenth century sought to bring up-to-date the notions of absolute property, which they traced back to "Quiritary Law" or the early law of the ancient Romans. Dozens of legal scholars weighed in on the issue of how Roman and Lombard law had either accepted collective property or enshrined absolute "quiritary" ownership. The legal historian Paolo Grossi has lovingly charted the treatises of authorities now consigned to obscurity that kept a collectivist tradition alive, whether drawing on Maurer, Maine, or Laveleye. Neapolitan authorities in particular argued paradoxically toward 1880 that common rights had persisted not because of seigneurial generosity but as the bare minimal recourse that baronial power had left to villages as they subjugated them in the south to the latifundial regime.[83] The positivist historians of Roman and Lombard law whom Grossi has arrayed made the crucial point that even if private property had come to prevail, it was, pace Fustel, a human invention, not a fact of nature. "Laveleye is right," insisted the indefatigable legal commentator Francesco Schupfer, when he traced the evolution of property from the community to the family to the individual: "Only as a result of this final evolution, sometimes very long, was [the concept of] property definitively constituted and became that absolute, sovereign, and personal right that is defined by our law code."[84]

The 1870s opened a period of difficulty for European agriculture in general, as North American grain production—revived after the Civil War and extensive rail construction in Canada and the United States—combined with deflationary monetary management to drive down commodity prices. Russian grain exports also leaped ahead with the settlement of new agricultural land and an increase in rail lines. Faced with the distress of farmers, major countries, first France, then Germany, Britain, and Italy undertook official investigations. Italy's "Agrarian Inquest" *(Inchiesta Agraria)* was the most notable, proposed in parliament and carried out under the supervision of the Catholic Senator Stefano Jacini between 1874 and 1877; its volumes of statistical findings were published continually into the 1880s and beyond. Jacini was a landowner but, unlike the investigators elsewhere, encouraged, or allowed, his inquest to highlight the distress of the agrarian working class. "Agricultural Italy is a world unknown even to Italians," Jacini told the parliament.[85] A century and a quarter earlier, the bureaucrats of Lombardy had carried out a major survey in the fiscal interest of the Enlightenment state. Jacini's survey spoke for rural civil society as a whole. His final report of 1884 pointed out how the taxes of the new Italian state had thrown rural Italy into crisis. Political Italy, he charged, claimed to desire an agrarian Risorgimento but had seized all of agriculture's savings through multiple heavy taxes: wartime "tenths," the tax on landed revenue, the stamp tax on documents, and local imposts. He called for a renewal of the rural world. But what Jacini and agriculture had to settle for was a protective tariff, as in most of the advanced world, Britain alone resisting.[86] By the late 1870s agricultural "depression" hovered over much of the world. Conflicts over collective rights were being displaced by the stagnation of returns on agriculture.

In political terms the Jacini report encompassed a conservative plea for the countryside—its landowners allegedly overwhelmed by the land tax, its workers afflicted with poverty and compelled to stream abroad— that might be carried out under a government of the center-left: a social monument to the premier Agostino Depretis's formula of ideological fusion or *trasformismo*. On the left, the Sicilian deputy Agostino Bertani had added an appendix to the report, emphasizing that one must tread warily in lumping together all property rights. It was wrong, argued Bertani, to sacrifice to the landowner the peasants' rights of sowing, grazing, or gathering wood. Bertani, however, was an erratic politician, financially dependent on the skillful centrist premier while ideologically pressured by his comrades on the parliamentary left, and marginalized in the debates.[87] The staff researcher Gino Valenti, who contributed the chapter on the mountainous regions of the Romagna, found that communal rights of usufruct rather than the absolute ownership that Roman law had codified still played a role. Valenti did not ask for a resurrection of a pre-Roman collectivist vision, but he urged that the legal order might be flexibly applied according to the region—allowing property to exist in many forms. Valenti went on in the next decade and a half to document the collective customs that marked his native region and finally the role of cooperatives in agriculture.[88]

But agricultural cooperatives, which would spread among the rural producers of the West over the decades to come, were associations among individual enterprises for common purposes—the sharing of machinery, the refinement of olive oil, the marketing of cheese. They did not have to claim rights of ownership over land. The sensitive issue was the residual common rights over rural territory, which had been the target of landed proprietors and of liberal party politicians for decades. In 1884 Depretis's minister for agriculture, Bernardino Grimaldi, introduced a motion to get rid of the remaining collective customs or usages *(usi civici)* in the former papal lands, residual rights for villagers that he insisted derived from "the barbarian and feudal era," and that supposedly remained sources of "immense harm" to agriculture. These included the so-called *Servitù del Pascere* (or *Pascolo* in the Veneto), the reserves kept open for animal grazing, which the state had been slowly abolishing from locality to locality since the 1860s. Common lands and pastures were to be wrested from collective custom and put up for sale.[89] The era seemed propitious: the 1880s was an era of extensive land reclamation schemes *(bonifiche)* in the Po Delta and the Veneto.[90] Marshy lands were to be made productive under the aegis of landlords who would settle not independent peasants, but an agrarian proletariat on their new holdings. Within a decade or two American threshers and combines would make their appearance in this recovered agrarian land and an era of combative labor relations would begin. As of the 1880s, four years of tortured debate were required for Grimaldi's proposal to become law in 1888. The law affirmed the norms of private property, but the debates suggested an attention to the rights of the tenant and the collective.[91]

Communalism was under siege throughout the world in the second half of the nineteenth century, not just by conservatives but by liberals. Often they acted not in the cause of individual acquisition but a vision of agricultural productivity, as had the Enlightenment reformers. Nostalgic efforts to preserve or restore collectivism, they believed, meant an inevitable loss of productivity. Nonetheless, if the adherents of agricultural communalism never won legal battles, they did not entirely lose them, either. The framework of law could still provide a foothold for defense of collective as well as individual property. In Brazil the major land law of 1850 supposedly would regularize possession of lands through public registration, but provided a field of legal contestations (and sometimes direct occupation) between those who claimed ownership of the large estates and those who persisted in their resistance.[92] The Ley Lerdo had loopholes for Indian communities. Law was a referee; it regularized and facilitated conflict but did not eliminate it.

So long as private property in land exists, Henry George wrote after his unsuccessful fling with electoral politics, "our democratic institutions are vain, our pretence of equality but cruel irony. . . . Until we in some way make the land what Nature intended it to be, common property . . . we have not established the Republic in any sense worthy of the name, and we cannot establish the Republic."[93] Such radicalism would require revolution, however. When collectivist visions next emerged, they no longer seemed realizable in terms of legislation within a bourgeois order. Alongside other impulses, such as resentment of foreign exploitation they motivated the great revolutionary upheavals of the early twentieth century in Russia, China, and Mexico. But before these radical challenges to private landholding erupted again, another specter triggered political foreboding: arable land might simply be running out. Territory was bounded, but now the border might seem a corset, the frontier finite, and democratic institutions endangered. The finitude of available land raised new problems.

Farewell to Free Land

The dilemma with respect to land for many nineteenth-century critics was not just that unequal property holdings produced class privilege or deprivation. Access to land, or lack of access, played a major role in scaffolding capitalism as such. Modern production demanded wage labor. Wage labor would be forthcoming only when families could not establish their own self-sufficient agricultural enterprises. "Land as productive element, in our opinion, is the prime cause of economic relationships. . . . Land is the fundamental basis of the economic system; the theory of the land is the supreme principle of all political economy, which follows ultimately only a logical and natural deduction from the analysis of landed property."[94] Now almost forgotten, but widely cited toward the end of the nineteenth century, Achille Loria (1857–1943) proposed the most encompassing theory, insisting that free or unclaimed land was not just the source of surplus, but that it determined all class relations:

> When free land exists, when every man can so soon as he
> wishes, occupy a terrain and commit his own labor for his
> own account, capitalist property is impossible, since there is
> no laborer who will be disposed to produce for a capitalist
> while he can produce for his own account on a terrain that
> has no [scarcity] value. . . . The formation of unearned
> income *(inoperoso)*, the creation of capitalist property can be
> obtained only by means of the violent suppression of the free

land to which the laborer owes his force and his liberty. So long as all the land has not been occupied, the suppression of free land can be achieved only by the violent appropriation of the worker, which first assumes the brutal forms of slavery and then, when the declining productivity of soil requires a greater productivity, gives way to a milder form of service more suited for effective labor. Thus ownership of men is the primary base, the first pedestal of the capitalist economy.[95]

It was logical enough that an analysis such as Loria's should be developed in the later decades of the nineteenth century. Marx had already emphasized the role of land appropriation in his discussion of so-called primitive accumulation as the basis for capitalist domination.[96] He was thinking of England's conquest of Ireland and other colonies at the dawn of British commercial development. But even as he wrote, vast global spaces were being enclosed and developed—in the U.S. West, in the Canadian prairies, in Russia's steppes, in Australia's fertile circumference, in Patagonia, and in the Amazon. The Berlin Conference of 1884–1885 attempted to demarcate the huge areas of Africa that the European powers had appropriated in their feeding frenzy of the previous half decade. In the United States, settlers succeeded in opening the last territory reserved for Indian settlement, the Oklahoma Territory, in 1889. For all the annexations, however, influential commentators were signaling future Malthusian limits with foreboding. Josiah Strong (*Our Country,* 1885), C. Wood Davis, and others drew the conclusion that America could succumb to Europe's ills, especially if immigration were not restricted.

Fatefully, much of this land had not merely been explored and wrested from its often-nomadic inhabitants; it had also been placed into private hands whether as the result of religious conviction, state inducements to railroad investors, or the policy of attracting family proprietors. As Thorstein Veblen wrote a decade later, the great American adventure was the transformation of the public domain into private wealth. Nineteenth-century states needed to populate their new interiors; landholders needed the state to arbitrate among land claimants and to subjugate or enclose the earlier inhabitants. Loria's analysis became widely known in the 1880s: his *Economic Theory of the Political Constitution* (1886) appeared in French translation and then was noticed by Columbia

University professor Edwin Seligman. Seligman urged Loria's student Ugo Rabbeno to write a major evaluation, "Loria's Landed System of Social Economy," for the *Political Science Quarterly* of 1891, where it followed an earlier if briefer review by E. Benjamin Andrews.[97] Rabbeno would contribute a second presentation in June 1892. Résumés appeared simultaneously by Loria himself in the *Annals* of the American Academy of Political and Social Science and the *Quarterly Journal of Economics* also in October 1891. As the historian Lee Benson pointed out in 1950, Loria's theory had a major impact on Richard Ely, who dropped the Ricardan "iron law of wages," in the second 1893 edition of his *Outline of Economics* to cite "free land . . . which has kept up the wages of labor," and predicted that "if that resource disappears we may look for different results unless new safeguards take its place." And, as Benson explained, Ely's Wisconsin colleague Frederick Jackson Turner declared in 1892, a year before his famous address on the closing of the frontier, "The ever retreating frontier of free land is the key to American development."[98] Striking in all these essays was the preoccupation with colonial land—as Loria emphasized in his *Analisi della Proprietà Capitalista*. The colony recapitulated the historical evolution of the motherland, and thus in a span of decades allowed the social scientist to track the long-term developmental laws of civilization. Loria himself cited Henry George's dictum that the basic cause of inequality was the inequality of landed property; *Progress and Poverty* (1879) was possibly one of his eclectic sources.[99]

Loria's analysis, however, had to wrestle with a major potential objection. Why should regions that had the largest proportion of free land, namely, the colonies of North America and Australia, become so nakedly capitalist? Since unoccupied land could be claimed and worked by ordinary workers, "free land" always represented an alternative to industrial labor. This meant that the capitalist class had to use coercion of one form or another to secure its workforce. As explained below, the nature of that pressure, however, could become less severe, not more so, as the quantity and quality of free land diminished over time. Still, the enforcement of class hierarchies by law and social discipline arose not because land was used up but because it remained a potential recourse for the landless.

For Loria, the distribution of colonial lands thus became a crucial stake in economic life. Colonies with extensive territories proved the point. Those studying the early period of the United States would understand "the historical necessity of slavery and serfdom in the Greco-Roman and feudal eras and in modern colonies, as the only means to obtain a profit in the period of free land and . . . the tenacity of proprieties to defend an economic system of such low productivity and so harmful to capitalism itself."[100] But how did capitalism arise when the vast lands of the United States (or Australia, as his student Ugo Rabbeno had studied alongside the United States) could not become totally appropriated? Rabbeno, who died prematurely of malaria at age thirty-three, had become an organizer of agrarian cooperatives. He found in Australia a laboratory of capitalist development based on limited access to land whose "fateful" class polarization—moderated only by the extralegal prevalence of squatters' rights—Rabbeno attributed first to the availability of large tracts for sheep raisers, then in the 1830s to the policies of Edward Gibbon Wakefield's ideas of a "sufficient price."

Edward Gibbon Wakefield, a restless genius, wrote his 1829 "Letter from Sydney," at the age of thirty-three, while serving three years in Newgate Prison for abduction of a minor, his second infatuation with a propertied heiress. He believed England overpopulated, the colonies underpopulated. But the reason was not the cost for colonists of acquiring the crown's land abroad, but in fact, the state's policy of granting it for free or low prices. The land had only an illusory value without labor and would soon be abandoned. The key was to set a price high enough that labor first accumulated in colonial towns such that the demands for rural produce drove land prices up but ensured rural development. Paradoxically counted in England as the tireless advocate of opening up Australian territory to immigrants who would be free to purchase farms, Wakefield aspired to development and the transplanting of civilization. He praised the industry of immigrants, citing the activity of the Chinese in Singapore.[101] But Rabbeno and Loria read him fifty years later as the designer of a policy designed to limit access and to forestall democracy. The "sufficient price" that Wakefield believed would ensure development Rabbeno understood to price calibrated high enough to prevent workers from buying their own farms. The ills of the home society, not its civilization, were thus recapitulated.[102]

Loria wrestled with the same general problem. Even after the best land in any territory of the world filled up, "there remained an ample zone of unoccupied lands whose cultivation certainly could not be undertaken without [some] capital but did not require major capital investment." To prevent workers from diffusing into these lands, "the condition *sine qua non* for the persistence of capitalist economy is the reduction of wages to a minimum so that the worker cannot save." Contemplating the United States, Loria was not, be it noted, claiming that once upon a time land was communal, only later to be privatized as the basis for capitalism. He was arguing rather that so long as land was available to individuals at no more than a modest cost, capitalism could not have arisen spontaneously. Since land was plentiful, wage restriction was therefore necessary for capitalism; the means included salary reductions, depreciation of money, the introduction of machinery that cost more than the workers displaced, expansion of unproductive capital and unproductive jobs—all of which limit profits but also "remove any danger of the reconstitution of free land, which would sound the death knell *(trarebbe alla tomba)* for the capitalist economy. . . . The basis of capitalist property is thus always the same: the suppression of free land and exclusion of the worker from the land—exclusion obtained by diverse means according to the diversity of the degree of occupation and the productivity of the terrain."[103]

But this result, Loria insisted, must not be the final one. Although capitalism was more productive than the precapitalist interlude of free land and unconstrained workers, there was potentially even a higher stage of economic life: cooperative production. "At this precise point free land must be reconstituted, and the right for everyone to occupy the land he might cultivate on his own has to be reinaugurated in order to construct the 'mixed association' and with it an adequate form of social equilibrium." By maintaining slavery or salaries, the capitalist class thus ultimately advanced the association of labor. The course of history was dialectical: "Suppression of free land is technically superior to free land and is a factor of progress and civilization, but less than free association would yield if spontaneously organized."[104]

Loria built on Ricardo's theory that as population increased, less productive lands had to be pressed into service, with the consequence that the higher cost of producing wheat produced on the most recently cleared land (its marginal cost) determined the price of grain and the price of land in general. Thus owners of previously cleared and more fertile acreage enjoyed an increasing revenue without effort—what economists meant technically by "rent"—from what they produced or received from tenants for letting their land out. Ricardan theory had helped justify the British manufacturers' crusade against wheat tariffs ("corn laws") that had culminated in repeal of the duties in 1846. "Thus it was the immortal glory of the greatest of the economists, Ricardo, to embark boldly on scientific argument with a theory of land."[105]

But Ricardo, Loria regretted, derived his analyses only from the decreasing productivity of soil, not from the role of free land, and he missed the notion of unlimited accumulation, excess of population, or the systemic role of commercial crises. "We admit a general law, but . . . the general economic law is this: *terra libera* determines the negation of the capitalist economy, which can be founded only on the suppression of free land, obtainable with methods that vary according to the successive grades of the occupation of land. . . . This is truly the *law of laws* and the vaunted natural laws discovered by Smith are only the historical laws of the capitalist economy, as the theory of the canonists and physiocrats are the historical laws of the medieval economy."[106]

Loria was not modest. He believed that his analysis provided an explanation for much of history and compared it to the breakthroughs of science, evolution, and sociology. "This theory explains the passage of civil nations from protection to free trade, from the indirect taxes that fall particularly on wage earners to the direct taxes that hit revenues." And it finally answered the riddle of why a capitalist class tolerated and supported private ownership of the land, which raised food prices and thus the wages capitalists had to pay. Even if the rent from land cost ate into capitalist profits, it was its "fundamental basis, and cannot be destroyed without overturning in its own ruins the entire edifice of capitalist fortunes." His theory, Loria claimed, showed how political economy provided a basis for sociology and revealed why all biological and social organization moved from multicellular and atomistic organization toward cooperative functioning. From the mechanical association imposed by slavery, thence to individual appropriation of the conditions for production, finally to the stage where association becomes possible and thus immune from the brakes that cooperation might impose on efficiency. Not race but landed endowments separated the progress of nations, and Loria concluded by showing how the theory of empty lands and decreasing fertility accounted for the economic history of nations and societies.[107]

Loria claimed both to praise socialism and to reject it. "We bow reverently," he concluded, before the critique it makes of today's economic life and before its mission "in favor of the disinherited and the defeated in the balance of life." Still, the socialists' theory would bring "not the dawn of equality but the sunset of liberty. Certainly the economic form that we are seeking as the fundamental institution of the future society is very different—the mixed association, the free association of workers and producers of capital is completely different." It "responds better than the socialist ideal to our national character because that terrible omnipotence of the collective that so pleases the German intellectuals has something terrifying and repulsive to us Latin peoples." On the other hand, "it has been the merit of socialism to have revealed the undeniable truth of capitalist property's usurpations . . . socialism is a beneficent and fertile force in the social and mental evolution of humanity."[108]

Loria's wavering on socialism, however, did not constitute the significant contribution of his analysis, which rested rather on his premise rather than his aspirations. What accounted for his widespread influence was his vision of the end of free land. The exhaustion of free land—whether already a transition in progress or one to be faced imminently—was a fundamental threshold of societal development: the mother of all constraints established by nature. It had already progressed far enough to bring about the unnatural condition of wage labor and thus modern capitalism. For Loria's reader Frederick Jackson Turner (who apparently had an Italian-speaking student translate and summarize portions of the text in the fall of 1892), the end of free land could undermine political democracy. For nascent ecologists it mandated preservation of wilderness. For imperialists it was an argument for annexations abroad or opening up the American Indian lands. There were still vast swathes of unexploited land, of course. But increasingly it must be redeemed from arid waste or taken from tribal occupiers who were not deemed worthy of improving it.

It is easy to find irony in history since it is created by the gaze of the historian. But assuming that it is a valid sensibility, the pervasive sense among intellectuals, at least those of a progressive bent, that the end of free land was at hand even as continental-size tracts yielded to exploration, settlement, and annexation counts as ironic. The ills of industrial capitalism, the undermining of democratic possibilities, the loss of individual autonomy darkened the progressives' fin-de-siècle perception of global space, fraught now with constraint rather than possibility. The significance of territory had changed over a century; its promise was no longer that of the cornucopia, the capacity to generate grains, fruits, and fibers that would enrich families and states. When Marx had prepared his notes on "Theories of Surplus Value"—the intended final volume of *Capital*—he had paid tribute to the Physiocrats for focusing on the question of surplus, which he understood to be the key to capitalist accumulation and the political economy of the bourgeois era (see Chapter 3). But surplus, he explained, could arise only from unremunerated labor power, not land itself. In fact, the agrarian reformers of the late eighteenth and nineteenth centuries had implicitly agreed when they kept emphasizing that labor had to be settled in place that, in effect, despite formal freedom workers must be tied to the land if possible through the gentle ideology of the pastoral and the neo-Georgian idyll, or, more likely, by means of the harsher restrictions on poor relief and laws against vagrancy—and in all cases, by the rational discipline of clear property lines.

By 1890, to take Turner's canonic date, the frontier had been closed, but the problem of agricultural yield no longer seemed preoccupying. Such a stance might be judged provincial in view of the terrible famines that afflicted India, China, and Brazil in the late 1870s, followed by the starvation in Ethiopia a decade later. But in Europe and North America, adverse agricultural terms of trade and not underproduction seemed the cause of hardship, a condition that aside from periods of war would continue into the 1950s. A bounty of grains, though, did not mean that territory lost its relevance for the structuring of collective life. Rather, its contribution was changing. Territory provided not just the foundation of economic production or static geopolitical security but a more diffuse sense of vitality. Above all, the possession and penetration of great landed spaces seemed essential to preserve or supposedly primeval national and racial survival. Size counted in a world of competitive nation-states. Just as filling in European maps had earlier made vivid the concept of a territorial state, coloring cartographic spaces in Africa and Asia signified global status: one's country's own "place in the sun." Along with size in its own right, infrastructure, hygiene, and national efficiency became prominent as the new values that inhered in political space and must be encouraged. The construction of territory would play a crucial, even obsessive, role, no longer because of what it might grow but because of the national energy it signified and enhanced.

5

"An Invincible Force"
Railroads, Continents, and Colonies

THE FIRST INTERCITY RAILROADS—the Manchester and Liverpool, and the Baltimore and Ohio—had made initial runs in 1830, only eight years before the enthusiastic Saint Simonian economist Michel Chevalier proclaimed, "Railroads seem truly called to change the face of the globe." The invention transported goods and passengers only twice as fast as canals—perhaps twelve miles an hour rather than six. It was the political and spatial dimension that prompted his vision: the noble dream of world association might be chimerical, but no one could contest that "the sentiment of unity that animates so many peoples today and the need of expansion that devours some of the nations that have recently emerged in the old world and the new, must work to change the political balance. An invincible force batters, shakes and undermines the barriers within which men today are parked in small states and consequently prepares the way for vast empires."[1]

The invincible source was the energy tapped by the Industrial Revolution, and this chapter follows its implications for constructions of territory, which it transformed with respect to size and vitality. The eighteenth century had seen historic provinces in Europe continually transferred from sovereign to sovereign. The kingdom of France had annexed Belgian borderlands and added the province of Lorraine; Prussia had wrested Silesia from the Habsburg domains; Russia took Crimea from the Ottomans; and the Romanovs, Habsburgs, and Prussians eliminated the Polish Commonwealth. Republics, often confined to small wealthy cities with some hinterland, seemed particularly vulnerable. Piedmont annexed Genoa in 1754. In 1797, a little more than a year after the last remnant of historic Poland was liquidated, the ancient republic of Venice would disappear. The wars of the French Revolution and Empire meant continual reshuffling as different pieces of German and Italian states were passed around, eliminated, or eventually annexed to France. Napoleon encouraged the midsize German states to absorb the religious jurisdictions and micro-principalities of the Holy Roman Empire, then helped eliminate that territorial expression of European public law altogether. He kept moving the border posts in northern Italy and supervised the Scandinavian trading of sparsely settled Norway from Denmark to Sweden, briefly removed the western provinces of Prussia, and annexed Belgium, Holland, Piedmont, the Swiss Confederation, Holland, Venice, and even the Habsburgs' Dalmatian provinces.

Just as the age of steam was dawning, the European powers engaged in a major effort to stabilize their territorial space following the Napoleonic effort at continental conquest. The diplomats at the Congress of Vienna paid relatively little attention to the economic potential or the ethnicity of the territories they restored or combined. Inhabitants of territory were important as a potential resource for military or agricultural purposes—but their preferences as to state affiliation did not count unless they might actively cause disorder. In its concern with stabilizing a geospatial order (and the land-based social order) that had been overturned and continually reshuffled during the preceding quarter century, the statesmen at Vienna effectively closed an era and followed an older agenda of territorial balance that was to become less and less capable of dealing with the new energies and ideologies of the industrial era. Nonetheless, in one major respect the Vienna settlement certainly incorporated a principle of resilience. This was not so much the idea of equilibrium that many historians have emphasized, but rather the unavowed reaffirmation of inequality that structured the new international order.

The statesmen at Vienna did not originate the idea of the great powers, which was at least a century older. But they frankly used it as the basis for negotiating the system of inequalities that they wished to preserve. This is no condemnation; it is unlikely that any durable effort at minimizing international violence can dispense with allowing powerful states greater voice in governance than others. The Vienna settlement reasserted the privileges and responsibilities of the great powers both for negotiation and subsequent enforcement, as expressed in the congress system or the Concert of Europe or the subsequent major congresses: Paris 1856,

Berlin 1878, Paris 1919, and Yalta 1945, to name only a few of the most salient. Vienna closed an era in another respect: it focused on the European territories that French ideological and military success had thrown into turmoil. Except for the British whose objectives were global, the geographical inequalities Vienna confirmed were designed to perpetuate the distribution of European territories. But what lay ahead—decisively impacted by the "invincible forces," of steam, electricity, coal, and eventually oil)—was a far more expansive set of territorial imperatives, continental in ambition and often imperial in execution. As Henry Adams, shortly after 1900, looked back on the prior era:

> he historian needs not much help to measure some kinds of
> social movement; and especially in the nineteenth century,
> society by common accord agreed in measuring its progress
> by coal-output. The ratio of increase in the volume of coal-
> power may serve as dynamometer. The coal-output of the
> world, speaking roughly, doubled every ten years between
> 1840 and 1900, in the form of utilized power, for the ton of
> coal yielded three or four times as much power in 1900 as in
> 1840. . . . Since 1800 scores of new forces had been discovered;
> old forces had been raised to higher powers, as could be
> measured in the navy-gun; great regions of chemistry had
> been opened up, and connected with other regions of physics.[2]

Continental and imperial visions certainly existed before the age of steam and steel. Whether in antiquity, the Renaissance, or the century before the railroad, continental expansion beckoned to those states that had the opportunity to border on vast tracts of thinly settled lands. This included the American nations—the United States, Canada, Argentina, and Brazil, components of earlier empires that came to see themselves as destined for imperial size if not institutions—but also older landed empires: Romanov and Qing, who assisted each other in absorbing inner Asia. Continentalism, though, took on renewed life with the transformation of railroads from short lines connecting close cities to long roads that could knit together remote points. Territorial thinking assumed new promise and new dimensions as it absorbed the potentials of the energy age.

The accepted inequality of greater and lesser powers would evolve into a far more dangerous vision of great continentalist powers destined to collide in a limited global space. Continentalism, to give a name to the ambition for controlling vast territories, brought with it the reveries and doctrines of geopolitics, as the size and orientations of large powers were seen as determining the course of history. It went hand in hand with a new world of global capital flows and labor migration—what Lenin would seek to describe as the highest stage of capitalism. It may have created an intellectual milieu that made it plausible in fact for students of the deep global past to suggest (over much resistance) that continents might physically change their shape, location, and size, as Alfred von Wegener proposed in 1912.[3] With the emergence of ambitious ideologies that could claim the imagination of large publics at the end of the nineteenth century for at least another hundred years, continentalist enthusiasm could fuse with ideological fervor to contribute to the unparalleled political violence of the past century. Political belief systems alone did not bring the Soviet Union and the United States to their dangerous and constant readiness after World War II to contemplate mutual nuclear destruction: but the identification of their respective doctrines with the extensive global surfaces they controlled did.

Railroad Nationalism

Michel Chevalier himself did not believe that "we are on the eve of a universal monarchy or that humanity will ever acknowledge one king alone or even just one God." Still, it might be hazarded that "we shall not wait long to see the organization, whether through federation or conquest, or whatever unknown auspices, of immense states that will englobe dozens of the kingdoms, principalities and duchies among which Europe's population is now divided." "This new civilization . . . this new political and social equilibrium that is now starting to preoccupy statesmen will have no material agent more prevalent, more powerful than the railroad. To prepare this *novus ordo* and to maintain it no more efficacious material instrument will be placed at the disposition of the human species."[4] A few years later, the German poet Heinrich Heine added his voice: "The railroads are . . . a providential event, giving humanity new momentum and changing the color and shape of life. A new chapter in world history begins, and our generation can be proud to have witnessed it. What changes must now enter our outlook and imagination. Even the elementary notions of time and space have become unstable."[5] Karl Marx agreed: railways meant "the annihilation of space by time." This murky dictum could easily have been reversed, however. The railroad was vastly expanding the space that humans could dominate. Even as it linked remote destinations it enlarged the territory that they inhabited.[6] Commentators offered the same unbridled predictions for transformative effects—call it railroad hype—that today's prophets of the social media proclaim daily. But with an important difference. The railroad and telegraph promised to extend not the connectivity of individuals, but the reach and authority of states and nations.[7] Whereas the Internet and social media are celebrated today as undermining the boundaries of national space, the railroad and the telegraph were supposedly destined to transform the scale of the political, not to dissolve it. These great innovations of the nineteenth century were still wedded to a territorial vision.

Successful telegraphy was developed within a few years of the first railroads but evoked different spatial images. The railroad depended on a system of communication that ran parallel to a system of physical conveyance. Telegraph and railroad operated in tandem, the one for information, the other for transporting personnel (and within a couple of decades military personnel) and commodities. Their material traces—wires on high, tracks below—snaked alongside each other through the countryside. The early railroad train captured the imagination in a more vivid way; its belching engine and untiring pistons carried individuals whose life experience was enlarged. It united vast landed areas ultimately of continental extent, but conversely it stopped at the ocean's edge.

Telegraph cables did not. In spatial terms they had a different potential. Particularly when undersea intercontinental cables were laid from the late 1860s on, the thickening networks introduced a metaphor of globality and commercial interconnectivity. They suggested the threads and fabrics of a nascent world economy—a term that appeared first in German analysis. Atlases depicted their figurative density. While they could be read as traces of imperial power, especially the British strategic cables to South Asia, they also stood for the intercourse of civil society and the axons of commerce on a world scale.[8] Certainly railroads served empire insofar as they would be laid down in the vast territories acquired overseas, as in India, which meant that they remained wedded to a vision of size and competition. But the telegraph (like the steamship) traversed the ocean and served globality, as well. It promised the fraternity of news and information. Railroads carried soldiers; the telegraph conveyed ideas.[9]

Chevalier early on calculated the social power of the innovation in terms of territorial control, and derived the latter by squaring multiples of speed. If railroads might be brought up to ten leagues or thirty miles per hour, that is, five times the velocity of ordinary coaches, a national space twenty-five times that of France, or four times that of Western Europe from Portugal to the Russian frontier, "would be centralized to the same degree as today's France and could be administered with the same speed." Skepticism about the transformative claims of speed and space would make little difference: even the skeptics recognized that railroad enthusiasm was "one of those sentiments against which all reasoning and remonstrance would fail . . . for one reason or another in their favor there was a universal acclamation: *consensus gentium.*" In the interests of civilization, one needed the *grandes lignes* (the term one still encounters in French railroad stations). "They are the ones that must contribute the most to transform the relations of people and things, that will connect provinces to provinces and peoples to peoples."[10]

Thus the territorial space that the railroad promised to enlarge was to make far greater claims on collective loyalties than had earlier state space. Sovereigns gave their territory a frontier but not necessarily a sentiment of loyalty and belonging. As proprietors and tax collectors, they mapped the territory in order to collect revenues. But the railroads they bankrolled served in particular as the sinews for the nation-state—a population supposedly feeling a common fate (or so its elite insisted), engaged in common military activity, often sharing a language, believed to rest on ethnic cohesion, united by loyalties not just to a monarch, but to a people shaped by historical continuity, demanding voice and representation. They enlarged communities of belonging.[11]

It is not that railroads were necessary for nationalism whether for political or economic reasons. Nor were they sufficient. The claims of nationalism certainly predated the steam locomotives that slowly trundled across the countryside. Centuries of warfare had helped to create senses of national community. So, too, had efforts to develop and rationalize territory that eighteenth-century monarchs and administrators had undertaken. Although nature had divided the national space by rivers and mountains, the conviction grew that such divisions could be overcome.

Despite appealing to the justification of "natural frontiers," when it suited plans for expansion, administrators worked to diminish the importance of natural geographical features for governing at home. "Men have never accepted natural divisions; they've divided the earth according to their ambitions," an early French geographer wrote. "They have settled the limits of their possessions by force and power, whence the origin of disputes between neighboring peoples."[12] The political map shows the territory as an "administered" space. The French Revolutionaries early on tackled the question of territorial division anew, dividing the country's historic provinces into a national space of eighty-three departments. Although even champions of the early revolution such as Mirabeau hesitated to break up what they valued as the natural solidarities of France, the advocates of territorial rationalization followed the Abbé Sieyès's lead in urging not a confederation of tiny autonomous republics but one cohesive monarchy: "France is capable of forming an integral whole, uniformly submitting in every part to a single legislation and one common administration."[13] "What does one really expect from the department? That it brings about mechanically the best conditions for a collective participation in the nation, by making sure that between Paris and every point of the territory a regulated division of authority and initiative, by counterbalancing the town privileges such as guaranteeing to every citizen access to his local capital within a day of horseback riding. Authority will be spread homogenously."[14] Territorial cohesion was emerging as a significant attribute of nationalism.

So too the elites of the late eighteenth and nineteenth centuries tracked indexes of progress on a spatial basis. The French national society of physicians asked for a "topography" of health and illness with respect to the provinces of the kingdom in 1776, which led to the *Annales d'hygiène publique* in 1830.[15] More generally, the Saint Simonians measured the productive forces of the departments; industrial development and levels of wealth were calculated geographically. Baron Charles Dupin, one of the pioneers of welfare economics, who developed chloropleth maps that showed how chosen social indicators varied over territorial units, calculated the "Forces productives et commerciales de la France" in 1826: "I am comparing each department's productive forces and the product of these forces with the French average," checking out the inequalities of north and south, east and west.[16]

The new American republic faced some of the same problems—preventing the aggregation of power in certain large provincial units, in this case the states whose colonial charters suggested they might extend their territory to the Pacific shore, But the new confederation had an additional challenge—how to provide for the acquisition of the vast lands hitherto not organized by white settlers. The Northwest Ordinance passed by the Continental Congress in 1784 and then reenacted under the federal government of the United States established the principle that the new lands were to be acquisitions in common, given republican constitutions and prepared for statehood with congressional and senatorial representation to follow the intermediate stage of becoming a "territory." The ordinance became in effect the spatial constitution of the new country—establishing an ambiguous guarantee of indigenous rights, as well as inscribing what would become the first ten amendments in the federal charter.[17]

Enhancing territorial consciousness probably involved more than administrative reform. Territory as a political resource for nationality could be self-evident for an island or a region long tucked within a recognized frontier, but it was problematic and contested in many cases. What allowed the triadic identification of state, land, and sense of an overriding public community known as a nation to become far more cohesive in the nineteenth century?[18] Enlightenment and revolutionary ideologies of public participation in government provided one impetus. Democratic claims originated in a given space even if their spokesmen claimed that they were based on rights that transcended any one territory: they inhered in humanity and not just in custom or historical precedent. Revolutionary constitutions were very different from so-called ancient constitutions. New regimes had to establish procedures for "naturalization," or the granting of citizenship, as did the United States. The idea of furnishing identity documents and passports took hold, as well.[19] Citizenship became in larger measure an appurtenance of residency certainly for those born within a national space. In Central European cities and even in a large state, such as the kingdom of Poland before its partition, citizenship had been a gradated quality, enjoyed fully only by a patrician or noble elite, meaningless for many simple laborers on the land. The simple peasant was often in effect a colonial subject at home. In the Ottoman lands it was gradated by religious affiliation; non-Muslims faced relative disabilities. In the societies of the Americas where slavery existed, such as the United States, Caribbean colonies, Brazil, and elsewhere, it was a set of privileges largely denied to people of African descent. Constitutional reform throughout the nineteenth century and into the twentieth century, often requiring revolution and war, was needed to abolish differentiated citizenship, and to declare that for most individuals their location was the decisive determinant of their legal status.

It was easier to legislate a new administrative ordinance than to ensure infrastructure. Here the railroad would contribute more decisively. Canals and roads had been improved through the eighteenth century and especially in the decades before the Revolution but they required winds, currents, or animal muscles. By 1836 there were 34,500 kilometers of roadway; however, they retained a languidness, for all the territory they might cover. By the opening of the railroad age, say, 1840, half of the freight traffic within France was carried by road and half by waterway, shared roughly equally between internal routes (canal and river) and by coastal shipping *(cabotage)*. Still, navigable waterways, though less unequally distributed between north and south than roads could contribute to economic growth only along water axes. Only in the Paris basin was the density of development sufficient to liberate the territory from a linear dependence, such that small towns could prosper throughout.[20]

It is not surprising then that the railroad promised much for the national state. But it was not because of simple economic growth. Ever since Albert Fishlow and Robert Fogel's work of the 1960s, economic historians have tended to downplay the direct gain or economic savings contributed by railroads. If some setback had destroyed the nineteenth-century railroad networks, cliometric calculations suggest that GNP might have fallen by 4–6 percent in Belgium, the United States, Russia, and Germany, and up to 18 to 25 percent in Spain and Mexico. The social savings increased as rail lines increased and travel became more efficient. Alternative water routes—navigable rivers and canals, say, in France or coastal shipping in Italy—meant that savings varied by geography. Water routes (not roads, however) could carry the heavy bulk traffic (coal, ore) that railroads also made possible. Still, "nowhere in Europe did railways make the difference between development and stagnation."[21]

Such calculations, however, capture too little of the transformative impact of the rail networks. A similar problem emerges when measuring the direct productivity gains provided by computers; these seem surprisingly low, even though it defies imagination to think that these technologies have not profoundly transformed life. We live in networked societies; as the developed world of 1900 lived in a world where the railroad journey was taken for granted. No matter how the economic impact be measured, the railroad was the emblematic technology of the nineteenth-century nation-state. Although local loyalties to city or province, *pays* or *Heimat,* could persist and even ease the transition to wider allegiances, state authorities felt a heightened need to knit together the reaches of the nation by rapid and smoother communication.[22] The forty years of network development from 1850 to 1890 coincided with the decades constructing and reconstructing nations, often through war. The energetic elites of Europe and the Americas claimed new territories and consolidated those that had been nominally within their frontiers—vast frontier regions far from their original sites of settlement: prairies and steppes or remote highlands and river-pierced interiors. They reaffirmed central authority at the expense of semiautonomous magnates on the perimeter. They constructed cross-class connections, knitting together old titled aristocrats with up-and-coming industrialists in the new subscriptions to railroad companies, making a national territory plausible both by extending distant lines or building dense networks around central "hubs."

The reverse also held—the increased "capacity" for mastering or penetrating territory in terms of resources, of communication throughout its area, of enhancing its cultural claims, was to become itself a condition for the emergence and growth of nationalism. Intensified territoriality was empowering. Territory was no longer merely a container but a source of communal energy and self-realization. Arguing in 1859 for an end to restrictions on economic enterprises in the German Confederation, A. E. F. Schäffle wrote that "economic energy" must be allowed to flourish unconditionally in any degree and in any place to achieve the freest unleashing of "national economic energy."[23] Railroad development had to be spatial and national. An early advocate of economic development, such as Carlo Cattaneo, still thought in terms of railroads for Lombardy, but Friedrich List, who during his early U.S. residence was influenced by Alexander Hamilton's concept for an American commercial future protected by tariffs, called for a "national system" of political economy to stand up to the industrial lead that Britain had exploited for its own powerful export energies.[24] Somewhat counterintuitively, Prussian civil servants exploited their free-trade orientation—which alongside political liberalism dominated policy in the late 1850s and 1860s—to strengthen German nationalism vis-à-vis Habsburg protectionism.[25] Whether believers in the ultimate power of free trade, or convinced that homeland industries required protection, entrepreneurs associated economic progress with a national space. For the bankers, bureaucrats, and entrepreneurs who were seizing a share of leadership in the 1850s and 1860s throughout the Western world, political territory had become the underlying framework for industrial strategies. What the appropriate scale of that territorial base should be, however, would remain open for debate. Ultimately, nations carried the day as the imputed spatial scaffolding for industrializing Europe and then for cultures outside Europe. Nationalism was an export product.

Railroads quickly became, openly or not, state projects. Eighteenth-century administrators believed that agricultural productivity was crucial for sustaining state and society. The Netherlands and Britain and later the United States believed that commercial seaborne success was also critical and maintained the naval power they believed necessary for successful maritime ventures. Railroads, too, were urgent for strategic needs, as the Prussians understood early on and the French learned painfully in the war of 1870. Nation-states were reknit in midcentury by virtue of heightened international competition.[26] Technology provided new opportunities for the application of military power, such that state prestige, national purpose, territorial maintenance, and railroad projects (along with telegraph and steamships) could no longer be divorced, even if states supposedly abjured ownership of the rails. But how should they be paid for? Private investment was never enough; nor were the great finance houses of London—so important for loans the world over—an unlimited resource. The railroad demanded state subsidies even when private companies had the right to build the lines. Tax and tariff and resource policy had to be shaped—and in effect new national-financial policies developed. The railroads were necessary for the nation; a more centrally organized and activist nation necessary for the railroads. This was as true for

France, Italy, Argentina, Canada, and the United States as for Germany and later Russia.[27]

Early rail projects in the 1830s and 1840s attracted authorities who wanted short prestige lines and investors who envisaged a source of commercial success alongside canals, rivers, and roads. In Britain, Parliament authorized the expropriation of land, rural and urban, needed for right-of-way. The legislature repealed the Bubble Act in 1825, allowing investors to organize corporations without an act of parliament or royal charter. But to buy or expropriate land still required parliamentary approval. Landowners resisted the cutting up of their estates, the intrusion of surveyors and crude construction gangs, the interruption of the hunt, and the competition for canals. Companies had to buy off noble landowners in particular, but negotiate continuously—some gentry understood how to extract very high prices for patches of land. The Eastern County Railway paid Lord Petre the grand sum of £120,000 for a small tract—he sold not only acreage as proprietor but his ongoing influence in the Lords. If no agreement was reached with landowners, the companies could appeal to juries where they might finally be authorized to seize the right-of-way for a stipulated price. Railroad agents insisted they paid more than the lands were worth; by the mid-1840s, landlords felt they were being coerced. Small proprietors felt they did not have the bargaining power of the larger gentry; the railroad companies felt that the sheriffs' juries would side with their local owners. But despite an escalation of claims and counterclaims, the general upshot was a cash settlement both sides could agree on.[28] The railroad firms insisted that absolute property rights did not exist. A country that probably protected property more effectively than any other in Europe was now lectured that land was entrusted to its proprietors for the common good. "The prevailing necessity of the time is that the public should have certain and rapid communication . . . and railways are the medium by which, according to the universal public voice, that necessity shall be accommodated."[29]

As with so many celebrated schemes, the promise of railroads was accompanied by a great deal of shabby dealing, undercapitalized schemes, hollow-shell companies, incompetent organizers, and, in Britain, perhaps above all by lawyers. Oversubscribed companies came crashing down in 1825, slowly recovered, and produced a new boom; by July 1836 eighty-eight new joint-stock companies were selling shares, many without the needed parliamentary go-ahead—only to crash again in the second half of that year. The process repeated itself. As late as 1844, a Lancashire MP recalled that "a good many railway schemes" were marked by "more fraud and felony that he had never heard of before in connexion with public matters." Another member said, "One of the grossest frauds ever perpetrated had been called a railway company."[30] Organizers escaped civil or criminal jurisdiction. None of which prevented another significantly larger bubble in 1844–1845, as more than a thousand new joint-stock companies were sold to an eager public. "The whole population of the empire was infected by the railway mania. Like a fever it spread through every rank."[31]

From the end of the 1840s on, railroad development became ever more an instrument of national strategy. Earlier chapters have followed territory as the basis for sovereignty and security and for surplus and wealth. The railroads promised to draw both sorts of yield from territory. They depended on state support, but they were conducive to constructing national regimes. Three hundred years earlier, border fortifications embodied the idea of the frontier that represented sovereignty. In the mid-nineteenth century, the emerging railroad networks instantiated the creation of a national territory, denser and more extensive. Consider the countries that worked out their modern territorial form even as railroad mileage advanced decisively in the 1850s and 1860s. This did not mean that private interests counted for less than, say, in Britain. Equivalent profit seeking and legal manipulation marked United States railroad development, as Richard White has amply demonstrated.[32] Still, granted all the flimflam behind the stock offering and the testosterone-fueled search for wealth and influence on the part of the railroad magnates, given the fusion of railroad capitalism with public governmental agency (whether for giving out land, putting down strikes, or rewarding financiers, it is still possible to view this chapter within a different perspective. From the first decades of the new republic, American politicians evoked a future nation spanning the continent. By the time John L. O'Sullivan, the editor who coined the phrase *Manifest Destiny,* wrote sixty years later, "The far reaching, the boundless future will be the era of American greatness," with a "magnificent domain of space and time,"[33] it was apparent that the American realm must depend on technological sinews to bind together east and west, just as it depended on the great draining rivers of the Mississippi and its tributaries to bind north and south in the preceding half century. (See the *American Progress* illustration.)

A few alternative concepts of continental railroad development contended in the United States of the 1850s. The east-west links to California—the Union Pacific and the Southern Pacific—have captured most attention because of their dramatic completion in 1869, but the effort to connect Oregon and the mouth of the Columbia with the Mississippi was just as compelling for Asa Whitney, a merchant returned from China.[34] Whitney looked to acquire a trans-Mississippi area that it would run as an inland empire. His railroad, he predicted, "would revolutionize the entire commerce of the world; placing us directly in the centre of all . . . all must be tributary to us."[35] At the same time, an alternative imperial vision bound the Mississippi to the Caribbean with a renewed dependency on black slavery. Matthew Fontaine Maury, a staunch defender of Southern slaveholding and cotton interests (he served as the Naval Observatory's hydrographer and notably analyzed Gulf Stream currents before resigning to superintend Confederate Virginia's coastal defenses), envisioned a conjoined Amazon and Mississippi continental space linked through the Caribbean as an inland sea, and advocated a transcontinental Memphis to Monterrey railroad.[36]

In a still-fragmented Italy, policy makers were convinced that railroads were critical both for the existing states and any national unification in the future. Piedmont was the state that had the most advanced network by the time it attempted unsuccessfully to oust the Austrians from neighboring Lombardy in 1848. Carlo Pettiti's 1845 tract on railroads urged the regime to take charge of organizing them and helping them raise capital. Camillo Cavour, the key statesman of unification in the next decade read Pettiti with approval, although he argued for a larger role by joint-stock companies.[37] The great Lombard liberal federalist and revolutionary participant in 1848, Carlo Cattaneo, urged the states to develop their own lines; indeed, this followed through the 1850s. Austria meanwhile built a railway system designed to integrate its Italian possessions into an empire based on Vienna, but including a Lombard network based on Milan and a connection between Vienna and Trieste. Unification of most of the peninsula by 1861 convinced Italy's founders that a national network north to south was required. A hodgepodge of private companies and state enterprises was finally consolidated by the railway act of 1865, which enjoyed support both among the rightist liberals and parliamentary Left. It formed five groups—one for Alta Italia or the north, one for the Tuscany and the south, others for Romagna and the center, and for the islands, Sardinia, and Sicily. Differing levels of development, local interests, and rising costs, meant that provisions were continually revisited, until finally the state took over the lines in 1885. A state-organized merger into one unified company followed only in 1905.[38]

Where the state did not own railroads directly, it had to come to their aid continuously. As the new Italian finance minister Silvio Spaventa minister of finances and then of public works reported to the Italian parliament in 1876, believers in the application of free-market principles to railways were deluded. Railroads were natural monopolies; they were in "perfect antithesis" to free completion. . . . There is no great company that can live without state aid and thus there is no way railway operation can even have the appearance of being a free and independent industry."[39] In Italy between 1865 and state takeover in 1885, the state provided the lines with a sliding-scale subsidy per kilometer, which tapered off as the railway revenues increased; in return, however, it profited from taxes and free travel. Only the Meridionali Railway Company really made it into the black; the Alta Italia was in continuous conflict over whether its operations in Austrian territory (a legacy of pre-1866) should count toward profits and taxes due. Wars and floods meant that the northern railways always needed more aid.[40] The governments of the unifiers were convinced that Italy needed extensive north-south lines. Their economic contribution was questionable since coastal shipping allowed Italy more transportation possibilities than many other countries, but visibly they seemed to be the arteries of unification.[41]

Still, railroads attracted investment only if there were promise of populating the country they were to serve. Population was dense in Britain from the outset and in the eastern United States and the Midwest by the 1850s, but certainly not in the almost two thousand miles that stretched from midcontinent to the Pacific shore. Congress had considered land grants to railways as early as 1833—direct financing was deemed unconstitutional and public ownership not an option—and passed its first act distributing land to Illinois and Alabama on behalf of the Illinois Central and Mobile and Ohio Railroad. Railroads received lands and subsidized loans—each of which roused both defenses of the largesse and criticism. The United States already had 31,000 miles of railway when the Civil War began, 35,000 when it ended. But in 1862 it voted for the

Pacific Railway Act, ostensibly to keep California in the Union, and it chartered a new corporation, the Union Pacific, Two years later it modified the law to provide further bonds. The Central Pacific and Union Pacific were left to compete for right-of-way by laying track—the former starting east from Sacramento, the latter west from Kansas City—to meet in 1869 at the setting of Promontory Point in Utah, where the famous golden spike was inserted.

———

As almost universally the case, the availability of public guarantees led to the trough of private enrichment. Richard White has followed the skullduggery of bribes, distribution of bonds, and whiskey consumed at Willard's Hotel that lay behind the lobbying. Congress's loan to the railroads had to be paid only at maturity in thirty years; meanwhile the government would pay the interest to private purchasers of the bonds, interest would be repaid only at maturity, and the government's own claim would be downgraded from a first to a second lien.[42] The British surveyor of the Argentine mountain routes explained a procedure that had variations in the American states, the French Second Empire and then the Third Republic, the United States, and Canada. "The [Argentine] Government of the day is importuned in all directions to grant concessions to its friends and supporters. . . . With this precious philosopher's stone (that is to turn everything into gold) in his pocket, the *concessionaire* rushes over to London, but does not always find a ready market for what he has to sell. If unsuccessful at first, as is usually the case, he then hawks his concession about the City and Westminster. . . . Numerous alterations are suggested, and the concessionaire is forced to return home to try and induce the Government to modify the terms of his contract in the way suggested."[43] In all countries public investment produced private wealth; intermediaries counted as sleazy, recipients as dignified. The larger the scale, the more dignified.

The American railway act provided that for every mile of right of way built, the railways were given twenty square miles of land with mineral rights, allocating land in alternate checkerboard patterns. By the end of the process in 1941, the federal grants amounted to more than three-quarters the equivalent of Texas; add in the state grants and the area was a bit bigger than California and Texas combined.[44] In fact, the bond guarantees were probably worth more than the land.

Canada had to contend with the same great distances as the United States. As a national and imperial creation, it was as closely dependent on the organization and construction of railroads as any country in the world. Major initiatives were undertaken at two major points: the late 1840s and 1850s, and again in the 1870s. Railroad development was a strategic factor in a complex set of interests. The Colonial Office wanted to encourage private British loans for Canadian railroads to preserve the imperial tie, but budget constraints limited the extent of an interest-rate guarantee, and in pure financial terms British investments in the United States were far greater than in Canada. Railroad development, however, represented more than just an economic opportunity to be weighed, but a strategic stake in preserving a restive and precarious colony whose settlers might be tempted to think of joining the United States.

Political solutions still ultimately depended on economic viability. Even as the union of upper and lower Canada was being enacted, Thomas Keefer's popular pamphlet, the *Philosophy of Railroads,* presented a parable of two villages, Sleepy Hollow mired in a pre-railroad hibernation, and a counterpart awakened into progress and enterprise by the trains it welcomed. The villages could be allegories for Montreal or Toronto, on the one hand, Boston or New York, on the other. Canadians had to work "as a people, through our government" to build a railway system.[45] Canals and the Saint Lawrence seemed to accommodate Canadian trade well enough in the early 1840s while the British still preserved preferential tariffs for the empire, but when free trade triumphed under the Whigs after 1846 (and the rivers froze in 1849), railroad construction to the ports of New York or Boston seemed urgent. The repeal of the Corn Laws (the grain tariff) in Britain in 1847 created a clear incentive for linking overseas wheat suppliers whether in Canada, the United States, or Russia to maritime ports and the expanded English market. Montreal's Anglo-Tory establishment, hostile to British reconciliation with the Francophone leaders of the Quebec's rebellion ten years earlier, was also raising the threat of seceding to the United States. Lord Elgin, the resident governor general, suggested a Halifax-Montreal railway line as an inducement to preserve Canadian loyalty. The Whig ministry in London, however, aspired to cheap government and was skeptical about the subsidies that would be required by Canadian railway development. If the mother country balked, the Canadians did not. An otherwise bitterly divided United Canada Legislative Assembly of 1849 overwhelmingly approved a loan guarantee act that ensured investors of a 6 percent return on bonds for any railroad at least half completed and planned for a minimum of at least 120 kilometers.[46] But the Halifax-Montreal plan intended to connect eastern Canada to the maritime provinces of New Brunswick, Nova Scotia and Prince Edward Island was dropped for the more alluring Grand Trunk railroad designed to link Montreal with Hamilton in Ontario. The Grand Trunk project, however, might have helped develop Canada's midwest, but offered only an indirect outlet to the sea and itself became financially overextended by the 1850s.

Perhaps the answer was an even more grandiose plan extending even farther west. Construct a country large enough to justify a national railroad! As Edward Watkin, the British manager who tried to consolidate refinancing in London, wrote, the Grand Trunk "is both too extensive, and too expensive for the Canada of today." The alternative was to build westward, lest the country and Britain, too, become hostage to U.S. rail routes: "Try for one moment to realize China opened to British commerce; Japan also opened: the new gold fields in our own territory on the extreme west, and California, also within our reach: India, our Australian Colonies—all our eastern Empire, in fact, material and moral, and dependent upon an overland communication, through a foreign state. . . . Try to imagine again, a main through railway, of which the first thousand miles belonging to the Grand Trunk Company, from the shores of the Atlantic to those of Pacific, made just within—as regards the northwestern and unexplored district—the corn-growing latitude. The result to this Empire would be beyond calculation; it would be something, in fact, to distinguish the age itself, and the doing of it would make the fortune of the Grand Trunk."[47] Barings in London remained skeptical, and Watkin had to resign.

Delegates at the 1862 intercolonial conference at Quebec agreed to extend the Halifax–Quebec railway to the Pacific. The British, however, were less interested in dreams of a connection to the Pacific than in cementing the links between the united Canadian provinces with the still unfederated Atlantic maritime colonies. London, moreover, controlled the west through the Hudson's Bay Company, which was organized to exploit the fur trade, not to develop grain production. The British government demanded Canadian authorization for the Maritimes' railway in the east (Halifax–Nova Scotia) as a quid pro quo for turning over the western territory. However, the attractiveness of ties to the Unites States continued to grow in the Canadian west; by 1864 Victoria, on Vancouver Island in British Columbia was linked by telegraph to San Francisco. Time was pressing; the United States seemed poised to subdue its Southern states' rebellion and resume its expansion westward—a Canadian nation and a transcontinental railroad had to be projected together. It would take the formation of the dominion in 1867, the cession of the Hudson's Bay's residual territorial rights, and the opening of the western provinces to agree to a Pacific railroad: the iron road progressed in tandem with national (and imperial) awareness. Watkin himself lost his bid to make the Grand Trunk the key link; instead, the newly organized Canadian Pacific would get the guarantees needed, which, as in the United States to the south, consisted of generous land grants alongside the rails.

In the heated historiography of railroads, the central issue raised by the Canadian and U.S. land grants was whether they were needed: Was "building ahead of demand" justified or just a subvention for the already wealthy? Of course, the grants amounted to a tremendous enrichment of well-placed capitalists and bankers. But in the absence of any willingness to make railroad construction a state enterprise, the logic seemed compelling. Transcontinental railroads transformed unsettled territory into a real national asset. Since it required capital to build these lines, why not privatize, say, 5 percent of the territory to be transformed to achieve the development of it all?[48] There are rarely unambiguous answers to the question, *Cui bono?*

As with earlier projects that addressed the promise of appropriating wealth from land, the key to reaping a return was to have the territory that the railways served attract a stable workforce. Railroad lines might serve to link mines and agricultural depots with distant markets, but settlers would also be needed. For Matthew Maury in the pre–Civil War South, that meant expanding a slave labor force; for the northern states and the Canadians, it meant giving free farmers inexpensive land. The massive tracts that Canadians and U.S. legislatures awarded to the rail companies should be viewed alongside the Homestead Act of 1862, which culminated a long-held aspiration of the new Republican Party. Any adult who had not taken up arms against the United States could gain title for 160 acres (one quarter of a square mile) at $1.25 acres per acre provided he improved the land and continued in residence for five years. The rail-roads also involved importing labor as well as settling farmers—immigrants to the United States eventually from southern and eastern Europe and from China and Japan, to add to those from Ireland and Germany (and of course Africa) earlier. Secretary of State William H. Seward signed the Burlingame Treaty of 1868 to admit Chinese coolie labor for work on the Pacific railway and the western mines and celebrated America's expansion toward Asia. In South America, European migrants toiled on the construction projects. The railroads knit together countries by virtue of their needs for labor as well as the transportation they later provided. Even as they filled out national territories, they combined local land with British capital and workers from the great labor reserves of Asia and the peripheries of Europe.

Few enthusiasts objected that there was a population to be exported as well as one to be imported. The remaining problem was clearing out the aboriginals. Much of the land allocated was on tracts supposedly reserved for Indians: treaties were pushed through by which tribal agents sold their tracts to the companies. Despite their sparse population, their periodic armed resistance to white expansion along the railroad lines threatened the projects of settlement, certainly in the United States and Argentina. "The questions concerning the frontiers have always been among the most difficult that the Argentine Government had to deal with, nor was it till recently that the matter was taken in hand with a firm grasp," wrote a major British engineer about his experience in organizing Argentine railroad construction in the early 1870s. The problem of the frontier had always been acute for the South American nation. Half of the country was occupied by Indians and "therefore as only belonging to the Republic in theory."[49] The Argentine administration was to take the problem in hand by genocidal policies in the 1880s, and the United States and Canada would turn to resettlement in reservations. The railroads, moreover, did not contribute just to the macro-geography of the great lands of the Americas, but to their micro-geography, as well. They made a start at filling space: freight cars had to be moved from one line to another and trains reorganized at stations and roundhouses. There was to be a station every eight miles, so that farmers could bring their crops to a depot and return home within a day. The stations aggregated settlements. Indeed, the large stations in the big cities were areas of potential lawlessness and were an inducement to expansion of police forces, including

America's private militias of strikebreakers and labor enforcers organized by the Pinkerton agency.[50]

In 1877–1878 the National Conservatives succeeded to power in the Canadian Confederation organized a decade earlier, and with them came the project for a tariff (as almost every country but Britain would institute between the 1860s and the 1890s) and a railroad to the Pacific. Canada's "spike" would be hammered in 1885, and the Canadian Pacific became a symbol of the national epic, as the fur traders had been two centuries earlier. Tariff and railroad together allowed the national government to wean Canadian traffic from the south of the Great Lakes routes and the Saint Paul, Manitoba line. It opened the west for grain; it broke the monopoly of the Hudson's Bay Company, which ceded its giant territories to the Canadian government in 1870. It represented a giant nation: as the later Canadian theorist of his country's development, Harold Innis would affirm, the great railroad succeeded the fur trade and the canoe in uniting environment, technology, and nationalism. Large countries were different from small—they could revel (as had U.S. citizens) in their vastness and the good fortune that they were at the top of the Darwinian chain of states. "Small kingdoms are marked out by the destinies of the world for destruction," Lord Salisbury declared in 1871, twenty years before he administered Britain's empire. "The great organizations and greater means of locomotion of the present day mark out the future to be one of great empires."[51]

Continentalism

Chevalier had suggested early on that railroads seemed destined to make continental landmasses as well as nation-states a coherent unit for development. Even before rail travel went beyond the purely local level, the continent had begun to serve the geographical imagination of the nineteenth century as the oceans had in the three centuries after Columbus. There was an important difference: the oceans remained a passage to islands or distant shores, whereas the continent—if more than desert waste—could become a space for exploration, settlement, and conquest. The continent incorporated the aesthetics of "the sublime" that late Enlightenment thinkers had sought to define. The sublimity of the continent lay in the vastness that might be settled and the vertical heights so hard to conquer, but so compelling to depict. The artists and photographers who accompanied the explorers into the American and Canadian west had a "capacity for wonder" that matched the Tahitian dream of eighteenth-century mariners in the Pacific.[52] The plains were to be civilized, their peoples to be absorbed or made to disappear by one means or another as if by some hazy genocidal euthanasia.

Continental exploration took off in the age of Romanticism with Lewis and Clark and Alexander von Humboldt, among others, but continued into the age of positivism and science, with measurements of height and distance, weather, magnetism, rock formation. In the United States, the presidency of James K. Polk, with its acquisitions of immense western territory, encouraged a geopolitical fantasizing. The great agricultural interior of the country drained by the Mississippi and its tributaries and thus connecting to the Columbia river system and the Pacific coast ("the maritime wing of the Mississippi Valley upon the Pacific, as New England was on the Atlantic"), made the American continent both a barrier and a bridge between Europe and Asia according to William Gilpin, an admirer of Polk's annexationism.[53] The railroad promoters did not stint in their projections. For Matthew Maury, Americans had to think in terms of great circle routes, not Mercator's parallels of latitude. The transcontinental development of the enlarged U.S. South would link via the Caribbean to a Panama canal: "I regard the Pacific railroad and a commercial thoroughfare across the Isthmus as links in the same chain . . . these two works . . . are not only necessary fully to develop the immense resources of the Mississippi valley . . . but would place the United States on the summit level of commerce." Break down the land barrier that separated the United States from the markets of three quarters of the earth's population, and the Gulf of Mexico "becomes the centre of the world and the focus of the world's commerce."[54] Central to Maury's vision was the role of enslaved African labor in exploiting the resources of the Amazon and the Mississippi alike. In Canada, as noted, Edward Watkin was promising a continental link between Asia and Europe to leap over the threatening bankruptcy of the Grand Trunk: bail out the railroad, and "the result to this Empire would be beyond calculation; it would be something, in fact, to distinguish the age itself."[55]

Continental linkages envisaged as part of global space exerted their own appeal aside from the profits to be made, but the scale of capitalist investments and exchange kept pace. The globe was arriving at a renewed era of imperial expansion, and the railroad was critical. This was recognized by the railroad propagandists in Latin America as well. In 1868 Guillermo Rawson petitioned the Argentine Congress to authorize a Trans-Andean railroad, which would bring to the western plains of Argentina the wealth that U.S. railroads had already brought to Indiana, Illinois, Michigan, and Iowa. For the Pacific republics (Argentina and Chile) the Trans-Andean would establish solid links and "must be without dispute the most efficacious route for its gigantic development—a thousand times preferable to all existing routes," whether Cape Horn, the Panama Isthmus, Suez, and even the U.S. transcontinental line that was scheduled to be completed imminently.[56]

The Argentine Congress authorized Juan and Mateo Clark to build the lines west to Mendoza and then to the Chilean frontier. Over a decade later, however, the project was still stalled over British financial concerns, but also disagreement over which Andean pass to cross and which regions they would service, whether the Pampas or the Cuyo region farther west.[57] Benjamín Vicuña Mackenna, indefatigable propagandist, journalist, and later unsuccessful presidential candidate in Chile renewed the plea for the interocean line. Chile (following a generalized global economic crisis) had slipped into recession in the 1870s and early 1880s as production and prices fell for copper and wheat. Meanwhile the United States had hammered in its golden spike, and the North Americans were planning to span the isthmus of Panama. Chile and Argentina must embark on a railroad from Santiago to Mendoza (there to join the line to Buenos Aires). What had delayed the grand project but "the shared guilt of inertia . . . the eternal mañana of our race!"[58]

The very competent British engineer Robert Crawford allowed himself to share the enthusiasm: he urged crossing the Andean summit by Nahuel Huapi "at the wonderfully low level of 2756 feet above the sea . . . then to Valdivia on the Pacific . . . the best port in Chile." Settlements would follow, "which by comparison, would dwarf all the existing colonies of La Plata, flourishing though they be. . . . Indian invasions [would] cease . . . and then a glorious era would begin for the Argentine Republic, over whose fertile plains the bone and sinew of the overpopulated states of Europe would soon spread out in amazing number, unchecked by the dread of an unprotected frontier."[59]

What did it signify that the railroads had to be built by the industrializing countries of North America and Europe? Railroads in the United States, Britain, Germany, and eventually elsewhere in Europe, Japan, and belatedly China, contributed to the vertical integration of an iron and steel economy. Elsewhere, at least for a generation, they had to be built by outsiders. Historians have described the dominant role of foreign capital as "railway imperialism," and in countries where rail lines were planned and constructed by the colonial power, as in India, the term can be justified. The British endowed the subcontinent to unify the Raj strategically. Elsewhere the colonial power built roads to bring the products of the interior to ocean ports. The Germans crossed the Shandong Peninsula after claiming their concession of Kiaochow (Jiaozhou) and tried to dominate the Chinese market for locomotives.[60] By the end of the century, the Germans and Turks envisaged an Ottoman railway network from Istanbul to Baghdad and Basra that they would construct and maintain that could benefit each empire. For German enthusiasts, including the emperor, the enterprise promised to project strategic power throughout southeastern Europe and the Islamic world even as it would cut travel time to India to less than what the Suez route required. The stakes became even higher as farsighted naval and other planners realized that oil must replace coal as the fuel for future navies.[61] Within a decade the Germans had to accept sharing this strategic and economic pathway with the British in Mesopotamia and the French in Lebanon. Imperialist expansion was potentially evolving into what Karl Kautsky termed "super-imperialism," a cartel of the European powers to share in the exploitation of the huge territories in Asia and Africa.[62] Railroads could make that shared domination a reality even as they increased the viability for defense and extraction within each particular colony. Still, the concept of railroad imperialism flattens out the great divergences of dependence and independence. For countries with proud and touchy awareness of their own sovereignty, as in Latin America, the concept oversimplifies. It also underestimates how the would-be railroad builders had to come to terms with local regimes, whether the ancient and nuanced mechanisms of Ottoman rule, or the proud and irritable stance of the Argentinians. Foreign capital and engineering did not diminish their own contribution to a sense of national advance. They created relations of economic dependency but all the while remained dependent in turn on local decision making as to charters, subsidies, and routing.[63]

The principle of the continent is similar to that of imperial space as discussed in chapter one: its hugeness implies the impermanence of ordinary state boundaries, and instead the ever-onward beckoning of wealth and space. Kipling captured the mystique of the beckoning interior for Australia near the end of the nineteenth century:

"There's no sense in going further—it's the edge of
   cultivation,"
So they said, and I believed—broke my land and sowed
   my crop—
Built my bars and strung my fences in the little border
   station
Tucked away below the foothills where the trails run
   out and stop:
Till a voice, as bad as Conscience, rang interminable
   changes
On one everlasting Whisper day and night
   repeated—so:
Something hidden. Go and find it. Go and look behind
   the Ranges—
"Something lost behind the Ranges. Lost and waiting
   for you. Go!"
Ores you'll find there; wood and cattle; water-transit
   sure and steady
(That should keep the railway rates down), coal and
   iron at your doors.
God took care to hide that country till He judged His
   people ready,
Then He chose me for His Whisper, and I've found it,
   and it's yours!
Yes, your "Never-never country"—yes, your "edge of
   cultivation"
And "no sense in going further"—till I crossed the
   range to see.
God forgive me! No, *I* didn't. It's God's present to our
   nation.

> Anybody might have found it, but—His Whisper came
> to Me![64]

As Kipling sensed, the railroad and the great rivers were integral to the continental vocation. (Five years earlier he had written a poem on the capacity of "The Deep-Sea Cables" to unify mankind: his railroads, however, were for domination not fraternity.)

"Never-never country," the term Kipling borrowed that was used for the Australian interior, was an appropriate designation for railroad continentalism in the years that J. P. Barrie's *Peter Pan,* with its "Neverland" (staged 1904) filled with pirates and crocodiles, charmed London audiences. It had the same quality that Baum's "Oz" possessed—childhood fantasy, and the overcoming of space with almost magical transportation. Such continentalism could not really be envisaged without the idea of empire. Granted, the envisaged empires could be justified in terms of economic progress—the railroad allowed a coalition between dominators and developers in a relationship that would become particularly appealing in the twentieth century: In India, for example, one enthusiast explained relatively early on: "Every railway station becomes a market, to which the wealth of the soil is brought by the natives, and where it is sold to high profit, and where, in exchange, they can obtain all the newest products of modern civilization. A railway in an uncultured country is a social revolution, and, wisely conducted, is a measureless blessing to the people of the soil. The people travel and get knowledge; they labour and grow rich; their prejudices of caste and class and village disappear; they become, in short, cultured, educated, and civilized."[65] But far from self-governing.

Russian intellectuals were also awakening to the lure of continentalism. The first geographical encyclopedia, *Geographical-Statistical Dictionary of the Russian Empire,* edited by Pyotr Semyonov-Tyan'-Shanskij, an explorer of Central Asia, was published in 1876.[66] It prefigured an opening generation of "Eastern" enthusiasm. The Canadians and United States entrepreneurs looked west; Cecil Rhodes to the north; by the 1860s and 1870s, the Russians east. Not at first. The railroads—once they outgrew the tsar's little line from Saint Petersburg to the summer palace suburb of Tsarskoe Selo—were laid out to join the former to Moscow. This was the accomplishment of the 1840s and 1850s—a project that had to be contracted to German and British engineers and was entrusted to a military administrator. What resulted was not the capitalist hodgepodge of the British interurban lines, or the American baronial fusion of investors and legislative facilitators, but the project of an army and a bureaucracy. From Moscow the lines continued south to Odessa: imperial expansion was a project still fixed on Constantinople and control of the Black Sea. Military requisites meant that railroad development of the west—lines to Warsaw—were a priority: "When all other governments are crossed with railroads and gain the ability to focus their forces, bring them quickly from end [of the country] to the other, Russia will also need the same ability," wrote Aleksei Khomyakov as early as 1845. "It's difficult, expensive, but what can be done? It's necessary. . . . Communication between Moscow and the Baltic Sea in Petersburg is only the beginning, only a part of the transportation system that should criss-cross Russia. The final work will bring the full fruits, and that work is so big and its results will be so complex that it is impossible to even try to define them. . . . Russia is not yet trapped, as Europe in ancient times, by defunct lines and comfortable highways, and we will jump directly, so to say, without transition from our current general roadlessness to the most advanced roads."[67]

Expansion into the Turkic border regions helped shift the promise of the railroads to the East. A mission to the east or south required a railroad just as urgently as did defense of the European frontier. Dostoyevsky's fragments from 1881 signaled the connection: the Russian capture of the Turkomen stronghold at Geok-Tepe prompted a celebration of Russia's Asian vocation from Turkey to the Indian frontier, a mélange of resentment against a Europe who "under no circumstances . . . would believe that we can participate in the future destinies of their civilization." "She despises us whether secretly or openly; she considers us an inferior race" and a vision of expansion. "In Europe we were hangers-on and slaves, whereas we shall go to Asia as masters. In Europe we were Asiatics, whereas in Asia we, too, are Europeans. Our civilizing mission in Asia will bribe our spirit and drive us thither. . . . Build only two railroads: begin with the one to Siberia, and—to Central Asia,—and at once you will see the consequences."[68] At the same time the idea that Siberia would serve as the equivalent of an overseas colony for resettlement also become prominent. Nikolai Iadrentsev envisaged a new society taking shape in Siberia: lightly populated lands would play an enormous role in the future of humanity.

Ideas of Siberia had grown from a place for criminals, for mining or furs, to a productive constituent of western Russia."[69]

Such predictions, whether for Russia, South Africa, or Argentina, could not be justified in narrow financial terms. A year or so after Kipling wrote "The Explorer," Count Witte's financial ally, Adolf Rothstein, director of the Saint Petersburg International Bank, admitted that the Trans-Siberian project was not economically rational from the calculus of returns: "But nations appear to be sometimes possessed by an uncontrollable passion to bring together the uttermost ends of a continent, quite irrespective of rational motives. It is a kind of demon which drives them; and I can only suppose that the impulsion is intended to promote the general good of mankind." As the British publicist, William Thomas Stead, who was citing Rothstein, continued, the supposed material benefits of the Cape-to-Cairo line were also illusory: the proposed railroad "will not materially diminish the dimensions of the planet. After it is built no express will traverse the continent in less than eleven days. Add to this the four or five days between London and Cairo and we have fifteen or sixteen days for the overland route, as against seventeen or eighteen days by sea. Why the keenly practical and stolidly unimaginative Briton should be bending his energies and lavishing his resources in order to construct a line from Cape to Cairo, it is difficult to explain, except on the theory of Herr Rothstein—that the Providence that rules mankind has willed that the ends of the world should be linked together and that the continents should be bridged by the iron rail; and so, obedient to the Invisible Power behind the veil, mortal men hasten to carry out their appointed task."[70]

Stead understood that continentalism was indissolubly linked with ideas of domination. "It is true the railway, even when constructed, will not paint the African map British red from the Mediterranean to the Table Mountain. But it undoubtedly tinges the whole intervening region with the ruddy glow that heralds the dawn of empire." The origins of the line, Stead pointed out, lay almost entirely with Rhodes, and were intertwined with Rhodes's less famous, but at the time much more advanced, project for a transcontinental telegraph line. As of 1899 expectations were that the railway could be finished by 1909; however, only the telegraph line was anywhere close to completion. The long-distance telegraph had accompanied railroad space and, like the railroad, served both commerce and empire. Strategic and imperial concerns motivated the cables through the Indian Ocean as well as Rhodes's projected lines. The trans-Atlantic cable linked the more equal commercial centers. Both networks thickened together and began the transcendence of territory that we can associate with the "first" globalization between 1870 and 1914. "Especially along the axis from the North American East Coast via London and Europe in general and on to South Asia, communication space started to condense around 1870 at hitherto impossible rates. . . . By 1900 at the latest, the telegraph network had been developed to a degree where global communication space had been almost completely detached from geographic or navigational space."[71]

Nonetheless, these projects did not transcend concepts of territory, even though they opened up a new scale for what it might encompass by virtue of their continental imaginaries and embeddedness in imperial relations. They emancipated territory from localism and from place in the service of global capitalism and white dominion. As Samuel Verner explained to Americans in 1899, the Cape-to-Cairo line will mean that "the predominant English influence . . . will gradually pervade the whole and practically, if not formally, the Continent will be more Anglo-Saxon than America." Ultimately a "benevolent system of easy sovereignty, allowing and encouraging the largest possible amount of local self-government will retain the imperial connection" until the colonies were ready to "confederate into a republic, overshadowing all previous conceptions of government." For the conceivable future the relationship was clear: "Politically, the railway is intended to make Africa finally and predominantly British. If the Strait of Gibraltar were ever closed an enormous British colonial army could be thrown in seven days into Egypt from the south. . . . By the Cairo route the Cape could be reached in fourteen days, and all points along the line proportionately less. England will then have the three corner points of the African Triangle—the Niger, the Zambesi, the Nile. Military posts, manned by white soldiers, will spring up along the whole course of the line. . . . The domestic slave trade will cease. The native population will see the utter futility of resistance."[72] Slavery, in fact, was economically irrelevant for the Anglo-Americans; it served the domestic and sexual economies of the African interior, the Maghrib, and the Middle East. Collective contract labor had become the organizational form that brought needed African and South Asian workers to Western plantations and construction projects. Economic and racial hierarchies held firm without formal inherited servitude.

Even as Verner was writing, the African imperial dream was to bog down in the South African War. But the trans-Atlantic rapprochement of Anglo-Saxon domination—whose advocates envisioned under joint U.S. and British auspices a great racialized condominium—was taking more durable shape. The geographical space appropriate for these ambitions was no longer just the nation but the super-continent—or its eternal opposite, the global ocean envisaged in effect, as a counter-continent. Cables and ships were the instruments for activating that domain. That was the significance of the Anglo-American condominium that was envisaged by the turn of the new century, increasingly as a counterweight to an ominous giant Eurasia. For the theorists of geographic confrontation, of geopolitics, territory bifurcated into two encompassing global possibilities, sea and land, whose respective peoples confronted each other throughout history. Which would prevail? "A generation ago steam and the Suez canal appeared to have increased the mobility of sea-power relatively to land-power," Halford Mackinder, the advocate for political geography reflected in 1904. "Railways acted chiefly as feeders to ocean-going commerce. But trans-continental railways are now transmuting the conditions of land-power, and nowhere can they have such effect as in the closed heart-land of Euro-Asia, in vast areas of which neither timber nor accessible stone was available for road-making. . . . The spaces within the Russian Empire and Mongolia are so vast and their potentialities for population, wheat, cotton, fuel, and metals so incalculably great, that it is inevitable that a vast economic world, more or less apart, will there develop inaccessible to oceanic commerce."[73] The railroad called forth the continent—a territory vast and militarized, and obscurely threatening global domination.

Last Call for Territories

From the explorations of continental interiors (culminating in the race to the South Pole in 1911–1912), to the construction of transcontinental railroads and the stringing of under-ocean cables, likewise to the thickening networks of urban power and telephone wires, the great geospatial projects of the late nineteenth century deployed a geometry of lines and areas. They penetrated and they enclosed; they seized territory beyond the coastal strips, islands, and riverine shores they had seized in the early modern era. Non-European leaders and peoples had long constructed larger and smaller polities in the huge continental interiors. As they expanded inland before 1870, the Europeans appropriated polities that occupied relatively stable boundaries, redivided their own imperial and national units, muscled in on the Indian states of the subcontinent as the Mughal Empire disintegrated, established control over the Maghrib units that had gained autonomy from the Ottomans, and, in the case of Russia, pushed south into the Caucasus and Central Asian khanates. In Central Asia, Britain edged north from its Indian territories, both seeking decisive influence at a weak Persian court and drawing boundaries where the risks of colliding with other imperial contenders become too high. In 1873 the British and Russians jointly and hastily drew the boundaries of Afghanistan as a buffer state, then worked on refining it for almost twenty years. Between 1884 and 1885 between two thousand and three thousand members of the British Commission, soldiers, surveyors, and baggage handlers, crawled over the territory; by the 1890s the Pamir Boundary Commission defined the northeastern tongue of the country that extended to the Chinese border, only eight miles wide at its narrowest but separating the two contenders in the great game. Determining the boundary of Baluchistan (then in India and today in Pakistan) with Afghanistan took more than two years from 1894 to 1896; British and Afghans each brought about one thousand men. When tribes disagreed over the local lines, chiefs and elders swearing on the Koran traced the segments of boundaries.[74] In the 1880s British and French expanded into Southeast Asia, moving farther into Burma and the Indochinese kingdoms. Less boundary work was needed since Thailand served as a buffer between their outposts.

After 1882 the astonishing enterprise was the rapid "scramble" for Africa. Two conferences in Berlin within seven years marked the German transition from continental to imperial player.[75] In 1878 Bismarck presided as "honest broker" over the international effort to set limited frontiers to a Bulgaria that Russia helped pry loose from the Ottoman Empire and that

threatened to become Saint Petersburg's proxy in the Balkans. From November 1884 to February 1885 the chancellor presided over a second conference in Berlin that was designed to keep the edgy European colonial
powers from serious conflict over the great river deltas and coastal stations of West Africa. In theory Bismarck declared Germany had no interest in either of these regions: the Balkans were proverbially not worth
the bones of a Pomeranian grenadier; neither did Germany have any
wish to sponsor ambitious adventurers in steamy remote harbors. But, of
course, there always remained an interest in limiting the gains of others.
The balance of the European state system, of which unified Germany had
become a preeminent continental member, required equilibrium on its
Balkan perimeter where Russian ascendancy, Ottoman fragility, and
Austrian precariousness threaten to make any sudden change dangerous.
And by the mid-1880s, the competition for tribal African territory assumed strategic stakes for relations with Britain and France. Moreover, it
threatened the political balances within unified Germany that the chancellor was always rejiggering to keep his supremacy—challenged initially,
as he calculated, by Catholic resentments, but by the end of the 1870s
supposedly vulnerable to a doctrinaire left-liberal opposition and socialist
pretensions for working-class power. Germany, the chancellor declared
in 1878, was a satiated power. But the "security dilemma" of Europe's
great powers, each feeling continually vulnerable to combinations of the
others, meant that none could truly be happy with the status quo. The
finiteness of global territory made it an invidious resource. Territory for
the taking was running out; the African interior was the last unclaimed
reservoir except for the frozen wastes of Antarctica.[76]

The great expeditions into the African interior after the end of the
Napoleonic Wars established the vast stakes of play. Continentalism was
seductive the world over, whether nurtured by the great prairie and steppe
lands in the temperate northern latitudes, or the possible tropical and mineral resources of the equatorial belt. The regions washed by the Niger in
its long curved course from the border of today's Sierra Leone northeast
past Tombouctou in today's Mali, then southeast and south through
western Nigeria to the Gulf of Guinea attracted explorers in the 1820s
and 1830s. The French pushed inland and north from Senegal to Tombouctou and through the Sahara. Others of various nationalities trekked
south from Algeria and Libya, into Chad and toward the great lakes or

even the Nigerian coast at Lagos; still others sought the sources of the Nile into the Sudan. But these regions were not yet territories for the Europeans. David Livingstone pressed north from the Cape Colony, then east and west, for thirty years. In search of the aging missionary explorer, a British naval mission was to continue west from Lake Tanganyika into Portuguese coastal territory: the Congo still remained to be traveled from its southern sources out to its great delta. Finally in the mid-1870s Verney Lovett Cameron and Henry Morton Stanley established that the Congo was a single tremendous river draining the interior of central Africa.

The glory of exploration was hardly the only prize at stake. With the end of the trans-Atlantic slave trade between 1808 and the 1830s, local polities lost their utility as suppliers of African bodies for European slavers. But the chance to control native labor power in situ and extract resources—whether diamonds and gold, eventually copper and rubber, so important for transportation innovations—beckoned a new cohort of rapacious but often talented adventurers. At this point the major asset that native kings could provide was precisely the surrender of their locally recognized political preeminence, which the Europeans translated as sovereignty according to the formalized usages they had defined over the preceding centuries. African chiefs and monarchs would come to understand after the fact that what the Europeans claimed they were getting by treaty was a degree of power different from what the rulers believed they had been asked to approve.

Sovereignty within Europe implied the right to limit trade and investment on the part of foreigners, and tariff protection rose in the 1870s after an intervening period of trade liberalization. But for claims staked overseas, the economic rights of exclusion were more contested. The continental European colonizers sought exclusive trading access as part of their political prerogatives as did the Japanese in their later East Asian claims. But the need to preclude trade and investment barriers seemed essential for their rivals, the British in Africa, and by 1900, the Americans in China. The asymmetrical objectives were to be a major factor in global politics from 1880 to 1905.

Political control was the key to economic exploitation. It varied in method and degree. In modern times, the British had been cajoling and conquering the major territorial rulers under the Mughal umbrella to cede practical control of their states to the East India Company. Indeed the

Mughal emperor had granted the major administrative office of Bengal, the diwani, to the company and from 1757 (following the great contest over Canada and India in the Seven Years' War), the company assumed the rights of coinage, signing treaties, and making war, for another century with the acquiescence of the British state. In China after 1842, later in nominally Ottoman territories (or those of the Maghrib where quasi-independent rulers gained control), the Europeans and later Americans wrested particular privileges—sometimes extraterritorial jurisdictions within a larger state whose ultimate suzerainty over their enclave was still recognized (as in China), sometimes legal privileges for their nationals (capitulations), sometimes leases, sometimes control over finances and tax collecting (as in the Ottoman Empire or Persia). Occasionally when a preexisting state enjoyed recognition by European standards, control over its foreign and/or financial policy was claimed under the status of protectorate, but European colonizers such as de Brazza also described the treaties for transfer of sovereignty from African chiefs as protectorates, as did the French in Tunisia in 1883.[77]

Terms can be contested as to meaning, but establishing a significantly new regime over a landed territory usually entailed a claim of sovereignty. Transfers of sovereignty were hardly new; they had many ancient and recent precedents. The monarchs of Prussia, Austria, and Russia had absorbed the territory of the kingdom of Poland (and eliminated its shrinking claim to statehood) in the late eighteenth century. The French Republic and then the French Empire temporarily absorbed the Austrian Netherlands (Belgium), the Dutch United Provinces, German territories to the west of the Rhine and ultimately along the North Sea, the Swiss cantons, a good part of Hanover (as the duchy of Westphalia), and increasing chunks of Italy, including the republic of Venice and the kingdom of Savoy. The European wars between 1859 and 1871 saw further elimination of sovereign units within Italy and the significant redistribution of territories among recognized nations.

When Europeans and white Americans confronted indigenous polities or tribal units that they subdued by force, they either claimed supremacy by conquest, or by treaty, which could be imposed by conquest or threat of force. Conquest, obviously, had led to boundary changes since history was recorded. But sovereignty could also be purchased. Indeed, if sovereignty, as we have seen, meant control of economic surplus, why should it not be bought or sold? Sovereignty and wealth, political control, and economic returns were fungible—prerogatives that were rooted in territorial control. The young United States purchased the Louisiana Territory and later would pay to acquire the Gadsden Purchase, Alaska, and the Danish Virgin Islands. And if sovereignty could be sold to states, why not, by the rights of property that the bourgeois liberal legal order of nineteenth-century states so prided, to individuals or to corporations? The Dutch and the British, then the French and the Russians, very briefly the Austrians, devolved political powers on trading companies in the seventeenth and eighteenth centuries. The British revoked the writ of the East India Company only after the Indian "mutiny" in 1858.

Moreover, why should sales of sovereignty be surprising when legally enforced individual control over other individuals' personal rights, that is, slavery—including the rights of corporal punishment, forced deportation, family separation, and ownership of descendants—had been bought and sold for millennia? General agreement and British enforcement had largely terminated the trans-Atlantic shipment of Africans for New World plantations between 1808 and the 1830s, but the capture and transportation of Africans east and north across the continent to Ottoman and Asian destinations was still taking place vigorously through the second third of the century. Slavery itself was ending in the British Empire in 1833, in the French colonies in 1848, in the United States after the Civil War; but contract migrant labor delegated legal rights to control labor to private purchasers. Could not a local chief transfer rights over territory as well as over persons—and to private individuals, not just official bodies?

Nineteenth-century societies devoted tremendous energy to drawing clear legal lines. But for all the pretensions of the bourgeois liberal era, the possibilities for economic gain continued to muddy them. Where did the possibilities for privatization and acquisition begin and end? The search for acquisition of sovereignty by private purchase was renewed when Europeans and Americans encountered the tribal polities of the Southeast Asian archipelagos and of sub-Saharan Africa. The pattern, Steven Press suggests, began in Borneo, where in the 1840s the sultan of Brunei was pressured into ceding sovereign rights (including legislation and revenue collection) to the English adventurer James Brooke. By the mid-1860s, two Americans, one of whom began as consul to Brunei, had leased political as well as economic rights in nearby Sabah in Borneo, again from the sultan of Brunei. Eventually, as was often the case, the original adventurers being short on funds, sold their rights. Via a German intermediary, the firm of Alfred Dent in London acquired the lease and sought Foreign Office protection of its leased polity. Dent's plea was still being weighed when the anticolonialist Gladstone came to power in 1880 and to general astonishment opted to charter what would be the North Borneo Company. The idea of giving a private for-profit company the rights of sovereignty, he explained to Parliament, of life and death, legislation, or raising an army was "frightful," but since Dent's enterprise already existed as a state, better to regulate the outcome. The new North Borneo Company, he did stipulate, had to yield foreign-policy decisions to London when it requested.[78]

With the penetration of Africa, possibilities for the acquisition of territory by outsiders were suddenly augmented, perhaps for the last time. The Borneo example, Press demonstrates, was contagious and soon justified acquisitions in Africa, first by Leopold II, king of the Belgians since 1865, then by other national explorers, and soon by Bismarck. Most of the explorers and freebooters who flocked to African shores aspired to have their home country give them retroactive support and take over their rights for a profit. Verney Cameron returned from his exploration with a valise full of treaties by native chiefs supposedly recognizing the sovereignty of Queen Victoria. The Foreign Office and cabinet were skeptical about their validity. But Leopold had his own grand ambitions; faced with his parliament's reluctance to get involved in distant and expensive ventures, he wanted to acquire and run a private state. The profits that neighboring Holland had drawn from the cultivation system of de facto coerced labor in Java were a goad to his own frenetic manipulations; he would use the Borneo model of acquired (and then recognized) sovereignty to extract vast profits. Henry Morton Stanley, famed for his explorations and "finding" of David Livingstone, who became Leopold's PR agent and buyer of treaties, argued that international law agreed that local rulers could sell the rights of sovereignty and exploitation of their land and mines,[79] even as Leopold's agents energetically accumulated hundreds of titles. These treaties transferred sovereignty not to other states, but to employees of Leopold and to German and British trading companies. Leopold was himself a European ruler, but was collecting claims of African sovereignty, not for Belgium but on his own account and, so he claimed, for scientific and humanitarian ends.[80]

With the approval of the Germans, Leopold summoned what became known as the Brussels Conference in September 1876 to organize an international committee, the Association Internationale Africaine (AIA) for the process of "exploration" and benevolent work in the Congo region. Getting nationally organized geographic committees to cooperate proved difficult, and Leopold abandoned the AIA for a new creation, the Comité des Études du Haut Congo (CEHC), whose ostensible purpose was to buy stations to police an end to the trade in African slaves still being transported across the continent to the Arab and Indian Ocean world, but which was also empowered to explore opportunities for trade and industry. By 1879 Stanley entered the service of Leopold's CEHC to buy up all the rights he could for exclusive agricultural development, road construction, and the like, even as he was charged with the effort to organize a confederation of free Negro republics on the basis of the Sarawak precedent that Britain had recently recognized.

Even as he was creating one allegedly humanitarian enterprise after another, Leopold was in danger of being preempted by the naturalized French naval officer Pierre de Brazza, who had been seconded by the French government (after considerable lobbying) to Leopold's committee in order to establish two of its benevolent antislavery stations. Brazza, however, used his time to collect his own treaties on behalf of France and returned to France in 1881 having signed treaties with the "makoko"—described as the regional king—and other chiefs that allegedly ceded control of extensive territory on the north bank of the Congo river to the French. The French foreign minister hesitated; the ministry was under attack, but French recognition of Brazza's treaties followed in November 1882, after much pressure by the emerging colonial lobby. Leopold kept pace, sending Stanley and his agents a sheaf of blank treaty modules by which African chiefs could transfer sovereignty to his third royal fig leaf, the Association International du Congo (AIC), designed to sound like the earlier multinational efforts. Conditions varied from document to document and within a year several Congolese leaders abjured what they had signed. What the terms suzerainty and sovereignty meant on the ground was unclear in the local context. By early 1884 Leopold's new AIC cited the treaties to declare the formation of a free state, a move taken to neutralize British claims.[81]

From the perspective of the major European governments, the objective in the chartering of colonial ventures was probably less the often forlorn settlements than precluding acquisition by another great power.[82] During the same period, the French and British had fallen into wary competition over the far more strategically important prizes of Egypt and Tunisia. But these were clearly venerable organized states that had slipped from Ottoman control, no matter their degree of financial disorder, and long involved in Mediterranean international relations. The Congo and West Africa were sites of African kingdoms centuries old, some well organized with recognized institutions—the kingdom of Kongo and Benin, for instance—but soon to be subordinated as peoples without history. The Portuguese had recognized and traded with these polities as they established coastal colonies. They had planted their original outpost at the mouth of the Congo River and claimed additionally a large coastal strip south of it. Their presence was long recognized, but the extent of their territory vague. What seemed to bother the other powers were the prohibitive Portuguese customs duties and restrictions on trade that might follow their more formal claims. Given the free-for-all developing in the region, the Portuguese now threatened to extend their presence and claims upriver. Leopold faced the possibility that his few outposts might be isolated by French and Portuguese claims.

What saved Leopold's claims was Bismarck's entry into the African competition, occasioned by calculations about the ramifications for European politics. Until the early 1880s the chancellor had resisted colonial enthusiasms—a revanchist France to his west and a massive Russia to the east, he would later say, formed his map of Africa. But urged on by a well-placed official in the Foreign Office, Heinrich von Kusserow, he too paid attention to the Borneo precedent of allowing in effect a private government to claim state protection. In April 1884 Bismarck extended the Reich's protection to Adolf Lüderitz's coastal strip at Angra Pequena in today's Namibia purchased from the Hottentot chief Joseph Fredericks. By July Bismarck declared Togo and Cameroon protectorates, and by August he envisioned an Angra Pequena charter company and, soon thereafter, control over the whole coastal strip of southwest Africa (Namibia). Germany was a player.[83]

The Gladstone ministry was more concerned about French annexation of the Congo delta region after Paris had recognized Brazza's treaties than German claims to the inhospitable wastes of Namibia. Fearing that France could close the river to British trade, the British Foreign Office signed a treaty with Lisbon in February 1884 that recognized Portugal's claims over the mouth of the Congo in return for Portuguese acceptance of free trade of a joint Anglo-Portuguese commission that would let the British control river traffic. No one liked the Anglo-Portuguese treaty and the British seemed prepared to withdraw, when the Portuguese proposed that Bismarck convene a conference to deal with the imbroglio. The agenda was supposedly to regulate the scramble for claims and to regulate freedom of navigation on the Niger and Congo Rivers and freedom of trade in the Congo basin and mouth. The British made it clear from the outset that they retained a preeminent claim on the Niger. Indeed their agent George Goldie had been avidly purchasing the same sort of sovereignty agreements along Nigerian shores that Brazza and Leopold were collecting. Still, the Berlin conference effectively provided the occasion for a grand colonial bargain among the European powers. After debate over how large the free-trade zone must be, it was agreed that two abutting areas spanning the continent should be agreed on, one for the Congo basin on the Atlantic and extending to the great lakes, Victoria and Tanganyika, and another extending east from the lakes to the Indian Ocean, though leaving out the long east coast sultanate of Zanzibar, which was by now a ward of Great Britain. Conference debates tended to separate France and Germany. The opposition mobilized within Germany against Britain paid off in the elections of October 28, 1884, which delivered Bismarck a victory over the anticolonial Progressives or left-liberals, a continuing thorn in his side. Having achieved his domestic victory, Bismarck had freedom to warm again toward Britain and temper his earlier encouragement of France's Jules Ferry, whose government would soon collapse before the taunts of nationalists. The chancellor now grew angry at France's efforts to oppose precise boundaries for the tariff-free Congo basin. Bismarck now found Leopold's structure quite convenient; it would block French and Portuguese ambitions, and it encouraged Leopold's representatives to defer to his leadership at the conference.[84]

As for Leopold's private state, the United States recognized its intermediate avatar, the AIC, in April 1884 ostensibly as an analog to the foundation of Liberia and after lobbying by their ambassador to Belgium who had financial interests in the Congo. How large should the territory be? Leopold first proposed that it extend coast to coast, then drew a map together with Stanley approximating today's Democratic Republic of the

Congo, first without Katanga then adding it anew after ceding Paris a slice of territory to augment France's neighboring acquisitions. The Act of Berlin maintained Leopold's title as the personal sovereign over the gigantic Free State of the Congo, guaranteed free trade and navigation on its huge river corridors, piously declared an end to slavery, and established that future colonial claims could be recognized only for effectively occupied territories, not fictional jurisdictions The French were recognized as the inheritors of Brazza's accumulated claims to the north of the Congo River in what today is the Republic of the Congo. Germany emerged with a gratuity as the German Cameroons and Togo. In return for their having secured unhindered commercial access to the interior, the British belatedly accepted the borders of the Free State that included Katanga. The precedent of private sovereignty also let them build their own colonies of upper and lower Nigeria from the numerous treaties that George Goldie had purchased along the lower Niger River. The Portuguese firmed up their colonial region as the large colony of Angola, and the Germans claimed South-West Africa (today's Namibia).

Only the indigenous African communities paid the price as the free state in particular imposed conditions of coerced labor in mines and rubber collections that were as horrendous as the formal slavery that the conference claimed to abolish.[85] But this was typical of a larger story. The Conference of Berlin at one level supposedly strengthened a European commitment to the obligations of "civilized" countries over less civilized peoples who needed tutelage to join the community of nations at some remote, unspecified time. International lawyers had sought to strengthen the gossamer restraints they defended after the wars of 1856–1870 as a "gentle civilizer of nations." But its gentleness was in little evidence in the Congo's "heart of darkness." Indeed as the German reactionary theorist Carl Schmitt would later maintain with some justice, international law was a product of European colonization, whether in the Americas in the sixteenth century or in Africa in the late nineteenth century.[86]

Extending colonial territory in Africa and Southeast Asia was as much tied up with accessing and controlling labor as it had been in the Americas and as it had been in commodifying the European countryside. But in Africa or Southeast Asia, there could be no illusions about a yeoman peasantry that would be integrated into the agrarian productive process, as there had been for the Physiocratic or cameralist theorists. The "races" found offshore testified to a gradient of civilization, which for some commentators was ascribed to history and culture but for others testified to biological inferiority. The grueling work they did was organized by plantations and contractors enforced and perpetuated by long cycles of indebtedness.

The Congo settlement was just one of a global wave of European imperial expansion in the 1880s. The British and white South Africans, Portuguese, and Germans formalized the partition of East Africa from Zanzibar to the Central African lakes. The British and French shared out Southeast Asia as rival powers in the same years. As the British added northeastern highland Burma to their holdings in Southern Burma, Singapore, and the Malay states, the French took over the kingdoms of Indochina. Siam escaped protectorate status because it lay between the rival blocs. Americans moved into Samoa and by the end of the 1890s, the United States would add the Philippines from Spain, wearing down the islands' own independence fighters; the Japanese would vigorously pursue acquisitions from China; and the Dutch would move from Java into the farther reaches of Sumatra and east to Bali and Celebes.

But the Asian annexations (including the areas taken by Russia in Central Asia) represented takeovers of long-recognized monarchs and states. Conceptually they comprised reshufflings of organized territories. The monarchies and sultanates were absorbed into new empires. The African expansions, however, were envisaged as takeovers of lands whose aboriginal or tribal communities had not attained a mature political or economic consciousness. They were primitive and infantile. Why else would they sell their rights for copper wire or old uniforms, not to mention intoxicating drinks? On the margins or deep within the great continental landmasses, whether in the U.S. interior or Argentina's Patagonia, Australia, or Canada, annexation accelerated.

In effect, the African boundaries negotiated as a consequence of the rivalries were European boundaries; only later did exploitation of the territory become significant. Other borders were to be established in the next decades. Focusing on British policy on the Nile and East Africa, Robinson and Gallagher refer to them as "frontiers of fear." The small group of British policy makers "were driven into abandoning creative policy and replacing it by cold administration and control. Prestige became all important to them. So did insurance. Policy grew more and more committed to the warding off of hypothetical dangers by the advancing of frontiers."[87] Rarely did defensive concerns lead to ceding the acquisitions; every empire justified expansion with the turbulence beyond its most recent frontier. Lord Salisbury was indeed preoccupied with Mahdist threats to Egypt and Britain's position in central Africa; therefore, he needed to dominate the Kenya-Uganda region and remove the protectorate that the Germans had established over the neighboring sultanate of Zanzibar (not just the island but the mainland region approximating Tanganyika). A major agreement in 1890 drew the new lines; the sweetener for the Germans was the island of Helgoland in the North Sea. To win French acquiescence to the treaty, the British acquiesced in Paris's control over an expanded West African domain in the Sahara and the upper Niger and western Sudan, as well as the island of Madagascar.

For Joseph Chamberlain, colonial secretary after 1895, the country's colonies were a "great estate" that called out for development. For this money was needed, which meant more taxation, resisted by the cabinet as well as business opinion. Beyond economic rewards, there were strategic imperatives: "The tendency of time," he declared in 1897, "is to throw all power into the hands of the greater empires." The minor kingdoms "seem to be destined to fall into a secondary and subordinate place." Salisbury had said the same thing twenty-six years earlier, but Chamberlain's vision was more totalizing, less focused, and, as Prime Minister Salisbury thought, the colonial secretary was "a little too warlike."[88] Chamberlain was prepared to risk war with the French but had to accept a settlement in 1898 that established the Nigerian border south of where he wished. The French were to control the Sahara and Sahel territories of French West Africa, an area equal in size to the trans-Mississippi west, but left the British in control of the Nile. The Italians attempted to expand their territorial holdings on the Red Sea but were defeated by Menelik II, who came to an agreement in 1902 with the British on the boundaries between his state and the Anglo-Egyptian Sudan. The Germans and British agreed to spheres of influence over the decrepit Portuguese colonies, such as Mozambique. The Boer Republics of the Transvaal and the Orange Free State fell to British and Cape Colony forces after a prolonged and bitter war nurtured by Cecil Rhodes. Marshal Lyautey gradually encroached upon the sultan of Morocco, likening his tactics to a spreading spot of ink.

The European powers could come close to war as they partitioned the continent and drew its new borders. French and British expeditions faced off at Fashoda; German bluster over Morocco was unsuccessful in 1905 but secured a bit of Cameroon from France in 1911. But boundary disputes between the colonial powers were resolved short of war. When they faced the brink, the areas did not seem worthy of battle when the balance of territorial power in Europe still had such high stakes. Another factor was that although they opened potential conflicts between the colonizing powers, the boundaries in fact sanctioned their common enterprise. They facilitated a joint arrogation of land and human resources even as they seemed to separate the European colonizers from each other. Within the boundaries, "development" could take place; colonial railroads might be built; gold and diamonds mined; rubber harvested from jungle vines before plantations came to be seen as necessary. Legally defined slavery had been abolished, which allowed the Europeans to take pride in their civilizing mission. But for their enterprises formal slavery was not really necessary. Black workers could be recruited or dragooned and assigned to plantations and mines. Discipline was applied that would not be tolerated in Europe, nor even any longer on American plantations (although allowed for prison chain gangs). This is not to exclude the fact that many settlers took pride in planting successful agrarian enterprises that offered decent employment and raised crops where no cultivation existed. They made their home in landscapes that were sometimes bleak but often beautiful. Africa became their home as much as it was the home for anyone who grew up on its savannahs and hills. Nonetheless, beyond he farms and ranches were the mines and plantations that provided the profits for the Europeans far away. The private contractors had no compunction about working their labor close to death, and collecting the hands of the reluctant. Joseph Conrad, E. D. Morel, Roger Casement, and after the fact Adam Hochschild have each masterfully written the story of epic exploitation in Leopold's "Free State." Despite all the legal theory debated about the status of African land, despite Morel's staunch protest that it was the common patrimony of the Africans, the pragmatic truth (in the sense of William James's no-nonsense philosophy advanced in this very era) was King Leopold's: the territory and the state belonged to the colonizers. But the equally essential truth was that what made it a source of value were the bodies that worked it.

In the noted Insular Cases before the Supreme Court, Americans asked whether the Constitution "follows the flag." That is, did the rights of citizens inscribed in the corpus of constitutional law hold sway in colonial possessions abroad? They are still asking today with reference to Guantánamo. Territoriality—the properties and jurisdiction that are defined by an enclosed geographical area—wait on the lines that are drawn. "La carte est plus intéressante que le territoire," the contemporary dyspeptic French novelist Michel Houellebecq writes about the artwork of his protagonist, who transforms Michelin maps into photo montages.[89] That may or may not be true, but in Africa, the map established the territory and licensed the powers that flow from sovereignty.

Delineation overwhelmingly served the Europeans, not the locals. The borders, in effect, were extensions of European boundaries. They confirmed the conditions for exploitation, capitalism, labor discipline, and joint possession, but sometimes for acculturation, education, hybrid and cosmopolitan identities, for Tagore or, later, Senghor and Fanon. And in adding massive Africa to the populated world of bordered territoriality, they made territory as such an even greater stake for global politics. As Henk Wesseling states, "Playtime in Africa was over."[90] The map of Africa in 1914 was saturated with color. There were no unclaimed spaces— Ethiopia and Liberia alone were formally independent of European sovereignty (although the British-Boer fusion in South Africa had effective dominion status). Many of the colonial jurisdictions were vast in size. Europeans know that they dwarfed their own territories in Europe: a small Belgium ruled a Congo eighty-three times its size. Bismarck marveled that a German adventurer in Africa with no titles of preeminence at home could claim a region (which he was to make a Reich possession) as large as France. France itself claimed a region in Africa almost as large as the United States. Britain's dominions, counting Egypt and the Sudan, were also huge. Since when taken over they were carved out of a continent that Europeans claimed to believe was preterritorial in their own sense (although many knew better), drawing African boundaries emphasized the universality of territory, and, since the territories were so large, they also confirmed that sheer size was a preeminent political resource.

After 1890 there was really no territory "beyond the line" outside Antarctica, although many ambiguous and contested areas still existed. That saturation, along with the growing fixation with the decisive weight of continents that we saw emerging from the railroad age, confirmed the territorial obsession that weighed on world and domestic politics in the years after 1890 and up through most of the Cold War. Britons sang: "Wider still and wider shall thy bounds be set; God who made Thee mighty make Thee mightier yet." But they sang for all those enthused by empire.

Postscript: Territorial Geometry after 1890

Boundaries and continental spaces reverberate against each other in the late nineteenth century. The border is not just a simple perimeter of a territory; it ensures no spatial repose. Boundary lines, like railway lines actively define space, and there is a new restlessness as continental and colonial space is penetrated and claimed. The United States frontier, Frederick Jackson Turner wrote in 1893, had "closed" according to the decennial census of 1890. He meant that there was no longer a vacant continental wilderness yet to be settled by white Americans. Influenced as we have seen, by Achille Loria, he believed that the end of "free" land represented a challenge for democratic institutions.

In the year 1890, too, the Turin mathematician Giuseppe Peano described how a continuous one-dimensional line might pass through every point of a bordered two-dimensional surface, thus effectively filling it. In the following year David Hilbert elaborated the exercise; today they serve algorithms to generate pixel patterns that can provide smooth and continuous images. But these "space-filling curves" could not themselves be continuously smooth (differentiable). They were generated by increasingly short line segments turning at right angles.[91] Lines filled a surface under very tightly defined conditions, both for the mathematicians and the rail builders. Like Peano's "curves," however, the rails laid claim to space; the rails might carry the armies and the people and the commodities of a territory from one end to the other and, as they became denser and more complex, to all the points between. By 1890 the European and American maps of railroad development revealed their modern pattern.

Lines and areas, that is, borders and territories, long acquired or newly beckoning, maintained their shared grip on the imagination of policy makers and commentators through the nineteenth century. The spatial imagination empowered by the railroad—the vision of continental unification and large colonial acquisitions—became intoxicating for many statesmen and publicists. Lines and territories were the sites where nations and economic interests asserted their ambitions. The vigor and ambitions of their ceaseless redrafting in the nineteenth century corresponded to the technological possibilities allowed by the vast expansion of energy resources embodied in coal and steam, the railroad, the steamship, and "instantaneous" electric communication. But they also corresponded to the evolution of broadly shared reigning metaphors, what Foucault has labeled an epoch's episteme. Nineteenth-century leaders became restless if not obsessive about drawing lines and enclosing territory. Continental thinking and imperial ambitions pervaded democratic as well as autocratic societies. The border and the territory no longer provided a reassuringly stable geographic framework for collective life. As dynamic manipulations of global space, they were sites of insecurity. Lines of communication were always menaced. Territories needed rounding out. If the territories were coastal colonies, they required inland delineation.

There is no territory without a boundary and likewise no notion of filling territory without exploiting the lines within it, whether cables, rails, or rivers. And although the lines themselves (considered most abstractly) are one-dimensional and cannot take up space, by the late nineteenth century they are essential for defining space not only by enclosing it but by covering more and more of the points within. Scientists and surveyors revel in lines; they undertake trigonometric mapping and apply it to the new land areas they want to control. As Ian Barrow has written, the trigonometric survey of India is certainly a claim to scientific cartography, but it is also a claim of dominion over the land that is mapped: "Eighteenth- and nineteenth-century British maps of India are about control—control over land, over access to location, over names, over people, over representation, over the past. They exult in national victory and present British power in India as established, legitimate, protected by boundaries, and long-lasting. . . . Rather than being about foreign rule in India, the maps are about making into British territory what was once foreign land."[92] Not every colony required such trigonometric surveys—the British did not apply it in contemporary Ceylon; and the older route survey maps, fixed less on area and more on depiction, reemerged later in the nineteenth century. But the restless men of the nineteenth century certainly required the line, in fact constructed all sorts of lines.

The French and British signed 249 boundary treaties for West Africa between 1882 and 1905.[93] The Europeans constructed three-quarters of the boundaries, measured by length, that still divide the African states. Along with the Americans, they ended the century governing almost 90 percent of the globe's landed territories. By 1900 they built almost all of the railroad mileage existing by the mid-twentieth century. They had strung the telegraph and then telephone lines and laid the undersea cable to communicate virtually instantaneously across vast stretches of territory and to control their empires in real time. They obsessed about "blood" lines to justify racialized hierarchical rule. By the early twentieth century they would construct the assembly lines that characterized their most iconic industries. Perhaps, most revealingly, the dominant scientific metaphor of the epoch were the lines of force made famous by Michael Faraday and James Clerk Maxwell. Maxwell published his breakthrough article "On Physical Lines of Force," in 1861–1862, as rails and telegraph lines radiated through the western countryside. Along with his famous equations published in 1865, his findings implied that electromagnetic "waves" radiated outward from a source, filling space with energy of diminishing intensity; imagine rays of light projected from a central point across an infinite set of enclosing spheres. Every point on those spheres could be assigned a quantity of energy (which varied inversely as the square of the distance from the source). The positivist administrators of the nineteenth century state envisaged an analogous project: the center would radiate its energy outward along lines of communication (telegraphs and railroad) and implant local sources of national energy, whether schools or prefectures, throughout the territory. Every point on the map should contribute to the vitality and efficiency of the whole.[94]

This does not mean that the world of politics assimilated Maxwell in the 1860s any more than they were aware of Peano and Hilbert's space-filling lines in the 1890s as they carved up the last of the huge continents available for colonial rule. The claim cannot be one of simple intellectual causation between radically different domains of thought and action. Thousands of scientific and pseudoscientific concepts were being thrown off in the period, many irrelevant, many discredited. To select a couple that had echoes in society and politics is wantonly unhistorical. Still, it is worth asking, was there a type of "elective affinity" that fell somewhere between causation and coincidence? Historians have long done so in appealing to the realm of biological reasoning, as they have alleged the impact of Darwinist ideas, usually vulgarized, on the national competitions of the late nineteenth century. Ideas of struggle and selection served as a bridge. But Western publics knew about evolutionary theory and could easily if often misguidedly appeal to the concepts for guidance in their struggles. Physics was another realm, and when even as intelligent a commentator as Walter Bagehot wrote a book entitled *Physics and Politics* (1872), he referred really to anthropological and biological influences. All we can say here is that the late nineteenth century was obsessed by lines and borders in many realms of life. The need to enclose colonies, zone cities, lay down urban rail systems, string the dense telephone lines that ran overhead, reaffirm barriers of class and religion, trace lineages, later produce the tracery of art nouveau seemed to respond to some underlying linear compulsion.

By 1900 some of these linear systems no longer followed just parallel or radial patterns. They were becoming complex networks with crosscutting connections, especially those woven to distribute electrical power.[95] The network as a social metaphor would become dominant only later in the twentieth century, when electrical and radio linkages emerged in the interwar and postwar period, and when the logistical and military problems set by the world wars required new techniques of optimization such as systems analysis and economic planning. The ironic result of this new network consciousness by the second half of the twentieth century would be to help dissolve the territorial obsessions that the railroad reinforced across the second half of the nineteenth century. But not before continental obsessions helped to generate the violent political confrontations of the two world wars and the cold war.

6

From Fate to Function
The Twentieth Century and After

CONTINENTS COME WITH MYTHIC OVERTONES.[1] They beckoned
as unknown wilderness at the beginning of the nineteenth century when
Lewis and Clarke set out west across North America and Alexander von
Humboldt descended the chain of the Andes. By the end of the century,
they beckoned as the stakes of empire. They had been arenas of the sublime in 1800—gifts of God, a resource for freedom and wealth even
though shared with aboriginals or first peoples, who often welcomed the
explorers. The settlers who came later found the indigenous societies an
inconvenience and removed or liquidated them. As the prairies and wilderness filled with new settlers, observers worried that their bounty would
run out. By late in the century continental landmasses were envisaged as
a depleted endowment for individualism: whether Frederick Jackson
Turner's vanishing guarantee of democratic institutions or Achile Loria's
expropriated reservoir of "free land." For Halford Mackinder, the British
propagandist for what the Germans termed *geopolitics,* a four-hundred-
year interval of European discoveries and expansion, the Columbian Age,
was coming to an end in the early twentieth century: "There is scarcely
a region left for the pegging out of a claim of ownership, unless as the
result of a war between civilized or half-civilized powers. . . . Weak elements in the political and economic organism of the world will be shattered
in consequence."[2]

The size and arrangement of the continents now appeared a preeminent factor in a continual struggle for global power. Control of the
land had long been counterpoised to control of the sea, and anxious
political leaders and policy advisers at the turn of the century meditated
continually on the respective advantages that preeminence on land or

dominance of the oceans would provide antagonists. Napoleon's conquests across Europe and British naval resistance had most recently epitomized the countervailing struggle of global strategy that could be traced back to Persia and Athens. But the momentous changes in global politics since the mid-nineteenth century provoked renewed reflection about the strategic advantages of continental territory or control of the seas. The United States acquired vast territories to the Pacific and filled out most of its continental boundaries following the Mexican War. Victory for the North in the ensuing Civil War ensured that it would remain one gigantic national power, and the completion of its transcontinental railroad meant that it could draw on the resources from coast to coast. Having reached the Pacific, the United States looked warily at the emergence of Japan, fretted implausibly at Chilean sea power in the Pacific after that country's 1874 victorious war with Peru, and began its naval expansion. Within Europe the wars of 1864 through 1870 that forged a united German Empire, and, so too, the resumption of Russian expansionism in the 1870s, brought two new contenders for continental preeminence. The respective advantages conferred by territorial assets and/or oceanic power was ripe for rethinking. By the 1890s commentators speculated on the impending rivalries or combinations of the truly global powers—whether the United States versus Britain, perhaps the United States in tandem with Russia, or Germany versus Russia, or the truly frightening combination of Germany with Russia as a "Eurasian" challenger to Britain.

Alexis de Tocqueville's famous prophecy that Russia and America were destined to dominate resonated in an era preoccupied with global power. The historian Sönke Neitzel has scoured the authoritative weeklies and monthlies of the major countries to document what he terms the new doctrine of world empires *(Weltreichslehre),* which, he proposes, had its major support in Great Britain and Germany—declining in Britain after the electoral defeat of Joseph Chamberlain in 1906, but reaching its acme in Germany during the First World War.[3] Continental expansion and empire had inspired U.S. publicists in the early nineteenth century. Now maritime power gave rise to speculations of hegemony. John Bristed saw a fundamental Anglo-American rivalry: "As the world could not bear two suns, nor Persia two kings, so the day is fast approaching when the globe will not be able to endure the existence of these two mighty maritime empires."[4]

Admiral Mahan's celebrated study of 1890, *The Influence of Seapower upon History 1660–1783,* and subsequent historical and policy-oriented essays, provided readers with an authoritative account of the ever-recurrent rivalry between great landed powers, often despotic and imperial, and the plucky maritime societies, free and democratic. The Americans, as rivals to the British into the 1880s, but increasingly aligned with them thereafter as both faced ambitious German and Japanese expansion in the Pacific, envisaged maritime domination as the key to pushing back against the menace of continental military powers. Naval supremacy supposedly required battleship domination of the oceans (there were, though, some alternative concepts that wagered on lighter, more rapid cruisers), and this in turn rested on national character, political structure, population, and extent of territory. Geographical placement in the oceanic world and the nature of the coastline were relevant factors. But while geography was influential, it was not destiny: France had the assets in the eighteenth century to have outpointed Britain as a naval power, but subordinated naval development to its armies and did not press in battle the resources it had. It was easy to overlook Mahan's many subsequent essays that stressed the importance of commerce and contingency and to read his message as a simple affirmation that naval power could prevail over land power.[5] In the judgment of Mackinder, his leading British counterpart, the great continental land empires held the potential edge in global competition. Both men insisted on the lessons of strategic geography, Mackinder more sweepingly, although each thought the balance between land and sea power could be preserved with effort.[6]

The twentieth-century discipline that promised the key to understanding geographical destiny would become known as geopolitics, tarred for a half century by its association with the Nazis. This chapter follows that trajectory. But looking ahead, beyond the years of discredit and dismissal, there has been a rehabilitation of sorts. Among later advocates such as Henry Kissinger or Zbigniew Brzezinski, the term has tended to lose the connection with geography and to imply just a mode of strategic thinking that is realistic about calculations of power. Recent geographical theorists, less concerned with policy consequences, have also sought to rehabilitate a geopolitics that is not wedded to a plea for global primacy.[7] Whether such an antiseptic methodology can be sustained without aspirations for hegemony remains in question. As another modern commentator has written, "The geopolitical vision is never innocent. It is always a wish parading as analysis."[8] This was certainly the case for the first century of its existence.

The Geopolitical Ambition

The term *geopolitics* was designed to give scientific status to the study of geographical resources in the service of national power. The key to its strategic persuasiveness consisted of the fact that even though economic development, in particular the development of transportation networks, was recognized as crucial to the calculus of power, the underlying asset—the natural outlines of continents with their river systems, mountains, and desert barriers—seemed to confer decisive advantages or handicaps on ambitious peoples. German, British, or American, the geopolitical interpreter discerned and expounded this substructure of power, often with highly charged historical and geographical generalizations and a confidence designed to suggest profundity. As a sociopolitical movement, geopolitics represented one strand among many in the wide-ranging effort by professional elites in the late nineteenth century to assert the claims of the social sciences in the management of a society that would resist mass democratic claims and to claim leading roles hitherto dominated by aristocratic and military circles.[9] National efficiency and hierarchies based on expertise were the attributes required by a competitive international environment.

But this social role of geopolitical arcana is not what interests us here. Instead it was the content of the knowledge claimed—the alleged territorial determinism that is arresting. The word *geopolitics* was coined in 1899 (along with ecopolitics, ethnopolitics, demopolitics, and cratopolitics) by the Swedish geographer Rudolf Kjellén, whose influential compendium *Grossmächte der Gegenwart* (Great Powers of the Present Day) went through twenty-two editions between 1914 and 1930. Its practitioners became convinced that their discipline held the key to deciphering global rivalries and power and that they possessed a profound, almost secret knowledge.[10] It found German advocates above all, but British and American theorists, as well—and in recent years it has become a fashionable term among French pundits. In our current century the term has resurfaced to describe what can be called a postmodern approach to "the spatial practices underpinning world politics."[11] Earlier, it caught the geographical imagination of the twentieth century as an almost esoteric doctrine. As a German-American acolyte was to write in 1942, "Geography had been taught for too long a time by men who failed to grasp that politics is destiny, and politics had been directed and also taught for too long a time by men who failed to grasp that land and sea spaces, too, are destiny."[12]

"Space" or *Raum* was the key term in the German geopolitical vocabulary. *Raum* came with different overtones from "territory" but was obviously related. Territory implied a bounded global space divided into sovereign polities. *Raum* had no fixed borders, but it was envisaged as continually pressing against other spaces: in other words it was quasi-bordered. The world might be divided into stable *Räume* or global regions, but they were never merely peacefully accepted areas. On the contrary: they remained latently conflictual, compelling rivalry even in the absence of war. For Mackinder, the heartland and the rimlands had strained against each other; for Haushofer, there should in theory be vast strips of land: the Western Hemisphere, a European/African space, a central Eurasian space, a South Asian space, and an East Asian one, too. Each spatial realm harbored subrealms: the United States, for instance, controlled South America, but Argentina might organize a contending "space." Central Europe could dominate Europe and later the Berlin-Rome axis might ensure its Mediterranean and even African vocation against Britain's pretenses. The British Empire spilled across geographical regions, but was a politically preeminent unit, and Southeast Asia was identified as the "monsoon lands" with its own geopolitical integrity. In short global spaces quivered with unresolved boundaries and resources. Their geographical features were evoked in an almost promiscuous process of naming and shifting elements, and they were often graphically depicted with ellipses, arrows, and stylized jagged boundaries designed to suggest constant tension and confrontation.

In the Central European lexicon, "spaces" or *Räume* came with a subtext. In suggesting a set of territories or a zone dominated by a hegemonic state power, they were implicitly imperial constructions. *Räume* could be zones of unequal economic interdependence if consciously organized. They came with metropoles and lesser regions, sometimes smaller or less industrialized countries that were supposed to accept gratefully their assigned task in a system of hierarchical exchange. The most celebrated construct was Friedrich Naumann's *Mitteleuropa* of 1915, a plan for a German dominated Central Europe that went from the Dutch North Sea through Bismarck's Reich, Switzerland, and down the Danube to encompass Austria Hungary, Greece, Romania, and Turkey. In effect this was a peacetime prolongation of a victorious Central Powers built around an internal free-trade zone or what National Socialist economists would later call a common economic space *or Gemeinwirtschaftsraum*. Naumann counted as a politically progressive pastor, an organizer of a National Socialist Party, preoccupied by the "social question," and hoping to win the industrial work force for a nationalist coalition through ideas of economic expansion. The agenda was similar to the plans for social imperialism of Alfred Milner, Joseph Chamberlain, and others in Britain. Yet Mitteleuropa was not just a concept for a European Common Market: it remained strictly hierarchical.[13] Even before the defeat of 1918 shattered the vision and the reality, however, Mitteleuropa was in trouble because of the divergent aspirations for conquest on the part of Berlin and Vienna's policy makers. Austria-Hungary, which also disappeared in 1918, had created its own economic space through a common external tariff and free-trade between the two halves of the monarchy; this had required a tradition-laden political carapace painfully negotiated fifty years earlier in 1867. Perhaps today's European Union exemplifies an egalitarian economic space (although hegemonic tendencies can intrude), but it was constructed during long decades of German division and whether it can thrive without a greater dose of formal "stateness" has yet to be decided.

The origins of geopolitics lay in organic metaphors. States were organic creations in Romantic thought, above all Adam Müller's *Elemente der Staatskunst*—a conservative response to alleged French revolutionary rationalism, which envisioned prince and people in a mystical partnership. Territory provided the basis for their life cycle. Continuing the intellectual trajectory from such antirationalist tenets to supposed scientific doctrines in the second half of the century, Müller's friend, Moritz Wagner propagated "the law of migration of organisms." Movement in space in search of better nourishment and living conditions constituted the impulse to evolution of species. New varieties of species evolved through migration as new territories promised more or less favorable living conditions.

Ratzel transformed the necessity of migration into one of spatial expansion: higher cultures first rooted themselves in their inner territories *(Bodenhaftung)*, then went out after colonies. The requirements of species evolution flowed into a process of historical modernization manifested by intensive territorialization.[14]

For Ratzel, study of the earth was merged with a study of human evolutionary development in a discipline he dubbed "Anthropogeography." Peoples or nations—in German the terms flow into each other—were in "unceasing motion, which constituted their history," which he termed "biogeography." He envisaged the state as a form of geographically grounded organism *(bodenstandiger Organismus)* in which people and territory were so connected that they could not be conceived separately and political space became a category of life.[15] As a later disciple wrote, "The underlying idea of his 'biological' or 'organic' doctrine of the state is that the state is not merely comparable to an organism but is a real organism, that is born, lives, and dies."[16] Ratzel coined the term *Lebensraum* and proposed seven laws of territorial struggle. Among them: the growth of states correlated with other measures of development such as cultural achievement and economic activity; and growth proceeded by the absorption of smaller territorial units. The national frontier was the external organ of the state and the measure of the organism's health.[17]

Kjellén took over from Ratzel the idea of the state as an organism. The second chapter of his popular treatise on the Great Powers, "Der Staat als Reich (Geopolitik)," dealt with the body of the state and the geographical individuality of states. The fifth chapter treated "The State as an expression of the laws of life." He refined Ratzel's laws into the determinist doctrine of "necessary growth and political ineluctability" *(Zwangsläufigkeit)* that had to lead to expansion. The deeply conservative Swedish theorist further concluded that the United States, Germany, and Japan could rise to dominance over their continental hinterlands, just as the democratic values of the French Revolution were yielding to nationalist and conservative ones.[18]

Fin-de-siècle German commentators, political leaders, and military pundits enticed by their new Reich's claim on *Weltpolitik* popularized these dubious geographical claims. In an age of racialized empire and military innovation—for instance, the machine gun and the decisively improved Dreadnought battleship—the concepts were widely shared outside Germany, as well. Mackinder argued in his celebrated lecture of 1904 that the "pivot area" or Euro-Asia and the larger "world island" that surrounded it was the continuing source of contention for global supremacy: its expansionist thrust and the resources it contained (originally the grasslands of the steppe) provided the key to global history. The world island could be contained only by the rimland—a fluctuating defensive zone that might include Western Europe, the Americas, and East and Southeast Asia. (Mahan had endowed the maritime powers with the greater geographic and geopolitical capacity. Mackinder appreciated his assessment but believed that railroad development would shift the preponderance to the rulers of Eurasia.)

For Mackinder the tribal societies of Euro-Asia had pressed on the Chinese and the Europeans, forcing a regional unity not out of common ideas (as claimed by the "literary conception of history") but out of continued pressure from the steppe peoples. In an early iteration, "the Franks, the Goths, and the Roman provincials were compelled for the first time to stand shoulder to shoulder on the battlefield of Chalons, making common cause against the Asiatics, who were unconsciously welding together modern France."[19] Centuries later the hordes that came into Eastern Europe "gathered their first force 3,000 miles away on the high steppes of Mongolia." Meanwhile Seljuk Turks and their Timurid successors defeated the "Saracen" contenders and pressed into Eastern Europe. Mackinder summoned up great swathes of geographical description and centuries of tribal movements in his presentation. The great rivers of Asia flowed either to the Caspian and Aral Seas or to the Arctic Ocean; they were useless as channels of communication from outside the region. Rather the steppe peoples pressed on the region of the five seas: the Caspian, Persian Gulf, Red Sea, Black Sea, and Mediterranean. With dizzying verve Mackinder described centuries of invasions across the steppe and moving south to beset the great river or Potamic civilization—China on the Yangtze, India on the Ganges, Babylonia on the Euphrates, Egypt on the Nile. "This conception of Euro-Asia to which we thus attain is that of continuous land, ice-girt to the north, water-girt elsewhere, measuring 21 million square miles, or more than three times the area of North America, whose centre and north, measuring some 9 million square miles, or more than twice the area of Europe, have no available water-ways to the oceans, but, on the other hand, except in the subartic forest, are very generally favorable to the mobility of horsemen and camelmen."[20] This Euro-Asian landmass formed the great "pivot area" of history. A new mental map took shape—a central sprawling continent, surrounded by the riverine empires that were to remain isolated and vulnerable until discovery of the Cape Route to the Indies in the fifteenth century let the Europeans utilize "the one and continuous ocean enveloping the divided and insular lands" and finally to move northward from both east and west to contain the successive steppe peoples.[21] Faced with these permanent geographical configurations, history allowed little contingency. But where, in fact, the peoples of Euro-Asia met those of surrounding crescent, history remained open. When the Cape was rounded and then again the Suez Canal was constructed, the oceanic powers seemed to gain a strategic advantage and were able to impinge on Eurasia from the southwest and southeast simultaneously. Railroads, however, threatened to reverse this advantage once again: providing a decisive mobility and force to the organizers of the central empire.

Passing with breathtaking rapidity to the contemporary era, Mackinder evoked the Russians as heirs to the great steppe conquerors. "Russia replaces the Mongol Empire." The geographic context was crucial. "Nor is it likely that any possible social revolution will alter her essential relations in the great geographical limits of her existence."[22] Here was the core of the geopolitical doctrine, to be repeated continually over the century: geography trumped any political institutions. Russia's development of railroads was only a question of time. Switching labels with confusing alacrity, Mackinder saw Russia as the pivot state, and although the United States (having built the Panama Canal) might mobilize Atlantic resources to join the forces resisting Russia from the east, if Russia enlisted Germany she would gain access to the western oceans. This would require the Western powers to deploy their oceanic bases from Europe through India and ally with Japan. Even "the vast potentialities of South America might have a decisive influence upon the system." They might strengthen the United States or woo Germany away from its "pivot policy." The particular combinations could vary; "I have spoken as a geographer," Mackinder claimed. The actual balance was the product of geography and "the relative number, virility, equipment, and organization of the competing peoples." Still, "the geographical quantities in the calculation are more measurable and more nearly constant than the human. . . .

The social movements of all times have played around essentially the same physical feature. . . . The westward march of empire appears to me to have been a short rotation of marginal power round the south-western and western edge of the pivot area."[23]

The vision wobbled in decisive respects: geography trumped mere politics but not, apparently, national vigor. And geographical advantages required the development of territory, preeminently through railroads. Russia was the pivot state at one point, Germany at others. Interestingly, Russian geographers and policy makers hardly utilized the approach (until it was recently resuscitated by supporters of Vladimir Putin).[24] In 1919 Mackinder published a book-length tract, *Democratic Ideals and Reality*, which retitled the pivot area as the heartland; the resisting rimland reappeared as the inner and outer crescents. Somewhat confusingly he wrote: "The joint continent of Europe, Asia, and Africa, is now effectively, and not merely theoretically an island. Now and again, lest we forget, let us call it the World Island."[25] In another breathless description of global invasions, Mackinder wrote, "Not until about a hundred years ago, however, was there available a base of man-power sufficient to begin to threaten the liberty of the world from within this citadel of the World-Island. . . . Now is the time, when the nations are fluid to consider what guarantees, based on geographical and economic realities, can be made available for the future security of mankind."[26] In either case, the map looked uncannily like the shifting landmasses that the German geologist Alfred von Wegener would propose early in the twentieth century, and it would remain the imagery of world political dualism into the Cold War, with the latter's polar projections crossed by the bomber and missile routes linking Russia and America in a deadly confrontation. The continentalist and oceanic visions were taking flight into a metaphysics of geography that supposedly reflected the most sophisticated awareness of global territoriality.[27]

Containment of Russia remained at the heart of Mackinder's program which he promulgated from his post at the London School of Economics after leaving Oxford. Lord Curzon, the viceroy of India and fellow member of his geographical association, read him with appreciation, and indeed Curzon's 1907 Oxford lecture on frontiers reflected similar concerns.[28] For both men, Russia's potential expansionary vigor—toward the Mediterranean or India—remained preeminent dangers. The 1907 convention to partition influence in Persia was a strategic answer, an effort to combine accommodation and containment. Germany was a potential adversary, but presented the greatest menace only if it were to become an ally of Russia and extend the power of the heartland. In October 1919, Curzon, now foreign secretary, sent Mackinder as high commissioner to south Russia to be a liaison with the counterrevolutionary forces of General Denikin. The appointment was secret in light of the expected furor that such a mission might cause. After meetings with Polish general Pilsudski and discussions of a joint anti-Bolshevik campaign, Mackinder conferred with Denikin and then prepared a report for Curzon in January that recommended joint action on behalf the then beleaguered White Russian commander lest the Bolsheviks sweep into southern Asia and India. The task was not only strategic but political, given working-class hostility to such an adventure. "The working classes must be made to realise that whatever the communistic ideals originally characteristic of Bolshevism, there is today a growing threat from Moscow of a state of affairs which will render this world very unsafe for democracies."[29] *Democratic Ideals and Reality,* his tract of the same year, popularized the formula that whichever power controlled the heartland also controlled the world island, and whoever controlled the world island controlled the world. The book posed the dilemma of how democracy, whose basis was ethics, might counter the managerial authoritarianism that characterized the German system. It spoke to all the insecurities threatening the precarious Wilsonian moment, when a resentful and humiliated Germany might link up with a pariah Bolshevized Russia. Emerging geopolitics thrived on (and continued to batten on) specters of insecurity.

Mackinder's lessons were fairly straightforward: Russia was the keystone of Eurasian power; Germany was potentially dangerous as a strategic partner and developer of Russia. Britain was the organizer of the rimlands, and ultimately the United States must be an ally, although there could be scope for rivalry. German advocates of geopolitics faced a more pessimistic situation. They believed in the advantage conferred by size but were condemned to a small territory—one that looked even more shrunken after the cessions imposed by the Treaty of Versailles. Still, the Reich was hardly a rimland, and its theorists tended to avoid Mackinder's bipolarity, instead envisaging three or four zones of domination, running not in quasi-elliptical or crescent-like swathes across the globe, but along great north-south slices: pan-America under the hegemony of the United States; a European and African space, Eurafrica, that Germany would control; a Central and South Asian empire under Russian sway; and a far eastern space in which, according to Karl Haushofer, Japan steered Chinese resources. But these were continually in flux, shifting according to circumstance.

Haushofer, an army officer and a geographer, who founded the *Zeitschrift für Geopolitik* in 1924, dominated the interwar discussion. A graduate of the Bavarian military academy and a major general in World War I, he was perceived by Americans who followed his writing as exerting a critical influence on the National Socialists through his friendship with Rudolf Hess. He had spent three formative years in East Asia from 1908 to 1910 and always saw Japan as a privileged partner for Germany. Geopolitics he defined as a "science of the political organism in its natural living space, which seeks to grasp its subject in its terrestrial and its historically determined currents." It was a science particularly important for the task of "reestablishing and re-enlarging the constricted and mutilated living spaces of Central Europe."[30] Like Mackinder, whom he believed was an intellectual kin, he was preoccupied by the threat posed by continent-size countries—namely, Russia and the United States—to middle-size powers, but he did not have the consolation of rallying a rimland empire. Mackinder's politics resembled an isometric exercise calling for continuous resistance against Eurasia, but Haushofer could not take solace in the defensive. Instead global politics had to be a process of attempted reshuffling of territory. Geopolitics offered the laws of development and possibilities for foreign policy in an overpopulated world—especially since World War I had not really concluded an era, but created a geopolitical tabula rasa that would open an age of redistributing global power.[31] Until the invasion of Russia, he sought cooperation with both Russia and Japan. Traveling to Japan via sea and returning across Siberia, he never really had a sense of the United States.[32]

In his *Wehr-Geopolitik,* Haushofer sought to apply the purported lessons of World War I. Position *(Lage)* and space were the essential components of military geography. While Mackinder had taught the supremacy of space, that is, territorial size, Ratzel had pointed to the essential role of place. But Haushofer also turned to Ratzel for the essential lessons dictated by space: "Extending space enhances life . . . the larger organization of space inevitably conflicts with the smaller ones, but ultimately achieves victory."[33] As he expounded further, "The European system of rural but intensively used spaces is retrograde in the face of [states based on *Grossraum*] because it cannot be the [pattern] of the future, a pattern which today, as it has for millennia, strives after ever-larger spaces."[34] The very first article in the new *Zeitschrift für Geopolitik,* penned by Haushofer's collaborator Otto Maull, emphasized that although Ratzel had understood correctly that spaces were organisms, he had not generalized sufficiently: "History is the continual enlargement of territory and thus consequentially the continuing expansion of territorial influence. The expansion or contraction of states is always just a means to an end: the enlargement of the human concept of space, the continually renewed rejuvenation of expansionary forces into new spaces." At the same time Maull also claimed that being rooted in a national space testified to a more profound culture. Only a cyclical view of state life seemed to reconcile the opposed values of rootedness and expansion, depth and vigor. "The forces for state formation that are created by taking root are greater and more enduring than those created through mobility. Striking down roots is more productive than just moving into foreign territories at the cost of others. States that arise by moving into a territory can grow by leaps and bounds but they also collapse." The author connected these two processes to the venerable German distinction between a rationalist "civilization" and a more profound "culture." States created by migration and invasion revealed the virtues of civilization; they diffused technical knowledge and achievements. "But their impact is transitory. Lasting effects that survive millennia can only emerge through taking root. In place of historical states with a small territory for taking root but great capacity for movement, there must gradually emerge a progressive settlement of the earth with a greater scope for taking root though less mobility, a future federation of global states."[35]

Maull apparently intended to resolve his spatial dialectic by a federative notion that was probably far too modest and irenic for most that of his collaborators, who saw no conflict between being rooted and annexing new territory. The elusiveness of geopolitical teaching was revealed by the fact that the editors of the *Zeitschrift* took two years to propose a definition of their subject.[36] "Geopolitics is the doctrine of the terrestrial determination of political events. It is based on the broad foundation of geography, especially political geography, as the doctrine of political spatial organization and its structures." It aspired, the authors confessed, to an application of geography to international politics just as once mercantilism had sought to apply economics for state ends. In line with this recognition, "Geopolitics wants to provide a tool for political activity and serve as a guide for political life. . . . Geopolitics wants to and must become the geographical conscience of the state."[37] "It is only a means to an end," wrote another. "It was not a natural science and could not formulate universal laws. It was an applied science, a technology of power, that began when the possibility of prediction began."[38]

Geospatial thinking appealed to conservatives in Germany before 1914. It praised discipline, elites and expansion. Haushofer was a member of the annexationist Pan-German League. Taking geography as its field of expertise, geopolitics mobilized the same sort of nationalist yearning that Fritz Stern described as the Germanic Ideology in *The Politics of Cultural Despair*. After World War I it enjoyed greater popularity in light of the cessions imposed by the Treaty of Versailles, especially the significant territory taken for the new Polish state. "Versailles is no peace treaty."[39] Hans Grimm's popular novel of 1926, *Volk ohne Raum*, expressed the need to colonize Eastern Europe, and Haushofer's quadripartite division of the globe—the United States and Britain, Germany, Russia, and Japan and the Far East—would require hegemonic expansion.

The difficulty, Haushofer recognized, was that after 1918 Central Europe (he meant Germany in fact) began under great geographical limits: "The impossibility of [living] in the long run with the current Central European spatial constraints and confined perspectives in the face of global questions (without a simultaneous adverse effect on the race and Volk) . . . had to be a constant summons to maintain the capacity to think in far-sighted and spatially vast perspectives about military geography and geopolitics even in our mutilated and blunted spatial situation."[40] Could the territorial limitations be overcome? When Hitler came to power, the *Zeitschrift für Geopolitik* welcomed his advent, and Haushofer envisioned that Indo-Pacific colonial conflicts would decisively weaken Britain and the European imperial powers to the benefit of Germany.[41] Writing later from the perspective of 1940, citing the precedents of Alexander, Napoleon, and taking heart from Germany's recent conquests, he allowed himself to believe the Reich might prevail. Still, he could not shed a certain pessimism. Central Europe had built its power on coal and iron; however, oil now served as the primary military resource, whether to lubricate railroads or provide fuel for submarines and airplanes.[42] His third edition of *Wehr-geopolitik* ended with a rather breathless summary of events from the Munich Conference through the fall of France and developments in the Indo-Pacific region. Haushofer clearly blamed the expansionist Western powers for rejecting Axis efforts to negotiate a geopolitical military compromise.[43] Haushofer's rapid proliferation of geopolitical tracts became summaries of current events, illustrated by photographs of ports, machines and Asian cities—a sort of militarized *National Geographic*. (Freed from the *ressentiment* of the defeated and the dogmas of geopolitics, and open to far more subtle genderings of hierarchy, the American magazine could construct a far more attractive case for United States imperial aspirations.)[44]

In the last analysis, despite the citation of multiple factors, whether natural resources, economic development, or just plain ethnic vitality, land area quickly became the easiest variable to grasp for the geopolitical mindset. But herein lay a fundamental contradiction. Geopolitics supposedly guided politics, but in fact it followed it. As boundaries shifted or the fortune of states increased or declined, the supposedly constant features of land and seascape were deployed to explain their rise and fall. The doctrine did find critics: Adolf Grabowski of the rival *Zeitschrift für Politik* attacked Haushofer's monocausality, but he was marginalized by 1938.[45] Above all, in fact, the fortunes and prizes of war fed the fortunes of geopolitics.

Spaces of Ideology: World Wars and Cold War

America's geographers were also energized by war. The summer Institute of Political Geography convened at UCLA in late July 1942 to take stock of how their sub-discipline should react to the military challenge, including the unwholesome doctrines of German geopolitics. "Today's war is the first truly global war in history," they were exhorted. "We have been forced to learn from difficult experience that the world is neither a plane nor a cylinder, but actually a sphere. . . . We are compelled to acquire a new respect for the very magnitude of the earth as we follow the painful course of United Nations' convoys to Archangel and Murmansk, to

Capetown, to Massaua, Basra, and Bombay, and to Sydney and Brisbane."[46] The seminars and papers represented the United States' response to National Socialist geopolitics—ostensibly a rejection of the Nazi "pseudoscience," but in fact an unconsciously imperial translation of the same sweeping reconsideration of territory and space that General Haushofer was continuously redrafting. The years 1941 and 1942 had brought a new intensity of geopolitical discourse to America: the United States was at war in Europe and the Pacific and becoming the supplier of a global coalition.

At the same time that American geographers could gather in Los Angeles, German armies were deep inside Russian territory in the largest engagements of land armies in history. Inside Estern Europe the Germans were putting into effect the racial alternative to geopolitical determinism that the most ardent Nazis had always preferred to geopolitics. Heinrich Himmler's SS University at Posen/Poznan had been the center for hatching plans for ridding the region of its unhealthy urbanism, and above all of the Jews who crowded the area from the Baltic down to Ukraine. Respected professors of *Volksgeschichte* who had written the history of the allegedly beleaguered outposts of *Deutschtum* helpfully submitted memos that envisaged a settlement of healthy German peasants. The concepts had in fact originated in the planning staffs of the German armies of the First World War that had advanced deep into Russian territory by 1917. Organized as the command Oberost, their staff officers, above all Colonel Max Bauer, developed schemes for the racial cleansing of the east. These deadly reveries in which German settlers displaced the crowded Jewish settlements and primitive Slavic peasants were not geopolitics in any formal sense. But they breathed the same atmosphere of vast spaces, swamps, and plains, of the clash of peoples and supposedly civilizations that Haushofer's ruminations encouraged in Berlin. Whether according to formal geopolitics or the practices of imperial expansion, they expressed the grandiose ambitions of continental conquest. Americans were fortunate. By the time that they had to confront the German plans for conquest they had already filled up their own vast continental spaces and had faced a population vastly less dense and far easier to overcome.[47]

The new geography evoked at UCLA, which described the American world at war, did not even need to dwell on North American continental resources: it cited the subarctic Russian ports beyond the North

Cape, the southern tip of Africa, the Persian Gulf, the Indian Ocean, and the western edge of Oceana. Polar or azimuthal map projections, originating in the Renaissance, were redeployed for a global war in which airpower assumed a major role and convoys crossed arctic waters. The polar projections echoed Mackinder's maps of heartland and rimland. The Mercator projections prioritized, as they had since the sixteenth century, the routes for naval navigation or the painful reconquest of the islands and ports of the equatorial Pacific. The Second World War starkly outlined but could not resolve the great alternatives for decisive national power: whether the need to fight huge land battles, above all in the plains of western Eurasia or the capacity to project naval power with the great American task forces in the Pacific. But the war also added the new role of airpower, whether as a ferocious addition to conflicts for land, or as the new projection of power at sea. The Cold War was to elevate nuclear-armed airborne bombers and intercontinental ballistic missiles to what appeared as the most decisive force of all.

The military confrontations of 1939 to 1945, and then again from 1948 to 1989, thus raised the stark territorial alternatives that geostrategic discourse had inscribed as the two related visions of global rivalry: a simplified Mahanite history of democratic sea (and now air) power versus despotic land power, and Mackinder's ominous confrontation of the Eurasian heartland arrayed against the rimlands (Western Europe, Britain and its dominions, the United States and the Americas). Mackinder's strategic imperative had long been the containment of the Soviet Union and, as a consequence, the need to preclude Germany from becoming Moscow's ally whether by compact or conquest. This obvious prescription was of little guidance in the Second World War, when Churchill and Roosevelt felt it necessary to accept a Soviet alliance to stop Germany. From the Ribbentrop-Molotov Pact (August 23, 1939) to the German invasion of the Soviet Union ("Barbarossa," launched on June 22, 1941), Berlin and Moscow seemed on course to peacefully collaborate in ruling Eurasia under totalitarian auspices. Logically speaking, this should have been Karl Haushofer's preferred policy—allowing Germany to control Eurasia and Eurafrica (and become Russia's tutelary power), while consigning East Asia to the Japanese as a natural German ally that would be hegemonic in East Asia and the "monsoon lands." The scenario would have left the undervalued Americas to the United States, while Britain's dispersed empire slowly disintegrated.[48] But Barbarossa intervened, and geopolitical science had to follow the rude decisions of the Führer: politics trumped the alleged dictates of geography. With an effort at tactical agility that barely masked the policy's incoherence, Haushofer wrote that if it were rightly understood, the decision of June 22, 1941, "unveiled the greatest task of geopolitics, of the vitalization of 20th century space in the old world with the almost simultaneous necessity of overcoming its continental resistance—the task of forming Eurasia and Eurafrica as realities and as positive creative values."[49] Although a Russian-German collaboration might have earlier seemed most logical for creating this Euro-Asian territory, Haushofer now explained that the Soviet leadership had treacherously exploited neutrality to subvert German interests; thus the Reich was compelled to impose the Eurasian solution against Russia.

As of late 1941 this still seemed possible, although Haushofer accepted that even continents had become too narrow an arena for the full unfolding of geopolitical destiny. The resources of geography had to be viewed on a worldwide scale. If viewed globally, however, with the long-term potential of the United States seriously counted, an objective calculus might have suggested that the most likely alternative would be ultimate defeat for Axis ambition. Such a calculation, of course, did not deter the Japanese from their desperate wager in December 1941, and with German armies advancing so rapidly into Russia and storming the portals of Eurasia, the outcome remained open-ended.

The entry of both the Soviet Union and the United States against the Third Reich meant that this conflict would be defined in ideological as well as territorial terms. One of Haushofer's collaborators theorized that Roosevelt, "the man who bore the chief responsibility for the current war" (although when he wrote the United States was still neutral!), had chosen foreign expansion to escape his desperate political situation at home: "Roosevelt's Weltpolitik" was of a simply universal nature. Expansion allowed him to reconcile the hitherto irreconcilable: "New Deal and big capital, world trade and a planned economy, democracy and dictatorship. He is promising his people an American world in an American century and he wants to be its first president."[50] For the German theorists of territory and empire, it was long clear that Roosevelt's America (especially in alliance with the UK) represented a radical threat to their geopolitical aspirations. The United States enjoyed not only a naval supremacy (although preoccupied by the Pacific war) but as a would-be successor to Britain embodied global ambitions keyed to its advanced capitalism and industrial prowess. This challenge had already manifested itself with the Anglo-American partnership in World War I. Wilsonian America claimed to act on behalf of freedom of the seas and the democratization of European regimes, but in fact used these slogans to ensure the economic penetration of continental Europe as it had done earlier in Latin America.

The most far-reaching analysis came from the rightwing legal theorist Carl Schmitt. Not a geopolitician in any strict sense, Schmitt produced legal and historical writings that still combined geographic considerations and a ruthless sense of the primacy of conflict in the most challenging critique of liberal internationalism. Steeped in Catholic reactionary thought—returning continually to theological concepts and the need to restrain primal forces of rebellion—his writings on domestic politics argued that "the political" emerged from a confrontation of a people with its adversaries, the defining opposition of friend and foe. Parliamentary liberalism, as instituted in the Weimar Republic, was a facade for powerful interests; real sovereignty had to be entrusted to a leader whose constitutional prerogative was to override normal legal procedures with exceptional decisions when he decided there was an emergency. Indeed, all real political acts rested on decisions that administrative rules could not determine. Schmitt nurtured an ambition to become the major legal advisor for the National Socialist regime, but he was too rigorous an intellect and remained deeply distrusted, despite his efforts in the mid-1930s even to incorporate anti-Semitic tropes.[51]

Schmitt's international thought took shape in the wake of German defeat first in 1918 and then in World War II. The United States earned his particular disdain in a 1933 text on modern imperialism. America claimed that its demand for a world of market and investment access was neither "political" nor imperialist. In reality it was both. Since enunciating the Monroe Doctrine and later the Platt Amendment (guaranteeing the right of U.S. intervention in independent Cuba), America had created its own western-hemisphere *Grossraum* as a theater for imperial domination. At the same time through its military role in World War I and its economic prowess, it worked toward world domination. As if it were an implicit accomplice of American ambition, the contemptible League of

Nations (always "the Geneva League") facilitated a similar program of global leveling based on pacifist pathos. Refusing to formally become a member of the League of Nations, Washington could still steer the League through the Latin American republics that it dominated; even as the League Covenant denied great powers the right to regional domination (except for the exception granted the United States).[52] Six years later Schmitt reaffirmed his denunciation. By elevating the principle of non-interference by European powers that the United States claimed in the Americas into a general norm for international affairs, Wilson had levered the Monroe Doctrine from its function as declaration of a *Grossraum* into a *raumlose* or spatially unbounded search for world domination. "By transforming a specifically American spatial conception into a transnational and trans-ethnic world ideology, Theodore Roosevelt, Woodrow Wilson and the current President Franklin D. Roosevelt, have attempted to use the Monroe Doctrine as an instrument for the domination of the world market by Anglo-Saxon capital." By its insistence on an "open door" in China, Washington, furthermore, was denying Japan the right to organize its own *Grossraum* in East Asia.[53]

From the 1930s on Schmitt had separated *Seevolk* from *Landvolk*—taking the distinction between sea power and land power and enlarging it to create a theory of national psychology.[54] The land was man's natural element. As creatures of the land, men were impelled to construct enclosed spaces, no matter how large. Sea people, preeminently the British and Americans and Dutch, the French in part, were traders and made their living from economic processes that tended toward a borderless world. Behind the archetype stood the medieval representation of crafty and restless Ulysses, disappearing on his last voyage into the boundless ocean beyond Gibraltar, and consigned by Dante to hell because of his overreliance on reason. The sea could be marked by "lines of friendship" as the powers had arranged in the early modern era, but the sea people ensured that there was "no peace beyond the line." Indeed, beyond the lines lay a realm of unstructured chaos.[55] Land people organized the continental zones that for Schmitt became the basis of *Grossräume,* akin to those Hjalmar Schacht had organized in Central Europe around Nazi Germany in the 1930s. For Schmitt, imperial as the *Grossraum* was, it was limited in ambition; it constituted part of a plurality of states and empires. In his discussion, it sounded almost cozy.

Schmitt drafted his major reflection on space and empire while living in a devastated Berlin in the winter of 1944–1945, as it was clear that the Nazi *Grossraum* was soon to collapse. *The Nomos of the Earth* argued that certain metaprinciples (the nomos—the constitutive principle of a people that united their ordering and their spatial placement—*Ordnung und Ortung*) defined international order at any time. "For underlying every new age and every new epoch in the coexistence of people, empires, and countries, of rulers and power formations of every sort, are new spatial divisions, new enclosures, and a new spatial order of the earth."[56] In the age he saw coming to a close, this order was based on a "European public law," which encompassed the world of states and of *Grossräume,* and which despite continual adversarial encounters had protected peoples against the tyranny of universal empire.

International law was the European public law that had taken shape as a code of principles that would prevent a continental civil war as the great powers divided up the New World. Every new "nomos" expressed a new division of the world: Schmitt used the concept of *Landnahme* or appropriation. It was integrally connected with a new drawing of lines and boundaries. "The last phase of European international law, now coming to an end, rests on the great appropriation of land in the 16th and 17th centuries."[57] This had been "the fundamental event in the history of European international law to date" and marked the modern advent of "global thinking in terms of lines [of demarcation]."[58] The underlying set of principles had been worked out on the basis of the territorial regime within Europe, which allowed for territory itself, aside from populations, to be accumulated and exchanged.[59] This pluralist international order had served Europe well (the fate of its colonial subjects was irrelevant since the system was based on territory and not peoples, who remained unmentioned through the nineteenth century). It allowed flexible adjustments of territory and rankings of great powers—the United States would be admitted after 1865, the Japanese after 1894—although the Americans' effort to wall off Latin America and Asian intrusion into the ranks had already suggested that the European-constructed nomos might be challenged. Indeed unbeknownst to its participants the whole European public order was starting to dissolve.[60]

Paradoxically, Schmitt argued, the nineteenth-century colonial experience was to undermine the European order. European public and international law traditionally recognized that private property and the liberal market order would remain protected in any transfer of territory among its states. Territorial changes, such as the partitions of Poland or the 1871 annexation of Alsace-Lorraine, did not bring about a change in the underlying social and economic order. "So long as the internationally legal appropriation of land affected only the centers of empire, it basically preserved the ownership of land guaranteed by private property."[61] But the colonies were an arena where the property rights of "totally uncivilized" indigenous peoples as well as their political claims were defined as nonexistent. The supposed treaties they made with Europeans were invalid. The native chiefs exercised no formal rule, and their use of the soil allegedly represented no property interest. Whatever relationship the natives had with respect to land, agriculture, and hunting, depended exclusively on the decision of the appropriating state, and the Europeans adopted diverse solutions ranging from recognition of native property to trusteeships to simple expropriation. So long as colonial land was conceptually held separate from "normal state territory," no problem arose for Europe. But insofar as colonial land, with its absence of a private property status that might have protected indigenous rights, became assimilated legally to the territory of the metropole, "the structure of international law changed, and the international law that applied to Europe itself also came to an end," now to the disadvantage of the European owners of colonies.[62] As one looked at the years around 1890 and the turn of the century, a great change was becoming visible, but "Without any critical perception, indeed to the total cluelessness *(Ahnungslosigkeit)*" of the actors, European international law doctrine lost its awareness of its previous spatial structure. In the most naive way it regarded this ever more external and superficial universalizing process as a victory. . . . As Europe became displaced from the center of global international law, it saw the process as an elevation to its center."[63] By undermining the traditional immunities of private property relations from transfers of territory, colonial annexations weakened the territorial pluralism and the rights of property within European states.

For Schmitt this banalization of European territoriality was just preparing the way for the triumph of the Anglo-American campaign to impose an empire of economic universalism. "Precisely in the economic realm, the old global spatial order visibly lost its structure." Britain was too weak to impose a territorial order on the entire world, but remained strong enough to dominate the realm of the global ocean. International law lost its moorings as a regulation of territory, becoming instead an ad hoc series of measures, such as represented by the laws of war that had been negotiated at the Hague Conference. "With this abdication of international law Europe fell dizzily into a world war that dethroned the old continent from the middle of the globe and lost the capacity to insulate itself from the impact of war."[64] In contrast to the multiplicity of empires, states, and *Räume*—expressed in the flexible recognition of great powers—the British and Americans were imposing a commercial or market-based universalism based on control of the sea, as well as the pseudo equality conferred by the feckless "Geneva League"—Schmitt's slighting term for the League of Nations. Twentieth-century history through 1945 was to become the story of a rapacious unlimited effort by Anglo-American capitalism to overcome and penetrate the *Grossräume* that had scaffolded European order and international law.

The Paris Peace Conference of 1919 represented the first triumph of the new principles, "but left the world in its earlier disorder, just removed two European great powers, two pillars of the spatial order hitherto, and undertook a new division of European land."[65] Schmitt allowed himself a long anti-American excursus. Although the United States was not formally a member of the League, it was thoroughly present in Europe. The United States followed up its expansionism by its declaration at Panama in October 1939, which, he charged, transformed the concept of the Western Hemisphere from a landed continent into a vague zone of American power, effectively extending America's borders into the ocean. The "Western Hemisphere" represented a new spatial structure. It allowed for no "amity lines" such as the Europeans had agreed on during the colonial era to demarcate respective New World interests. The Western Hemisphere now was an expression of anti-Europeanism. "The new West, America, wants to remove the previous West, Europe, from its previous world-historical position. The Occident, with its entire moral, civilizational and political meaning, is not to be discarded or destroyed or even dethroned, but only displaced."[66]

The sweep of the *Nomos of the Earth,* its citations of international law, stylized historical pathos, and manipulation of dualisms, is impressive. So, too, is the effrontery of its claim: the Third Reich should be understood as the champion of territorial pluralism and as the bulwark of European international law against the rapacious domination of the

Anglo-Americans (echoing in its way the Italian Fascist demand that the powers of blood resist the powers of money). Accompanying the triumph of Anglo-American international principles were their new usages of war. These were disconnecting war from its hitherto normal but confined use to rearrange territory in order to unleash it against civilians, whether through the blockades of the First World War, or the unlimited aerial bombing of the Second. Although the Third Reich was also dying under the massive blows of the Soviet army, this fact was fading before the triumph of the British and Americans. The air had become a new theater, along with the sea, for overcoming the virtuous and limited land powers. The age of two-dimensional territoriality and warfare was ending; the humanistic separation of public European law and private property relations was likewise over. Schmitt was to have another four decades to refashion his own persona once again. Starting with his exculpatory memoir of 1946, *Ex Captivitate Salus,* he would similarly present himself as a European humanist, following in the steps of Erasmus and trying to preserve a spiritual commonwealth.

As the Cold War deepened, Schmitt realized that the great ideological conflict was leading to a renewal of imperial territorial organization. Schmitt had lamented that Anglo-American capitalism was an instrument for global domination that precluded the territorial organization of great spaces by large and medium powers. He did not stress the divergence of objectives that had intervened since 1919. By the Second World War, the British were trying to strengthen their waning international economic strength by organizing their Commonwealth as in effect, a *Grossraum* with a common tariff and a sheltered currency zone, whereas the United States was theoretically insisting on the dismantling of Commonwealth tariffs and the convertibility of sterling into dollars as conditions for lend lease and postwar aid. In fact, Washington continually relented and eased its requirements for liberalization. Still, British officials and parliamentarians felt that Washington was pressing to crack open their protected economic zone as a price for indispensable short-term assistance. Like the defeated Germans, they could no longer maintain their own *Grossraumwirtschaft.* Only the Soviets could, and did, even when tempted by the Marshall Plan.

On March 3, 1948, Ernest Bevin, the doughty trade unionist who had become British foreign secretary, commented on a Foreign Service memo that "physical control of the Eurasian landmass and eventual control of the whole World Island is what the Politburo is aiming at—no less a thing than that."[67] The language was Mackinder's; the context was the Cold War. The American journalist Dorothy Thompson, a long-term advocate of military responses to dictatorship, became an avid reader of Mackinder at least from 1942. The aspirations for the heartland she ascribed to Hitler in World War II she tagged on the Soviets in 1948–1949, who were moving to consolidate the heartland from which "all Eurasia can be conquered by land-based masses of manpower, and the Americas isolated." The Russian program "is based upon a concept of world strategy identical with Hitler's, which Hitler owed to his geopolitical adviser, Karl Haushofer, who, in turn, owed it to the great British geographer, Sir Halford Mackinder."[68] In the same year George Orwell's novel *1984* envisaged an eternal war between continental totalitarian states: Oceana and Eurasia. "Whoever controls the present controls the future. Whoever controls the past controls the present." Oceana's rulers declared, as Orwell played on Mackinder's formula from 1919: "Who rules East Europe commands the Heartland: Who rules the Heartland commands the World-Island: Who rules the World-Island commands the World."[69] The upshot was that the clash of ideologies and economic imbalances meant not the dissolving of geographical great spaces, but their reinforcement. It would bring the erection of new and more absolute borders in the postwar era, notably the thirty-eighth parallel in Korea and the division of Germany, manifested after 1961 by the notorious Berlin Wall.[70]

Often at odds with the United States on issues of international finance, London certainly shared Washington's hard line on the political divisions of the postwar world. Geopolitics was becoming the language of British and American policy makers alike. During the war, the War and Peace Studies Group of the New York–based Council on Foreign Relations discussed the geographical acquisitions needed to secure postwar predominance after the defeat of the Axis. Political émigrés from Central Europe and those who read the Old World's tracts familiarized Americans with the doctrines of German geopolitics. Only a few pundits seconded the vocation of geopolitics in formal terms. The most notable was Nicolas Spykman, who outlined his argument in the *America Political Science*

Review in 1938, and then in his 1942 book, *America's Strategy in World Politics:* "In this kind of world states can only survive by constant devotion to power politics. The struggle for power is identical with the struggle for survival. All else is secondary, because, *in the last instance, only power can achieve the objectives of foreign policy."* Spykman, who headed Yale's Institute of Strategic Studies from 1935 until 1940 but died by age fifty, sought to steer a fine line between the alleged geographic determinism of Haushofer and the French school of social geography, but he started from the premise that conflict was the natural condition of international society. The geographical area of the state was the territorial base occupied during wartime "and the temporary armistice called peace." It was the factor most important for influencing national policy since it was the most permanent. "Ministers come and ministers go, even dictators die, but mountain ranges stand unperturbed."[71] Size, location, and resources were the crucial parameters; resources, technological in part, now included airpower. Security for the democracies must be assured by an Anglo-American bloc in which the United States played the key role since it could buttress the rimlands both on the Pacific and the European flanks of Eurasia. Either the rimlands organized by America must encircle Eurasia, or Eurasia would encircle the United States.[72] Robert Strausz-Hupé would write along similar lines, insisting that Americans learn the lessons of unremitting antagonism between geographic blocs in his World War II book, *Geopolitics: The Struggle for Space and Power,* and in his 1959 study, *Protracted Conflict,* with the thesis refocused for the Cold War in the early 1950s.[73]

American experts who claimed to unravel the impact of geography usually avoided the term *geopolitics,* which seemed tainted by its connection with National Socialism. Indeed geopolitics as taught by Haushofer seemed to many the secret doctrine of Nazi expansion, to the point that the American team at Nuremberg weighed putting him on trial.[74] In fact, there were multiple sources of German ambitions for subjugating and organizing Eastern Europe; geopolitical tracts just provided one supposedly scientific rationale for conquest, but an argumentation notorious enough to put the term under a cloud for a generation. The new American experts called themselves political geographers; and they distinguished their discipline from the German notion of geography as destiny.[75] But while Jan Marius Otto Broek, who contributed the key lecture on geopoli-

tics during the 1942 institute held at UCLA, joined the majority in rejecting the German version as a pseudoscience, he also warned against
rejecting the idea of power altogether. Americans lacked "the understanding of foreign countries as distinct personalities, determined by
history and location."[76]

American political geography was compatible with democracy—
distinct from a determinist and German-tainted geopolitics—but accepted the same tasks of political guidance as the Germans. "The political
geographer uncovers and displays . . . those features of the physical world
that are related to the life of man and to his collective social effort. But
he had also to publicize and educate the leaders of public opinion in the
possibilities of exploiting the physical properties of the world for the public
good. . . . In the spirit of the scientific technician, he must be willing to
make his knowledge available to the political authority that requires it."[77]
There was no doubt for the professor/engineer that some politicians had
disregarded the lessons that should have been drawn. "The disparity between the political and the scientific view does much to explain the curious notions that gained credence in international relations in the interval
between the First and Second World War. American isolationists, serving
their own political interests, insisted upon national policies that brought
us close to national suicide because they disregarded our physical relationship—in time and distance—to other parts of the world. Pan-German
Nazis, indoctrinated with mystical notions of racial supremacy and prating
constantly of German 'honor' and 'destiny,' were eager to misuse Germany's geographic situation in Europe for the purpose of denying 'honor' and
'destiny' to every other European state."[78] The author assumed a politicized
geography, but at the same time said that he sought "the destruction of the
principle of geographic determinism" which in the nineteenth and twentieth centuries had become "a victim of mystical extremism." Rather than
states being constrained by their resources they could trade or, as with the
recent case of synthetic rubber, develop alternative resources. Ultimately
politics was determinative: democratic states utilized resources for peace,
totalitarian states for war.[79] At the same time, the state was still the creature
of its geography: "The character of a state is intimately bound up with the
particular earth conditions in which it evolves."

For Derwent Whittlesey, the professor of political geography at Harvard who insisted on this premise in 1939, the European state certainly

changed over time but served as template the globe over.[80] Great Britain, France, and Germany were the primal states; those of east central Europe were "geographically immature." And vulnerable. Whittlesey rejected the mystique of area; unless accompanied by population and transportation infrastructure, it accounted for little. The area of a nation that was developed with transportation infrastructure and a vibrant economy was its "ecumene": the United States "possesses the largest ecumene on earth."[81] Canada and Australia's size mattered less than the restricted extent of their ecumene—the southern edge in Canada's case and the coastal strip in Australia's. But in contrast to area, "the shape of a state" appeared to fit "an unchanging formula." It should be "chunky rather than elongate"; it should have its densest population (ecumene) in the center; it should have permanently marked natural barrier boundaries and be economically self-contained. No state possessed all the ideals; and other attributes being equal, large states had an advantage, assuming they had a unifying "emotion of nationality."[82] Whittlesey became an authoritative expounder of Haushofer and geopolitics, copublishing studies in 1941 and 1942.[83] Bigger was better, developed was better, self-sufficient was better, and territorially cohesive was better—was this really the basis for a science?

New Geographers, New Geographies

American political geographers distanced themselves from Nazi-tainted geopolitics, but they recognized that this fashionable discourse of spaces and power seemed to confer a new glamour on their field. They tended to elide difficult questions. Could the claims of political geography provide an equivalent but benign influence within a democratic state? Was the allegedly democratic intent of political geography really enough to prevent the misuse of geographical reasoning? Could a social science emerge that did not conceal, perhaps even unbeknownst to its practitioners, an aspiration for national hegemony? In a world where Germany sought to rule Europe and Japan to dominate China, they believed that political geography might provide lessons for resisting fascism and militarism and serve as a beneficial social science. But America's own policies of resistance to fascism entailed a major extension of geographical influence, which was hardly to be withdrawn after the Second World War ended. Just as fundamental from the viewpoint of developing a claim as a valid field of knowledge, could political geography claim to be a social science? Many of the supposed social sciences developed during the positivist enthusiasms of the late nineteenth century and after tended to serve agendas of domination, whether anthropological, eugenic, or genetic. In the postwar era, modernization theory emerged as the most notable interpretive key. Its proponents suggested that societies advanced along a path of scientific reasoning, market-oriented economic development, and multiparty welfarist democracy, to end up, if all went well, with institutions that not surprisingly would resemble those of the United States and its Western partners. Critics of American policy would suggest that the ubiquitous deployment of modernization theory legitimated a series of "interventions and penetrations that sought to subordinate, contain and assimilate the Third World as other." It "was a reflection of a will to spatial power."[84] Among its cruder advocates, political geography could also harbor a will to spatial power.

In fairness, two inflections of American political geography emerged over time. Its appearance in the 1940s testified to a fascination with German geopolitical discourse even when its practitioners sought to distance themselves. In recent years, geographer John Agnew has revived it as a more neutral study of "the geographical distribution of power," including its continuing shifts. It forswears any geographical determinism as a source of power but seeks to map contingent displacements in both dimensions and their relationship.[85] Its ambitions within the discipline faced opposition, in any case, as was revealed by the cameo controversy involving the professional fate of Whittlesey, the spokesman for political and social geography, as well as the fate of the geography department he chaired at Harvard. The issue played itself out (along with a great deal of personal politics) in the university's decision in 1948—admirably researched by Neil Smith, the biographer of Whittlesey's antagonist Isaiah Bowman—to close its geography unit nested in the Department of Geology, an outcome that shook the American discipline. The department was a troubled one. It had to contend with the importuning of the wealthy heiress Eleanor Elkins—who had already donated Widener Library in memory of her son, lost on the *Titanic* with her first husband—to have an independent geography institute founded that would be directed by her new husband, a Harvard instructor of geography. And Whittlesey himself was a reputed homosexual, living with a younger, supposedly mediocre instructor whom he championed for reappointment.

Bowman, trained as a geographer early in the century, had risen to become an eminent policy adviser since Woodrow Wilson enlisted him to head the committee of geographers and historians—the so-called Inquiry—who would deal with the contentious border issues at the Paris Peace Conference of 1919. By 1940 Bowman had become the president of the Johns Hopkins University, an adviser to Franklin Roosevelt, and the public face of geography. He also served on the governing Board of Overseers of Harvard. Bowman had been trained in an era when American geography was considered an offshoot of geology and his doctoral research had focused on geological formations that underlay the global surface. Subsequent research concentrated on forest sciences. The social and political geography championed by Whittlesey Bowman considered little more than a descriptive catalogue, and the Harvard program (as he casually remarked to Jean Gottmann, the young French-trained geographer in his own Johns Hopkins department) little more than a "kindergarten." In his report "Geography as a University Discipline," he condemned human geography as a wooly-minded activity. Despite reassurances to Whittlesey that he wanted to defend geographical studies, as a Harvard overseer Bowman remained silent when the department's fate was discussed (for which President James Bryant Conant wrote him to express his profound gratitude). Conant himself expressed his belief that the discipline was unworthy of being a university subject. And together with Bowman he fought to keep the funding mission of the newly founded National Science Foundation limited to the natural sciences. A left-wing aura, if not communist influence itself, surrounded the social sciences.

As Neil Smith further suggests, geography was vulnerable in the United States, as it was associated with a study integrally connected to the experience of frontier expansion that had come to an end. When under criticism, geographers seemed able to defend their subject only as a synthetic discipline, easily dispensed with. "The field was always defined so broadly that it was virtually all-inclusive or so narrowly that it had little raison d'être as an independent pursuit." For all the prejudices and personal frictions involved, the geographers could not make a convincing statement of what their research was supposed to achieve.[86]

Ironically a greater incorporation of German-style geopolitics might have done more to save the field in the decade after the Second World War. For the Cold War rivalry of the United States and Soviet Union—at once ideological and territorial—warped many scientific perceptions along its lines of force. The wars of the twentieth century, hot and cold, demanded new maps and competitive thinking about undeveloped regions. In particular the last and most inhospitable portions of the globe, the Arctic and Antarctic, were explored and charted. Mackinder's maps had shown Eurasia contained by the surrounding subcontinents of the "rimland" to the south, west, and east. These formed a defensive semi-circle holding in the heartland. Spykman's maps showed a variant in which Eurasia clamped down on the Americas from two sides, or conversely, the United States, helping the small states of Europe, pressed east and west from its ocean coasts. There was no reason to take account of the relatively impenetrable north. Still, when Henry Luce's *Fortune Magazine* applied Spykman in Technicolor and published its 1942 map of the world at war, the cartographer placed the United States and Canada "right-side-up" at the visual center of an azimuthal projection in which the other anti-Axis allies were "upside down" and the Arctic opened as a key barrier from Eurasia. Like World War II itself, the map allowed a visual transition from a global alliance dominated by America to a possible confrontation across Atlantic, Pacific and Arctic (See illustrations.)

As the Cold War quickly took on military aspects, the Soviet ally across the pole became the enemy. By the 1950s long-range bombers and intercontinental missiles placed each country within striking distance of the other across the arctic ice. New azimuthal projections—in which the meridians of longitude radiated outward from the North Pole and emphasized the territorial proximity of the United States, Canada, and the Soviets—dramatically suggested the terrifying possibility of Armageddon. They visually simplified the Cold War antagonism and emphasized the new potential long-range bombers and ICBMs whose hydrogen bombs held the potential for national extinction. At the same time, the post-Stalin "thaw" in the Soviet Union permitted conspicuous cooperation between the powers, in part to demonstrate scientific prowess. The International Geophysical Year of 1957–1958 saw the launch of Sputnik and many rocket probes into the upper atmosphere.

Systematic mapping activity filled out the hitherto vaguely charged spaces of both polar regions. Air expeditions as well as the landings on the Antarctic ice shelves facilitated the process. Advances in cartography were also an encouragement. After some faltering efforts in the 1930s the Soviets began systematically mapping the Arctic sea floor, motivated by the old dream of a northeast passage from Europe to the Pacific. By 1949 they had essentially completed the survey, which they revealed to the world in 1954. The Second World War spurred Canadian aerial mapping as the inadequacy of existing maps became apparent. In 1947 Canada and the United States began a joint meteorological program for weather mapping and in 1948 the U.S. Air Force and Canadian air force combined to report on the aerial reconnaissance of Arctic North America.[87]

Perhaps surprisingly, but certainly logically enough, the two polar regions ended up (at least to date) under two separate "regimes." In the public imagination they had been the two remaining unpenetrated global regions. But as a landed continent the Antarctic was a potential source of rivalry. A sense of competition prompted flag planting and expeditions at the edge of the ice shelves by the British, French, Russians, Norwegians, Argentines, and Americans. Claims were made on the basis of proximity or bases. The Australians and New Zealanders supposedly acting with Britain (looking south from the Falklands) were prepared to lodge claims from the 1920s. The Argentines contested these and speaking supposedly on behalf of Chile, as well, cited their proximity to extend a claim from Tierra del Fuego. Aerial photography began (aside from shipborne balloons) in 1928–1929 and its scope increased in the 1930s. By a decade later German and American crews were surveying the interior by plane, and Admiral Byrd later attributed to Franklin Roosevelt the encouragement of systematic photography as the basis for eventual U.S. control. An American National Academy of Science in July 1939 pondered undertaking a comprehensive aerial survey, and U.S. efforts intensified after the war. Meanwhile Americans also cited their bases on the ice-shelf as a basis for a dominant role. The Americans' Operation Highjump in 1946–1947 took seventy thousand photos, although by 1952 only a quarter of the continent had been photographed.[88]

Australia's composite map of Antarctica in 1939 was judged a major cartographic achievement, produced to buttress its claim to 40 percent of the continent. The map (a South Polar azimuthal projection) was intended to support the joint British, Australian, and New Zealand efforts to establish a common empire claim to east Antarctica, which Australia formally registered in 1933.[89] The history of the Australian map as well as of the diverse nationally sponsored expeditions to Antarctica that were to serve as the basis for claims underscores the diverse geopolitical and geostrategic valence of the two polar regions. There was no traditionally conceived territory to claim in the North although the stakes of oil and minerals in the ocean floor and control of coastal passage made the circumpolar states—the United States by virtue of Alaska, Canada, Denmark (by virtue of Greenland), Norway, and Russia—acutely aware that a major strategic resource was at stake. By international law the open sea had allowed no exclusive claims beyond the traditional three-mile limit of national jurisdiction. In war, the search and seizure of enemy vessels was sanctioned; so too was a coastal if not remote blockade, although in all the major conflicts—Napoleonic War, American Civil War, the two world wars—the rules had been disregarded.[90] The first major formal change to the prevailing international law came with the 1982 UN Convention on the Law of the Sea (UNCLOS), which raised the 3-mile limit to 12 miles and extended coastal powers' exclusive economic zones for fishing and oil drilling to 200 miles, and up to 350 miles for seabed minerals. Other countries had to seek authorization for any fishing or exploration within the wider limits of the exclusive economic zones. But all nations had the right to peaceful passage even within territorial waters and to lay cables and pipelines.

Without continued occupancy, national claims on islands or Antarctic territory had no international law status; they remained declarations of intent. Claimants did establish base camps and staked out Antarctic ice shelves. The United States and Russia, along with the southern hemisphere countries, who projected radial cones toward the Pole, remained interested parties and the Soviets published a superb atlas of Antarctica in 1962. Nonetheless, the South Polar continent was to escape an African-like "scramble" and for reasons easy to discern. There were no indigenous peoples to colonize or "protect"; there were no resources to dig out from below the permafrost, only the threat of being excluded from benefits that might materialize at some remote date. The average temperature was −50 degrees Celsius at the South Pole (versus −17 degrees Celsius at the North Pole). There were no permanent settlements aside from scientific encampments. Perhaps most important, by the 1940s and 1950s there was really no Cold War strategic stake. Antarctica was a continent surrounded by oceans and far from the preponderance of global territory and population in the northern hemisphere. No missile trajectories or B-52 patrols would follow an Antarctic trajectory. Despite some theorists' calls for carving the stratosphere into territorial segments, orbital space remained a global commons like the high seas. The Antarctic could thus be demilitarized by treaty in 1961 following the International Geophysical Year of 1957–1958—hardly a renunciation for any power given the absence of an indigenous population and its apparent military irrelevance. Eventually forty-six nations signed on to the Antarctic Treaty System. The agreement allowed claims to economic rights (though not sovereignty) based either on the wedges of continental land shelf extending south from states to the north, or established bases; therefore, all powers, Argentines perhaps excepted, found it relatively easy to chill.

The result was that Antarctica was the region governed by a well-accepted treaty system, whereas in the Arctic, the legal framework has remained a product of the neighboring countries' declaration. The Arctic remains almost enclosed by the five circumpolar powers, who convened in Ilulissat, Greenland, in 2008 to form an Arctic Council—admitting Sweden, Finland, and Iceland to a consultative role along with representatives of the Inuit and Sami peoples—and to sign a declaration that they would govern the arctic region by virtue of their bordering on it. The end of the Cold War meant that the direct military rivalry might ease, but since then melting Arctic ice and the possibilities for ship passages through Arctic waters have kept the stakes high.[91] In general the Arctic Council recognized the UNCLOS provisions of a 200-mile claim to exclusive fishing rights and a 300-mile limit for exploitation of seafloor mineral extraction. Formally this was an award of exclusive rights of dominion but not of sovereignty and international shipping was to remain unencumbered. The Canadians published maps showing a supposedly territorial claim extending to the North Pole, but they made no effort to enforce it. On balance, with a few concessions to national advantages in the future, as the authors of *Imagining the Arctic* suggest, the declaration confirmed the status quo: the Arctic Ocean coastal states made it clear that there was no need for an Arctic treaty. But the motivation and legitimacy of their own claims was unclear since Ilulissat seemed to amount to a quasi-territorialization or at least trusteeship over open water.[92] In contrast to the Antarctic, which might be partitioned, the Arctic was a sea, a passage where the freedom of the seas must be preserved. Lyrical commentators compared it to the Mediterranean, linking the nations on its shore. They forgot that the Mediterranean was rarely a peaceful lake. Ilulissat remains a regime of ambiguity. In 2001, the Chinese opened a research station on Norway's Svalbard Island, citing among other reasons the international law of the sea, Grotius's legal grandchild, which guaranteed that access to resource remain open to all comers.

The frigid waters of the polar seas offer a convenient stopping point for the twentieth century's history of obsessing over territory both as an expression of power and for its own sake. Likewise for the obsession with sheer size, and for the conviction that continent-size powers (or their archipelago adversaries) must grind against each other like the tectonic plates that were being discovered at the same time. The polar arrangements signaled as well an end to the experience of having fundamental secular ideologies legitimate control over such huge units by combining their geographical resources with doctrinal fervor and single-minded politics. The antipodes did not serve the logic of those confrontations well. They revealed that at the same time as the politics of the later 1950s and 1960s backed away from the atomic brink and as the clash between militant communism and the capitalist world tended to soften, geopolitical obsessions might also yield.

A century of brooding over the advantages of continents and massive regions was fading. Smaller countries that claimed immense financial power or vast oil resources exercised more of a geostrategic presence. New nonstate actors would take greater roles in international society. Finally there were new international regimes for contested regions, reconceived out of desperation, but suggesting an alternative to continued violence and bloodshed. The innovative effort to place interwar Danzig under the League of Nations in 1919 could not withstand the National Socialist movement's rise to power and the unleashing of World War II twenty years later. The League's efforts to create a domain for common associative domains of territory, citizenship, and law, such as emergency passports or the minorities treaties, were discredited by its general failure to help keep the peace. Consequently, the UN sought instead to regulate but not to transcend the regime of sovereign territorial states. For a generation after the Second World War, partition usually appeared the only feasible response to overcoming violence in ethnically mixed areas, where nationalists on both sides could inflame communal sentiments. Imposing a solution to the murderous wars of territorial succession in the former Yugoslavia by creating a UN provisional supervision of Kosovo in 1999 seemed to revive the Danzig solution of 1919–1939, although it slipped into an ambiguous legal limbo after 2008.

In the decades since the Second World War, however, the ambition to achieve ethnic exclusivity within territories—sometimes expressed as inflamed nationalism, sometimes as religious zealotry—continued and continues, as of this writing, to produce millions of victims. It is only decent to recall the tremendous costs of the territorial obsession, which in so many areas of the world exacted its toll of uprooted peoples, misery, and death—especially in areas where empires had earlier enforced a certain side-by-side life among mingled peoples but then left these communities to work out bitterly divided states. The long list would include Armenians and Greeks in the late Ottoman Empire, Protestants and Catholics in Ireland, Jews in Central and Eastern Europe, ultimately Germans, too, in east Central Europe, Bosnians in a disintegrating Yugoslavia, Ukrainians in a brutal Stalinist empire, Poles who neighbored both that empire and the German Reich, Chinese in Southeast Asia or the Tibetans and Uighurs in an expanding China, Jews and increasingly Christians in Arab-speaking lands, Arabs in the aspiring Jewish state of Israel, Muslims in a new India, Hindus in Muslim territory, Tutsis and Yoruba in postimperial African nations. To evoke them all as a group, of course, is not to imply that they suffered equally or merely shared a common status. All tears are salty, but the causes and reasons for weeping are particular.

To be sure, they were victims as representatives of a minority ethnicity, sometimes religious, sometimes linguistic, sometimes just by virtue of a label. But they were victims within a framework that fetishized territory and borders. The reader might argue that to ascribe to sentiments of territorial attachment the toll in life, expulsion, rape, and loss of homes and possessions accumulated over generations misattributes the wellsprings of violence, rooted as they are in nationalism or communal hatreds and fears.[93] But the claim in this book has been different. It is that the continuing sociopolitical recourse to territoriality as a dominant mode of establishing the spatial reach of legal regimes for citizenship and property has infused and structured other differential properties of social and cultural organization. "Blood and soil" was kin to faith and soil, or to labor and soil—and the "soil" was implicitly a bordered turf that became increasingly prized in own right. It established possession and validated allegiances.

But the very acts of bordering might also point to more instrumental alternatives for territoriality. Carl Schmitt fumed at the denial of territory inherent in the universalist claims for Anglo-American capital. Instead he offered the alternative of a *Grossraum* while like-minded Germans constructed their *Grossraumwirtschaft,* in effect a Zollverein with a Gestapo. The continental imperial spaces that geopolitics envisaged might be coexistent, but they were hardly gentle within and hardly irenic without. Still, there was always a multipolar element to Schmitt's vision: there were spaces as well as space. The problem for a liberal view of the world was that these territories and their inhabitants—as for the theorists of geopolitics in general—constructed their life worlds through conflictuality. How might one think of pluralistic geographies without basing them on the Hobbesian premises that Schmitt had studied? What could not emerge in the second half of the twentieth century was a simple liberation from territoriality. Certainly not when the UN enshrined the idea that the globe must comprise a mosaic of equally legitimate nation-states.

But what did appear were alternative and pluralistic concepts for territorial organization, and it is to these alternatives, labeled here as functional, that we turn in conclusion. "If territories have always been the essential base of geographical reflection . . . at the threshold of the third millennium they are increasingly becoming its fundamental stake . . . and are multiplied in the domains where they've been absent." For Jean Michel Hoerner, territory meant an appropriation as a spatial domain (that is an imposition of a dominant center and a periphery) in any life sphere— religion and economy, as well as pure politics.[94] At the same time currents of globalization acted to erode such territorial structures, to undermine their geographical bases. The implication of such a view was that territory was always being created and dissolved, like sand castles heaped up on the beach, to be lapped away by the incoming surf.

In such a view, geography was hardly determinative and geopolitics potentially archaic. But so, too, was the perspective, such as the one in which Bowman had been trained, that derived geography from geology and its determination of where men might settle and enforce their states. Rather territories emerged from the human construction of exchanges and relationships that filled a space. This was an approach that had largely dominated the earlier French school of human geography identified closely with its founder, Paul Vidal de la Blache, originally educated in Greek history and archeology and a member of the generation that had to absorb the power of German science after the shocking defeat at the hands of Germany in 1870. For Vidal the positive influence was that of Michelet, who declared, "Without a geographic base, the historical subject, the people, seems to walk in air as in those Chinese paintings where the ground is lacking."[95] Vidal was familiar with the German contributions to geography from Humboldt and Ritter and more recently Ratzel. Ratzel stressed a planetary organism of which human settlement and states were products while Vidal emphasized how over long eras, societies shaped their global environment, a concept expressed today in the idea of the anthropocene. Still Ratzel's idea of the earth as organism was not entirely absent from Vidal's work: geography in this emerging conception sought the unity of species grounded in a region. Appealing to the precedents of Humboldt and Ritter and Buckle, and citing the English term *environment* as well as *milieu*, Vidal wrote, "The idea that underlies all the progress of geography is that of planetary unity *(l'unité terrestre)*."[96] This almost mystical commitment would be shared by the great historians Lucien Febvre, Marc Bloch, and in the postwar period by Fernand Braudel, and would in part inspire their celebrated journal, *Annales*.

In traversing the Atlantic in 1948 Isaiah Bowman had unburdened himself about the Whittlesey case to Jean Gottman, a member of his own faculty who chanced to be his fellow traveler on a liner bound for Europe. Gottmann himself, born of a Jewish family in Kharkiv with a doctorate in geography from Paris, was twice a refugee: as an infant migrant from the Russian Revolution in which his parents died, and as a young adult from the Nazi occupation of France. Gottman's own research pointed to approaches that might provide an alternative orientation for academic geography and particularly a way to escape the preoccupation with state power. His work emphasized "circulation" and "iconography" (ideas and images and symbols) in the spatial construction of a human community. Circulation and iconography were complementary principles of energy and stability that Gottman saw as essential, de-emphasizing the fixity of traditional territory and boundaries. In 1952 he set out his views in work still focused on states, but nine years later he published a major volume labeled *Megalopolis* that treated the Boston-Washington corridor as a unified region of human ecology: "the cradle of a new order in the organization of inhabited space."[97] This region cut across political lines within the United States and had no unified authority. Although greeted with enthusiasm as an imaginative approach to rethinking territory it remained unclear what were the principles that created a unity of this space besides the railway lines and highways that traversed it, that is, the principles of a "corridor"—the sense of dense human interaction with thirty million inhabitants. Megalopolis was not really a territory with a frontier, but it might be a proto-territory, a sort of flat galactic system with its major cities as the places where energies and communication were concentrated. Cities were crucial nodes in the symbolic and logistical creation of this proto-territory although surprisingly almost half of Megalopolis's territory was still woodland. Just as important, the cities and the corridor formed the West Coast of the North Atlantic and opened themselves outward across the ocean to cities on the other shore.

In the era when it appeared, such a geography, based as it was on a space of communications and shared values, appealed in particular to thinkers who sought to ground the North Atlantic Alliance (NATO) on a regional trans-Atlantic unity of ideals that transcended mere military security concerns. Cultural exchanges, sister cities, and economic missions would fill out the communication energies that allegedly made the North Atlantic a geographical unity or what one of its expounders, Alan Henrikson, called "one vast transatlantic orbit."[98] But the shadow of NATO and then after 1990 the debated frontiers of a post–Cold War Europe revealed that the issue of borders—of the reach of "circulation," and of the shared "iconography"—might be bracketed but hardly removed. Once political issues intruded, the attractive methodology of founding geographical thinking on the energies within a community raised the issue of where and why such a community was finite. Gottmann himself retreated from his early exuberance about the potential of the megalopolis to a concern for all its urban ills, including the absence of any unified planning capacity, in the 1970s. And in 1971 lectures he chose "the significance of territory" as a theme. The artifacts of Megalopolis that remain a half century later—"the Shuttle," the Acela, and "Easy Pass"—suggest its limits as well as achievements.

Perhaps most unexpected was the emergence of a geopolitics of the Left. Angered by the American intervention in Vietnam, Yves Lacoste proposed to enlist geographical expertise as social criticism. In his celebrated tract of 1976, *La géographie, ça sert, d'abord, à faire la guerre* (Geography Is Useful, First of All, for Making War), he analyzed the impact of U.S. bombing on the population, villages, and the ecology of the Red River delta in Vietnam. "[The science of] space is not a neutral support, a passive framework or an innocent science, but memory, terrain itself, the stake of social practices."[99] Lacoste's journal *Hérodote* announced in 1982 that it was to be a journal of geography and geopolitics. Christian Grateloup has endeavored to describe and visualize the spatial logics of paradigmatic historical formations, but causality and post hoc geographical description tend to blur into each other.[100] French geopolitics is commendable as an effort to revive a strong disciplinary tradition in the milieu of Vidal de la Blache and Braudel, but it has achieved public notice at the price of a certain disciplinary dilution. The casual browser of geography titles in a French academic book store and even newsstand could see that almost every description of places and politics was announced as a geopolitics of one sort or another. But then dilution remained an abiding peril of the discipline in all countries. Geography in France had a weakness for schematized maps with zones and arrows; in the United States GIS (geographical information systems) techniques allowed the visual correlation of economic activities, population demographics and social or political indices with the spatial features of a territory. The challenge remained establishing causal connection. That required temporalizing the changing spatial and territorial structures, whether at the local or global levels—or preferably taking account of both. In short, whatever the technique, to resort to history.[101]

———

Developing in parallel with the theorizing were the institutions: the continual modification of traditional nation-state self-sufficiency. There were many forms for this and most had existed a long time. Even as Socialist Party internationalism was largely suppressed in the 1870s and 1880s, lawyers and administrators entered a period of international cooperation, including the foundation of the 1873 Society for International Law. This was no mere coincidence: European bourgeois leaders were seeking to occupy a secular transnational "social" domain (even as their countries might confront each other as rivals), which could reinforce a social order capable of resisting the revolutionary dangers that had erupted in 1848, during the Paris Commune of 1870–1871, and subsisted in radical labor organization.[102] In an age of class conflict, the question of which great grouping might preempt the social realm as it cut across national lines lurked as a major issue.

Not all these initiatives involved territory per se: the International Telegraph Union (1865) and Universal Postal Union (1874) and the Red Cross (1865) recognized sovereign members and their shared interests. The geography of the great rivers that washed many national shores was another obvious locus for cooperative action. International authorities had been created in the early nineteenth century for the Danube and for the Rhine to establish navigation and maintenance of the waterway. The Rhine Commission began in 1804 with a treaty between a fading Holy Roman Empire and Napoleon's France, which was further elaborated in 1815, 1831, and 1868. It included the representatives of the river touched, while the Danube Commission became a great-power supervisory commission. A Congo and a Niger River Commission were envisaged at the Berlin Conference, although they did not come into being. The Danube and Rhine River Commissions inspired further twentieth-century efforts. In Latin America the 1971 Mixed Commission for the Rio Paraná representing Argentina and Paraguay was followed in 1973 by a similar body for the Rio de la Plata (Argentina and Uruguay) and an Amazon Cooperation Treaty Organization in 1995—the Organisation pour la Mise en Valeur du Fleuve Sénégal in 1993, a Niger Basin authority of 1964, and a Mekong River Commission (1995).[103]

Shared harbor geography, interregional highways, and the challenges of natural resource management had long compelled new approaches to traditional administrative divisions, whether (to take U.S. examples) Robert Moses's Port of New York Authority or the New Deal's TVA. Within countries, regimes instituted special purpose authorities to cope with particular challenges that local governments could not easily manage, what the French called *l'aménagement du territoire,* expressed most concretely by the 1963 creation of DATAR (Délégation à l'aménagement du territoire et à l'action régionale), a bureaucracy attached to different ministries and charged with thinking about the reorganization of national territory along regional and functional life. Behind such institutional innovations often lay utopian, visionary, or just megalomaniac plans. The liberal planning impulse that motivated a David Lilienthal—chair of the TVA and a democratic technocrat—was balanced by the schemes cited above on the part of German military and National Socialist planners to reorganize the eastern territories conquered by Germany—whether Colonel Bauer's visions for "Oberost" in World War I, or the SS schemes in World War II for de-urbanizing and de-Judaizing the Baltic, Poland, and the region Timothy Snyder has aptly named "Bloodlands."

When not the product of conquest, schemes for functional reterritorialization were complemented by international regional authorities—most famously after the Second World War, the European Steel and Coal Community in 1950, which morphed into the European Economic Community (with the 1957 Treaties of Rome), and thereafter the European Union. The continued debates over what sort of institution the EU actually was revealed that the legal stipulations of sovereign nationhood retained a strong grip on Western thinking. But constructing the EU also entailed a debate over an imagined European space, the rights and obligations it encompassed, and the appropriate frontiers it included.[104] Usually to bring such new territorial organization into play required the nation-state. Nonetheless in many respects the nation was being displaced—delegating many of its prerogatives "upward" into such associations as the EU, and devolving others downward, into reorganizations of national space that merged old provinces into regions with new leaders and stronger budgets and greater powers.

Also increasing in number and scope were the nonstate institutions of governance, the NGOs that proliferated to provide medical care or aid, to help with building local infrastructure or community organizing—would-be suppliers of benevolence who naturally developed their own aspirations for permanence and influence. They allegedly came without national ties. The term *governance* was the revealing descriptor: it meant the capacity or aspiration to govern without a state. But it also suggested that the programs represented were legitimated by rational choice and should somehow transcend the conflict of wills that muddied ordinary national or local politics. Of course, these had a long history—the International Red Cross, cited above, had been organized in the 1860s, missionaries and church groups far earlier. Where Franciscans or Jesuits or Presbyterian educators had earlier been active, *Médecins Sans Frontières* now followed. But the fabric of these groups became far denser. In effect, NGO land crowded out some of the fragile state institutions of Central Asia and Africa.[105]

Internationally negotiated associations were not the only ones that chipped away at what might be called territorial purity. Economic agents organized associations to advance common interests: starting in the nineteenth century, labor leaders and socialist theorists had created the First International from the Revolution of 1848 until its disintegration in the 1870s, and then a new generation created the imposing Second International from 1889. In theory these associations posited allegiance to a higher commitment than the nation-state, that is, the organized proletariat. In practice when national loyalties collided, they were revealed as fragile commitments, overpowered by older allegiances to state and nation.

With fewer manifestos, international business representatives and bankers have continued to weave a dense fabric of associations and contracts. These never seemed stronger than in the early twenty-first century, when the principles of "the market" that governed them generally came to be accepted as a set of laws that possessed a far higher rationality than the old norms of national territoriality. Yes, markets arose under the protection of national states or empires—they had a spatial logic and history—but they were interpreted to possess a dynamic that shattered political divisions. The "space" of capital could include offshore territory—protected postcolonial islands or onshore enterprise zones in which states ceded tax immunities for the sake of "development."[106] Corporations could deterritorialize their operations, separating management from manufacture. Some of this activity aimed merely at tax avoidance, squirreling wealth out of reach of the headquarters' fiscal suzerain, not the investment and reinvestment that "accumulated" capital or generated surplus. Some involved efforts to combine labor inputs across state lines. Along with deterritorialization came selective reterritorialization. Determining meaningful categories for this politically interstitial entrepreneurial activity was not easy. In economic terms it seemed akin to the "dark energy" that physicists and cosmologists theorized to account for the inflationary expansion of the universe. Where Carl Schmitt had based a theory of sovereignty on control of "the exception," here was a realm in which exceptions were granted precisely to let privileged elites escape sovereignty.

And with markets came "flows"—not only investments and remittances, and in fact the migration of corporate headquarters, but the millions of peoples on the move, whether as refugees from despotism or civil war, or as migrants who would feed the massive demands for labor, skilled and unskilled. Peoples settled elsewhere but brought the languages and traditions of their originating countries, making the ambiguities of diaspora an almost universal condition. The peoples of the globe seemed by the end of the second millennium to have passed quickly from an era in which national territoriality had been the most absolute of human institutions and loyalties into an era when it was revealed as an archaic, even feckless principle. Sovereignty and territoriality did not disappear as a consequence of some epochal struggle, whether military or otherwise. But suddenly observers had the sensation that these attributes of worldwide social organization had become depleted, displaced, and delegitimized even as they had been enshrined in theory and description and history. Territoriality, sovereignty: Were they the morning dew of a few millennia, perhaps, now evaporating under the sun of a global capitalism, social media, and mass migration?

Still within Borders?

Twentieth-century film directors understood the power of borders. "Don't shoot; they're in Switzerland," cry the German Stalag guards in *La Grande Illusion* as French prisoners of war flee across the snow. We hold our breath lest the prisoner exchange across the "bridge of spies" between West Berlin and East Germany in the adaptation of John Le Carré's novel break down in a hail of bullets. The tension in these scenes reminds us how remarkable it remains that crossing a border can radically change our rights and security. Few institutions so fundamentally structure our legal and sometimes physical existence as a frontier. This hardly stops border crossers, indeed often incentivizes their efforts. Wars and brutal regimes in particular set people in motion across frontiers, that is, from one territory to another. An estimated twenty million refugees had been uprooted by local turmoil as of early 2016. Migrants in search of work and even tourists have added to the flux of humanity and the need to create national and international responses.

For the last third of the twentieth century the responses tended to be in the direction of openness. Before Schengen referred to the removal of boundaries within the EU, it was just an unimposing village on the Moselle River where the southeastern corner of Luxemburg nudges the French and German frontiers. In 1985 delegates from Belgium, Luxembourg, the Netherlands, France, and Germany convened at this common vertex to eliminate border controls and visa requirements between their countries. Over the course of the next dozen years, "Schengen" grew to become a noble country of the mind that notionally overlays the European Union (less Ireland and the UK but with the addition of Switzerland and Norway), enclosing it in a common external frontier while abolishing frontiers within.[1] Americans cross the Schengen border when their passport is stamped at their first EU airport.

Concerns about terrorism in our current century have increased surveillance efforts but have not yet staunched the flow of humanity. As this book nears completion, thousands upon thousands of uprooted families from disintegrating states across the neighboring Mediterranean have also been crossing, often on perilously overloaded boats, hoping to win a foothold "inside" Schengen on Greek islands or Apulian shores and from there to trek further north, settle within the EU and share in its wealth and safety. Schengen rules specify that asylum seekers are supposed to be processed—given asylum or sent home—by the country where they enter. If they are not to be returned to the often violent milieus they fled, they must supposedly be allocated among EU states. Even the more welcoming countries and towns that take them despair at their integration, and several within the Schengen area have simply refused. Thirty years after Schengen, even the liberal German weekly *Die Zeit,* which deplored the Populist mobilization and the unpunished attacks against refugee shelters, was calling for a quota: "Everyone in politics or public administration knows that [the flood of asylum seekers: one million for Germany in 2015 and eight hundred thousand expected for 2016] cannot and must not continue in this way because integration demands an effort, above all in terms of humane guidance and fellowship, that every country in the world can provide only within limits." The German word *Grenze* refers to figurative limits as well as geographical frontiers and figurative limits: The country had to reassert its frontiers and acknowledge the boundaries of the possible.[2] Despite the dramas at the borders, the underlying stake for both those seeking asylum and those summoned to offer it was the safety, wealth, and civility of the respective societies within. As this book went to press, these attributes looked rather fragile.

Borders Besieged

The challenges to the Schengen regime are a good place to take stock of the current state of territoriality. Europe, of course, is not alone—millions of migrants from Mexico and South America have scrambled across the U.S. border, some legally, some not, some in search of work, others, even children, fleeing the violence that the narcotics habits of the country to the north helped implant. Millions of Asians have traversed the lands and archipelagos of Southeast Asia throughout the past century and in recent decades ventured to the Gulf states as well as the Americas and Europe. Borders are no longer to be taken for granted—not because they can be redrawn as the result of war, but because they function best only under conditions where they seem hardly necessary. The Canadian-U.S. frontier need only signify territory and sovereignty, but is hardly required as a barrier, whereas the Mexican-U.S. frontier has become an inflammatory issue for American policy, even as it processes tens of thousands of transiting laborers and tourists daily.[3]

Ultimately Schengen's crisis suggests not the fragility of borders but the contradictions and anomalies of territoriality in the twenty-first century. Setting aside for the moment the atrocities and terrorist rampages, the differential life chances for raising a family transform territories into zones of differential privilege. International borders can become steep gradients of inequality. A gradient, however, is not a glacis. In an age of global communication and possibilities for mobility, boundaries are still scaled or circumvented. Can global regions that maintain conspicuously unequal levels of material welfare and development—not to mention divergent moral and religious values—really sustain robust territorial regimes? To focus exclusively on frontiers in the face of massive differentials of opportunity—whether measured by economic and educational outcomes, levels of criminal violence, or the choice of work or intimate partner—might well be dubbed a policy of mass excarceration. But the vulnerability of borders means that they are likely to be defended all the more rigorously; whether successfully or not remains to be seen. As I write this conclusion, Hungary has erected a fence along its borders to keep out Middle Eastern refugees; Turkey has downed a Russian jet that allegedly trespassed into its airspace over a narrow tongue of Turkish territory; Donald Trump calls for an emergency ban on Muslim immigrants to the United States and a more impenetrable wall along the Mexican border. National territories—still guarded, still militant.

Territories, defined as geographical spaces controlled by means of borders, are not only constructed on the basis of sovereign states. Within countries and cities, the micro-territories of neighborhoods, *arrondisements,* or suburbs can become abutting cantons of mistrust and hostility.[4] To construct a territory at any scale often entails an effort to preserve distinctiveness and/or inequality once linguistic differences, sentimental allegiances to local "place," the habits inculcated by familiar landscapes, or the material barriers to migration all fail to do so. Territories on any scale impede the momentum of geographical homogenization or spatial entropy. National territories in particular, are inscribed into treaties and international law. International law, however, treats movements of peoples asymmetrically, as the Syrian refugee crisis poignantly illustrates. International agreements recognize the right to emigrate and condemns its infringement, but except for claims of political asylum, it simultaneously accepts the right of a state to limit entry. Early UN conventions recognized the right to flee persecution, and efforts by Soviet bloc countries to limit the right of dissenters to emigrate (whether Jewish "refuseniks" in the Soviet Union or the East Germans confined by the Berlin Wall) led to further codification of principles. Although 148 states have agreed to admit political and religious refugees under one of the applicable UN conventions, there is no generally recognized right to enter a host country. Sovereignty in short implies the authority to exclude but not to confine.[5]

Should there be a general right to immigrate? Speaking realistically, no state would accept such a norm, even though large extra-European nations—the United States, Canada, and Argentina, among others—welcomed many migrants into the twentieth century. Even these sprawling nations, however, imposed restrictions on the basis of health and race, and no country renounced the right to exclude or to limit naturalization. The presumption prevails that citizens already in place construct a society of mutual obligation as well as enjoy preexisting rights to citizenship on the territory that their ancestors have in fact themselves sometimes forcibly appropriated.[6] But they have also built a common life; they have a claim to abode. Still, if would-be immigrants accept the obligations—paying taxes, the possible summons to national service, perhaps an effort to learn a dominant vernacular—should there not be an unlimited right to immigrate (subject only to restrictions, say, on criminal behavior or infectious disease)? If migrants have the right to leave a place, it might plausibly be maintained, ought they not possess the right to enter someplace else? The responses, when it comes to refugee politics, traditionally reverse the questions: Why "our" territory in particular? Will not opening the gates in general just facilitate the violation of human rights by offending states? Even if we take them as more than cynical efforts to deflect criticism for inaction, the Evian Conference of July 1938 and the Bermuda Conference of April 1943 summoned to discuss the plight of Germany's and then Europe's Jews lamentably revealed how difficult the collective action problems were.[7]

Political refugees are just the most poignant component of migration issues. More general questions intrude, as well. How tenaciously can territorial principles of sovereignty persist when states remain so unequal in conditions of life that the more advantaged find it hard to exclude the less advantaged? To date, wealthier nations have contended themselves with accepting a general commitment to raising welfare abroad though foreign aid—though never the fundamental redistribution demanded at times by the UNCTAD or other advocates of the "Global South." The latest long effort to ease the barriers in the industrialized world to the agrarian exports of poorer countries—the so-called Doha Round—ended unsuccessfully in 2015.[8] Raising income in societies abroad to forestall the flow of migrants is difficult enough; settling political and sectarian strife in conflict-torn regions, whether by diplomacy or military action, has proved even more fruitless and counterproductive. Borders have not insulated countries from the violence that emanates from civil strife originating elsewhere. Neither do they offer security against those already settled within who take up the causes being fought out abroad. Perhaps we have reached the limit of territoriality as an instrument of order and welfare.

In any case, today's turmoil threatens—to recall the distinction treated in Chapters 1 and 2—to transform the "space of states" with its clear border regimes into what was described as the "space of empires" with its more permeable frontiers and the difficulty of excluding "barbarians." Even when they build great walls, empires continually face border challenges. Imperial politics continually returns to debates over how to stabilize or expand or otherwise contest the frontiers.[9] In the postwar decades, Western societies tended to open their borders: the United States decisively amended its restrictive legislation of the 1920s with the Hart-Celler (Immigration and Nationality) Act of 1965 and continued to enlarge categories of acceptable migrants. Despite some early illusions that it was merely importing temporary labor, Germany opened its borders first to southern Europeans and then to Turks as permanent settlers. France and Britain accepted large privileged categories of immigrants from the empires they were relinquishing.[10] Between the late 1960s and the mid-1970s, many countries entered an epoch in which the territorial frameworks that had defined so much of their organizational lives seemed to crumble and erode. The Western public's confidence that bounded, customary, and viable national states could rely on their borders to secure their well-being seemed to founder. Faced with crises of migration, is that confidence likely to collapse further?

The movement of peoples has gone hand in hand with the movement of capital, the displacement of industries, and the reemergence of Asia as major actor in the world economy after an eclipse of two to three centuries. Social theorists might muster indexes to claim that globalization was an exaggerated development, but the frequent recourse to the term was a symptom of the malaise in its own right.[11] Political economists, often drawing on neo-Marxist analyses, focused on the worldwide search to maintain rates of profit, prompting capitalist firms to evade state regulation by burrowing their activities down into the local level and simultaneously upward into the international realm—a tendency called by some "denationalization," and by others "glocalization."[12] Responses have polarized. Conservatives and Populists alike have decried cultural cosmopolitanism and the forsaking of communal roots along with unregulated movement of peoples. Sociologists and cultural critics—often from the ancient societies now so headily resurgent—have celebrated the flux as a rather kaleidoscopic form of emancipation.[13]

Social scientists usually search for the deeper or underlying "causes" of visible events and trends. But can the historian account for the past generation's transformation of territoriality on its own terms, that is, as a consequence of a geographic or spatial evolution? Geopolitics, as discussed in Chapter 6, represented one such attempt. Consider briefly the suggestive but frankly nonmeasurable categories and schemata proposed by Gilles Deleuze and Felix Guattari's *Thousand Plateaus,* in which the logic of territoriality continually contends with forces of deterritorialization. For the authors, territoriality remains a manifestation of "striated space," a term they use to describe the regions administered by states or regulated by capitalist economic processes and "assigned constant directions, divisible by boundaries" with respect to other states and regions. In constant opposition, according to Deleuze and Guattari's account, micropolitical life forces are escaping along "lines of flight" from these macropolitical structures, finding their refuge in "smooth space" and spreading themselves in "rhizomic" patterns of decentralized growth. The authors' account is not just a poetic version of James Scott's wistful account of tribes that evade the regulatory state, nor an echo of Max Weber's rationalization blues. Despite the term, smooth space is not really smooth but rather an assembly of multiple localities and points that provides the shelter for "nomads" who challenge the striated territorial spaces of the state and mount "war machines" against them. And not all attempts at lines of flight are praiseworthy rebellions; some, such as fascism in modern times, specialize in violence and become the creators of war machines: assemblages for conflict that dominate by violence, not law.[14]

History is not linear for Deleuze: its spatial categories recur and Rome still provides a model of what happens at the frontier: "on the horizon, there is an entirely different kind of line, the line of the nomads who come in off the steppes, venture a fluid and active escape, sow deterritorialization everywhere. . . . The migrant barbarians are indeed between the two: they come and go, cross and recross frontiers, pillage and ransom, but also integrate themselves and reterritorialize."[15] It bears emphasis: nomads and migrants are not identical. The nomad is territorial, but his space is smooth and outside the walls. He will not inhabit state space, but he starts a process that uproots the migrant from one point in a state space to another.[16] Deleuze and Guattari deploy "reterritorialization" as a key concept. It involves for them not merely a geographic counteroffensive but also nonspatial processes of asserting state control over economic actors.[17]

Of course, this is not empirical anthropology or documented history, but it captures the spatial dynamic that challenge empires in particular: the very distinction, created by the border, between space within, that is, territory, and space without. Establishing a frontier, imposing territorial order on the "civilized" side, creates incentives on the other to penetrate the boundary either for economic gain or reversing the encroachments of empire. The very effort by an imperial power to take over territory often involves a policy of dividing tribal adversaries, sowing rivalries, and in the process provoking the recourse to violence in general. "They make a wilderness and they call it peace," to cite the Caledonian chief who resisted the Romans as reported by Tacitus. Those on the side of Rome, however, interpret wilderness as the milieu of those resisting, nomads or nations. They label it as ethnic, sometimes as tribal, today often as sectarian, in any case, fundamentally perverse or irrational.

Faced with such resistance today, the guardians of the administered world within borders offer two different strategies for achieving stability, one territorial, the other global. The first is to extend the boundaries of political and economic control, wresting ever-wider regions from "nomad" autonomy by spreading technology, markets, and orderly politics. The program can be presented as a progressive campaign against entrenched privilege and hierarchies: remember the reformist theorists discussed in Chapter 3—Turgot, Jovellanos, and Belgrano, among others—or the architects of recent European Union enlargement. Even when progressive, though, confirming political borders and clear property divisions remain prerequisites for this program. So, too, does the control of migration. The movement of individuals and families ideally becomes a function of the labor market. Wanderers without work or promised land—for example, gypsies, hoboes—are categorized as vagrants by officials, though often celebrated as folkloric by those resisting. As suggested in Chapters 3 and 4, one of the crucial if unavowed tasks of agrarian political economy in the Enlightenment was to tie the laborer to the soil in an era when outright bondage was no longer possible. If the charms of pastoralism wore thin, for plantation cultivation there were always the mechanisms of deepening indebtedness or contract labor. In the nineteenth century the champions of public hygiene, social surveys, and censuses took up similar efforts.

The territorial strategy can also be presented under conservative auspices, by spokesmen preoccupied by encroaching anarchy. Samuel Huntington, Henry Kissinger, and Francis Fukuyama have seen the issue as one of creating political "order" (a continuing trope) against the dark forces of utopian radicalism or political decomposition: "Mere anarchy is loosed upon the world,"[18] Conservative territorialists wager on states and indeed on imperial states—whether on United States interventions or even wistfully on a Chinese-American condominium. Securing capitalism and markets may be a part of that agenda but are hardly primary.

In contrast to this reliance on stabilizing and enlarging territorial stability, globalizers aim to transcend bordered territories as much as possible and to make them irrelevant for the rational organization of the world. Rather than yearning for a de facto reanimation of empire to subdue allegedly religious and tribal violence, as conservatives advocate, globalizers hope to overcome transcend territorial limits. They seek to establish a domain where market transactions and economic growth (or "accumulation" in Marxist parlance) or such good causes as global health align us all in a pursuit of rational interest; they share Thomas Friedman's ambition to make the world "flat."[19] Although the globalizers traditionally inveigh against inherited privilege and sometimes inequality, their program is hardly egalitarian in its premises: It proposes benevolent guardians—the G20, central bankers, and so on—but guardians nonetheless. And in so doing it must also arouse resistance, no longer just from nomads without but those defending their own home territory and turf.

The political resources of territory—control of immigration, protection of domestic industries—thus appeal to two potentially opposed constituencies: those wanting to stabilize the world through a neo-imperial politics and those wishing to resist globalization. The second group can in fact often be recruited to sign on to the objectives of the first by virtue of shared nationalist commitments. In today's world the first coalition constitutes an influential but restricted group building on a fear of great-power decline. The second constituency, often viewed as benighted and labeled as Populist, appears as ascendant or threatening, according to the observer's politics. The contest that dominates the headlines today is between them and the globalizers.[20] Their signature artifact is the wall that will control immigration: in the United States they call for a more effective wall against migrants in the Southwest, in Israel they work to seal off the Occupied Territories, in Hungary the government walls off the Serbian border to prevent Middle Eastern refugees from landing in the Magyar state. Every strong state needs a strong border, a leading GOP candidate for the presidency stated in his campaign for the nomination in mid-2015.

Territory Transformed

The renewed cry for robust borders should not conceal the fact that the attributes and significations of territory have significantly evolved since the great rivalries of the mid-twentieth century. Contests over territory have largely eased between established European nation-states of western Europe, although not along the Black Sea, nor in the Middle East, South Asia, and the seas off China, where claims to offshore territorial rights threaten dangerous conflicts. Aside from an occasional cockfight, such as between Ecuador and Peru over their border or between Argentina and Britain over the Falklands/Malvinas they have ceased in South America.

But it would be superficial to declare that the significance of territory is simply waning. The importance of spatial governance and special contestation has not diminished. States still use spatial segregation to enclose the unwanted within a state as well as an expedient to exclude them. European ghettos, Indian reservations in the United States since the nineteenth century, and Bantu "homelands" in the Republic of South Africa were exemplary ways of investing troublesome and challenging peoples with a pseudo-territoriality of their own. The enclosed "camp" or Lager became an iconic recourse for states from the beginning of the twentieth century, when the British invented the tactic of "concentration" of a hostile population in South Africa. In the West it reached its ugliest and most vicious form with the Nazi concentration camps and Soviet Gulag. Even democratic regimes resorted to the refugee or resettlement camp when confronting masses of wandering humanity in the wake of war. In the Middle East, life in confined territories, such as Gaza or the refugee camps of Syria and Lebanon, has become a normal feature of civic organization. State authorities have no monopoly on exploitation of micro-territorial sites. Opposition challengers occupy symbolic spaces with increasing frequency. Television and social media allow small arenas to become the surrogates for the larger control of national territories.

Such a displacement from national to local contests should hardly surprise us. Territoriality has long been a dynamic resource and, as earlier chapters have documented, has provided a bounded spatial structure for more than just raw political authority. It quickly became more than just the cage where stripped-down sovereignty met "bare life."[21] It has secured different resources essential for governmental capacity and hierarchical social structures more generally. These resources, material and ideological, evolved and accumulated over time.

Recall briefly the history we have traced. The fortified frontier that came to define territory in the sixteenth and seventeenth centuries was essential (though not sufficient) to stake a claims to sovereignty. Extending or defending it encouraged advances in ballistics and mathematical reasoning, including analytical geometry and calculus. *"Ces espaces infinies m'effraient,"* Pascal confessed as he contemplated the heavens; territories were precisely finite. They created security, not the unease of the infinite. By the eighteenth century in Europe and its overseas dependencies, the properties of territory were conceptually well accepted. Territory could be traded, annexed; it might be compensated; it came with the rights of sovereignty. It could be passed to different rulers without regard for the ethnicity of inhabitants, assuming (but only after the mid-seventeenth century) that their religious convictions were not brutally suppressed.

With the seventeenth and eighteenth centuries, the properties inhering in territory expanded: economic productivity became an essential basis for state ambitions. The rationalization of the rural countryside, trade, and finances became all-important, as rulers and reformers sought to generate material surpluses, income beyond subsistence that might contribute to subjects' welfare and certainly to the regime's fiscal resources. Surveying and assigning values to the multiple properties of a realm—the achievement of the cadaster—seemed as critical as defining the borders of states. The cameralist regimes of the European and American continents, as well as the market oriented societies of England, Scotland, and the Netherlands, devoted sustained reflection to the production of national wealth. Economic activity often crossed borders, but territorial states had to provide protection for the agents who produced its wealth. The growth of trade reinforced territorial thinking and practices even as commerce surged across borders. The passages of the open sea that were the portals to distant colonies had to be allocated between common usage and claims of sovereign states.[22] On land, merchant capitalism and agrarian production both required the spatial stability of a labor force, achieved for three centuries by slavery and indenture in plantation settlements, by agrarian reform elsewhere (although well-intentioned schemes often went awry).

The technologies of the Industrial Revolution transformed the scale and resource potential of great landmasses. "Filling" national space along transportation networks became a plausible project, so that appropriating more of it promised grandeur and success in the eternal competition among nations. Undifferentiated lands were annexed from the interior of continents—in North America as well as elsewhere—and their "primitive" inhabitants spatially confined if not liquidated. The steel rails and copper wires allowed wilderness to be incorporated into expanding countries, as at the same time they let citizens and firms establish their "ownership" of the resources harbored by the soil.

The late nineteenth and twentieth centuries brought a fevered interval of territorial consciousness—expansion for its own sake. Territory became the spatial stake of global ideological contention. The huge African interior presented itself for penetration and claims of sovereignty, as well as ownership. The world wars and the Cold War intensified the stakes—freezing global rivalry in territorial form. And then, in the last third of the twentieth century, when territorial confrontations had become more encompassing than they had ever been before, the framework seemed to loosen. Global capitalism seemed to resume its relentless progress, now often at odds with territorial governance. To the surprise of social theorists, religious commitments once thought in decline kindled passionate alternative loyalties.

As the possibilities for acting territorially increased, the epistemological frameworks for conceptualizing space grew more encompassing. Organizers of territory got the tools they required and their innovations seemed to exploit new scientific knowledge. The early modern state and European expansion overseas drew on the analytical geometry that described location and movement on a plane surface, the advances in map projection suitable for navigation and visualizing territory, and the mathematics, including calculus, useful for ballistics. The preoccupation with maintaining fiscal solvency in the seventeenth and eighteenth and nineteenth centuries accompanied the early development of statistical surveys. The effort to energize and to penetrate national territory made possible by railroads and telegraph was accompanied by the analysis of electromagnetic fields. Europe's sovereigns were convinced they could allocate remote riverine territories in Africa's interior by agreeing on lines on the map; mathematicians within a decade proposed that one-dimensional lines would in fact fill two-dimensional surfaces. Theories of space accompanied its economic and political appropriation. Without our ascribing any simple one-way causality, it remains the case that the construction of analogous spatial frameworks advanced in different domains at the same time. The construction of territory was an encompassing activity.

So, too, in the late twentieth century orientations shifted again. Intuitive concepts of space and time, codified by Descartes and Newton as universal laws, became interpreted as special conditions of the broader frameworks findings of relativity and quantum theory, even as totalizing territorial aspirations started to become more pluralist and functional. Relativity suggested that simultaneity was impossible to determine and there could be no single universal spatial and temporal coordinates. By the 1920s quantum physics in particular set limits on the possible determinations of location and directions. Over the next few decades, theorists decided that it implied the "entanglement" of two particles at a distance, which meant that each simultaneously determined basic properties of the other, no matter how far apart they were, a counterintuitive finding that led further to the concept of "nonlocality," the inability to specify the parameters of one region of space without reference to others.[23] Nonlocality was a logical complement of many of the perspectives, and actual developments that were weakening the older reassurances of ideas of bordered territory: physical theories and geographical thinking themselves remained entangled as they had throughout history. Not—to paraphrase Gertrude Stein's quip about Oakland, California—that there was no there there, but there was there everywhere. Territory, too, became disarticulated and plural—a carpet of localisms toward the end of the twentieth century.

Territory for Whom?

To envisage the possible futures for territorial order we might ask the question so basic for political analysis: *Cui bono?* whose interest is served in a given territorial framework? As a preeminent attribute of political life, territoriality came to eclipse other pillars of identity and allegiance relatively late and with great unevenness. It always needed to compete with other principles of loyalty. In the Christian West, religion made powerful and sometimes conflicting claims across political territories or within them ever since spiritual authorities claimed independence from secular rulers. These claims and those of other faiths—Islamists in the Middle East and Africa, Buddhists in Southeast Asia—have revived to a surprising degree within the last half century. Kinship, friendship, and sex also weave strong bonds that often outweigh territorial political loyalties. In the "criminal" societies known as gangs or mafia, members in fact can build up their own territorial organizations within and across states with coercive sanctions that pursue their enterprises in the face of legal territorial jurisdictions. Economic associations—IBM, GM, BP, UBS, Goldman Sachs, Mittal, Siemens, and so on—sanctioned by law in modern capitalism, have come to spill over territorial and state boundaries. Even more successfully than illegal gangs they have created challenges to territorial political organization; these are the ones usually referred to under the idea of globalization. Capitalist economic organizations first allied with the early modern state and then penetrated the liberal state, for a while enhancing its scope but in the long run undermining its claim to independence. In so doing they blurred the spatial framework of states, as well.

From the mid-nineteenth century to the mid-twentieth century, it appeared that international working-class organizations or anticapitalist parties might have mounted their own successful threat to the territorial order. But the workers of the world did not really unite; trade union power waned and social democratic aspirations grew modest in the face of a competitive international economy and burdened welfare states. The latter, in any case, were precisely state achievements. International NGOs today often provide basic health and welfare services where governments fail; jihadists claim to combat the decadent states of the West. But until the explosion of legal and nonreligious associations, territoriality still seemed to have provided the normative framework for organizing societies.

Let me propose that in many aspects of life, territorial allegiances have become a class-specific property; they have in effect bifurcated. Those who tend to occupy the supervisory positions in politics and the economy—in the nonprofit or the electronically based economy, the research centers and financial firms, but in many units, too, of the manufacturing, agriculture, and mining sectors—claim to transcend territory. They aspire to make it archaic, depriving it both of real power over their particular activities and of symbolic power, as well. To use the term reserved earlier for intellectuals, or in the Soviet sphere for Jews, they are "cosmopolitan." They weekend far away from their work addresses. At the upper end of the income distribution, besides the universal apparel of jeans they like to sport identifiable products, whether recreational or cultural, supposedly associated with an international elite, but in fact now merely a badge of belonging. One finds them displayed in the *Financial Times'* self-parodying consumerist supplement "How to Spend It."[24]

This does not mean that global elites actually depend less on territorial segmentation. Their nonchalance about territorial loyalty takes for granted the capacity to wall themselves off from foreign or poor or dark-skinned intruders. They are more immune from foreign economic competition; indeed, they face little impact in terms of employment. To revive the terms of school-busing disputes a generation ago, they are often the "limousine liberals" of globalization. But for those who produce and exchange commodities and manufactures or contribute to the basic and less exalted services of life—administrative and military, custodial— territory remains an important principle of structuring existence in the world. The protection they derive from borders is fragile, but they are dependent on them, and their sense of national or ethnic identity remains higher. And, of course, they find political spokesmen who articulate their unease. Territorial orientations are thus not archaic, but they have become more socially specific. The territorial instinct tends to be a Populist one, and I do not intend the term in a derogatory sense. What remains of territory if the bifurcation of cosmopolitans and Populists continues? Obviously, interruptions are possible. Armed conflicts and wars make even cosmopolitans into defenders of national space. The First World War temporarily overcame the rationality of capitalism such as Norman Angell had outlined it in *The Great Illusion.* But assuming that societies are not at war, participants in many spheres of life activity have cast loose from some aggregate sense of territorial affiliation in order to weave a set of intense functional relationships that compel their energies and loyalties. Professional bonds replace territorial loyalties. These spheres of intense interaction, call them domains perhaps, are not spatial. Spatiality becomes perhaps one such "field" of interaction, privileged but not exclusive.

Territorial consciousness, moreover, has changed not just with respect to the socio-occupational-classes where it persists. It has been transformed with respect to the geography it delimits. Territory still defines national space in a world of states, though with less effectiveness in many respects. But, as noted above, territorial orientation increasingly defines authority within states. Territory is contested less exclusively as a question of frontiers than as an issue of public legitimacy at home. When the visible control of public space is lost (lost on television in particular), the power of a regime dissolves with it. This is not new: revolutions have usually involved the dramaturgy of the city square, but it highlights the changing importance of scale. If for geopolitical theorists, size of territory appeared as a crucial property, today size is less important; intensity of commitment is crucial. Territory is contested at the micro level in front of the television cameras such that a small bit of acreage becomes a synecdoche for national space. The public square—whether the Sorbonne in 1968, Tiananmen and Leipzig in 1989, or Tahrir 2013 and Kiev's Maidan shortly after—reveals the power or impotence of the national regime. The public square is a pure artifact of partisan engagement. It has no permanent residences; it is not a preexisting village or commune, not even a stadium or arena. Within a couple of days it gathers a population that has to set up basic supply lines and medical facilities, ensuring access to the media. It becomes in effect a counterterritory to contest a regime's hold on the wider country. Its occupants do not aspire to spatial aggrandizement, although they hope their movement and protest will spread. Acquiring macro-territory fades as an aspiration; micro-territory intrudes as the theater of legitimacy. The conflicts we face then over territory involve not the effort to aggrandize it but to manifest control, to illustrate that those who claim it preclude others from sustaining their hitherto legal order. A paradoxical situation emerges. Territory can do less for its inhabitants, deliver less assurance as to livelihood or even safety, but occupying acreage in the capital can reveal what forces can claim to rule.

The size of territory has lost importance in another way. What counts is a state's role within the networks of global capital: think Singapore or the Emirates.[25] The nexuses of finance lose their relationship to any hinterland and subsist on financial services that unite them in an archipelago of international banking or perhaps a tissue of logistics. They are geographical nodes on the necklaces of securities issues, art auctions and luxury hotels.[26] The geography of the classic nineteenth-century city followed the dynamics of Johann von Thünen's market center that gathered in rural products from the countryside and exported manufactures. Its labor force in Europe, if not the Americas, derived from the children of nearby agricultural regions. Today's world metropolises have become more independent of their hinterlands; they draw their labor services from overseas immigrants many from distant continents—Filipinos or Africans as household servants in the Middle East, Jamaicans for geriatric care in New York, Turks as taxi drivers in Berlin—and they generate wealth by trading claims on capital with each other.

We turn finally to a notion that the author has avoided so far—that of "place." In some ways it overlaps with the idea of "identity space," introduced in the introduction to convey the bonds of allegiance and sentiment to our homelands as contrasted with the "decision space" or political capacity and autonomy that these homelands possess.[27] Place, however, conveys a limited and specific manifestation of identity space. It usually summons up local and physical features; it manifests variously itself as landscape or turf or *Heimat.* Place had long been contrasted with space, a specific site versus the universe as an infinite container. Newton had left the idea of absolute space—identical and linear in all directions without orientations. Place was location, reassuring to hold on to and a repository of memory and identity. Place could become a sentimental-ized concept often deployed for a conservative preservation of old priv-ileges and hierarchies, but one with powerful appeal. The idea of "place" rarely escapes the pull of nostalgia. It has been associated with the charm of the picturesque, often of ruins evocative of decay but endowed with museological status such that the observer is not personally threatened by transience: a distillate of past strivings and contention preserved in the interim as folklore and restoration. Theorized originally by William Gilpin at the end of the eighteenth century (and soon contrasted with the Kantian Sublime), the picturesque testifies precisely to the rapid social change inducing melancholy but not protest—recall the theme of *"Et in Arcadia ego"* (Even I, death, am present in Arcadia), or the Romantic project of Wordsworth: "That what we feel of sorrow and despair from ruin and from change, and all the grief the passing shews of being left behind, ap-peared an idle dream that could not live where meditation was. I turned away and walked along my road in happiness."[28] More recently, the phi-losopher Martin Heidegger suffused his writing across two decades with concepts of place to convey his fundamental concept of "being in the world," *Dasein.* He welcomed a regime that fetishized places and OD'd on *lieux de mémoire.* Among the places of special importance, Heidegger emphasized the city-state or polis, where man created his historical life, or the woodland clearing—*die Lichtung,* a site of revelation within which he could create art and, according to his interpreter, could return to "nearness"—or, finally, the border where place was constructed, at times by violence.[29]

It would be unfair to associate the sense of place entirely with the conservative or rightist thinkers who often deploy it. There are privileged places that convey a shared community: Fenway Park or Yankee Stadium (although the "sky boxes" restratify the experience). Under some conditions place can serve social critics on the left. E. P. Thompson invoked William Morris for this role. Donna Landry finds the picturesque politically ambivalent: although it can lead observers to acquiesce in the inequalities it sentimentalizes, it can also depict its marginalized inhabitants—from eighteenth-century peddlers to contemporary Palestinians—as mute rebukes to history's winners. Raymond Williams offered perhaps the most eloquent evocation of the rural world as a site of communal values for contemporary society and not merely as a source of the picturesque and the folkloric.[30]

Without transforming place into territory, however—without bounding geographical space to assert a political claim—place as such, I think, offers deceptive hopes for redressing injustice. But even then territory's promise to control collective or communal autonomy must progressively weaken. Even without waves of migration and the power of capital, global environmental change and the explosive technology of data transmission will continue to undermine "decision space." "Data is shaking territoriality at its core," concludes one legal commentator. "Whereas territoriality depends on the ability to define the relevant 'here' and 'there,' data is everywhere and calls into question which 'here' and 'there' matter."[31] But, of course, the guardians of territory, national security services, seek to monitor the explosion—whether successfully or not will be undecided for many years.

Those who yearn for place have a different agenda than security services do. But to some degree they are engaged in a common quest—both search for some real-place orientation. For many global residents place is tantamount to territory, as common nouns attest: *pays, paese, Heimat*. They remain stubbornly grounded within segments of the earth's surface that have provided assurances of common life and continuity. Should we wish to weaken these? Is there any way, besides just decomposing the world into Populists enamored of territory and capitalists who feel no dependence on it, of diminishing the almost magical power territory has over our public lives? Dual citizenship is far more generalized today: nation-states are less jealous of exclusive loyalties than they were even a generation ago.[32] Legal financial regimes have also progressed toward diminishing the hold of single jurisdictions through tax treaties and exemptions on earnings abroad. But the expat shopper for tax avoidance hardly beckons as a model global citizen. We hesitate to describe him or her as part of a fiscal diaspora. To generalize such legal transnationalism might involve stepping backward into the distant medieval eras, where peoples were judged by their tribal law. The European citizenship of the EU seems to offer a rather pallid supplement to national citizenship, and ultimately it, too, is based on territorial principles. Still, the fact that territory can "do" less and less for us hardly means it becomes less important for our identity. And indeed perhaps we should not try to transcend territoriality too rapidly. Territory is still the emotional reference point for legal belonging. To give it up may not merely advance cosmopolitanism but also allow all sorts of even more "primitive" loyalties: family, race, ancestry, and religion. It may seem a primal source for allegiance, but it is often less brutal compared with many of the others.

––––––––

As of now most readers of this work will have experienced dual pulls. "We" live in a moment of global space, even as we still live within borders. The "non-we"—those whose livelihoods, health, sometimes basic personal choices concerning sex and marriage remain precarious, those whose life horizons, in short, are circumscribed more than we the readers or critics, those whose welfare "we" sometimes make our livelihood but often ignore—certainly live within borders. But almost all of us have inherited centuries of institutional habits structured by territory. The legal and personal and group expectations created thereby are not easily shed. We cannot renounce territory, even if it does less for us. Diasporas, multinationality, and advanced capitalism have all attenuated its significance; however, its sentimental importance has not thereby weakened, at least not yet. Certainly we are creatures caught in segments of time, not just time without end, but in given epochs and thus in history. But we are beings also set in defined places, defined by boundaries as well as by landscapes within. For now, even those who transplant themselves, whether from desperation or opportunity, for work or for love, remain still within borders.

NOTES

INDEX

NOTES

Introduction

1. As the early legal anthropologist Henry Sumner Maine pointed out, "From the moment when a tribal community settles down finally upon a definite space of land, the land begins to be the basis of society in place of the kinship." See *Lectures on the Early History of Institutions: (A Sequel to "Ancient Law")* (New York: Henry Holt, 1888), 72.

2. See the effort to summarize a territorial epoch since the sixteenth century by Jean Gottmann, *The Significance of Territory* (Charlottesville: University Press of Virginia, 1975); Jean Gottmann, "The Evolution of the Concept of Territory," *Social Science Information* 14, nos. 3–4 (1975): 29–47; summarized by Georges Prévélakis, "La notion du territoire dans la pensée de Jean Gottmann," *Géographie et Culture* 20 (1996): 72–83; also discussed in Chapter 6, this volume; and Peter Taylor, "The State as Container: Territoriality in the Modern World System," *Progress in Human Geography* 18, no. 2 (1994): 151–162. See also Alexander B. Murphy, "The Sovereign State System as Political-Territorial Ideal: Historical and Contemporary Considerations," in *State Sovereignty as Social Construct,* ed. T. J. Bierstecker and C. Weber (Cambridge, MA: Harvard university Press, 1996), 81–120. For an importantant intellectual history of the idea of territory from antiquity to the Enlightenment by Stuart Elden, *The Birth of Territory* (Chicago: University of Chicago Press, 2013). Elden also comments on the overlooking of territory as a historicizable category. See Stuart Elden, "Missing the Point: Globalization, Deterritorialization and the Space of the World," *Transactions of the Institute of British Geographers* 30, no. 1 (2005): 8–19, esp. 10. Although he traces the concept to that of *terre* or lands in his history, he has also suggested that there is a close relationship to *terrere,* to exert terror. See Stuart Elden, *Terror and Territory: The Spatial Extent of Sovereignty* (Minneapolis: University of Minnesota Press, 2009), xvii–xxxii. Related debates about the claims of early political organization are treated by Martin Thom, *Republics, Nations and Tribes* (London: Verso, 1995). The present work is conceived less as a history of ideas than the sociopolitical practices in which early modern and modern concepts of territoriality have been embedded. For recent contributions by political scientists that point to central questions for historians, see Miles Kahler and Barbara F. Walter, eds., *Territoriality and Conflict*

in an Era of Globalization (Cambridge: Cambridge University Press, 2006); in that work, I found particularly useful I. Hein Goemans's chapter, "Bounded Communities: Territoriality, Territorial Attachment, and Conflict" (25–61), and Beth A. Simmons's chapter, "Trade and Territorial Conflict in Latin America: International Borders as Institutions" (251–287).

3. Jean-Jacques Rousseau, "Discours sur l'origine et les fondements de l'inégalité, II," in *Oeuvres complètes,* vol. 2, *Oeuvres philosophiques et politiques 1735–1762,* ed. Michel Launey (Paris: Seuil, 1971), 228. Note the role of "belief" in the claim. Rousseau suggests that property finds acceptance from "progress and enlightenment" and prior cultivation of the land.

4. Max Weber, "Staat ist diejenige menschliche Gemeinschaft, welche innerhalb eines bestimmten Gebietes—dies: das Gebiet gehört zum Merkmal—das Monopol legitimer physischer Gewaltsamkeit für sich (mit Erfolg) beansprucht," in "Politik als Beruf," (1919) in *Gesammelte politische Schriften,* ed. Johannes Winckelmann, 3rd rev. ed. (Tübingen: J. C. B. Mohr [Paul Siebeck], 1971), 506. Without the article, *Staat* conveys "statehood" as much as "state." The term *Gebiet* implies a defined area. As Robert David Sack wrote in one of the classic texts, "Territoriality for humans is a powerful geographic strategy to control people and things by controlling area." See Robert David Sack, *Human Territoriality: Its Theory and History* (Cambridge: Cambridge University Press, 1986). See also Robert D. Sack, "Human Territoriality: A Theory," *Annals of the Association of American Geographers* 73, no. 1 (1983): 55–74. For other points of orientation, see Assi Paasi, "Territory," and David Newman, "Boundaries," both in *A Companion to Political Geography,* ed. John Agnew, Katheryne Mitchell, and Gerard Toal (Oxford: Blackwell, 2003), 109–137. On boundaries, see Georg Simmel's 1908 observation: "The border is not a spatial fact with sociological effects, but a sociological fact that is formed spatially." Georg Simmel, *Soziologie. Untersuchungen über die Forme der Vergesellschaftung,* ed. Otthein Rammsted (Frankfurt: Suhrkamp Verlag, 1992), 696—a citation I have taken from Andreas Rutz, "Grenzen im Raum—Grenzen in der Geschichte: Probleme und Perspektive," in *Grenzen im Raum—Grenzen in der Literatur,* ed. Eva Geulen and Stephan Kraft (Berlin: Erich Schmidt Verlag, 2010), 24. John A. Agnew has provided an admirable short survey with respect to Europe: "National Boundaries and Europe's Borders," in *Reinventing Geopolitics: Geographies of Modern Statehood. Hettner Lecture 2000* (Heidelberg: University of Heidelberg, Department of Geography, 2001), 7–26. Recent perspectives are collected in Henk van Houtum, Olivier Kramsch, and Wolfgang Zierhofer, eds., *B/ordering Space* (Aldershot: Ashgate, 2010). For a typology of exchange across borders, see Oscar J. Martinez, "The Dynamics of Border Interaction: New Approaches to Border Analysis," in *Global Boundaries,* ed. Clive H. Schofield (London: Routledge, 1994), 1–15; Ilidio do Amaral,

"New Reflections on the Theme of International Boundaries," in Schofield, *Global Boundaries,* 16–22. Owen Lattimore called attention to the shared society of the borderland in *Inner Asian Frontiers of China* (Oxford: Oxford University Press, 1940). Further citations in Chapter 2, this volume. In his pioneering study *Boundaries: The Making of France and Spain in the Pyrenees* (Berkeley: University of California Press, 1989), 1–7, Peter Sahlins rightly emphasizes that there is no simple progression from zonal borderland to delineated frontier, nor from authority over groups to territorial sovereignty: the two forms of boundary can coexist.

5. On walls in particular and the transformations of sovereignty, see Wendy Brown, *Walled States, Waning Sovereignty* (New York: Zone Books, 2010).

6. Toward the end of the last century the fashionable trope of decline was usually stated in terms of state sovereignty and not territoriality as such. For an early diagnosis, see John H. Herz, "Rise and Demise of the Territorial State," *World Politics* 9, no. 4 (1957): 473–493. For a useful antidote to the claims that globalization has largely erased territorial states and sovereignty, see John Agnew, *Globalization and Sovereignty* (Lanham, MD: Rowman and Littlefield, 2009). And for a major contribution to putting globalization in its place (indeed, as a force operating within the modern national state), see Saskia Sassen, *Territory, Authority, Rights: From Medieval to Global Assemblages* (Princeton, NJ: Princeton University Press, 2006): the engagement of the state in the contemporary transformation "cannot be reduced, as is common, to the victimhood of national states at the hands of globalization" (1).

7. Sir Walter Scott, "The Lay of the Last Minstrel," Canto Sixth.

8. It is important to keep in view a third spatial domain that has never been bordered so rigidly, indeed that challenges the territorial limits that prevail at any moment—what might be called the *communication space* in which ideas and cultural goods have been exchanged. The circulation of news, of telephone messages, or of e-mail; the exchange of scientific results and researchers; the transmission of nonterritorial religions; the rapid diffusion of cultural forms—consider the rapid implantation of operas and opera houses, later cinema, soaps, and rock—have always challenged territorial space. Theorists such as Benedict Anderson, and earlier, Jürgen Habermas, Karl Deutsch, Harold Innis and Marshall McLuhan proposed what amounted to histories of communication in different ways. The Internet and web have further freed this domain from the constraints of territory. Whereas identity space and decision space remain dimensions of territory that seem recently to have become decoupled, communication space has continually challenged given limits, even as it has sometimes become the basis for subsequently more encompassing territorial units.

9. For a summary of the dissenting literature, see Henry Wai-chung Yeung, "Capital, State and Space: Contesting the Borderless World," *Transactions of the Institute of British Geographers* 23, no. 3 (1998): 291–309. See also Agnew, *Globalization and Sovereignty.*

10. See Pekka Hämäläinen, *The Comanche Empire* (New Haven, CT: Yale University Press, 2008); Thomas J. Barfield, "The Shadow Empires: Imperial State Formation along the Chinese-Nomad Frontier," in *Empires,* ed. Susan E. Alcock et al. (Cambridge: Cambridge University Press, 2001), 10–41. For African polities, see Jan Vansina, *Paths in the Rain Forest: Toward a History of Political Tradition in Equatorial Africa* (Madison: University of Wisconsin Press, 1990). For a tribute to those peoples who have avoided state integration, see James C. Scott, *The Art of Not Being Governed: An Anarchist History of Upland Southeast Asia* (New Haven, CT: Yale University Press, 2009).

11. Marc Bloch, *Les caractères originaux de l'histoire rurale française,* rev. ed. (Paris: Armand Colin, 1961–1964); Fernand Braudel, *The Mediterranean and the Mediterranean World in the Age of Philip II,* trans. Siân Reynolds (New York: Harper & Row, 1972); Emilio Sereni, *History of the Italian Agricultural Landscape,* trans. E. Burr Litchfield (Princeton, NJ: Princeton University Press, 1997); Simon Schama, *Landscape and Memory* (New York: A. A. Knopf, 1995); Richard White, *The Organic Machine* (New York: Hill and Wang, 1995); John F. Richards, *The Unending Frontier: An Environmental History of the Early Modern World* (Berkeley: University of California Press, 2003); Mark Elvin, *The Retreat of the Elephants: An Environmental History of China* (New Haven, CT: Yale University Press, 2003); David Blackbourn, *The Conquest of Nature: Water, Landscape, and the Making of Modern Germany* (New York: W. W. Norton, 2006). See also John McNeill, *Mosquito Empires: Ecology and War in the Greater Caribbean* (Cambridge: Cambridge University Press, 2010); Alf Hornborg, John R. McNeill, and Joan Martinez-Alier, eds., *Rethinking Environmental History: World-System History and Global Environmental Change* (Lanham, MD: AltaMira Press, 2007).

12. For the notion that space as such is socially constructed, see Henri Lefebvre, *The Production of Space* (Cambridge, MA: Blackwell, 1991); and David Harvey, *The Condition of Postmodernity: An Enquiry into the Origins of Social Change* (Cambridge, MA: Blackwell, 1990). I find this claim problematic in its blurring of the uses of, and even of the lived experience of space with its physical attributes.

13. John Agnew outlines different combinations of territorial consolidation and claims of sovereignty in, "Sovereignty Regimes: Territoriality and State Authority in Contemporary World Politics," *Annals of the Association of American Geographers* 95, no. 2 (2005): 437–461. For the complexity of what the

Treaties of Westphalia formalized, see Andreas Osiander, "Sovereignty, International Relations, and the Westphalian Myth," *International Organization* 55, no. 2 (2001): 251–287. Granted the actual stipulations of the settlement, "Westphalia" as a metaphor remains important.

14. Michel Foucher, *L'invention des frontières* (Paris: Fondation pour les études de défense nationale: Documentation française, 1986); cf. Daniel Nordman, *Frontières de la France: De l'espace au territoire, XVIᵉ–XIXᵉ Siècles* (Paris: Gallimard, 1998).

15. I summarized these changes in Charles S. Maier, *Leviathan 2.0: Inventing Modern Statehood* (Cambridge, MA: Harvard University Press, 2014), esp. chap. 2.

16. Karen Elazari, "How to Survive Cyberwar," *Scientific American* 312, no. 4 (2015): 66. Cf. Jack L. Goldsmith, *Who Controls the Internet? Illusions of a Borderless World* (New York: Oxford University Press, 2006).

1. Spaces of Empire (1500–1650)

1. Marguerite Yourcenar, *Memoirs of Hadrian,* trans. Grace Frick (London: Penguin, 1959), 76.

2. Gudula Linck, "Visions of the Border in Chinese Frontier Poetry," in *China and Her Neighbours: Borders, Visions of the Other, Foreign Policy 10th to 19th Century,* ed. Sabrina Dabringhaus and Roderich Ptak, with Richard Teschke (Wiesbaden: Harrassowitz Verlag, 1997), 99–117 (the citations from poet Nalan Xingde [1684–1685] on 112–113); see also Arthur Waldron, *The Great Wall of China: From History to Myth* (Cambridge, MA: Harvard University Press, 1990); and Gudula Linck, "Realität und Mythos einer steinernen Grenze," *Sozialwissenschaftliche Informationenen (Sowi)* 3 (1991): 170. On the poet-soldier, see Kathleen Ryor, "*Wen* and *Wu* in Elite Cultural Practices during the Late Ming," in *Military Culture in Imperial China,* ed. Nicola Di Cosmo (Cambridge, MA: Harvard University Press, 2009), 219–241.

3. The tsars, according to Willard Sunderland, focused on their realm as a territory only by the early eighteenth century; see "Imperial Space: Territorial Thought and Practice in the Eighteenth Century," in *Russian Empire: Space, People, Power, 1700–1930,* ed. Jane Burbank and Mark von Hagen (Bloomington: Indiana University Press, 2007), 33–67. The maps of the era depict approximate territories (though with the Amur River as a clear frontier) characterized by settlements distinguished by yurts and churches. See Valerie A. Kivelson, *Cartographies of Tsardom: The Land and*

its Meanings in seventeenth-century Russia (Ithaca, NY: Cornell University Press, 2006).

4. Michael Roberts, *The Swedish Imperial Experience, 1560–1718* (Cambridge: Cambridge University Press, 1979).

5. Citations in Charles S. Maier, *Among Empire: American Ascendancy and its Predecessorss* (Cambridge MA: Harvard University Press, 2006), 1. On the European maritime ascendancy, see Adam Clulow, "European Maritime Violence and Territorial States in Early Modern Asia, 1600–1650," *Itinerario* 33, no. 3 (2009): 72–94.

6. See Martha A. Pollak, *Cities at War in Early Modern Europe* (Cambridge: Cambridge University Press, 2010); and for discussion of how observers in the eighteenth century understood the moral and political implications of these fundamental categories, see Martin Thom, *Republics, Nations and Tribes* (London: Verso, 1995).

7. Daniel R. Richter, *Facing East from Indian Country: A Native History of Early America* (Cambridge, MA: Harvard University Press, 2001), 164.

8. Richard White, *The Middle Ground: Indians, Empire, and Republics in the Great Lakes Region, 1650–1815* (Cambridge: Cambridge University Press, 1991). White claims that using such designations as polities or confederations exaggerates the spatial scope of American Indian tribes in the Great Lakes region where authority barely reached beyond the village. But his narrative documents that confederal efforts were persistent, especially when rival European authorities encouraged alliances. See also David J. Weber, *The Spanish Frontier in North America* (New Haven CT: Yale University Press, 1982).

9. On the campaign against the Zhungar, see Peter Perdue's great study, *China Marches West: The Qing Conquest of Central Eurasia* (Cambridge MA: Harvard University Press, 2005), 128–289.

10. Lois Beck, "Tribes and the State in Nineteenth- and Twentieth-Century Iran," in *Tribes and State Formation in the Middle East,* ed. Philip S. Khoury and Joseph Koistiner (Berkeley: University of California Press, 1990), 185–225. Other essays in this collection illuminate the thorny concept of tribe and usefully point out that "tribes and states have created and maintained each other in a single system, though one of inherent instability." Richard Tapper, "Anthropologists, Historians, and Tribespeople on Tribe and State Formation in the Middle East," in Khoury and Koistiner, *Tribes and State Formation,* 51.

11. Carl Schmitt, *Der Nomos der Erde im Völkerrecht des Jus Publicum Europaeum,* 4th ed. (Berlin: Duncker und Humblot, 1997), 54.

12. Marc Bloch, *Feudal Society,* trans. L. A. Manyon (London: Routledge and Kegan Paul, 1961), 15–31; for the geography of medieval expansion, see also

Robert Bartlett, *The Making of Europe: Conquest, Colonization, and Cultural Change* (Princeton, NJ: Princeton University Press, 1993). For specialized studies, see Société des Historiens Médiévistes de l'Enseignement Supérieur Public, *L'Expansion occidentale (XIe–XVe siècles): Formes et consequences,* XXXIIIe Congrès de la S. H. M. E. S. Madrid 2002 (Paris: Sorbonne, 2003). Lauren Benton has recently suggested how the legal regimes of empire responded to the geographical features encountered in *A Search for Sovereignty: Law and Geography in European Empires, 1400–1900* (Cambridge: Cambridge University Press, 2010).

13. Suraiya Faroqhi, *The Ottoman Empire and the World Around It* (London: I. B. Tauris, 2006), 21. Palmira Brummett, "Imagining the Early Modern Ottoman Space: From World History to Piri Reis," in *The Early Modern Ottomans: Remapping the Empire,* ed. Virginia H. Aksan and Daniel Goffman (Cambridge: Cambridge University Press, 2007), 24.

14. This distinction between the frontier as a zone, and the border as a line has become well established. For the period covered in this chapter, see Peter C. Perdue's introduction to *Shared Histories of Modernity: China, India, and the Ottoman Empire,* ed. Peter C. Perdue and Huri Islamoğlu (London: Routledge, 2009), 25–26. See also his instructive discussion of two imperial styles of enforcing or accommodating frontier separation in "Coercion and Commerce on Two Chinese Frontiers," in Di Cosmo, *Military Culture in Imperial China,* 317–338. For a useful reminder that elements of both zonal and linear frontiers can exist simultaneously, see Peter Sahlins's description of the 1659 negotiations in the middle of the river boundary between France and Spain in *Boundaries: The Making of France and Spain in the Pyrenees* (Berkeley: University of California Press, 1989), 4–7. Jeremy Adelman and Stephen Aron "From Borderlands to Borders: Empires, Nation-States, and the Peoples in Between in North American History," *American Historical Review* 104, no. 3 (June 1999): 814–841. On the fundamental importance of the frontier as an institution for empire, see Charles S. Maier, *Among Empires American Ascendancy and Its Predecessors* (Cambridge, MA: Harvard University Press, 2006), chap. 3.

15. For a splendid reflection on the ubiquity and social role of colonial warfare, see Jacques Frémaux, *De quoi fut fait l'empire: Les guerres coloniales au XIXe siècle* (Paris: CNRS Éditions, 2010).

16. Richard White, *The Middle Ground: Indians, Empires, and Republics in the Great Lakes Region 1650–1815,* 2nd ed. (Cambridge: Cambridge University Press, 2011); Christine Daniels and Michael V. Kennedy, eds., *Negotiated Empires: Centers and Peripheries in the Americas, 1500–1820* (London: Routledge, 2002). See the introduction by Jack P. Greene and Amy Turner Bushnell (2–14) for the argument: the negotiation in the title is that between what

used to be called the periphery and the center. Perhaps this is an alternative formulation to the notion that much of imperial politics is determined at the edge.

17. Dina Rizk Khoury, "Administrative Practice between Religious and State Law on the Eastern Frontiers of the Ottoman Empire" makes the same point in Islamoğlu and Perdue, ed. *Shared Histories of Modernity*, 46–74.

18. C. H. Alexandrowicz, *An Introduction to the History of the Law of Nations in the East Indies* (Oxford: Clarendon, 1967).

19. See Derek Croxton, *Westphalia: The Last Christian Peace* (Basingstoke: Palgrave Macmillan, 2013).

20. George Nathaniel Curzon, *Frontiers: Lecture Delivered in the Sheldonian Theatre, Oxford (1907)* (Westport, CT: Greenwood Press, 1976). For the discussion of the Ghazi theory of Ottoman development, see Cemal Kafadar, *Between Two Worlds: The Construction of the Ottoman State* (Berkeley: University of California Press, 1995). For Russia, see James H. Billington, *The Icon and the Axe: An Interpretive History of Russian Culture* (New York: Knopf, 1966). Frederick Jackson Turner's lecture on the significance of the frontier for American history was delivered in 1893; for the Italian influences on his ideas see Chapter 4 of this book. For German stimuli for his thinking, see Matthias Waechter, *Die Erfindung des amerikanischen Westens. Die Geschichte der Frontier-Debatte* (Freiberg: Rombach, 1995), 112n146. Friedrich Ratzel, one of the pioneers of geopolitics (see Chapter 5 of this book), discussed borders in *Anthropo-Geographie oder Grundzüge der Anwendung der Erdkunde auf die Geschichte* (Stuttgart: J. Engelhorn, 1882)—all cited by Andreas Rutz, "Grenzen im Raum—Grenzen in der Geschichte: Probleme und Perspektive," in *Grenzen im Raum—Grenzen in der Literatur*, ed. Eva Geulen and Stephan Kraft (Berlin: Erich Schmidt Verlag, 2010), 7–32.

21. Christopher Marlowe, Tamburlaine the Great, part I, Act IV, Scene 4 (Project Gutenberg E-text).

22. Ludwig Dehio, *The Precarious Balance: Four Centuries of the European Power Struggle,* trans. Charles Fullman (New York: Knopf, 1952). German original *Gleichgewicht oder Hegemonie* (1948).

23. For cultural approaches to the centuries between Han and Tang, emphasizing the role of the Northern Wei and Sui dynasties in inner China, see the catalogue for the Metropolitan Museum of Art exhibition: *China: Dawn of a Golden Age 200–750 AD,* ed. James C. Y. Watt and Prudence Oliver Harper (New Haven, CT: Yale University Press, 2004), esp. 3–36. For Central Asia, the Mongols, and successors, see Nicola di Cosmo, Allen J. Frank, and Peter B. Golden, eds., *The Cambridge History of Inner Asia: The Chingissid Age* (Cambridge: Cambridge University Press, 2009). These gen-

eralizations obviously omit the dynastic and cultural domains of South and Southeast Asia, whose expansionist legacies have usually been discussed in terms of their Hindu and Buddhist religious impacts.

24. Overviews by Beatrice Forbes Manz, "Timur and the Early Timurids to c. 1450," and Stephen C. Dale, "The Later Timurids c. 1450–1526," in Cosmo, Frank, and Golden, *The Chingissid Age,* 182–217. For a survey of the Mughals, see John F. Roberts, *The Mughal Empire,* The New Cambridge History of India (Cambridge: Cambridge University Press, 1993). For Iran from Timur through the Safavids, see the fine survey by Hans Robert Roemer, *Persien auf dem Weg in die Neuzeit: Iranische Geschichte von 1350–1750* (Beirut: Orient-Institut der deutschen Morgenländischen Gesellschaft, and Stuttgart: Franz Steiner Verlag, 1989).

25. Marshall G. S. Hodgson. *The Venture of Islam: Conscience and History in a World Civilization* (Chicago: University of Chicago Press, 1974), vol. 3; William H. McNeill followed this explanation, a hypothesis apparently first proposed by the Russian historian V. V. Bartol'd. See the discussion of historiography in Douglas E. Streusand, *Islamic Gunpowder Empires: Ottomans, Safavids, and Mughals* (Boulder, CO: Westview Press, 2011), 6–10, and the bibliographic essay, 323–333.

26. Peter Turchin, "A Theory for Formation of Large Empires," *Journal of Global History* 4 (2009): 191–217.

27. Without posing the same question as I have here, Jeremy Adelman has provided a thick description and analysis of early modern imperial interactions. See Jeremy Adelman, "Mimesis and Rivalry: European Empires and Global Regimes," *Journal of Global History* 10 (2015): 77–98, doi:10.1017/S1740022814000291.

28. Samuel P. Huntington, *The Third Wave: Democratization in the Late Twentieth Century* (Norman: University of Oklahoma Press, 1991).

29. See Thomas J. Barfeld, "The Shadow Empires: Imperial State Formation along the Chinese-Nomad Frontier," in *Empires,* ed. Susan E. Alcock, Terence N. D'Atroy, Kathleen D. Morrison, and Carla M. Sinopoli (Cambridge: Cambridge University Press, 2001), 10–41.

30. *Os Lusiadas,* III, 20.

31. Stephen Saunders Webb, *The Governors-General: The English Army and the Definition of the Empire, 1569–1681* (Chapel Hill: Institute of Early American History and the University of North Carolina Press, 1979).

32. For a recapitulation of the long-standing views, see Anthony Pagden, "Occupying the Ocean: Hugo Grotius and Serafim de Freitas on the Rights of Discovery and Occupation," in Pagden, *The Burdens of Empire:*

1539 to the Present (New York: Cambridge University Press, 2015), 153–173, esp. 159–160.

33. Cited, R. J. Barendse, *The Arabian Seas 1640–1700* (Leiden: Research School CNWS, 1998), 100. For a discussion of the law of the sea in the context of empire, see Lauren Benton, *A Search for Sovereignty: Law and Geography in European Empires, 1400–1900* (Cambridge: Cambridge University Press, 2010), 104–161.

34. See in this connection Berendse's critical observations on the proponents of various forms of the world-systems thesis in *Arabian Seas*, 433–442.

35. The question arises: Why did the Ottomans not become a stronger force? The ships that would ply the Indian Ocean could have been Turkish as well as European. The usual answer, ratified by Fernand Braudel and Colin Imber, was that the Ottomans lost the battle for naval military power. The galley, powered by rowers and sails and carrying fighting men for deck combat, lost out to the Genoese and Portuguese carrack with square and lateen rig and armed with cannon. See Colin Imber, *The Ottoman Empire, 1300–1650: The Structure of Power*, 2nd ed. (London: Palgrave Macmillan, 2009), 295–323; also J. F. Guilmartin, *Gunpowder and Galleys: Changing Technology and Mediterranean Warfare at Sea in the Sixteenth Century* (Cambridge: Cambridge University Press, 1974). The recent historian of Turkish maritime activity Svat Soucek suggests instead that neither the Ottoman state nor its mercantile classes committed themselves to long-distance ocean trade to the degree the West Europeans did; see "The Ottoman Merchant Marine," in Soucek, *Studies in Ottoman Naval History and Maritime Geography* (Istanbul: Isis Press, 2008), 171–180.

36. C. Boone, cited in Berendse, *Arabian Seas*, 438.

37. Written in 1604–1605 but unpublished as a whole until 1868, although Grotius published the chapter on *Mare Liberum* in 1608.

38. Richard Tuck, *The Rights of War and Peace: Political Thought and the International Order from Grotius to Kant* (Oxford: Oxford University Press, 1999), 82–94; see also Martine Julia van Ittersum, *Profit and Principle: Hugo Grotius, Natural Rights Theories and the Rise of Dutch Power in the East Indies, 1595–1615* (Leiden: Brill, 2006). I am not entering here into Grotius's involved arguments about the relationship the "countries" of the United Provinces (among others, the "States" of Holland) had to the union as a whole. More generally on Grotius, see Renée Jaffrey, *Hugo Grotius in International Thought* (New York: Palgrave Macmillan, 2006); Christian Gellinek, *Hugo Grotius* (Boston: Twayne, 1983) with brief but close attention to the origins of the texts.

39. Alexandrowicz, *Introduction*, 42–49. The most recent commentator, Peter Borschberg, has argued that the Dutch claim to wrest trading privileges

from Asian sultans was unjustified because it attributed more sovereign power for conceding trade monopolies to the diverse Malaysian princes than Asian usages allowed. But as Grotius understood, the patchwork of privileges and quasi sovereignties in the Holy Roman Empire was not so fundamentally different from the nested sovereignties and delegations of agency along the Indian Ocean. The sovereignty claimed by early modern European empire and perhaps empire more generally partakes of the same fluidity as that of the world of Southeast Asia. See Peter Borschberg, *Hugo Grotius, the Portuguese and Free Trade in the East Indies* (Singapore: National University of Singapore Press, 2011), 102–104, 153–162.

40. Alexandrowicz, *Introduction,* 49–59. See also Pagden, *Burdens of Empire,* esp. 165–170.

41. John Selden, *Mare Clausum,* cited by Tuck, *Rights of War and Peace,* 63–65.

42. Cited in ibid., 119.

43. Carl Schmitt, *The* Nomos *of the Earth in the International Law of the Jus Publicum Europaeum,* trans. G. Ulmen (New York: Telos Press, 2003); Schmitt is treated in more detail in Chapter 6 of this volume. For recent commentaries, see the collection edited by Stephen Legg, *Spatiality, Sovereignty and Carl Schmitt* (London: Routledge, 2011); the essays by Stuart Elden and Claudio Minca get at basic implications.

44. The three-mile limit was long attributed to the Dutch lawyer Conelius van Bynkershoek (1673–1743), but it seems to have existed already. See Wyndham L. Walker, "Territorial Waters: The Cannon Shot Rule," *British Year Book of International Law* 22 (1945): 210. I am indebted to Steven Press for this reference.

45. I take these accounts from Adam Clulow, "European Maritime Violence and Territorial States in Early Modern Asia, 1600–1650," *Itinerario* 33 (2009): 72–94. Francisco de Vitoria argued that a war for expansion alone could not be deemed just; Alberico Gentili, an Oxford lecturer, argued that a war might be just on both sides—but these early international jurists were thinking of war between organized states, not conflicts with tribal societies. For the debates on colonization, conversion, and compulsion, see Bernice Hamilton, *Political Thought in Sixteenth Century Spain: A Study of the political Ideas of Vitoria, Soto, Suárez, and Molina* (Oxford: Clarendon, 1963). See also Theodor Meron, *Henry's Wars and Shakespeare's Laws* (Oxford: Clarendon, 1993), 37–42.

46. Barendse, *The Arabian Seas,* 101. Berendse cites Frederick C. Lane to argue that the local rulers were selling armed protection for a rent, not engaged in trade to reap a profit on the commodities.

47. Van Dam ("evil and treacherous nature") and Grotius cited in Berendse, *Arabian Seas,* 104–105; Van Rheede cited 109.

48. See Anthony Pagden, "Dispossessing the Barbarian: The Language of Spanish Thomism and the Debate over the Property Rights of the American Indians," in *The Language of Political Theory in Early Modern Europe,* ed. Anthony Pagden (Cambridge: Cambridge University Press, 1986), 79–98; John H. Elliott, "The Seizure of Overseas Territories by the European Powers," in *The European Discovery of the World and Its Economic Effect on Pre-Industrial Societies: Papers of the Tenth international Economic History Congress, Louvain, 1990,* ed. Hans Pohl (Stuttgart: F. Steiner Verlag, 1990), 43–61—both now included in *Theories of Empire, 1450–1800,* ed. David Armitage (Aldershot: Ashgate, 1998).

49. Again Pagden indispensably analyzes the diverse positions in detail. See "Conquest, Settlement, Purchase, and Concession: Justifying the English Occupation of the Americas," now in Pagden, *Burdens of Empire,* 120–152. The formulations attempted in my text inevitably reduce the subtleties of claims over time.

50. Robert Gray, *A Good Speed to Virginia* (London, 1609); John Donne, Sermons, and Samuel Purchas all cited in Tuck, *Rights of War and Peace,* 123–124.

51. Besides Tuck, *Rights of War and Peace,* see Paul Keal, *European Conquest and the Rights of Indigenous Peoples: The Moral Backwardness of International Society* (Cambridge: Cambridge University Press, 2003), esp. chap. 3: "Dispossession and the Purposes of International Law" (84–112).

52. Brummett, "Imagining the Early Modern Ottoman Space," 52–54.

53. See Kivelson, *Cartographies of Tsardom.*

54. Jane Burbank and Frederick Cooper, *Empires in World History: Power and the Politics of Difference* (Princeton, NJ: Princeton University Press, 2010); Karen Barkey, *Empire of Difference: The Ottomans in Comparative Perspective* (New York: Cambridge University Press, 2008).

55. Eugenio Alberi, *Relazioni degli ambasciatori veneti al Senato,* ser. 3, vol. 1 (Florence: Al Insegno del Giglio, 1844), cited in Brummett, "Imagining the Early Modern Ottoman Space," 41.

56. Stephen Haliczer, *The Comuneros of Castille: The Forging of a Revolution, 1475–1521* (Madison: University of Wisconsin Press, 1981); José Antonio Maravall, *Las comunidades de Castilla: una primera revolución moderna,* 2nd ed. (Madrid: Revista de Occidente, 1970).

57. J. H. Elliott, *The Revolt of the Catalans: A Study in the Decline of Spain, 1598–1640* (Cambridge: Cambridge University Press, 1963); J. H. Elliott, *Riche-*

lieu and Olivares (Cambridge: Cambridge University Press, 1991); Rosario Vilari, *La rivolta antispagnola a Napoli: Le origini 1585–1647* (Rome: Laterza, 1994).

58. Gábor Ágoston, "Information, Ideology, and Limits of Imperial Policy: Ottoman Grand Strategy in the Context of Ottoman-Habsburg Rivalry," in Askan and Goffman, *Early Modern Ottomans,* 75–103, esp. 94.

59. Brummett, "Imagining the Early Modern Ottoman Space," 49, 47. For the justifications as ghazi, and of lineage, see Imber, *Ottoman Empire,* 107–115; see also Kafadar, *Between Two Worlds.* For general approaches, see Suraiya Faroqhi, *Approaching Ottoman History: An Introduction to the Sources* (Cambridge: Cambridge University Press, 1999). For a guide to the literature, see Cem Emrence, "Imperial Paths, Big Comparisons: The Late Ottoman Empire," *Journal of Global History* 3 (2008): 289–311.

60. Cornell H. Fleischer, *Bureaucrat and Intellectual in the Ottoman Empire: The Historian Mustafa Ali (1541–1600)* (Princeton, NJ: Princeton University Press, 1986), 273–292.

61. M. Athar Ali, "The Mughal Polity: A Critique of 'Revisionist' Approaches," in *Mughal India: Studies in Polity, Ideas, Society, and Culture,* ed. Athar Ali (New Delhi: Oxford University Press, 2006), 82–92. For Athar Ali the heavy land tax that the Mughals could collect throughout their empire testified to their effective penetration of society and belied a confederal structure. On religious justifications, see Athar Ali, "Towards an Interpretation of the Mughal Empire," in *Mughal India,* 59–81. For territorial concepts, see Athar Ali "The Evolution of the Perception of India: Akbar and Abul Fazl," in *Mughal India,* 109–118. Cf. Richards, *Mughal Empire,* esp. 36–40; Richards supports Athar Ali's view of a centralized empire. For a stimulating comparison, see Sanjay Subrahmanyam, "The Fate of Empires: Rethinking Mughals, Ottomans, and Habsburgs," in Islamoğlu and Perdue, *Shared Histories of Modernity,* 74–108.

62. For an insistence on how religiously oriented (rather than proto-national) it remained, see Gabriele Haug-Moritz, "The Holy Roman Empire, The Schmalkald League, and the Idea of Confessional Nation-Building," *Proceedings of the American Philosophical Society* 134, no. 4 (2008): 427–439. The conjunction of vigorous empires with world religions has been frequently noted. Religion exerts an obvious impact, but it sometimes serves as a force for cohesion and sometimes as a powerful solvent on central power. Established religions, or those the sovereigns chose to favour, Latin and Orthodox Christianity, Suni Islam under the Ottomans, or Shi'a Islam under the Persian Safavids, serve rulers. But the local fringes of large territorial units traditionally generate charismatic prophets. They exploit the resentments

of the underdeveloped edges of empire to denounce the opulence at the center. Less embedded in the bureaucratic structures and social hierarchies of the core, they claim direct mediation to the judgmental gods of the desert or prairie. Their doctrines can sometimes tear an empire apart, or lead to a generalized subversion, but they can also be patronized by an empire to provide a new lease on life. Even where desert prophets are not available, alternate dispensations can find territorial champions against the center: the elector of Saxony helped a fervent Augustinian monk challenge the orthodoxy of Latin Christian in Central Europe. In any case, religious doctrine and the claims to order political space have a vital interconnection.

63. For the background of provincial administration from the Han on, see R. Kent Guy, *Qing Governors and Their Provinces: The Evolution of Territorial Administration in China, 1644–1796* (Seattle: University of Washington Press, 2010), esp. 3–78.

64. Subrahmanyam in Islamoğlu and Perdue, *Shared Histories of Modernity*, 84–85.

65. For background, see Richard Hellie, *Enserfment and Military Change in Russia* (Chicago: University of Chicago Press, 1971). For the Ottomans, see Imber, *Ottoman Empire*; and Hallil Inalcik and Donald Quaetart, eds., *An Economic and Social History of the Ottoman Empire, 1300–1914* (Cambridge: Cambridge University Press, 1994).

66. Muzaffar Alam and Sanjay Subrahmanyam have included important descriptions of this immensely variegated system in their collection, *The Mughal State, 1526–1750* (New Delhi: Oxford University Press, 1998), including W. H. Moreland, "Rank (mansab) in the Mogul State Service" (1936); A. Jan Qaisar, "Distribution of the Revenue Resources of the Mughal Empire among the Nobility" (1965); Tipan Raychaudhari, "The Agrarian System of Mughal India: A Review Essay" (1965), summarizing and discussing Irfan Habib, *The Agrarian System of Mughal India* (1963); and S. Nurul Hasan, "*Zamindars* under the Mughals" (1969), 213–298; also the editors' own critical stance to this literature in their introduction, 12–16, 39–55, and their general insistence on regional differentiation and evolution over time, 57–71.

67. See the preface to the fourth edition of Satish Chandra, *Parties and Politics at the Mughal Court, 1707–1740* (New Delhi: Oxford University Press, 2002); see also the introduction from the first edition (1959), 1–39, for a general exposition.

68. Fleischer, *Bureaucrat and Intellectual*, 294–307.

69. See the subtle study by Najwa AlQattan, "Inside the Ottoman Courthouse: Territorial Law at the Intersection of State and Religion," in Askan and Goffman, *Early Modern Ottomans*, 201–212.

70. Ray Huang, *1587, a Year of No Significance: The Ming Dynasty in Decline* (New Haven, CT: Yale University Press, 1981), 210.

71. See Pierre Laederich, *Les limites de l'Empire: Les Stratégies de l'impérialisme romain dans l'ouevre de Tacite* (Paris: Economica, 2007).

2. Spaces of States (1550-1700)

1. See Guillaume Montsaingeon, *Vauban: un militaire très civil. Lettres; présentées par Guillaume Montsaingeon* (Paris: Éditions Scala, 2007).

2. See George A. Rothrock, The Musée des Plans-Reliefs," *French Historical Studies* 6, no. 2 (1969): 253–256; Isabella Warmoes, *Le Musée des Plans-Reliefs* (Paris: Éditions du Patrimoine, 1997); Joël Cornette, *Le roi de guerre: essai sur la souveraineté dans la France du Grand Siècle* (Paris: Payot et Rivages, 2002), 167–169. Unfortunately the far denser barrier of fortifications designed to protect France's eastern land frontier from the armies of the Empire, the Dutch, or the Germans, extending from today's Belgium to the key river valleys of the Meuse and Moselle, thence through Lorraine and to the Alpine regions, now remains in storage or displayed in Lille. Perhaps when the Vichy regime officially constituted the collection as a museum in 1943, they did not want visitors to dwell on the planned impregnability of the eastern frontier, where the Maginot Line had been so easily bypassed three years earlier. For the northeast fortifications, see Gaston Zeller, *L'organisation des frontières du Nord et de l'Est au XVIIᵉ Siècle* (Paris: Berger-Levrault, 1928). On the plans and models that fortification and sieges required, see the chapter on "siege views," in Martha A. Pollack's major survey, *Cities at War in Early Modern Europe* (Cambridge: Cambridge University Press, 2010), 109–154.

3. Marquis de Sourches, *Mémoires sur le règne de Louis XIV (1681–1712)*, 2:51–53, cited in Joël Cornette, *Le roi de guerre: essai sur la souveraineté dans la France du Grand Siècle* (Paris: Éditions Payot & Rivages, 1993), 168.

4. Local authorities might raze their own fortifications, as did some of the independent cities in the Holy Roman Empire after Westphalia that could not afford to construct up-to-date bastioned fortifications, and began removing their obsolescent walls for the sake of light and air. See Yair Mintzker, "What Is Defortification? Military Functions, Police Roles, and Symbolism in the Demolition of German City Walls in the Eighteenth and Nineteenth

Centuries," *Bulletin of the German Historical Institute* 48 (Spring 2011):
33–58.

5. Descartes's actual military itinerary is contested at points in the early sources.
   See Geneviève Rodis Lewis, "Descartes' Life and the Development of his
   Philosophy," in *The Cambridge Companion to Descartes,* ed. John Cottingham
   (Cambridge: Cambridge University Press, 1992), 21–57, esp. 29–35.

6. René Descartes, *Discourse on Method,* in *Discourse on Method and Meditations
   on First Philosophy,* ed. and trans. Donald A. Cress, 4th ed. (Indianapolis:
   Hackett, 2006), part 2, §§ 17–22.

7. René Descartes, *Meditations on First Philosophy,* ed. and trans. John Cut-
   tingham (Cambridge: Cambridge University Press, 2013), 2nd Meditation,
   § 31–43. Analysis in John Carriere, *Between Two Worlds: A Reading of Descartes's Meditations* (Princeton, NJ: Princeton University Press, 2009), 105–127;
   see also Daniel Garber, *Descartes Embodied: Reading Cartesian Philosophy
   through Cartesian Science* (Cambridge: Cambridge University Press, 2001).
   For the reference to his German stay, see Descartes, *Discourse on Method.* For
   the relationship with Beeckman, first enthusiastic, later full of reproaches,
   and the military events, see A. C. Grayling, *Descartes* (London: Simon and
   Schuster, 2005).

8. These constant-bearing rhumb lines are known technically as loxodromes;
   on a globe they would spiral toward one pole or another. Constant bearing
   means that a straight line drawn on a map would cross each azimuth or meridian of longitude at the same angle; the navigator would not have to
   curve his route (as he would on a great circle) to arrive at the chosen destination. Predrawn rhumb lines drawn from individual destination (say, a
   Mediterranean port) to numerous others would produce the oblique crisscrossing grids called portolans. The first known portolan map was the "Pisan
   Map" (bought at Pisa but made in Genoa) of 1290. Nunes published treatises in 1537 that differentiated navigation by loxodromes from great circles
   or orthodromes, and was named royal cartographer in 1547. Mercator knew
   his work, used rhumbs on his globe on 1541, and could avail himself of
   Nunes's mathematical elaboration of 1566 for his projection of 1569. For a
   detailed study, see Raymond D'Hollander, Henri de Sousa Leütai, Bernard
   Leclerc, and Henri Marcel Dufour, *Loxodromie et Projection de Mercator* (Paris:
   Institut Océanographique, 2005). The Wikipedia entry allows a clear and
   simple introduction. The Mercator cylindrical projection was also con-
   formal, which meant that not only did it necessarily stretch out east–west
   distances as they went from the equator to the poles to keep the meridians
   of longitude parallel, but it also lengthened the north–south distances on
   the same scale. This meant that the rhumb angles a navigator needed on the
   globe would be preserved on the flat map, but at the cost of vast distortions

of the polar areas. In an era before the development of logarithms and the calculus, the calculations of the angles was intensely laborious.

9. Valerie Kivelson, *Geographies of Tsardom: The Land and Its Meanings in Seventeenth-Century Russia* (Ithaca, NY: Cornell University Press, 2006). Cf. Valerie Kivelson, ' "Between All Parts of the Universe': Russian Cosmographies and Imperial Strategies in Early Modern Siberia and Ukraine," *Imago Mundi* 60, no. 2 (2008): 166–181. On the cartographies of China, Korea, and Japan, see *The History of Cartography,* vol. 2, *Cartography in the Traditional East and Southeast Asian Societies,* ed. J. B. Hartley and David Woodward (Chicago: University of Chicago Press, 1994). Svatopluk Soucek, "Ottoman Cartography," in his *Studies in Ottoman Naval History and Maritime Geography* (Istanbul: Isis Press, 2008) 225–238, charges that Ottoman cartography remained derivative in the sixteenth and seventeenth centuries although the copies of western maps became of high quality. Portolan charts were used, and Piri Reis's produced his famous world map of 1513 and its successors, but "the giant leap forward made by Piri Reis ran into a dead end. The exponential and unceasing progress of maritime cartography and geography taking place in Europe had no counterpart in the Ottoman Empire after Piri Reis, and in the last analysis the neglect of his contributions corresponded to the gradual stagnation of the Ottoman state and society" (ibid., 237–238).

10. Willard Sunderland, "Imperial Space: Territorial Thought and Practice in the Eighteenth Century," in *Russian Empire: Space, People, Power, 1700–1930,* ed. Jane Burbank and Mark von Hagen (Bloomington: The Indiana University Press, 2007), 38–39, and 53, as the basis for resource extraction and national consciousness. For maps of empire in general, see James R. Akerman, ed., *The Imperial Map: Cartography and the Mastery of Empire* (Chicago: University of Chicago Press, 2009).

11. See James R. Akerman, "The Structuring of Political Territory in Early Printed Atlases," *Imago Mundi* 47 (1995), 141. I am indebted to Benjamin Sacks for his research assistance on early modern maps.

12. Reproduced on page 41 of the contemporary reprinting of Joan Blaeu, *Atlas Major: Italy,* introduction and ed. Peter van der Krogt (Cologne: Taschen, 2006). Perhaps it is fitting that this large, beautiful volume was printed in China.

13. Jordan Branch, *The Cartographic State: Maps, Territory, and the Origins of Sovereignty* (New York: Cambridge University Press, 2014). For an elementary presentation of technical aspects, see Porter W. McDonnell Jr., *Introduction to Map Projections* (New York: Marcel Dekker, 1979); for more advanced, see Lev M. Bugayevskiy, *Map Projections: A Reference Manual* (London: Taylor and Francis, 1995). For a brief summary of Western cartographic development that presents but also critiques what might be called the Foucauldian view

in which maps become instruments of domination, see Jeremy Black, *Maps and Politics* (Chicago: University of Chicago Press, 1997). As a naive empiricist, I remain awestruck when the views of global coastlines from the airplane window at 10,000 meters or from satellite transmissions at 200 kilometers faithfully seem to follow the lines on maps.

14. Martha D. Pollack, *Cities at War*. For the neo-Stoic circle in Antwerp, I am indebted to Jessica Maier's study, "The Parergon of Abraham Ortelius" (MA thesis, Columbia University, 1999).

15. Claude Wenzler, *Architecture du Bastion: l'Art de Vauban* (Rennes: Éditions Ouest-France, 2000), 14. Wenzel's small but beautifully illustrated book is based on the museum exposition. Pollak, *Cities at War*, 49–59, covers Vauban and the eastern border fortresses. For a survey, see also Jean-Denis G. G. Lepage, *Vauban and the French Military under Louis XIV: An Illustrated History of Fortifications and Strategies* (Jefferson, NC: McFarland, 2010).

16. See Sebastien le Prestre de Vauban, *A Manual of Siegecraft and Fortification*, ed. and trans. George A. Rothrock (Ann Arbor: University of Michigan Press, 1968); Nicolas Faucherre, *Places Fortes, Bastions du Pouvoir* (Paris: Rempart, 1986); Christopher Duffy's two-volume work, *Siege Warfare*, issued as *Siege Warfare: The Fortress in the Early Modern World 1494–1660* (London, Routledge & Kegan Paul, 1979) and *The Fortress in the Age of Vauban and Frederick the Great 1660–1789* (London: Routledge & Kegan Paul, 1985). See also Christopher Duffy, *Fire & Stone: The Science of Fortress Warfare 1660–1860* (London: Newton Abbot: David & Charles, 1975).

17. For a critical defense of Cartesian concepts and a review of the controversies, see, most recently, Edward Slowik, *Cartesian Spacetime: Descartes' Physics and the Relational Theory of Space and Motion. Archives Internationales d'Histoire des Idées, nr. 181* (Dordrecht: Kluwer, 2010).

18. Jozsef Kelenik insists that Hungary participated in the innovations of fortress architecture. As of the 1570s there were large fortresses that accommodated defensive artillery at Szatmár, Eger, Komárom, and Gyor, and numerous palisades and smaller forts. He also provides a highly informed discussion of muskets and other individual firearms, which became far more extensively deployed from the 1560s or 1570s on and took an increasing toll among Ottoman sipahi or cavalry (increasing the role of the Janissary infantry and contributing to the crises of feudal tenures). The artillery power deployed in Hungary was comparable to that available for sieges in France and the Low Countries. Jozsef Kelenik, "The Military Revolution in Hungary," in *Ottomans, Hungarians, and Habsburgs in Central Europe: The Military Confines in the Era of Ottoman Conquest,* ed. Géza Dàvid and Pál Fodor (Leiden: Brill, 2000), 71–159 (with a plan for the hexagonal citadel of Érk-

sekújvár); and in the same volume, Klara Hegy, "The Ottoman Network of Fortresses in Hungary," 163–192, which was keyed to the geography of the provinces conquered.

19. Above all, see Geoffrey Parker, *The Military Revolution; Military Innovation and the Rise of the West, 1500–1800* (Cambridge: Cambridge University Press, 1996); J. R. Hale, *Renaissance Fortification, Art and Engineering* (Norwich: Thames and Hudson, 1977). For Vauban's designs, see Vauban, *A Manual of Siegecraft and Fortification.* On the political consequences, see Brian M. Downing, *The Military Revolution and Political Change: Origins of Democracy and Autocracy in Early Modern Europe* (Princeton, NJ: Princeton University Press, 1992); Charles Tilly, ed., *The Formation of National States in Western Europe* (Princeton, NJ: Princeton University Press, 1975).

20. On the technology of pre-gunpowder weapons and forts, I rely on Ronnie Ellenblum, *Crusader Castles and Modern Histories* (Cambridge: Cambridge University Press, 2007), 189–230.

21. Jean Deloche, *Studies on Fortification in India* (Paris: Ecole Française d'Extrême-Orient, 2007), which summarizes a lifetime of specialized studies. See also J. Burton-Page, "A Study of Fortification in the Indian Subcontinent from the Thirteenth to the Eighteenth Century A.D." *Bulletin of the School of Oriental and African Studies* 23, no. 3 (1960): 508–522.

22. See Ellenblum, *Crusader Castles and Modern Histories.* The dispute, as its historian-archeologist brilliantly demonstrates, rests in turn on the imputed relationship of fortified site to territorial frontier: Did the pre-artillery (but not pre-catapult) castles protect the eastern border and the roads of a cohesive narrow state that extended from the northern half of today's Israel and West Bank up to Beirut? Or had they originated, as he claims, as local centers in a frontier area that only after about sixty years became so threatened as to require enhanced fortification—and some of whose most monumental additions were added only by Muslims after reconquest? By implication, can they be construed as a remote claim to Zionist or to Palestinian patrimony?

23. For the calculations of sixteenth-century design, see Horst de la Croix, "Military Architecture and the Radial City Plan," *Art Bulletin* 42, no. 4 (1960): 263–290, esp. 279–281. See also John Hale, "The Early Development of the Bastion: An Italian Chronology c. 1450–c. 1534," in *Europe in the Late Middle Ages,* ed. J. R. Hale, L. Highfield, and B. Smalley (London: Faber & Faber, 1965), 464–494. Heavy cannon had a range of perhaps four hundred meters or a quarter mile if fired directly at a target; lighter artillery had about half of that. Effective demolition required horizontal fire—not the parabolic arc of forty-five degrees that engineers soon learned provided the maximum range. Claude Wenzler, *Architecture du Bastion: l'Art de Vauban* (Rennes: Éditions Ouest-France, 2000).

24. Pollack, *Cities at War,* 63–78.

25. Francesco di Giorgio Martini's *Trattato di architettura civile e miliare* is presented—along with de Busca's and other contributions—in de la Croix, "Military Architecture and the Radial City Plan," 268–71.

26. Michael S. A. Dechert, "The Military Architecture of Francesco di Giorgio in Southern Italy," *Journal of the Society of Architectural Historians* 19, no. 3 (1990): 161–180. For the towers of the Romagna, see 162n3.

27. Ibid. Dechert provides extensive bibliography on the history of fortification.

28. Simone Pepper and Nicholas Adams, *Firearms and Fortification: Military Architecture and Siege Warfare in sixteenth-century Siena* (Chicago: University of Chicago Press, 1968), 28–30. For the Maghrebian forts, see Néji Djelloul, *Les fortifications côtières ottomanes de la Régence de Tunis (XVIe–XIXe siècles)* (Zaghouan: Fondation Temimi pour la Recherche Scientifique e l'Information [FTERSI], 1995).

29. Details in Pepper and Adams, *Firearms and Fortifications,* 32–78.

30. For surveys of these developments, see Quentin Skinner, *The Foundations of Modern Political Thought,* vol. 1, *The Renaissance* (Cambridge: Cambridge University Press, 1978), 113–118.

31. Most recently on the implications for territory, see Luca Vannoni, "Il dominio territoriale di Firenze in Guicciardini e Machiavelli: Alcune Considerazioni," *Annali della Storia di Firenze* 7 (2012): 73–96.

32. Dechert, "Military Architecture of Francesco di Giorgio," 179.

33. Pollack, *Cities at War,* 9.

34. De la Croix, "Military Architecture and the Radial City Plan," 279.

35. Ibid., 287–289.

36. Text from Tommaso Campanella, *The City of the Sun* (eBooks @Adelaide: University of Adelaide Library).

37. Franco de' Marchi cited by Pepper and Adams, *Firearms and Fortifications,* 28.

38. Pollack, *Cities at War.* See also Walter Barberis, *Le Armi del principe: La tradizione militare sabauda* (Turin: Einaudi, 1988).

39. For the interplay of map and image, see Jessica Maier, *Rome Measured and Imagined: Early Modern Maps of the Eternal City* (Chicago: University of Chicago Press, 2015).

40. Ramon Gutierrez and Cristina Esteras, *Territorio y Fortificación: Vauban, Fernandez de Medrano, Ignacio Sala y Felix Prosperi. Influencia en España y America*

(Madrid: Ediciónes Tuero, S. A., 1991). On the Italian connections, see 61–65. On Latin America, see 127–160.

41. Ibid., 52–59.

42. Fernando Giron cited in Christopher Duffy, *Siege Warfare: The Fortress in the Early Modern World 1494–1660* (London: Routledge and Kegan Paul, 1979), 58.

43. See Duffy, *Siege Warfare*, 102 and 103. The passing of the edge to the offensive, often concealed by the visual impression made by the great fortifications, had a parallel in late 1917 and 1918, when the primacy of the defensive, indelibly envisaged after three years of trench warfare, actually began to yield to the new British and German tactics of offensive action.

44. Tavannes, cited in Duffy, *Siege Warfare*, 100. The provinces of Holland and Zeeland had more of these difficult obstacles than the more open country below the Great Rivers, which was the area that the Spanish ended up holding.

45. Vincent A. Smith, *Akbar, the Great Mogul 1542–1605,* 2nd rev. ed. (Oxford: Clarendon, 1919), 86–91. On Akbar's quadrilateral, see John F. Richards, *The Mughal Empire* (New York: Cambridge University Press, 1995), 27–28.

46. Cf. Jos J. L. Gommans, *Mughal Warfare: Indian Frontiers and High Roads to Empire, 1500–1700* (London: Routledge, 2002).

47. Deloche, *Studies on Fortification in India,* 75–142, regrets the fragmentary sources available but provides details on multiple sites and techniques. Gommans stresses that for the Mughals the roads of the interior as well as the frontiers formed an integral concept of military expansion (see *Mughal Warfare*).

48. I rely on Mark L. Stein, *Guarding the Frontier: Ottoman Border Forts and Garrisons in Europe* (London: Tauris, 2007), 29–61.

49. William E. Whittaker, ed., *Frontier Forts of Iowa: Indians, Trader, and Soldiers, 1682–1862* (Iowa City: University of Iowa Press, 2009), 2, 4. For American Indian forts, see 42–54.

50. Gutierrez and Esteras, *Territorio y Fortificación,* 32–39.

51. The French fortification at Louisbourg in Quebec did not serve particularly well; the French did not use it to project power outward into the Gulf of Saint Lawrence as the Spanish used Havana. John Robert McNeill, *Atlantic Empires of France and Spain: Louisburg and Havana, 1700–1763* (Chapel Hill: University of North Carolina Press, 1985); Samuel Wilson, *Colonial Fortifications and Military Architecture in the Mississippi Valley* (Urbana: University of Illinois Press, 1965).

52. Horacio Capel, *Geografía y matemáticas en la España del Siglo XVIII* (Barcelona: Ikos, Tau, 1982). Cited in Gutierrez and Esteras, *Territorio y Fortificación,* 78.

53. Gutierrez and Esteras, *Territorio y Fortificación,* 114–116.

54. Andreas Osiander, "Sovereignty, International Relations, and the Westphalian Myth," *International Organization* 55, no. 2 (2001): 251–287; see also Andreas Osiander, *The States System of Europe, 1640–1990: Peacemaking and the Conditions of International Stability* (Oxford: Clarendon, 1994), 16–89. For good brief discussions of the treaties and their context, see the essays for the catalog *1648: War and Peace in Europe,* ed. Klaus Bussmann and Heinz Schilling (N.p.: Münster,1998). For a general survey, see Stephen D. Krasner, *Sovereignty: Organized Hypocrisy* (Princeton, NJ: Princeton University Press, 1999).

55. Text taken from Yale Law School's Avalon project with online documentation: avalon.law.yale.edu/17th_century/westphal.asp.

56. Text of Abschied is at www.lwl.org/westfaelische-geschichte/portal /Internet/finde/langDatensatz.php?urlID=739&url_tabelle=tab_quelle.

57. Ulrich Zasius, *The Custom of Fiefs,* cited in Skinner, *Foundations,* 2:129. For the application of international law to German public law, see Michael Stolleis, *Geschichte des öffentlichen Rechts in Deutschland,* vol. 1, *Reichspublizistik und Policeywissenschaft 1600–1800* (Munich: Beck, 1988).

58. For the citations, see Skinner, *Foundations,* 2:281–285. Jean-Fabien Spitz's effort to make this doctrine coherent escapes me. See Jean-Fabien Spitz, *Bodin et la souveraineté* (Paris: Presses Universitaires de France, 1998).

59. M. Athar Ali, "The Evolution of the Perception of India: Akbar and Abul Fazl," *Mughal India: Studies in Polity, Ideas, Society, and Culture* (New York: Oxford University Press, 2006), 109–128.

60. Skinner, *Foundations,* 2:349.

61. Ibid., 2:286–287.

62. Peter Sahlins, *Boundaries: The Making of France and Spain in the Pyrenees* (Berkeley: University of California Press, 1989), 25–61.

63. See Annabel S. Brett, *Changes of State: Nature and the Limits of the City in Early Modern Natural Law* (Princeton, NJ: Princeton University Press, 2011), 198.

64. Michel Foucault, *Sécurité, Territoire, Population: Cour au Collège de France, 1977–1978* (Paris: Gallimard-Seuil, 2004), 98–100.

65. Ibid., 236: "on entre dans l'âge des conduits, dans l'âge des directions, dans l'âge des direction."

66. Ibid., 252–253.

67. Giovanni Treccani degli Affaria, *Storia di Milano,* vol. 10, *L'età della riforma cattolica, 1559–1630* (Milan: Fondazione Treccani degli Alfieri per la Storia di Milano, 1958).

68. *Henry V,* act 3. Cf. Thedor Meron, *Henry's Wars and Shakespeare's Laws: Perspectives on the Law of War in the Later Middle Ages* (Oxford: Clarendon, 1993). Also Maurice H. Keen, *The Laws of War in the Late Middle Ages* (London: Routledge and Kegan Paul, 1965), 119–133. See Henry V's catalogue of horrors that awaited Harfleur if the town resisted (act 3, scene 3). But if the commander of a city or fortress did surrender while he still had ammunition and civilian supplies, he could, if caught, be charged with treason. Keen cites the remarkable case in which Henry, acting as an executive for the internationally accepted laws of siege warfare executed a French officer who negotiated the surrender of Cherbourg to his own English forces (46–47). See also Jim Bradbury, *The Medieval Siege* (Woodbridge: Boydell Press, 1992), chap. 10, "The Conventions and Laws of Siege Warfare," 296–334.

3. Contesting the Countryside

1. Jacob Viner, "Power versus Plenty as Objectives of Foreign Policy in the Seventeenth and Eighteenth Centuries," *World Politics* 1, no. 1 (October 1948): 1–29. On mercantilism—which was more encompassing a policy than mere bullionism—see Joyce Appleby, "Ideology and Theory: The Tension between Political and Economic Liberalism in Seventeenth-Century England," *American Historical Review* 81, no. 3 (1976): 499–515.

2. Michel Foucault, *Sécurité, Territoire, Population: Cour au Collège de France, 1977–1978* (Paris: Gallimard-Seuil, 2004). See also Graham Burchell, Colin Gordon, Peter Miller, eds., *"Governmentality," the Foucault Effect: Studies in Governmentality* (Chicago: University of Chicago Press, 1991), 87–105. For Foucault, the program of governmentality, with its stress on physical welfare, indeed the hygiene of the commonwealth, was at the origin of what he labeled biopolitics.

3. Daniel Defoe, *A Tour through the Whole Island of Great Britain,* abr. ed., ed. Pat Rogers (Harmondsworth: Penguin, 1971).

4. See the discussion of terra nullius as related to the acquisition of private or sovereign rights in Anthony Pagden, "Conquest, Settlement, Purchase, and Concession: Justifying the English Occupation of the Americas," in *The Burdens of Empire, 1539 to the Present* (New York: Cambridge University Press, 2015), 120–154.

5. Vauban, *La Dîme royale,* introduction by Emmanuel Le Roy Ladurie (Paris: Imprimerie Nationale, 1992), 33, 70, and 200–207. This edition is based on the *Projet de dime royal,* edited by J.-F. Pernot in 1998. The book is composed of an extensive preface, then a more extended argumentation (such that topics cited arise in different places), followed by statistical tables. For a discussion that unifies Vauban's concern with economic management of the domain (*domaniales Wirtschaften*) in *La dîme royale* with his spatial concepts, see David Bitterling, "Marschall Vauban und die absolute Raumvorstellung," in *Vermessen, Zählen, Berechnen: Die politische Ordnung des Raums im 18. Jahrhundert,* ed. Lars Behrisch (Frankfurt am Main: Campus, 2006), 65–74.

6. Vauban, *La Dîme royale.*

7. Cited in Wilhelm Abel, *Agricultural Fluctuations in Europe from the Thirteenth to the Twentieth Centuries,* trans. Olive Ordish (London: Methuen, 1980), 161–162.

8. Vauban, *La Dîme royale,* 59–60.

9. Ibid., 70.

10. Ibid., 61.

11. Ibid., 67.

12. Ibid., 157–158.

13. For British developments, see John Brewer, *The Sinews of Power: War, Money, and the English State, 1688–1783* (New York: Knopf, 1988). For a defense of Law's Mississippi scheme as well as the British South Sea Bubble, see Larry Neal, *The Rise of Financial Capitalism: International Capital Markets in the Age of Reason* (Cambridge: Cambridge University Press, 1990), 62–117.

14. See the papers presented at the conference: "Beschreiben und Vermessen. Raumwissen in der östlichen Habsburgermonarchie im 18. und 19. Jahrhundert," Tübingen, October 29, 2009–October 31, 2009. Conference report on line from <H-Soz-Kult> 15.12.2009. See also the essays in Behrisch, *Vermessen, Zählen, Berechnen.*

15. Geoffrey Parker, *Global Crisis: War, Climate Change and Catastrophe in the Seventeenth Century* (New Haven, CT: Yale University Press, 2013); Abel, *Agricultural Fluctuations,* 158–197. On the Spanish crises at the end of the sixteenth century, see Andrew B. Appleby, "Epidemics and Famine in the Little Ice Age," *Journal of Interdisciplinary History* 10, no. 4 (1980): 643–663; Vicente Pérez Moreda, *Las crisis de la mortalidad en Espana interior, siglos XVI–XIX* (Madrid: Siglo XXI, 1980). Celebrated fictional depictions of the plague appeared in such masterpieces as Manzoni's *I promessi sposi* (c.1827 and rev.1840–1842), modern ed., ed. L. Caretti, 2 vols. (Turin: Einaudi, 1971), chaps. 31–37; and Daniel Defoe, *A Journal of the Plague Year* (c. 1722), ed. Louis Landa, with an introduction by David Roberts (New York: Oxford University Press, 2010).

16. See Witold Kula, *An Economic Theory of the Feudal System: Towards a Model of the Polish Economy, 1500–1800,* trans. Lawrence Garner (London: NLB, 1976); Jack A. Goldstone, *Revolution and Rebellion in the Early Modern World* (Berkeley: University of California Press, 1991). Goldstone, like Le Roy Ladurie, sees the early modern state breakdown as caused by a Malthusian squeeze on the resource base of agrarian economies.

17. Vauban, *La Dîme royale,* 30.

18. On silver, see Dennis O. Flynn and Arturo Giráldez, "Born with a 'Silver Spoon': The Origin of World Trade in 1571," *Journal of World History* 6, no. 2 (1995): 201–221; William S. Atwell, "Notes on Silver, Foreign Trade, and the Late Ming Economy," cited in Robert B. Marks, *Tigers, Rice, Silk, and Silt: Environment and Economy in Late Imperial South China* (Cambridge: Cambridge University Press, 1998), 128n125; William S. Atwell, "International Bullion Flows and the Chinese Economy circa 1530–1650," *Past and Present* 95 (May 1982): 68–90.

19. See Marks, *Tigers, Rice, Silk, and Silt,* 84 (for catastrophe), 120–121 (for the interdependencies of the earlier productive era), 135 (for the forty-year period).

20. For recent consideration of the general crisis thesis, see the forum in the *American Historical Review* on the fiftieth anniversary of Hugh Trevor Roper. For Asia, see the essays in *Modern Asian Studies* 24, no. 4 (1990), including William S. Atwell, "A Seventeenth-Century 'General Crisis' in East Asia" (664–665).

21. Kenneth J. Andrien, *Crisis and Decline: The Viceroyalty of Peru in the Seventeenth Century* (Albuquerque: University of New Mexico Press, 1985).

22. Colin Imber, *The Ottoman Empire: The Structure of Power,* 2nd ed. (New York: Palgrave Macmillan, 2009), 181–192 provides a description. See also Halil Inalcik, "Military and Fiscal Transformation in the Ottoman Empire," *Archivum Ottomanicum* 6 (1988): 281–337. Also Bruce McGowan, *Economic Life in Ottoman Europe: Taxation, Trade and the Struggle for Land, 1600–1800* (Cambridge: Cambridge University Press, 1981), 48–51; Halil Inalcik, *The Ottoman Empire: The Classical Age, 1300–1600* (London: Phoenix, 1994). The timar system was based on feudal rents not on the assignment of taxes, which had different ramifications for those liable if village tenants fled. Max Weber used the term *prebendal* to distinguish the ancien regime's offices that came with rent or income (*Pfründe*) from landed fiefs (*Lehen*) bestowed personally on vassals, and differentiated both from a modern salaried bureaucracy; see Max Weber, *Wirtschaft und Gesellschaft: Grundriss der verstehenden Soziologie,* 5th revised ed., ed Johannes Winckelmann (Tübingen: J. C. B. Mohr [Paul Siebeck], 1972), 625–640.

23. McGowan, *Economic Life in Ottoman Europe,* 56.

24. Imber, *The Ottoman Empire,* 196.

25. For an in-depth study of western Macedonia, extending into the early nineteenth century, see McGowan, *Economic Life in Ottoman Europe,* 58–79, and 135–710: "To a degree Ottoman villages were fiscal collectivities, as we see from the fact that they took loans as collectivities" (158). See also Halil Inalcik, "Centralization and Decentralization in Ottoman Administration," in *Studies in Eighteenth Century Islamic History,* ed. T. Naff and Roger Owen (Carbondale: Southern Illinois University Press, 1977), 27–52.

26. W. H. Moreland, *The Agrarian System of Moslem India: A Historical Essay with Appendices* (Allahabad: Central Book Depot, 1929), 147.

27. See the thick and detailed description in ibid., esp. 79–123, 136–139. The chief source is the final section of Abu'l Fazl's *Akbarnama,* his historical memoir of Akbar's reign, the final section of which included a description of the empire and its revenues (see Chapter 1 of this book). See also A. K. Khalid, *The Agrarian History of Pakistan* (Lahore: Allied Press, 1998), 4–10, 75–115. For the later developments, see B. H. Baden-Powell, *The Land Systems of British India,* 3 vols. (Oxford: Clarendon Press, 1892).

28. Moreland, *Agrarian System,* 168, 175, 207–208.

29. Luke S. Roberts, *Mercantilism in a Japanese Domain: The Merchant Origins of Economic Nationalism in 18th-Century Tosa* (Cambridge: Cambridge University Press, 1998). Peter Perdue, *China Marches West* (Cambridge, MA: Harvard University Press, 2006).

30. On French mapping, see the important work by Josef W. Konvitz, *Cartography in France 1660–1848: Science, Engineering, and Statecraft* (Chicago: University of Chicago Press, 1987), chap. 1.

31. While the longitude problem appeared most urgent for navigation at sea and required highly accurate chronometers so "simultaneity" of time might be established (within limits), establishing the measurements on land required accurate observation of eclipses and the Earth's deviation from a perfectly spherical shape. The coasts had retreated inward; the Cassinis preference for a prolate earth had to yield to the Newtonian calculation of an oblate sphere, but it would be completed almost thirty years later. For British surveys, see the cumulative work of Matthew Edney, in particular his *Mapping an Empire: The Geographical Construction of British India, 1765–1843* (Chicago: University of Chicago Press, 1997). For the efforts to survey and map Ireland, see William O'Reilly, "Charles Vallancey and the *Military Itinerary* of Ireland," *Proceedings of the Royal Irish Academy* 106C (2006): 125–217. The military itinerary combined elements of a geographic and cadastral survey.

32. See Jordan Branch, *The Cartographic State: Maps, Territory, and the Origins of Sovereignty* (New York: Cambridge University Press, 2014).

33. Jean Nicolas, "Quand le Duc de Savoie arpentait ses domaines," in *Le cadastre sarde de 1730 en Savoie*, Musée Savoisien exhibition catalogue (Chambéry: Musée Savoisien, 1980), 27. As a quid pro quo for French assistance in the 1859 war of unification, the Kingdom of Sardinia ceded today's department of Haute-Savoie to France, such that the cadaster for the region ended up in French departmental archives.

34. David Warren Sabean, *Power in the Blood: Popular Culture and Village Discourse in Early Modern Germany* (Cambridge: Cambridge University Press, 1984), 202–206. See also Sabean, *Power, Property, and Family in Neckarshausen* (New York: Cambridge University Press, 1990); Fritz Redlich, *The German Military Enterpriser and His Work Force: A Study in European and Social History*, 2 vols. (Wiesbaden: Franz Steiner Verlag, 1964–1965).

35. Roger J. P. Kain and Elizabeth Baigent, *The Cadastral Map in the Service of the State: A History of Property Mapping* (Chicago: University of Chicago Press, 1992), 50–51, but cited in reverse order.

36. Ibid., 119.

37. Werner Buchholz, *Geschichte der öffentlichen Finanzen in Europa in Spätmittelalter und Neuzeit: Darstellung—Analyse—Bibliographie* (Berlin: Akademie Verlag, 1996), 72.

38. Kain and Baigent, *Cadastral Map in the Service of the State*, 118.

39. Cited in Maria Schimke, *Regierungsakten des Kurfürstenstum und Königsreichs Bayern 1799–1815* (Munich: Oldenburg, 1996), 72. See also Eberhard Weis, *Montgelas. Der Architekt des modernen bayerischen Staates 1799–1838* (Munich: Beck Verlag, 2005).

40. Kain and Baigent, *Cadastral Map in the Service of the State*, 160–161; cf. Josef Heider, *Das Bayerische Kataster* (Munich: Verlag Bayerische Heimatsforschung, 1954). I am indebted to Stefan Link's research assistance on the Bavarian tax reforms.

41. Pompeo Neri, *Relazione dello Stato in cui si trova l'opera del censimento universale del Ducato di Milano nel mese di Maggio dell'anno 1750* (Milan: Franco Angelì, 1985), 106.

42. Kain and Baigent, *Cadastral Map in the Service of the State*, 181–185.

43. Renato Zangheri, *Catasti e storia della proprietà terriera* (Turin: Giulio Einaudi, 1980), 52–57. On the Milan cadaster, see Sergio Zaninelli, *Il nuovo censo dello Stato di Milano dall'editto del 1718 al 1733* (Milan: Vita e Pensiero, 1963). Average yields and prices were used to arrive at a notion of net yield similar to the Physiocratic "net product" or the fair taxable base.

44. On the history of the First Giunta, the report of Gian Rinaldo Carli—and a resume of Neri's work and the historiographical debates surrounding it, see the introduction by Franco Saba, "La 'relazione' di Pompeo Nera e la storia lombarda dei secoli XVI–XVIII: una fonte, una interpretazione," in Neri, *Relazione,* 7–34. The 1985 edition is a photo-reproduction of the original 1750 report.

45. Ibid., 22–24, which summed up methods and processes, and—though interpreted in different lights—is a major summary of Austro-Lombard cameralism.

46. Ivan Cadenne, "En Campagne," in *Le cadastre sarde,* 38–67.

47. Nicolas, "Quand le Duc de Savoie arpentait ses domaines," 32–34. The government had decided that feudal dues and tithes of a sufficient age were to be deductible so as to arrive at a parcel's net value, but owners were reluctant to claim the exemption. Savoy authorities established "general delegations" in 1729–1730 to weigh the many claims they expected for this deduction, but few landowners came forward. Noble proprietors ended up claiming that only 12 percent of their property was "feudal," because they feared they might face claims for payment of overdue fees long in arrears to the sovereign.

48. Nicolas, "Quand le Duc de Savoie arpentait ses domaines," 36.

49. Richard Herr, *Rural Change and Royal Finances in Spain at the End of the Old Regime* (Berkeley: University of California Press, 1989), 8–9. See also Richard Herr, *The Eighteenth-Century Revolution in Spain* (Princeton, NJ: Princeton University Press, 1958); Tascón Matilla, *La única contribución y el catastro de la Ensenada* (Madrid: Servicio de Estudios de la Inspección del Ministerio de Hacienda, 1947).

50. Zangheri, *Catasti,* 195. See also Edith Murr Link, *The Emancipation of the Austrian Peasant, 1740–1798* (New York: Columbia University Press, 1949), 132–142; for the citation of Chancellery, see 138.

51. For the protests, see Link, *Emancipation,* 135–142; Karl Grünberg, *Die Bauernbefreiuung,* 2 vols. (Leipzig: Duncker und Humblot, 1894), 2:441; Pavel Mitrofanov, *Joseph II: Seine politische und kulturelle Tätigkeit,* trans. V. von Demelic (Vienna: C. W. Stern, 1910), 639–640.

52. Zangheri, *Catasti,* 205–213. For a survey of the nineteenth-century and twentieth-century French cadasters, with some comparative references, see Stéphane Lavigne, *Le cadastre de la France* (Paris: Presses Universitaires de France, 1996). See also the papers presented at three major conferences on cadastral history sponsored by the French Ministère de l'Économie, des Finances, et de l'Emploi: *De l'estime au cadastre en Europe, le Moyen Age: colloque des 11, 12 et 13 juin 2003 sous la direction scientifique d' Albert Rigaudière*

(Paris: Comité pour l'histoire économique et financière de la France [CHEFF], 2006); *De l'estime au cadastre en Europe: L'époque moderne. Colloque des 4 et 5 décembre 2003.* Sous la direction scientifique d'Albert Rigaudière (Paris, CHEFF, 2006); *De l'estime au cadastre en Europe: Les systèmes cadastraux aux XIXe et XXe siècles. Colloque des 20 et 21 janvier 2005 sous la direction scientifique de Florence Bourillon, Pierre Clergeot et Nadine Vivier* (Paris: CHEFF, 2008). In the final collection see above all, Alfredo Buccaro, "Les cadastres italiens avant et après l'unité," 99–114.

53. On the role, techniques, and cultural importance of mapping, see Martin Brückner, *The Geographic Revolution in Early America: Maps, Literacy, and National Identity* (Williamsburg: Omohundro Institute of Early American History and Culture, 2006), 20–21. For the diverse patterns of colonial landholding over the long term, see Edward T. Price, *Dividing the Land: Early American Beginnings of Our Private Property Mosaic* (Chicago: University of Chicago Press, 1995). See also David Buisseret, ed., *Monarchs, Ministers, and Maps: The Emergence of Cartography as a Tool of Government in Early Modern Europe* (Chicago: University of Chicago Press, 1992).

54. Cited in Vivian Walsh and Harvey Gram, *Classical and Neoclassical Theories of General Equilibrium: Historical Origins and Mathematical Structure* (Oxford: Oxford University Press, 1980), 17; citing Petty, *The Economic Writings of Sir William Petty,* ed. Charles H. Hull (Fairfield, NJ: A. M. Kelley, 1986), 1:43.

55. For Cantillon, see Joseph A. Schumpeter, *History of Economic Analysis,* ed. Elizabeth Boody (Oxford: Oxford University Press, 1954), 221.

56. Victor de Riquetti, Marquis de Mirabeau, "Fertilité incommensurable de la terre," in *Les Devoirs* (Milan: Au Monastère Impérial de St. Ambroise, 1780), 56–57, cited in Georges Weulersse, *La physiocratie sous les ministères de Turgot et de Necker (1774–1781)* (Paris: Presses Universitaires de France, 1950), 248.

57. I follow the exposition of Joyce Oldham Appleby, *Economic Thought and Ideology in Seventeenth-Century England* (Princeton, NJ: Princeton University Press, 1978), who summarizes literature. See also B. E. Supple, *Commercial Crisis and Change in England, 1600–1642* (Cambridge: Cambridge University Press, 1959). See Eli Heckscher's standard history, *Mercantilism,* trans. Mendel Shapiro (London, G. Allen & Unwin, 1935). See also Bruno Suviranta, *The Theory of the Balance of Trade in England* (Helsingfors: Suomal Kirjall Kirjap, 1923).

58. Cited in Appleby, *Economic Thought and Ideology,* 40.

59. P. D. Groenewegen, *The Economics of A. R. J. Turgot* (The Hague: Martinus Nijhoff, 1977), 97, 102. See also "Observations on a Paper by Saint-Péravy on the Subject of Indirect Taxation" (1767), 109–122, and "Observations on the Paper by Graslin in Favour of the Indirect Tax" (1767), 123–132 (both in

ibid). For the role of surplus, see Ronald L. Meek, "The Physiocratic Concept of Profit," in *The Economics of Physiocracy: Essays and Translations* (Cambridge, MA: Harvard University Press, 1963), 297–312, esp. 300–305.

60. Voltaire cited in Renzo De Felice's introductory note to Pietro Verri, *Meditazioni sulla economia politica,* ed. Renzo De Felice (Milan: Bruno Mondadori, 1998), 17.

61. Ibid., 3:23; on the infinite expandability of agriculture, see 3:87–88. For Adam Smith's two balances, see *An Inquiry into the Nature and Causes of the Wealth of Nations,* ed. Edwin Cannan (Chicago: University of Chicago Press, 1976), 1:522–523. See also Peter Groenewegen, "Il significato delle Mediatazioni del Verri nella storia del pensiero economic: ampie influenze europee," in *Pietro Verri e il suo tempo,* ed. Carlo Capra (Milan: Cisalpino, 1999), 2:969–982, esp. 977–978.

62. See Verri's vigorous dissent to this characterization in *Meditazioni,* 24.

63. Ronald L. Meek, "Problems of the Tableau Économique," in *The Economics of Physiocracy* (Cambridge, MA: Harvard University Press, 1963), 265–396, esp. 293 on absence of growth.

64. Verri, *Meditazioni,* 3.

65. Smith, *Wealth of Nations,* 1:523

66. Ibid., 1:401.

67. Ibid., 1:358–360 ("parsimony").

68. Ibid., 2:185–209 ("Of the Agricultural Systems"), 195 ("capital error of this system").

69. Ibid., 1:403.

70. Ibid., 1:445.

71. Anne-Robert Turgot, *The Formation and Distribution of Wealth: Reflections on Capitalism,* trans. Kenneth Jupp (London: Othila Press, 1999), 3=§5. The Turgot citations are identified by paragraph numbers in the text.

72. Étienne Bonnot, Abbé de Condillac, *Commerce and Government Considered in Their Mutual Relationship,* trans. Shelagh Eltis (Cheltenham: Edward Elgar, 1997).

73. Karl Marx, *Theories of Surplus Value* (London: Lawrence and Wishart, 1969), 44–65; on Verri, see ibid., 64–65. The praise of James Steuart for distinguishing between "relative profit" as redistribution from "positive profit" as augmentation of societal wealth (42–43). *Theories of Surplus Value* was published late; it was a history of economic ideas that anticipated Marx's system and thought of as the basis for an eventual fourth volume of *Capital.*

74. Philippe Paillard, "Cadastre et réforme économique," in *Le Cadastre sarde,* 76–80.

75. Cited by Weulersse, *La physiocratie,* 76. For the subsequent vicissitudes of the reform, see ibid., 273–277. The corvée amounted to about a week to ten days of labor conscription; administration was assigned to the parishes.

76. For the reforms enacted and proposed—there was hardly time to push them all through—see Weulersse, *La physiocratie,* 79–102.

77. Cited by Nicolas, "Quand le Duc de Savoie arpentait ses domaines," 36.

78. Carlo Capra, "Kaunitz and Austrian Lombardy," in *Staatskanzler Wenzel Anton von Kaunit-Rietberg 1711–1794, Neue Perspektiven zu Politik und Kultur der europäischen Aufklärung,* ed. Grete Klingenstein and Franz A. J. Szabo (Graz: Andreas Schneider Verlagsatelier, 1996), 245–260, esp. 254–255.

79. Verri, *Meditazioni,* 23. See also his the critique, on page 24, which explained that the artisan received more than just his raw materials and family survival required. Wealth was created and economic growth, *accrescimento,* followed from the fact that more was produced (Verri uses the term *reproduced*) than consumed. "The growth of the annual product [not just its steady state] ought to be the goal of political economy" (33). On Verri and the influence of the Physiocrats, see Peter Groenetwegen, "Pietro Verri's Mature Political Economy of the *Meditazioni:* A Case Study in the Highly Developed International Transmission Mechanism of Ideas in Pre-Revolutionary Europe," in *Political Economy and National Realities: Papers Presented at the Conference Held at the Luigi Einaudi Foundation, Palazzo d'Azeglio, Turin, September 10–12, 1992,* eds. Manuela Albertone and Alberto Masoero (Turin: Fondazione Luigi Einaudi, 1994), 107–125.

80. Francesco Maria Gianni, *Meditazione sulle teorie e sulla pratica delle imposizioni, e tasse pubbliche* (n.p., 1792), http://find.galegroup.com.ezp-prod1.hul.harvard .edu/mome/infomark.do?&source=gale&prodId=MOME&userGroup-Name=camb55135&tabID=T001&docId=U102442178&type=multipage &contentSet=MOMEArticles&version=1.0&docLevel=FASCIMILE.

81. Neri devoted a chapter, "Della Stima dei Terreni," to assessments. See *Relazione,* 127–152.

82. Richard Herr, *Rural Change and Royal Finances in Spain at the End of the Old Regime* (Berkeley: University of California Press, 1989), 43–44; Bartolomé Yun Casalilla, "La venta de los bienes temporalidiades de la Compañia di Jesús, una visión general y el caso de Valladodid (1767–1808)," *Desamortizacion y hacienda publica,* 2 vols. (Madrid: Ministerio de Agricultura, Pesca y Alimentación, Secretaría General Técnica: Ministerio de Economía y Hacienda, Instituto de Estudios Fiscales, 1986), 1:293–316.

83. Herr, *Rural Change and Royal Finances,* 47–50.

84. F. Gaspar Melchior de Jovellanos, *Informe de la Sociedad Económica . . . de el expediente de ley agraria* (Valladolid: Lex Nova, 1795), photo reproduction of the 1795 original, §24, 8. Further source paragraphs have been identified in the text and in note 85 below.

85. Citation from ibid., 55–60. In addition to paragraphs cited in the text, on the evils of tranhumancy and the Mesta, see §§125–146; on amortization and entail, see §§147–225; on American productivity (rice from Philadelphia, Jovellanos noted, sold cheaper in Constantinople than rice from Italy or Egypt), see §156; on the evils of the *mayorazago*—civil entail—see §§186–210.

86. Francesco Renda, *La grande impresa: Domenico Caracciolo viceveré e primo ministro tra Palermo e Napoli* (Palermo: Sellerio, 2010), 77.

87. Ibid., 90–91.

88. Ibid., 26–31.

89. Ibid., 88.

90. Ibid., 112. See also Augusto Placanica, *Alle origini dell'egemonia Borghese in Calabria: La privatizzatione delle terre ecclesiastiche (1784–1915)* (Salerno-Catanzaro: Societá Editrice Meridionale, 1979), 29–48.

91. Placanica, *Alle origini dell'egemonia borghese.*

92. Ibid., 347–358.

93. Ibid., 15, 371.

94. Franklin to Kames, February 21, 1769, in Leonard W. Labaree and Whitfield J. Bell, eds., *The Papers of Benjamin Franklin* (New Haven: Yale University Press, 1959–), 16:107–109, as cited by Drew R. McCoy in *The Elusive Republic: Political Economy in Jeffersonian America* (Chapel Hill: Institute of Early American History and University of North Carolina Press, 1980), 56. On the politics of the Republicans, see Lance Banning, *The Jeffersonian Persuasion: Evolution of a Party Ideology* (Ithaca, NY: Cornell University Press, 1978), 126–173, 197–207.

95. For Adams on commerce see McCoy, *Elusive Republic,* 97; and for the logic behind the view that active commerce was a benevolent force, Albert Hirschman, *The Passions and the Interests: Political Arguments for Capitalism before Its Triumph* (Princeton, NJ: Princeton University Press, 1977).

96. Ezra Stiles, *The United States Elevated to Glory and Honor* (New Haven, CT: Printed by Thomas and Samuel Green, 1783), 52; cited in McCoy, *Elusive Republic,* 89.

97. Ibid., 100–104.

98. Ibid., 140–165.

99. Jefferson invoked the "empire of liberty" to Indiana political leaders in 1805 and then in an 1809 letter to Madison as he indulged in ideas about acquiring Florida and perhaps Cuba; for his fuzzy ambitions, see Peggy K. Liss, *Atlantic Empires* (Baltimore, MD: Johns Hopkins University Press, 1983), 110.

100. Walsh and Gram, *Classical and Neoclassical Theories of General Equilibrium,* 57.

101. Cited in Ranajit Guha, *A Rule of Property for Bengal: An Essay on the Idea of Permanent Settlement* (Paris: Ecole Pratique des Hautes Études, 1963), 11. For the evolving nineteenth-century debate on the legitimacy of the permanent settlement and the rights of landlords versus ryots, see Andrew Sartori, *Liberalism in Empire: An Alternative History* (Berkeley: University of California Press, 2014), esp. chaps. 2–4.

102. Guha, *Rule of Property,* 54–55.

103. The disastrous despoliation of Bengali property rights since 1765, Francis believed, derived from the mistaken view on the part of the East India Company that "by the constitution of the Mogul Empire the governing power was the proprietor of the soil; consequently that they ought not to content themselves with a fixed tribute as government, since they had a right to engross the entire produce as landlord." As successors to diwani, Francis argued, we have a right to revenue, he argued, but "we are not Proprietors of the Soil." In fact, he argued, the Mughal conquerors had not dispossessed the landlords of the territories they conquered, but had demanded only a fixed pecuniary tribute. Francis, cited in Guha, *Rule of Property,* 98–102.

104. Guha, *Rule of Property,* 124–125, 196–197.

105. Ibid., 177–178.

106. Ibid., 172, 173.

4. Projects for an Agrarian Regime (1770–1890)

1. Events in Eastern Europe taken from Franco Venturi's magisterial, *Settecento Riformatore,* vol. 3, *La prima crisi dell'Antico Regime (1768–1776)* (Turin: Einaudi, 1969), as translated by R. Burr Litchfield, *The End of the Old Regime in Europe, 1768–1776: The First Crisis* (Princeton, NJ: Princeton University Press, 1989). For the Austrian enthusiasm for tax simplification and a single tax, see Helmuth Feigl, "Die Auswirkungen der Theresianisch-Josephinischen Reformgesetzgebung auf die ländliche Sozialstruktur Österreichs," in *Österreich im Europa der Aufklarung: Kontinuität und Zäsur in Europa zur Aera*

Maria Theresias und Josephs II, ed. Richard Georg Plascka and Grete Klingenstein, vol. 1, *Österreich im Europa der Aufklärung* (Vienna: Österreichischen Akademie der Wissenschaften, 1985), 45–66. For the analysis of interest-group sclerosis, see Mancur Olson, *The Rise and Decline of Nations: Economic Growth, Stagflation, and Social Rigidities* (New Haven, CT: Yale University Press, 1982).

2. See, especially, Feigl "Auswirkungen der . . . Reformgesetzgebung," in Plascka and Klingenstein, *Österreich im Europa der Aufklarung,* 45–66, esp. 56–66 for the focus on peasant productivity. See the discussions of Jan van Thys, Johann Jakob Reinhard, and Johann August Schlettwein, Phillip Joseph Sinzendorf, and Ludwig Zinzendorf—with their influence on the Austrian debates—cited in Franz A. J. Szabo, *Kaunitz and Enlightened Abolutism, 1753–1780* (Cambridge: Cambridge University Press, 1994), 161–163. Otto Stolz, "Die Bauernbefreiung in Süddeutschland im Zusammenhang der Geschichte," *Vierteljahrshefte für Sozial- und Wirtschaftsgeschichte* 33 (1940): 1–4; Karl Grünberg, *Die Bauernbefreiung und die Auflösung des gutsherrlich-bäuerlichen Verhältnisses in Böhmen, Mähren und Schlesien,* 2 vols. (Leipzig: Duncker und Humblot, 1894); Domokos Kósary, *Culture and Society in Eighteenth-Century Hungary* (Budapest: Corvina, 1987). See also Helen P. Leibel, *Enlightened Bureaucracy versus Enlightened Despotism in Baden, 1750–1792* (Philadelphia, PA: American Philosophical Society, 1965).

3. Edith Murr Link, *The Emancipation of the Austrian Peasant, 1740–1798* (New York: Columbia University Press, 1949), 60–61.

4. Joseph to Leopold, January 16, 1777, cited by Szabo, *Kaunitz and Enlightened Abolutism,* 176. I have relied on Szabo, *Kaunitz and Enlightened Abolutism,* 154–180 for this narrative. But see also Stolz, "Die Bauernbefreiung in Süddeutschland," 1–4; Grünberg, *Die Bauernbefreiung und die Auflösung des gutsherrlihc-bäuerlichen Verhältnisses;* Kósary, *Culture and Society in Eighteenth-Century Hungary.* For a Marxist emphasis on peasant unrest and flight from landlords after the takeover of Galicia, see Józef Busko, "Theresianisch-Josephinische Agrar- und Bauernpolitik in Galizien und ihre Folgen," in *Österreich im Europa der Aufklärung,* 1:66–86. For the Bohemian conditions, see Joseph Koci, "Die Reformen der Untertänigkeitsverhältnisse in den Böhmischen Ländern unter Maria Theresia und Joseph II," in *Österreich im Europa der Aufklärung,* 1:121–137.

5. See, in addition to the previous sources, Jerome Blum, *Noble Landowners and Agriculture in Austria, 1815–1848* (Baltimore, MD: Johns Hopkins University Press 1948); Blum, *The End of the Old Order in Rural Europe;* Link, *Emancipation.*

6. Cited in Link, *Emancipation,* 75, and in general 89–105. For Sonnenfels's views of the countryside, see his fictional character Capa-Kaum in "Der Mann ohne Vorurteil," in *Gesammelte Schriften* (Vienna: Baumeister, 1783), vol. 2.

7. Marc Raeff, *The Well-Ordered Police State: Social and Institutional Change through Law in the Germanies and Russia, 1600–1800* (New Haven, CT: Yale University Press, 1983).

8. Brissot cited in Franco Venturi, *The End of the Old Regime in Europe, 1776–1789: II. Republican Patriotism and the Empires of the East,* trans. R. Burr Litchfield (Princeton, NJ: Princeton University Press, 1991), 755–756.

9. Manuel Belgrano, *Escritos econonómicos,* ed. Gregorio Weinberg (Buenos Aires: Editorial Raigal, 1954), 65–66.

10. Ibid., 156.

11. Ibid., 163. See also "Cria de Ganados," August 18, 1810, 179–185.

12. For studies that downplay the ranchers' role in the political elite and the importance of ranching before independence, see Carlos A. Mayo, *Estancia y sociedad en la Pampa (1740–1820),* 2nd ed. (Buenos Aires: Biblos, 2004); Jorge Gelman, *Campesinos y Estancieros; Una region del Rio de la Plata a fines de la epoca colonial* (Buenos Aires: Editorial Los Libros del Riel, 1998). See also Osvaldo Barsky and Jorge Gelman, *Historia del Agro Argentino desde la Conquista hasta fines del siglo xx* (Buenos Aires: Grijalbo Mondadori, 2001), 73–113; and the introduction by Raúl Fradkin to the reprinting of Tulio Halperin Donghi, *La formación de la clase terrateniente bonaerense* (Buenos Aires: Proeteo Libros, 2007), esp. 19–22. Belgrano's biographer, the nineteenth-century liberal Sarmiento, used Belgrano's critique to affirm the strength of Argentine liberalism.

13. For reassertion of the primacy of the large *hacendado* landlords, see the articles on land distribution and rancher organization in the Buenos Aires region reproduced in Eduardo Azcuy Ameghino, *La otra historia: Economia, estado y socidad en el Rio de la Plata colonial* (Buenos Aires: Imago Mundi, 2002): among others, see "Comercio Exterior y comercio de cueros en el virreinato del Rio de la Plata," 17–89, esp. Cuadro 10, 49. The annual average of hides (1792–1796) was about 800,000 versus the 150,000 maximum before 1778 and the removal of Spanish restrictions on trade and shipping. See also "La propriedad de la tierra en los campos bonaerenses y el censo de haciendado de 1789," 165–175.

14. Manuel Belgrano, "Agricultura," in *Correo de Commercio de Buenos Aires, Article of March 10, 1810,* in *Escritos Económicos,* ed. Gregorio Weinberg (Buenos Aires: Editorial Raigal, 1954), 118–119.

15. Doblas cited in Guillermo Wilde, *Religión y Poder en la misiones de Guaraníes* (Buenos Aires: Editorial Sb, 2009), 282.

16. Ibid., 310–325 (letter on music, 311).

17. Jorge Gelman, ed., *Un funcionario en busca del Estado: Pedro Andres Garcia y la cuestion agraria bonaerense, 1810–1822* (Buenos Aires, Universidad Nacional de Quilmes, 1997), memo of November 26, 1811, 81. For the widespread pre-occupation of officials, including Andres Garcia with the semi-squatters *(agregados)* of the pampas—small wheat growers employed on the ranches but outside the regular labor market—see Mayo, *Estancia y sociedad,* 73–86. The status of Argentina was cloudy: a local junta had taken power in 1810 and was fighting Spanish forces, although it had not formally declared independence. South Americans sent delegates to the reformist Cortes of Cadiz as would-be autonomous kingdoms of Spain, but the returning Ferdinand VII reversed all the constitutional innovations in 1814. Belgrano's co-commander to the north, Juan José Castelli, imposed a policy of terror and lost Paraguay to its own dictator, "Dr. Francia." See Jaime E. O. Rodriguez, *The Independence of Spanish America* (Cambridge: Cambridge University Press, 1998), 56–64, 123–136; Jeremy Adelman, *Sovereignty and Revolution in the Iberian Atlantic* (Princeton, NJ: Princeton University Press, 2006). On the general constellation of political forces, see Fernando López-Alves, *State Formation and Democracy in Latin America, 1810–1900* (Durham, NC: Duke University Press, 2000).

18. C. K. Meek, *Land Law and Custom in the Colonies* (London: Oxford University Press, 1946), v.

19. Karl Polanyi, *The Great Transformation: The Political and Economic Origins of Our Time* (Boston: Beacon Press, 1957), 3.

20. For other examples of the trends taken up here, see the splendid work by Andro Linklater, *Owning the Earth: The Transforming History of Land Ownership* (New York: Bloomsbury Publishing, 2013), which appeared after I drafted this chapter. While my work seeks to relate property relations to the prior establishment of political rights, Linklater follows property rights as his fundamental parameter.

21. For an earlier survey, see Charles M. Haar, ed., *Law and Land: Anglo-American Planning Practice* (Cambridge, MA: Harvard University Press, 1964).

22. Meek, *Land Law and Custom in the Colonies,* 24.

23. Not all land was transferred by purchase and sale. Where monarchical protection was weak, landlords often just seized the commons and peasant properties, for instance, in the Baltic and areas of Eastern Europe. See Jerome Blum, *The End of the Old Order in Rural Europe* (Princeton, NJ: Princeton University Press, 1978), 203–206.

24. Herr, *Rural Change and Royal Finances in Spain* (Berkeley: University of California Press, 1989), 7–9.

25. Ibid., 522–524.

26. Ibid., 537.

27. Germán Rueda Hernanz, *La desamortización en España: un balance (1766–1924)* (Madrid: Arco/Libros, 1997), 60–65. For recent work, see also F. Simón Segura, *La desamortización española del siglo XIX* (Madrid: Instituto de Estudios Fiscales, 1973); F. Tomás y Valiente, *El marco político de la desamortización en España* (Madrid: Ariel, 1971); Germán Rueda Hernanz, ed., *La desamortización de Mendezibal y Espartero en España* (Madrid: Cátedra, 1986). For comparative impacts, see G. Rueda Hernanz, "Estudio comparative de las consecuencias de la desamortización de tierras en tres zonas de Europea: Departamento del Norte (Francia), Napolés Italia) y Vallalodid (España)," *Hacienda Publica Española* 69 (1981): 107–124.

28. Manuel Roso Díaz, *La desamortización urbana en la provincia de Cáceres, 1836–1900* (Cáceres: Universidad de Extremadura, Servicio de Publicaciones, 2006), 207–208, 222–223, 270–277. The heaviest participation of the urban bourgeoisie took place under the Mendizábal legislation during the liberal Isabellan period (1837–1854) and slackened off subsequently. In contrast to some traditional affirmations to the contrary, the nobility, so Roso Díaz found, played only a small role in the acquisition of Cáceres's urban properties.

29. Jan Bazant, *Alienation of Church Wealth in Mexico. Social and Economic Aspects of the Liberal Revolution 1856–1875* (Cambridge: Cambridge University Press, 1971), 13.

30. On the Jesuit confiscations, see Harold Bradley Benedict, *The Distribution of the Expropriated Jesuit Properties in Mexico, with Special Reference to Chihuahua (1767–1790)* (Ann Arbor: University of Michigan Press, 1971); Nancy Farriss, *Crown and Clergy in Colonial Mexico. The Crisis of Ecclesiastical Privilege 1759–1821* (London: Athlone, 1968); Abelardo Levaggi, "La desamortización eclesiástica en el virreinato del Rio de la Plata," *Revista de Historia de América* 102 (1986): 7–90; Magnus Mörner, ed., *The Expulsion of the Jesuits from Latin America* (New York: Knopf, 1965); Peter Schmidt, *Desamortisationspolitik und Staatliche Schuldentilgung in Hispanoamerika am Ende der Kolonialzeit* (Saarbrücken: Verlag Breitenbach, 1988); Margarita Menegue Bornemann, "Los bienes de comunidad y las Reformas Borbónicas (1786–1814)," in *Estructuras agrarias y reformismo ilustrado en la España del siglo XVIII,* ed. Antonio Miguel Bernard Rodriguez (Madrid: Ministerio de Agricultura, Pesca y Alimentación, 1989), 383–389.

31. John Tutino, "Desajustes Sociales," in *La construcción de las naciones latinoamericanas, 1820–1870, Historia General de América Latina,* ed. Josefina Z.

Vázquez and Manuel Miño Grijala (Paris: UNESCO, 2003), 6:445–463, esp. 458–459.

32. Bazant, *Alienation of Church Wealth,* 55–56. Tithes had been made voluntary in 1833; "temporalities" of the Inquisition and various orders had been seized in the turbulent years after independence, often just taken as a forced loan. The Lerda Law allowed tenants three months to acquire title; after that "denouncers" could claim the property. Failing denouncers, the property would be auctioned or "adjudicated" (ibid., 53–55). Besides Bazant, see also Robert J. Knowlton, *Church Property and the Mexican Reform 1856–1910* (DeKalb: Northern Illinois University Press, 1976).

33. Bazant, *Alienation of Church Wealth,* 156–157, 167, 178–183, 287–290. Herr arrived at a more optimistic judgment for Spain than Bazant did for Mexico, who saw mostly a new *hacendado* fusion. Herr saw impediments to agrarian growth removed.

34. Jesús Gómez Serrano, *Ciénaga de Mata: Desarollo y ocaso di la propriedad vinculada en Mexico* (Aguascalientes: Universidad Autónoma de Aguascalientes, and Guadalajara: Colegio de Jalisco, 1998), 160–161.

35. Jonathan Ocko, "The Missing Metaphor: Applying Western Legal Scholarship to the Study of Contract and Property in Early Modern China," in *Contract and Property in Early Modern China,* ed. Madeleine Zelin, Jonathan K. Ocko, and Robert Gardella (Stanford, CA: Stanford University Press, 2004), 202–203.

36. Michael T. Ducey, "Liberal Theory and Peasant Practice: Land and Power in Northern Veracruz, Mexico, 1826–1900," in *Liberals, the Church, and Indian Peasants: Corporate Lands and the Challenge of Reform in Nineteenth-Century Spanish America,* ed. Robert H. Jackson (Albuquerque: University of New Mexico Press,1997), 73. Brigida von Mentz, *Pueblos de Indios, mulatos y mestizos, 1770–1870: Los campesinos y transformaciones proto-industrales en el poniente de Morelos* (Mexico City: CIESAS, 1988).

37. Donald J. Fraser, "La politica de desamortización en las comunidades indigenas, 1856–1872," *Historia Mexicana* 21, no. 84 (1972): 615–652; Robert J. Knowlton and Mario Zamudo, "La división de las tierras de los pueblos durante el siglo XIX: El caso de Michoacán," *Historia Mexicana* 40 (1990): 3–25.

38. Ducey, "Liberal Theory and Peasant Practice," 85–86; Ethelia Ruiz Medrano, *Mexico's Indigenous Communities: Their Land and Histories, 1500–2010* (Boulder: University Press of Colorado, 2010), 163–184; Antonio Escobaar Ohmstede, ed., *Los pueblos indios in los tiempos de Benito Juarez (1847–1872)* (Mexico City: Universidad Autónoma Metropolitana, 2007). See also Fraser, "La politica de desamortización."

39. See the assimilationist view of Rutgers president Merrill Edwards Gates, *Land and Law as Agents in Educating Indians: An Address Delivered before the American Social Science Association at Saratoga, N.Y., Sept. 11th, 1885. The Making of Modern Law* (Gale Cengage Learning, 2016). See also Stuart Banner, *How the Indians Lost Their Land* (Cambridge, MA: Harvard University Press, 2005); Janet A. McDonnell, *The Dispossession of the American Indian, 1887–1914* (Bloomington: Indiana University Press, 1991).

40. Martha Mundy, "Shareholders and the State: Representing the Village in the Late 19th Century Land Registers of the Southern Hawran," in *The Syrian Land in the 18th and 19th Century,* ed. Thomas Philipp (Stuttgart: Franz Steiner Verlag, 1992), 5:217–218, 1858 law cited, 217. The author asks whether the legislation innovated or formalized trends toward privatization already under way in the hope of more effective taxation. See also Martha Mundy and Richard Saumarez Smith, *Governing Property, Making the Modern State: Law, Administration and Production in Ottoman Syria* (London: I. B. Tauris, 2007).

41. Eugene L. Rogan, *Frontiers of the State in the Late Ottoman Empire* (Cambridge: Cambridge University Press, 1999), 82–94. See also P. Sluglett and M. Farouk-Sluglett, "The Application of the 1858 Land Code in Greater Syria: Some Preliminary Observations," in *Land Tenure and Social Transformation in the Middle East,* ed. Tarif Khalidi (Beirut: American University of Beirut, 1984), 409–421; G. Baer, "Land Tenure in Egypt and the Fertile Crescent, 1800–1950," in *The Economic History of the Middle East 1800–1914: A Book of Readings,* ed. Charles Issawi (Chicago: University of Chicago Press, 1966), 80–90; Joseph Chaoui, *Le régime foncier en Syrie* (Aix-en-Provence: Éditions Paul Roubaud, 1928).

42. Mundy and Saumarez Smith, *Governing Property, Making the Modern State,* 235. The book is an exemplary interdisciplinary study.

43. Raymond Williams, *The Country and the City* (New York: Oxford University Press, 1973).

44. Still very rich, though perhaps downplaying the restless commerce that was percolating, and writing in the shadow of the revolutions ahead, is Geroid Tanquary Robinson, *Rural Russia under the Old Régime: A History of the Landlord-Peasant World and a Prologue to the Peasant Revolution of 1917* (London: George Allen and Unwin, 1932), esp. 64–132.

45. For a recent discussion emphasizing statistical research and with a superb summary of the massive bibliography that has appeared in Russian and non-Russian languages (10–22) and a rejection of Alexander Gerschenkron's model of a state-centered industrialization at the cost of the peasantry (113–115), see Heinz-Dietrich Löwe, *Die Lage der Bauern in Russland 1880–1905: Wirtschaftliche und soziale Veränderungen in der ländlichen Gesellschaft des*

Zarenreiches (St. Katharinen: Scripta Mercaturae Verlag, 1987). Löwe maintains that the *obshchina* was hardly the brake on progress later claimed; that the smallholding peasantry increased its wealth; and that the sources of industrial capital and labor resembled Western European development much more closely than traditionally claimed.

46. Robinson, *Rural Russia,* 125.

47. J. H. von Thünen, *Der isolerte Staat in Beziehung auf Landwirtschaft und Nationalökonomie,* 2nd ed. (Berlin: Akademie Verlag, 1990), 27. Michael Chisholm, *Rural Settlement and Land Use* (London: Hutchison, 1962), 21–35. See also Klaus Brake, ed., *Johann Heinrich von Thünen und die Entwicklung der Raumstruktur-Theorie* (Oldenburg: Heinz Holzbreg Verlag, 1985); Walter Isard, *Location and Space-Economy* (Cambridge, MA: MIT Press, 1956).

48. Thünen, *Der isolierte Staat,* 15. For his further reflections on what later economists would call a "model," see ibid., 28 ("the isolated state is only a visual representation, a form that extends and eases a view of the whole, which we cannot renounce because it yields so many results") and 284–287.

49. Ibid., 389–414.

50. Henry George, *Progress and Poverty: An Inquiry into the Cause of Industrial Depressions and of Increase of Want with Increase of Wealth, the Remedy* (San Francisco: W. M. Hilton, 1879).

51. Numa Denys Fustel de Coulanges, *The Origins of Property in Land by Fustel de Coulanges,* translated by Margaret Ashley, with an Introductory Chapter on *The English Manor* by W. H. Ashley, M.A. (London: Swan Sonnenschein, 1891), xii.

52. "La politique d'envahissement: Louvois et M. de Bismarck," *Revue des Deux Mondes,* January 1, 1871, cited in Claude Digeon, *La crise allemande de la pensée française (1870–1914)* (Paris: Presses Universitaires de France, 1959), 236. Digeon follows Fustel's continuing denunciation of "the historians who merged their admiration for Germany and democracy," claiming to oppose theory, generalization, and imagination with documents and facts (248).

53. Fustel de Coulanges, *The Origins of Property in Land,* 1–2. Fustel cites G. L. von Maurer, *Einleitung zur Geschichte der Mark-Hof- und Stadtverfassung* (1854), 93, as well as P. Villet and the Belgian Émile de Laveleye, *De la propriété et de ses formes primitives* (Paris: Librairie G. Baillière, 1874).

54. Preface to *The Origins of Property in Land,* xx.

55. Fustel, *Questions Historiques,* 408, cited in Digeon, *La Crise allemande,* 249n1.

56. Citations from Fustel de Coulanges, *La cité antique* and Fustel de Coulanges, *Recherches sur les idées,* etc. in Paolo Grossi, *"Un altro modo di possedere":*

L'Emersione di Forme alternative di proprietà alla coscenza giuridica postunitaria (Milan: Giuffré, 1977), 136.

57. Ibid., 67, citing Henry Sumner Maine, *Ancient Law: Its Connection with the early History of Society and its Relation to Modern Ideas* (London: J. Murray, 1861).

58. Sir Henry Sumner Maine, *Lectures on the Early History of Institutions: (A Sequel to "Ancient Law")* (New York: Henry Holt, 1888), 81–87.

59. Sir Henry Sumner Maine, *Village-Communities East and West: Six Lectures Delivered at Oxford* (London: John Murray, 1871), 164–166. Maine relied heavily for comparative insights on the just published study by a German historian of English medieval institutions, Erwin Nasse, *Über die mittelalterliche Feldgemeinschaft und die Einhegungen des sechszehnten Jahrhunderts in England* (Bonn: C. Georgi, 1869); H. A. Ouvry, trans., *On the Agricultural Community of the Middle Ages and Inclosures [sic] of the Sixteenth Century in England* (London: Macmillan, 1871).

60. Maine, *Village-Communities,* 197. The market was an area where men of autonomous communities could trade and seek the best price, "unshackled by customary rules" (193).

61. For the context of Laveleye's work in international law, see Martti Koskenniemi, *The Gentle Civilizer of Nations: The Rise and Fall of International Law 1870–1960* (Cambridge: Cambridge University Press, 2002), 60–61.

62. Emile de Laveleye, *De la propriété et ses formes primitives,* 5th ed. (Paris: Alcan, 1901); English translation, *Primitive Property,* trans. G. R. L. Marriott (London: Macmillan, 1878).

63. Ibid., xviii–xxx.

64. Ibid., 82.

65. Ibid., 516.

66. Grossi, *Un altro modo di possedere,* 146–147, citing Fustel de Coulanges, *Le probléme des origines de la propriété foncière,* 88.

67. Grossi, *Un altro modo di possedere,* 160–161.

68. Émile Belot, *Nantucket. Essai sur les diverses sortes de propriété primitive. Annuaire de la Faculté de Lettres de Lyon* (Paris: Ernest Leroux, 1884).

69. Friedrich Engels, *The Origin of the Family, Private Property and the State (Preface to the First Edition 1884),* in *Karl Marx and Friedrich Engels, Selected Works in Two Volumes* (Moscow: Foreign Languages Publishing House, 1958), 2:171. Engels refers to the impact of Johann Jacob Bachofen's "Mother Right" *(Mutterrecht)* (1861); the ignoring of Lewis Morgan's *Ancient Society* he attributes to the British contempt for an American author.

70. Engels, *The Origin of the Family;* on the Zadruga, 218, and Greek monogamy, 224, citing Maxim Kovalevsky, *Tableau des origines et de l'évolution de la famille et de la propriété* (Stockholm: Samson & Wallin, 1890).

71. Engels, *The Origin of the Family,* 2:224–225.

72. Ibid., 202–204.

73. Ibid., 319.

74. Ibid., 321–322.

75. Ibid, 327.

76. Alexander Herzen, "The Russian People and Socialism: Letter to J. Michelet," in *Selected Philosophical Works,* trans. L. Navrozov (Moscow: Foreign Languages Publishing House, 1956), 489.

77. Engels, "On Social Relations in Russia" (1875), in *Origin of the Family,* 2:49–61. The idea that a peasant revolution was needed to secure a bourgeois one foreshadowed Trotsky's 1905 concept of permanent revolution, which argued that the proletarian revolution must secure the bourgeois upheaval.

78. Karl Marx and Friedrich Engels, *Sochinenniya* (Moscow: Gosudarstvennoe izdatel´stvo, 1928–), 15:261, cited in E. H. Carr, *The Bolshevik Revolution, 1917–1923* (London: Macmillan, 1952), 2:389.

79. Karl Marx and Friedrich Engels, "Preface to the 'Manifesto of the Communist Party,'" 2nd Russian ed. of 1882, included in Marx and Engels, *Karl Marx and Friedrich Engels, Selected Works in Two Volumes* (Moscow: Foreign Languages Publishing House, 1958), 1:24.

80. Carr, *The Bolshevik Revolution,* 391.

81. Ibid., 393. Be it said, though, that Carr seeks to make Marx and Engels prophets of collectivization as it eventually took place.

82. See John Laurent, ed., *Henry George's Legacy in Economic Thought* (Cheltenham: Edward Elger, 2005).

83. Grossi, *Un altro modo di possedere,* 232–233, "The *usi civici* arose, at least among us, as a counterweight to feudal power"; they were "primitive rights, absolutely inviolable and on a par with every other natural right, and thus prior not only to baron, but also to the king."

84. Francesco Schupfer, "Degli usi civici e altri diritti del commune di Apricena," in *Atti della R. Accademia dei Lincei, Classe di scienze morali, storiche e filogiche, seria IV, II* (1886), 282; cited in Grossi, *Un altro modo di possedere,* 247n159—and in general, see the chapter on Italian social descriptions and legal doctrines, southern and northern, in the same work (191–247).

85. Stefano Jacini, *L'Inchiesta Agraria, with a Foreword by Francesco Coletti and a Biographical Note by His Grandson, Stefano Jacini* (Piacenza: Federazione Italiana dei Consorzi Agrari, 1926), 292. The edition is a selection from the full report parliamentary report, *Atti della Giunta per la inchiesta agraria e sulle condizioni della classe agricole,* 23 vols., reprinted (Sala Bolognese: A. Forni, 1978). For the politics of the investigation, see Alberto Caracciolo, *L'Inchiesta agraria Jacini* (Turin: Einaudi, 1973).

86. Caracciolo, *L'Inchiesta Agraria,* 96–120. See also "Relazione finale," in Jacini, *L'Inchiesta Agraria,* 122–276.

87. For Bertani's position, see Grossi, *Un altro modo di possedere,* 284–285. For a highly critical view of his personal difficulties and political posturing, see Caracciolo, *L'Inchiesta agraria Jacini,* 66–82, 98–99. Caracciolo, however, implies that a non-socialist Left was doomed to inconsistencies.

88. Grossi, *Un altro modo di possedere,* 286–305.

89. Is the issue so open and shut? While Paolo Grossi treats the *servitù del pascere* as a right of commoners, the historian of the Friuli region of the Veneto in the northeast of Italy treats the right of pasturage, including the *pensionatico* or winter pasturage for sheep, as a noble and clerical privilege, obstructing modernization of property relations. Economists and Venetian administrators might disdain their rural ignorance. But the writer also admits that the inhabitants of the commons *(i comunisti)* defended their rights, which survived the French occupation and lasted until unification. See Furio Bianco, *Nobili castellani, comunità, sottani: Il Friuli dalla caduta della repubblica alla restaurazione* (Monfalcone: Edzioni della Laguna, 1997), 39–62.

90. For a case study, see Carlo Fumian, *Possidenti: le élites agrarie tra Otto e Novecento* (Catanzaro: Meridiana libri, 1996).

91. Grossi, *Un altro modo di possedere,* 312–325.

92. Marcia Maria Menendes Motta, *Nas Fronteiras do poder: Conflito e direito à terra no Brasil do século XIX* (Rio de Janeiro: Arquivo Público do Estado do Rio de Janeiro, 1998).

93. Henry George, *The Land Question: What It Involves, and How Alone It Can Be Settled* (New York: Doubleday and McClure, 1898), 60.

94. Achille Loria, *La terra ed il sistema sociale: Prolusione al corso di economic politica nella R. Universitá di Padova 21 novembre 1891* (Verona: Fratelli Drucker, 1892), 28–29.

95. Ibid. The lecture summarizes the massive *Analisi della proprietá capitalista,* 2 vols. (Torino: Fratelli Bocca, 1889), which Loria presented as the fruit of a decade of reflection since his 800-page tract, *La rendita fondiaria e la sua*

elisione natural (Milan: Ulrico Hoepli, 1880) had first stated that the relations determining the returns on agriculture lay at the basis of the social organism. See Loria, *Analisi*, xiii–xiv. But whereas Ricardo argued that agrarian rent, based on the differential quality of land pressed into service, would increase to the benefit of the holders of the better land at the expense of urban manufacturers, Loria stressed instead the falling rate of agricultural profits and their impact on the class confrontation between large landowners and deprived peasants. "The root of the modern social malady does not arise from the separation of the worker from his product, but of the cultivator from landed property" (Loria, *Analisi, 576*). Nonetheless, falling returns on land would stabilize the purchasing power of industrial workers and allow them to buy smallholdings. They would, to be sure, succumb to debt and foreclosure in turn—but then form the basis of a future agrarian collectivism: "Like the liberty embodied in the medieval communes, which was extinguished by the political absolutism that restricted it everywhere only to revive more completely in a subsequent age, so contemporary smallholdings are condemned to vanish in the latifunda that absorb them—but to reappear more efficient and universal in a successive period. On the tomb of agricultural property we shall engrave the epitaph of the believer: *Resurrectura*" (581). For Loria's influence, see Marcela Varejão, *Achille Loria: Saggio sulla fortuna di un positivista in Italia e all'estero* (Milan: Edizioni Unicopli, 1997).

96. See "Historical Tendency of Capital Accumulation," in *Capital,* vol. 1, chap. 32.

97. Ugo Rabbeno, "The Present Condition of Political Economy in Italy," *Political Science Quarterly* 6 (1891): 439–473; Rabbeno "Loria's Landed System of Social Economy, *Political Science Quarterly* 7 (1892): 258–293, cited in Lee Benson, "Achille Loria's Influence on American Economic Thought: Including His Contributions to the Frontier Hypothesis," *Agricultural History* 24 (1950): 182–199, now included in Lee Benson, *Turner and Beard: American Historical Writing Reconsidered* (New York: Free Press, 1960), 1–40.

98. Benson, *Turner and Beard,* 19–20, 23–24.

99. Ibid., 4n9, 39. Cf. Ray Allen Billington, *Frederick Jackson Turner: Historian, Scholar, Teacher* (New York: Oxford University Press, 1973), 121–124.

100. Loria, *La terra ed il sistema sociale,* 31.

101. Edward Gibbon Wakefield and Robert Gouger, eds., *A Letter from Sydney: The Principal Town of Australasia* (London: J. Cross, 1829). For the idea of "sufficient price," see Stephen H. Roberts, *History of Australian Land Settlement, 1788–1920* (London: Frank Cass, 1969), 77–101. With seven million acres held in property but lacking agrarian labor, "Australia had work

and no labourers and no work; England had labourers and no work"
(ibid., 83).

102. Ugo Rabbeno, *La questione fondiaria nei paesi nuovi,* vol. 1, *La questione fondiaria nelle grandi colonie dell'Australasia* (Turin: Fratelli Bocca Editori, 1898),
12–26. Loria disagreed on the cause, which he believed followed from the
early nineteenth-century seizure of public lands under theories of no-man's-
land or *terra nullius.* See his introduction (ibid., xi–xvii).

103. Loria, *La terra ed il sistema sociale,* 32–34.

104. Ibid., 34.

105. Ibid., 44.

106. Ibid., 45, 52–53.

107. Ibid., 35, 39–40.

108. Ibid., 60–61.

5. "An Invincible Force"

1. Michel Chevalier, *Des intérêts matériels en France: travaux publics, routes, canaux,
chemins de fer,* 6th ed. (Paris: C. Gosselin, 1841), 149–151.

2. Henry Adams, *The Education of Henry Adams: A Centennial Version,* ed. Edward Chalfant and Conrad Edick Wright (Boston: Massachusetts Historical Society, 2007), chap. 34: "A Law of Acceleration, 1904," 385.

3. For the intellectual currents in which Wegener's theories originated, see
Naomi Oreskes, *The Rejection of Continental Drift: Theory and Method in American Earth Science* (New York: Oxford University Press, 1999); and for his
original publication, see Alfred L. Wegener, "Die Entstehung der Konti-
nente und Ozeane," *Geologische Rundschau* 3 (1912): 276–292.

4. Chevalier, *Des intérêts matériels en France.*

5. Heine, May 5, 1843, in Manfred Windfuhr, ed., *Heinrich Heine: Historisch-
Kritische Gesamtausgabe der Werke* (Hamburg: Hoffmann und Campe, 1990),
14:57–58, cited in James M. Brophy, *Capitalism, Politics, and Railroads in
Prussia, 1830–1870* (Columbus: Ohio State University Press, 1998), 22. For
other German enthusiastic prophecies, including Friedrich Harkort's early
boosterism, see Brophy, *Capitalism, Politics, and Railroads in Prussia,* 23. They
were disappointed that the Prussian state seemed so reluctant to encourage
construction. A major reason was that a state bond issue would have required summoning a Prussian legislature—resisted until 1847; indeed the
strictures placed on private railroad companies brought them near bankruptcy. A more supportive attitude followed under the new and initially

more liberal monarch Friedrich Wilhelm IV after 1840s. Business leaders lamented bureaucratic impediments even as they sought to work with the state and the situation really changed only in the 1850s under an activist but often resented minister of trade and former banker, August von der Heydt, yielding finally a mixed system that Brophy characterizes as uneasy accommodation. Nationalization followed in 1879 and acceptance by major private lines: railroads were not the money machine they were in the United States. See Colleen Dunlavy, *Politics and Industrialization: Early Railroads in the United States and Prussia* (Princeton, NJ: Princeton University Press, 1994), which emphasizes that the Prussian state was less interventionist than the United States was.

6. For a discussion of the contemporary relation of territory to transportation, see Severino Escolano, "Territory and High-Speed Rail: A Conceptual Framework," in *Territorial Implications of High-Speed Rail: A Spanish Perspective,* ed. José M. de Ureña (Farnham, UK: Ashgate, 2012), 33–53; A. Beyer, "La capacité d'articulation des territoires, enjeu majeur de la grande vitesse ferroviaire européenne," *Bulletin de l'Association de Géographes Français: Géographies* 85, no. 4 (2008): 427–430.

7. For the Internet comparison, see Tom Standage, *The Victorian Internet* (New York: Walker and Co., 1998). On social and political control, see F. C. Mather, "The Railways, the Electric Telegraph and Public Order during the Chartist Period," *History* 38 (1953): 40–53; Iwan Rhys Morus, *Frankenstein's Children: Electricity, Exhibition and Experiment in Early Nineteenth-Century London* (Princeton, NJ: Princeton University Press, 1998), 224–225. See Morus's catalogue of delinquents apprehended by telegraphy in " 'The Nervous System of Britain': Space, Time and the Electric Telegraph in the Victorian Age," *British Journal for the History of Science* 33 (2000): 462. The emphasis is on the metaphors of the nervous system.

8. At the same time they became important for the German "historical school" of economists who focused on spatial economic development as a traffic among national units, formed by history. Quinn Slobodian, "How to See the World Economy: Statistics, Maps, and Schumpeter's Camera in the First Age of Globalization," *Journal of Global History* 10 (2015): 307–332.

9. Although he focuses on the intercontinental units that could compose a British imperial federation and not on continents, Duncan S. A. Bell emphasizes how the capacity to master distance and space helped shape political ideas and ambitions. See "Dissolving Distance: Technology, Space, and Empire in British Political Thought, 1770–1900," *Journal of Modern History* 77 (2005): 523–562. Bell also usefully distinguishes between the national scale of spatial "contraction" heralded before midcentury and the global scale that captured the imagination after 1870 (ibid., 556). For more

burbling on the potential of the railroad, see A. A. Den Otter, *The Philosophy of Railways: The Transcontinental Railway Idea in British North America* (Toronto: University of Toronto Press, 1997), esp. in the discussion of technological nationalism, 3–32.

10. Ibid., 152.

11. Daniel Nordman and Jacques Revel, "La formation de l'espace français," in *L'espace français,* ed. Jacques Revel (Paris: Seuil, 1989), 102–113.

12. "Mais l'homme n'a point reconnu cette division naturelle; il a partagé la terre au gré de son ambition; it a reglé les bornes de ses possession sur ses force et son pouvoir. . . . De là l'origine des contestations entre des Peuples voisins." The geographer Jean Nicolas Buache de La Neville cited in ibid., 117.

13. "La France puisse former un seul tout, soumis uniformément, dans toutes des parties, à une legislation et à une administration commune" (cited in ibid., 134).

14. Ibid., 137. Marie-Vic Ozouf-Marignier, *La Représentation du territoire français à la fin du xviiie siècle, d'après les travaux sur la formation des departments* (Paris: Ed. De l'EHESS, 1989); P. Gremion, *Le pouvoir périphérique* (Paris: Éditions du Seuil, 1976).

15. Marcel Roncayolo, "L'aménagement du territoire, xviiie–xxe siècle," in Revel, *L'espace français,* 512–13.

16. "Je compare les forces productives et le produit de ces forces, dans chaque department, avec la France Moyenne" (cited in ibid., 541).

17. Peter S. Onuf, *Statehood and Union* (Bloomington: Indiana University Press, 1981).

18. Johann Gottfried Herder, *Ideen zur Philosophie der Geschichte der Menschheit, Werke Bd. 6* (Frankfurt: Deutscher Klassiker Verlag, 2001). On nationalism, see the editors' introduction in Ulrike von Hirschhausen and Jörn Leonhard, eds., *Nationalismen in Europa: West und Osteuropa im Vergleich* (Göttingen: Wallstein Verlag, 2001), 11–45. And among the other essays that discuss theorists and theories, see Stefan Berger, "Britischer und deutcher Nationalismus im Vergleich: Probleme und Perpektiven," 96–116; and Adrian Lyttelton, "Between *piccola patria* and *grande patria:* National Identify and Nation-Building in Nineteenth-Century Italy," 154–177, both in Hirschhausen and Leonhard, *Nationalismen in Europa.* For the connection of nationalism and war, see also Jörn Leonhard, "Vom Nationalkrieg zum Kriegsnationalismus—Projektion und Grenze nationaler Integrationsvorstellungen in Deutschland, Grossbritannien und den Vereinigten Staaten im Ersten Weltkrieg," in *Nationalismen in Europa,* 204–240. Cf. Jörn Leonhard,

Bellizismus und Nation: Kriegsdeutung und Nationsbestimmung in Europa und den Vereinigten Staaten, 1750–1914 (Munich: R. Oldenbourg, 2008).

19. John Torpey, *The Invention of the Passport: Surveillance, Citizenship, and the State* (New York: Cambridge University Press, 2000).

20. Bernard Lepetit, *Chemins de terre et voies d'eau: Réseaux de transports et organisation de l'espace en France 1740–1840* (Paris: Éditions de l'École des Hautes Études en Sciences Sociales, 1983), 1, 17–18, 21–26, 32, 81, 98–103.

21. Patrick O'Brien, "Transport and Economic Development in Europe, 1789–1914," in *Railways and the Economic Development of Western Europe, 1830–1914* (New York: St. Martin's Press, 1983), 7–14.

22. For an early statement, see Karl Deutsch, *Nationalism and Social Communication* (Cambridge, MA: MIT Press, 1953).

23. Cited by Theodore S. Hamerow, *The Social Foundations of German Unification 1858–1871: Struggles and Accomplishments* (Princeton, NJ: Princeton University Press, 1972), 51.

24. Friedrich List, *The National System of Political Economy,* trans. G.A. Matile (Philadelphia: J. B. Lippincontt & Co., 1856).

25. Helmut Böhme, *Deutschlands Weg zur Grossmacht. Studien zum Verhältnis von Wirtschaft und Staat während der Reichsgründungszeit (1848–1881)* (Cologne: Keipenheur und Witsch, 1966); Hamerow, *Social Foundations;* Hans Ulrich Wehler, *Deutsche Gesellschaftsgeschichte,* vol. 3 (Munich: C. H. Beck, 1991), 228–230, 287–290.

26. See Charles S. Maier, *Leviathan 2.0: Inventing Modern Statehood* (Cambridge, MA: Harvard University Press, 2014), chap. 2.

27. For the state guaranteed loans and subsidies that characterized French railway construction, pressed decisively by Minister Charles Freycinet, see Kimon A. Doukas, *The French Railroads and the State* (New York: Columbia University Press, 1945).

28. R. W. Kostal, *Law and English Railway Capitalism 1825–1875* (Oxford: Oxford University Press, 1994), 147–153. It was probably no accident that the rhetoric against the landowning obstructionists or the cupidity of the railroad companies escalated at the same time the conflict over the Corn Laws was also reaching its peak.

29. *Railway Times,* July 2, 1849, cited in ibid., 179.

30. Kostal, *Law and English Railway Capitalism,* 24.

31. "The Railway Director," January 9, 1846, cited in ibid., 30.

32. Richard White, *Railroaded: The Transcontinentals and the Making of Modern America* (New York: W. W. Norton, 2011). For the role that the military played

in the development of American systems, see Robert G. Angevine, *The Railroad and the State: War Politics, and Technology in Nineteenth-Century America* (Stanford, CA: Stanford University Press, 2004), esp. 165–230, on the post–Civil War era in the West.

33. See the citations from David Ramsay in Charles S. Maier, *Among Empires: American Ascendancy and Its Predecessors* (Cambridge, MA: Harvard University Press, 2006), 1 and taken from Robert L. Brunhouse, ed., *David Ramsay, 1749–1815: Selections from His Writings* (Philadelphia: American Philosophical Society, 1965), 183–190; Anders Stephanson, *Manifest Destiny: American Expansion and the Empire of Right* (New York: Hill and Wang, 1995), 40. But in James A. Ward, *Railroads and the Character of America, 1820–1887* (Knoxville: University of Tennessee Press, 1986), 128–129, Ward claims that the language of railroad development narrowed from a visionary picture of the nation's expansive future to one of commercial rivalry, which seems to make more sense for the competitive lines of the east than the still unbuilt enterprises of the west.

34. George L. Albright, *Official Explorations for Pacific Railroad 1853–1855* (Berkeley: University of California Press, 1921).

35. Charles Vevier, "American Continentalism: An Idea of Expansion, 1845–1910," *American Historical Review* 65, no. 2 (1960): 323–335. Whitney is on 327.

36. Ibid., 327. For Maury's correspondence with John C. Calhoun, see J. D. B. DeBow, ed., *The Industrial Revolution of the Southern and Western States*, 3 vols. (New Orleans, Office of De Bow's Review, 1852–1853), 1:257. For Maury's vision of a racist empire, see Walter Johnson, *River of Dark Dreams: Slavery and Empire in the Cotton Kingdom* (Cambridge, MA: Harvard University Press, 2013), 289–302.

37. Carlo Ilarione Pettiti di Roreto, *Delle strade ferrate italiane e del migliore ordinament di esse. Cinque discorsi* (Capolago, Tipografia e Libreria Elvetica, 1845); Camillo Benso de Cavour, "Des chemins de fer en Italie," *Revue Nouvelle* (May 1, 1847): 446–479, now in Camillo Cavour, *Scritti di economia,* ed. Francesco Strugo (Milan: Feltrinelli, 1962), 225–248.

38. Albert Schram, *Railways and the Formation of the Italian State in the Nineteenth Century* (Cambridge: Cambridge University Press,1997), 41–44; Aldo Berselli, "La questione ferroviaria e la 'rivoluzione parlamentare' del 18 marzo 1876," *Rivista Storica italiana* 46 (1958): 188–238.

39. Sllvio Spaventa, reviewing the experience of railway costs in Britain, France, the United States and elsewhere in *Lo stato e le ferrovie. Sul riscatto ed esercizio* (Milano: Fratelli Treves, 1876), 10. See also Schram, *Railways and the Italian State,* 49, 55.

40. Schram, *Railways and the Italian State,* 46–53. See also Spaventa, *Sul riscatto ed esercizio delle ferrovie italiane.*

41. Schram, *Railways and the Italian State,* 115, argues that they were rather frivolous; I think it's harder to measure the imponderables.

42. White, *Railroaded.*

43. Robert, Crawford, *Across the Pampas and the Andes* (London: Longmans, Green, 1884), 320–321. Crawford offered some recommendations for the government to avoid either deluding investors or making unwise guarantees: "To grant no railway concessions except for such lines as were expected after a few years working, to pay a fair dividend upon the capital employed in their construction. Such lines as were not likely to have a good traffic at once, but which might be desirable for strategical purposes, or to open up the country, the government to construct itself" (321–323).

44. For amounts, see Lloyd J. Mercer, *Railroads and Land Grant Policy: A Study in Government Intervention* (New York: Academic Press, 1982), 6–8. Mercer covers the large historiography up until 1982—notably the exchanges in the *Mississippi Valley Historical Review,* vols. XXXII and XXXIII (1946) and after (see 8–15). See also Stanley L. Engerman, "Some Economic issues Relating to Railroad Subsidies and the Evaluation of Land Grants," *Journal of Economic History* 32, no. 2 (June 1972): 443–463. The issue is different from the question famously raised by Robert Fogel, *Railroads and Economic Growth: Essays in Economic History* (Baltimore: Johns Hopkins University Press, 1964) as to whether railroads qualitatively transformed economic growth.

45. Otter, *Philosophy of Railroads.*

46. Ibid., 32–33.

47. Ibid., 110.

48. White, *Railroaded,* 23–26; Mercer, *Railroads and Land Grant Policy.*

49. Robert Crawford, *Across the Pampas and the Andes* (London: Longmans, Green, 1884), 268.

50. I am indebted to Jonathan Obert's unpublished paper, "The Co-Evolution of Public and Private Security in the Nineteenth Century City," for this point.

51. Salisbury remarks in Hansard [Parliamentary minutes], ser. 3, vol. 204 (6 March 1871): cols. 1366–1367.

52. William H. Goetzmann, "A 'Capacity for Wonder': The Meanings of Exploration," in *North American Exploration,* ed. John Logan Allen (Lincoln: University of Nebraska Press, 1997), vol. 3 of *A Continent Comprehended,* 542.

53. Vevier, "American Continentalism," 325–326. Vevier's valuable article followed Bernard DeVoto's explorations of American geopolitical hype (which given the conflict with Nazi Germany had been a timely topic) in "Geopolitics with the Dew on It," *Harper's Magazine* 188 (1944). He skewered

William Gilpin's imagery of the West. See John L. Thomas, *A Country in the Mind: Wallace Stegner, Bernard DeVoto, History and the American Land* (New York: Routledge, 2000), 80–81. See also DeVoto's history of Polk's expansionism in *The Year of Decision: 1846* (Boston: Little, Brown, 1943); *Across the Wide Missouri* (Boston: Houghton Mifflin, 1947); and *The Course of Empire* (Boston: Houghton Mifflin, 1952). Chapter 6 of this book takes up the theme of geopolitics more systematically.

54. Vevier, "American Continentalism," 328.

55. Otter, *Philosophy of Railroads,* 110.

56. Cited in Benjamín Vicuña Mackenna, *A Través de los Andes: Estudio sobre la major ubicación del future ferrocarril interoceánico entre el Atlántico i el Pacifico en la América del Sur (La República Arjentina i Chile)* (Santiago: Imprenta Gutenberg, 1885), 203–204.

57. For an account of the conflicts over finance and planning of the lines, see William J. Fleming, "Profits and Visions: British Capital and Railway Construction in Argentina, 1854–1886," in *Railway Imperialism,* ed. Clarence B. Davis and Kenneth E. Wilburn, with Ronald E. Robinson (New York: Greenwood Press, 1991), 71–83. For a theoretically informed discussion of the development of Argentine rail networks, see Juan Alberto Roccatagliata, *Los Ferrocarriles en la Argentina* (Buenos Aires: Docencia, 2010), esp. 59–83.

58. Mackenna, *A través de los Andes,* 255. For a long description of the geographical challenges to the Trans-Andean, see Robert Crawford, *Across the Pampas and the Andes* (London: Longmans, Green, and Co., 1884). Crawford was the chief of an engineering staff sent by Waring Bros. of London to survey the projected Trans-Andean line in 1871–1872. Of the two routes he preferred the Planchon pass from Buenos Aires to Valparaiso; it would have been longer but required less climbing than the route to Santiago (8225 ft. versus 10,658 ft.). Construction to Valparaiso would also be "decidedly light for a railway across such a mountain range as the Andes. There are no engineering novelties in the undertaking from first to last" (307). For the impact of the railroad on local economy, see María C. Vera de Flachs, *El Ferocarril Andino y el Desarrollo socioeconomic del Sur de Cordoba 1870–1880* (Buenos Aires: Fundación para la Educación, la Sciencia y la Cultura, 1982).

59. Crawford, *Across the Pampas and the Andes,* 324–325.

60. See the essays collected in Davis, Wilburn, and Robinson, *Railway Imperialism.* See also Liat Spiro's discussion of Germany's railroad enterprise in Shandong, "Griff nach dem Weltmarkt: The German New Middle Class, Overseas Infrastructure-Building, and Empire, 1885–1913" (seminar paper, Harvard University, Cambridge, MA, 2014).

61. Jonathan S. McMurray, *Distant Ties: Germany, the Ottoman Empire, and the Construction of the Baghdad Railway* (Westport, CT: Praeger, 2001). McMurray contests any view of the project as merely one for German imperial domination. See also Helmut Mejcher, "Die Bagdadbahn also Instrument deutschen wirtschaftlichen Einflusses im Osmanischen Reich," *Geschichte und Gesellschaft* 1 (1975): 447–481; Dietrich Eichholz, *Die Bagdadbahn, Mesopotamien und die deutsche Ölpolitik bis 1918* (Leipzig: Leipziger Universitätsverlag, 2007); Sean McMeekin, *The Berlin-Baghdad Express: The Ottoman Empire and Germany's Bid for World Power* (Cambridge, MA: Harvard University Press, 2010), which is really a study of the Ottoman-German alliance emphasizing developments in World War I.

62. Karl Kautsky, *Sozialismus und Kolonialpolitik: Eine Auseinandersetzung* (Berlin: Buchhandlung Vorwärts, 1907).

63. See Davis, Wilburn, and Robinson, *Railway Imperialism*. The theory rests on the notion that "locomotives generated informal imperial influence in preindustrial societies, whether or not lines were supported by the political intervention of an imperial power" (3). Yes—but a line built in a settler colony of Kenya or a British-run India revealed different power relations than those constructed in Brazil and Argentina. Cf. William J. Fleming's effort at differentiation in "Profits and Visions," in ibid., 71–83. For a careful periodization and review of the literature, see Colin M. Lewis, "Britain, the Argentine and Informal Empire: Rethinking the Role of Railway Companies," in Brown, *Informal Empire in Latin America: Culture, Commerce and Capital* (Oxford: Blackwell, 2008) 98–123. See also the harsh judgment on British owned railways in Winthrop R. Wright, *British-Owned Railways in Argentina: Their Effect on Economic Nationalism, 1854–1948* (Austin: University of Texas Press, 1974), esp. 70–88.

64. Rudyard Kipling, "The Explorer" (1898), *Collected Verse of Rudyard Kipling* (New York: Doubleday, Page and Company, 1915), 19–22.

65. F. Scott Russell, "The Service of Steam: The Romance of Railways," *Good Words* 17 (1876): 615–624.

66. Pyotr Petrovich Semenov-Tyan'-Shanskij, *Geografichesko-statisticheskij Slovar Russkoj Imperii*, vol. 1 (Saint Petersburg: Tip. Bezobrazova, 1863–1885). I am indebted to Joshua Kucera for research on the Russian sources. For a major study, which I learned of too late to consult fully, see Frithjof Benjamin Schenk, *Russlands Fahrt in die Moderne: Mobilität und sozialer Raum im Eisenbahnzeitalter* (Stuttgart: Franz Steiner Verlag, 2014).

67. Cited in S. F. Dmitrenko, *Zheleznia Doroga v russkoi Literatur: Antologiia* (Moscow: Izdateles'skii dom 'Zheleznodoroznoe Delo', 2012).

68. F. M. Dostoyevsky, "Questions and Answers," in *The Diary of a Writer*, ed. Boris Brasol (New York: Charles Scribner's Sons, 1949), 2:1048. The Aus-

trian resistance to Russian ambitions during the Russo-Turkish war over Bulgaria ignited the writer's anger in the late 1870s; successes in Central Asia allowed an alternative. For a discussion of Russia's Asian vocation, see Mark Bassin, "Asia" in *The Cambridge Companion to Modern Russian Culture,* ed. Nicholas Rzhevsky (Cambridge: Cambridge Companions Online, 2014), 65–93, available at http.//dx.doi.org/10.1017/CCOL9781107002524.005.

69. N. M. Iadrinstev, *Sibir' kak Koloniia* (Saint Petersburg: Tip. M. M. Stasiülevicha, 1882), ix–x, 14, 708–709.

70. W. T. Stead, "The Cape to Cairo Railway," *McClure's Magazine,* August 1899, 320–333.

71. Roland Wenzlhuemer, *Connecting the Nineteenth-Century World: The Telegraph and Globalization* (New York: Cambridge University Press, 2013), 257. See also Simone Müller-Pohl, *Wiring the World: The Social and Cultural Creation of Global Telegraph Networks* (New York: Columbia University Press, 2016).

72. Samuel Phillips Verner, "The Cape to Cairo Railway," *Conservative Review* 1 (1899): 245–254.

73. Halford Mackinder, "The Geographical Pivot of History," *Geographical Journal* 23 (1904): 434.

74. Thomas Hungerford Holdich, *Countries of the King's Award* (London: Hurst and Blackett, 1904), 20; Thomas Hungerford Holdich, *The Indian Border-land, 1880–1900* (London: Methuen, 1901), 99, cited in S. Whittemore Boggs, *International Boundaries: A Study of Boundary Functions and Problems* (New York: Columbia University Press, 1940), 141–145. The celebrated McMahon line separating India and Tibet was traced in 1913; the Afghan-Persian border, approximately stabilized in the seventeenth century, was finally traced in detail during 1913–1914; and the Turkish-Persian border in 1913–1914 (see Boggs, *International Boundaries,* 145–147).

75. Eric Weitz makes the connection between the two Berlin conferences in "From the Vienna to the Paris System: International Politics and the Engangled Histories of Human Rights, Forced Deportations, and Civilizing Missions," *American Historical Review* 113, no. 5 (2008): 1313–1343, esp. 1319–1321.

76. Among the numerous treatments of Bismarck's motivation, see Otto Pflanze, *Bismarck and the Development of Germany,* 3 vols. (Princeton, NJ: Princeton University Press, 1990) 3:113–142; Hans Ulrich Wehler, *Bismarck und der Imperialismus* (Cologne: Kiepenheuer & Witsch, 1969); and, in the context of German imperialism, Dirk van Laak, *Über alles in der Welt: Deutscher Imperialismus im 19. und 20. Jahrhundert* (Munich: C. H. Beck, 2001), esp. 64–73.

77. See the discussion of the status of the Makoko in H. L. Wesseling, *Divide and Rule: The Partition of Africa, 1880–1914,* trans. Arnold J. Pomerans

(Westport CT: Praeger, 1996), 94–95, and on the implications of protectorate, 28–30.

78. I draw on Steven Press's account in this section, "The Private State" (dissertation, Harvard University, 2013).

79. Henry M. Stanley, *The Congo and the Founding of its Free State,* 2 vols. (New York: Harper and Bros., 1885), 2:2.

80. Leopold's effort was seconded by international lawyers, some associated with the Brussels-based Institut du Droit International, founded in 1873, including Émile Levaleye, who had weighed in on collective property and now supported Leopold's venture. Members of the Institut divided over the issue of empire, some claiming that "no power on earth has the right to impose its laws upon wandering or even savage peoples," others defending the project in the name of a higher "civilization." See Andrew Fitzmaurice, "Liberalism and Empire in Nineteenth Century International Law," *American Historical Review* 117, no. 1 (2012): 127. The British lawyer Sir Travers Twiss effectively put his casuistry at the service of Leopold, refashioning an older idea of *territorium nullius. Territorium nullius,* Twiss argued, meant not that territorial sovereignty could not be claimed, but that it did not exist to date. Although territorial sovereignty as understood in Europe was still unknown in the Congo, personal sovereignty, that enjoyed by the African chief, did exist and they had the capacity to sell their rights to personal sovereignty to European purchasers who could exercise both *dominium* (or ownership) and *imperium* (or territorial sovereignty). To ensure that only certain claimants (not the Portuguese!) might prevail, the principle of effective occupation was also imposed. Fictional staking out of claims was not to be permitted, but those in the name of a higher civilization or welfare, the legal apologists explained, had the support of venerable legal principles. See ibid., 130–132. The even more radical *terra nullius*—an absence of private property rights and public rights of sovereignty—according to Fitzmaurice, was not really applied to Africa, though it was used in Australia and later in the Arctic (see ibid., 132–133). Cf. Jörg Fisch, "Africa as *Terra Nullius:* The Berlin Conference and International Law," in *Bismarck, Europe, and Africa: The Berlin Africa Conference, 1884–1885, and the Onset of Partition,* ed. Stig Förster, Wolfgang J. Mommsen, and Ronald E. Robinson (New York: Oxford University Press, 1988), 347–375.

81. Press, "Private State," 102–116; Wesseling, *Divide and Rule,* 98, 103.

82. For a now classical account of British calculations essentially based on the idea that expansion follows from the impossibility of renunciation, see Ronald Robinson and John Gallagher, with Alice Denney, *Africa and the Victorians: The Climax of Imperialism* (Garden City: Doubleday Anchor, 1968).

83. The reasons have been analyzed repeatedly since. Colonial activists in France resented Britain pushing forward in Egypt. Bismarck was happy to encourage the rivalries, which might divert French nationalists from obsessing about Alsace-Lorraine, and would simultaneously prevent a German liberal opposition at home from becoming too cozy with the pro-British German crown prince Friedrich, whose apparently imminent accession to the imperial throne might threaten the chancellor's own future position. A detailed narrative with an emphasis on domestic interests is provided by A. J. P. Taylor, *Germany's First Bid for Colonies, 1884–1885: A Move in Bismarck's European Policy* (London: Macmillan, 1938). See also Wehler, *Bismarck und der Imperialismus*, 258–390.

84. Sybil Eyre Crowe, *The Berlin West African Conference 1884–1885* (London: Longmans, Green, 1942), esp. 105–118; Wesseling, *Divide and Rule*, 113–124.

85. Adam Hochschild, *King Leopold's Ghost: A Story of Greed, Terrorism, and Heroism in Colonial Africa* (Boston: Houghton Mifflin, 1999). For the British attitudes to the unfolding horrors in Leopold's estate from 1884 to its takeover by the Belgian state, see S. J. S. Cookey, *Britain and the Congo Question 1885–1913* (London: Longmans, 1968). See also the 1918 study of conditions since 1885 in Arthur Berriedale Keith, *The Belgian Congo and the Berlin Act* (Oxford: Clarendon, 1919).

86. See the authoritative history of international law by Martti Koskenniemi in *"The Gentle Civilizer of Nations": The Rise and Fall of International Law, 1870–1960* (Cambridge: Cambridge University Press, 2002). Carl Schmitt, *Der Nomos der Erde im Völkerrecht des Jus Publicum Europaeum*, 4th ed. (Berlin: Duncker & Humblot, 1997).

87. Ronald Robinson, John Gallagher, and Alice Denny, *Africa and the Victorians* (New York: Doubleday & Company, 1968): 288.

88. Chamberlain's speech to Royal Colonial Institute, March 31, 1897, and Salisbury comment cited in ibid., 404–405.

89. Michel Houellebecq, *La carte et le territoire* (Paris: Flammarion, 2010).

90. Wesseling, *Divide and Rule*, 258.

91. Peano, and after him the German mathematician David Hilbert, wrestled with the recent analyses of Georg Cantor, who explained that there had to be different orders of infinity, the second order infinitely more numerous than the first order, which had paradoxes enough.

92. Ian J. Barrow, *Making History, Drawing Territory: British Mapping in India, c. 1756–1905* (New Delhi: Oxford University Press, 2003), quote from 183. Barrow critiques Matthew Edney's study for universalizing the trigonometric map.

93. Wesseling, *Divide and Rule,* 128.

94. Maxwell had published "On Faraday's Lines of Force," in 1855 and would publish his developed system of equations in 1865. See David Gooding, "Final Steps to the Field Theory: Faraday's Study of Magnetic Phenomena, 1845–1850," *Historical Studies in the Physical Sciences* 11, no. 2 (1981): 321–275, http//www.jstor.org/stable/27757480. See also Bruce Hunt, "Michael Faraday, Cable Telegraphy, and the Rise of Field Theory," *History of Technology* 13 (1991): 1–19.

95. For a magisterial survey, see Thomas Hughes, *Networks of Power: Electrification in Western Society, 1880–1930* (Baltimore, MD: Johns Hopkins University Press, 1983).

6. From Fate to Function

1. Cf. Martin W. Lewis and Kåren Wigan, *The Myth of Continents: A Critique of Metageography* (Berkeley: University of California Press, 1997).

2. Halford Mackinder, "The Geographical Pivot of History," *Geographical Journal* 23, no. 4 (1904): 421–422. For useful commentary and assessments, see the centennial collection of articles in the *Geographical Journal* 170, no. 4 (2004).

3. Sönke Neitzel, *Weltmacht oder Untergang: die Weltreichslehre im Zeitalter des Imperialismus* (Paderborn: Schöningh, 2000), 25–27.

4. John Bristed, *The Resources of the United States of America, or A View of the . . . Capacity and Character of the American People* (New York, James Eastburn & Co., 1818), 246, cited in Neitzel, *Weltmachtlehre,* 69.

5. For a commentary stressing Mahan's nuances, see John Sumida, "Alfred Thayer Mahan, Geopolitician," in *Geopolitics: Geography and Strategy,* ed. Colin S. Gray and Geoffrey Sloan (London: Frank Cass, 1999), 39–63. The volume is a reprinting of the special issue of the *Journal of Strategic Studies* 22, nos. 2–3 (1999).

6. See Paul Kennedy, "Mahan versus Mackinder, Two Interpretations of British Sea Power," in *Strategy and Diplomacy 1870–1945: Eight Studies* (London: Allen and Unwin, 1983), 41–85. Also Paul Kennedy, *The Rise and Fall of British Naval Mastery* (New York: Scriber's, 1976).

7. See Gearóid Ó Tuathail (Gerard Toal), "Understanding Critical Geopolitics: Geopolitics and Risk Society," in Gray and Sloane, *Geopolitics,* 107–124. It is an effort to demonstrate how much of conventional geopolitics was socially constructed. See also Gearóid Ó Tuathail, "Postmodern Geopoli-

tics? The Modern Geopolitical Imagination and Beyond," in *Rethinking Geopolitics,* ed. Gearóid Ó Tuathail and Simon Dalby (New York: Routledge, 1998), 16–38. See also John Agnew, *Geopolitics: Re-Visioning World Politics* (London: Routledge, 1998); and John Agnew and S. Corbridge, *Mastering Space* (London: Routledge, 1995), which define successive geopolitical orders through the centuries that organize spatial relations according to stages of political economy. John Agnew, *Reinventing Geopolitics: Geographies of Modern Statehood. Hettner Lecture 2000* (Heidelberg: University of Heidelberg Geography Department, 2001), is actually a series of four lectures on boundary making and creation of national cohesion, marked by great historical range.

8. Gerry Kearns, "Imperial Geopolitics: Geopolitical Visions at the Dawn of the American Century," in *A Companion to Political Geography,* ed. John A. Agnew, Katherine Mitchell, Gerard Toal (Oxford: Wiley-Blackwell, 2003), 174. For an excellent recent survey, touching on all the figures taken up below, see most recently Patricia Chiantera-Stutte, *Il pensiero geopolitico: Spazio, potere e imperialismo tra Otto e Novecento* (Rome: Carocci, 2014).

9. This is one of the analytical approaches taken by Mark Polelle, *Raising Cartographic Consciousness: The Social and Foreign Policy Vision of Geopolitics in the Twentieth Century* (Lanham, MD: Lexington Books, 1999). For the most inclusive survey of authors, and of the Nazi agencies entrusted with issues of *Raum,* see Andrew Gyorgy, *Geopolitics: The New German Science* (Berkeley: University of California Press, 1944). For a summary of geopolitical thinking and other twentieth-century schools, see John Agnew and Luca Musara, *Making Political Geography,* 2nd ed. (Plymouth, UK: Rowman and Littlefield, 2012), 59–101.

10. Ulrike Jureit, *Das Ordnen von Räumen: Territorium und Lebensraum im 19. und 20. Jahrhundert* (Hamburg: Hamburger Edition, 2012), 152; Peter Schöller, "Wege und Irrwege der politischen Geographie und Geopolitik," *Erdkunde* 11 (1957): 1–20.

11. Ó Tuathail, "Postmodern Geopolitics?," 17. See also Agnew, *Geopolitics;* and Agnew and Corbridge, *Mastering Space.* Ó Tuathail suggests instead that the modern geopolitical imagination "is a legacy of the imposition of European territorial forms across the globe from the sixteenth century, an order of power over the Earth that sought to discipline its infinite spaces . . . around sovereign presence and immanent logos" (23), by which murky term he seems to mean geographical features. The conclusion of this volume returns to concepts of postmodern geopolitics.

12. Hans W. Weigert, *Generals and Geographers: The Twilight of Geopolitics* (New York: Oxford University Press, 1942), 4.

13. Friedrich Naumann, *Mitteleuropa* (Berlin: G. Reimer, 1915); Henry Cord Meyer, *Mitteleuropa in German Thought and Action, 1815–1945* (The Hague: Nijhoff, 1955).

14. Ratzel, "Studien über politische Räume," and "Gesetze des räumlichen Wachstums," manuscripts from Ratzel Nachlass, Institut für Länderkunde Leipzig, cited in Jureit, *Ordnen von Räumen*, 145–151.

15. Jureit, *Ordnen von Räumen*, 134–135. Cf. Ernst-Wolfgang Böckenförde, "Organ, Organismus, Organisation, politischer Körper," in *Geschichtliche Grundbegriffe*, ed. Otto Brunner, Werner Conze, and Reinhard Koselleck (Stuttgart: E. Klett, 1978), 4:519–622; Ernst-Wolfgang Böckenförde, "Der Staat als Organismus. Zur staatstheoretisch-verfassungpolitischen Diskussion im frühen Konstitutionalismus," in *Recht, Staat, Freiheit. Studien zur Rechtsphilosophie, Staatstheorie und Verfassungsgeschichte* (Frankfurt/Main: Suhrkamp 1991), 263–272.

16. Robert Sieger, "Rudolf Kjellén," *Zeitschrift für Geopolitik* 1, no. 6 (1924–1925): 339–346.

17. Cited in Polelle, *Raising Cartographic Consciousness*, 97.

18. Polelle, *Raising Cartographic Consciousness*, 99; Christian W. Spang, *Karl Haushofer und Japan: Die Rezeption seiner geopolitischen Theorien in der deutschen und japanischen Politik* (Munich: Iudicum Verlag, 2013), 226–228.

19. Mackinder, "Geographical Pivot of History," 426.

20. Ibid., 431.

21. Ibid., 432–433.

22. Ibid., 435–436.

23. Ibid., 436–437. For assessments of how Mackinder's views fit into the British strategic and foreign-policy debates of the 1904–1907 years, see the articles in the 2004 centennial retrospective cited in Klaus Dodds and James D. Sidaway, "Halford Mackinder and the 'Geographical Pivot of History': A Centennial Retrospective," 292–297, and Pascal Venier, "The Geographical Pivot of History and Early Twentieth Century Geopolitical Culture," 330–336, among other commentary in B. Blouet, *Halford Mackinder: A Biography* (College Station: Texas A&M University Press, 1987).

24. David J. M. Hooson, "The Heartland—Then and Now," in *Global Geostrategy: Mackinder and the Defence of the West,* ed. B. W. Blouet (London: Frank Cass, 2005), 165–176. Hooson, a British geographer and Soviet expert, did seek to apply Mackinder's ideas; see Ron Johnston, "David Hoson: Political Geography, Mackinder and Russian Geopolitics," *Geopolitics* 14 (2009): 182–189.

25. Halford J. Mackinder, *Democratic Ideals and Reality: A Study in the Politics of Reconstruction,* introduction by Stephen V. Mladineo (Washington, DC: National Defense University Press, 1992); from the 1942 printing of the 1919 original). The definition of the world island is on page 45. At the same time, though, he identified the "interior of Africa south of the Sahara as a second Heartland . . . the Southern Heartland" (58). Designations and regions were described with exuberant abandon—the heartland with northern forests and steppe, Arabia as a linking region to the southern heartland, the monsoon land in south and Southeast Asia, the East Asian coastland from southern China to Kamchatka, which with the European peninsula and its islands comprised four-fifths of the world-island population but measured only one-fifth of its area (58–60).

26. Ibid., 80.

27. Mackinder, "Geographical Pivot of History," 438.

28. Nathaniel George Curzon, Marquess of Keddleston, *Frontiers: The Romanes Lecture delivered in the Sheldonian Theatre* (Oxford: Clarendon, 1907). For Curzon, the frontiers of empire offered a moral education: "on the manifold Frontiers of dominion, now amid the gaunt highlands of the Indian border, or the eternal snows of the Himalayas, now on the parched sands of Persia or Arabia, now in the equatorial swamps and forests of Africa . . . is to be found an ennobling and invigorating stimulus for our youth, saving them alike from the corroding ease and the morbid excitements of Western civilization" (56–58).

29. Report printed in E. L Woodward and Rowan Butler, eds., *Documents on British Foreign Policy, 1919–1939,* first series, vol. 3, HMSO 1949, 768–787, and cited in Polelle, *Raising Cartographic Consciousness,* 105.

30. Cited in Jureit, *Ordnen von Räumen,* 251.

31. "Dass eine Zeit gepolitischer Flurbereinigung der Neuverteilung der Macht auf der Erde mit dem Weltkrieg nicht abgeschlossen ist, sondern angefangen hat." Cited by Jureit, *Ordnen von Räumen,* 252, from *Handbuch der völkischen Wissenschaften,* ed. Ingo Haar and Michael Fahlbusch (Munich: K. G. Sauer, 2008), 236–237.

32. Spang, *Karl Haushofer und Japan,* 288–289.

33. "Weiter Raum wirkt Leben erhaltend" and "Die grössere Raumaffassung gerät notwendig in Streit mit der kleineren. Sie hat endgültig den Sieg errungen," both in Karl Haushofer, *Wehr-geopolitik: geographische Grundlagen einer Wehrkunde,* 3rd ed. (Berlin: Junker und Dünnhaupt, 1941), 52. Wehrgeopolitik was paralleled by a geographical survey in the same period: Karl Haushofer, *Weltpolitik von heute* (Berlin: Zeitgeschichte-Verlag Weilhelm Andermann, 1934).

34. Cited from M. Bassin, "Imperialism and the Nation State in Friedrich Ratzel's Political Geography," *Progress in Human Geography* 11 (1987): 480; and Polelle, *Raising Cartographic Consciousness,* 98. "Die Geopolitik . . . fusst auf der breiten Grundlage der Geographie insbesonder die politischen Geographie als der Lehre von den politischen Raumorganisation und ihre Strukturen. . . . In Sinne dieser Erkenntnis will die Geopolitik Rüstzeug zum politischen Handeln liefern und Wegwieser im politischen Leben sein. . . . Die Geopolitik will und muss zum geographischen Gewissen des Staates werden." Ewald Liedecke, "Raumordnung und Geopolitik," *Zeitschrift für Geopolitik* 9 (1933): 481–496.

35. Fritz Hesse, "Das Gesetz der wachsenden Räume," *Zeitschrift für Geopolitik* 1, no. 1 (1924): 1–4.

36. For a brief outline of the journal's history that stresses the continuing tensions and disagreements among the editors (was Kjellén or Ratzel the real founder of geopolitics?), see Wolfgang Natter, "Geopolitics in Germany, 1919–1945: Karl Haushofer and the Zeitschrift für Geopolitik," in Agnew, Mitchell, and Toal, *A Companion to Political Geography* (Oxford: Wiley-Blackwell 2003), 187–203.

37. Haushofer, *Bausteine,* 27, cited in Spang, *Karl Haushofer und Japan,* 229.

38. "Für die reine Geographie ist der Raum Selbstzweck, für die Geopolitik ist er nur Mittel zum Zweck. . . . Die Geopolitik—als angewandete Wissenschaft—beginnt da, wo die Möglichkeit der Voraussage anfängt." Cited in Spang, *Karl Hauhofer und Japan,* 234.

39. Ernst Tiessen, "Der Friedensvertrag von Versailles und die politische Geographie," *Zeitschrift für Geopolitik* 1, no. 3 (1924): 205–220.

40. Haushofer, *Wehr-Geopolitik,* 57–58.

41. *Zeitschrift für Geopolitik.* See also Jan O. M. Broek, "The German School of Geopolitics," in *Global Politics: Lectures Delivered under the Auspices of the Institute of Political Geography University of California Los Angeles, Summer 1942,* ed. Russell H. Fitzgibbon (Berkeley: University of California Press, 1944), 167–179, esp. 169.

42. Haushofer, *Wehr-geopolitik,* 166–167.

43. Ibid., 171. For Gyorgy, who followed the group around Haushofer, his journal and his institute, most attentively, the theorist descended into increasing irrationality (*Geopolitics,* 186). But part of the evolution stemmed from Haushofer's need to follow the changing policies of the regime—Russia (and with it Eurasia) was always the entity that determined global landed space; Germany ultimately could retain parity or domination only insofar as it could guide Moscow or defeat it. Among the Haushofer circle (what

Gyorgy termed the Munich International), the role of his son Albrecht Haushofer was the most poignant. He contributed to the *Zeitschrift für Geopolitik* and presciently asked in January 1939 whether appeasement "in spite of Mr. Chamberlain's emphatically repeated view that concessions serve the cause of peace, only means preparing the ground for [a new world war]" (see 242n19). A contributor to the journal, later a functionary in the Foreign Ministry, he consorted with the conspirators of July 20, 1944, and was executed two weeks before the end of the war after having written a series of sonnets from Moabit prison that severely criticized his father. The parents committed suicide in 1946.

44. For the complexity of the messages created by this magazine, especially its photographs, see Catherine A. Lutz and Jane L. Collins, *Reading National Geographic* (Chicago: University of Chicago Press, 1993).

45. See Gyorgy, *Geopolitics*, 189–190. See also Grabowsky, "Das Problem der Geopolitik," *Zeitschrift für Politik* 22, no. 12 (1933): 765–802.

46. H. Arthur Steiner, "The Relation between Geography and Politics," in Fitzgibbon, *Global Politics*, 3.

47. On German plans for conquered Eastern Europe, see Vejas G. Liulevicius, *War Land on the Eastern Front: Culture, National Identity, and German Occupation in World War I* (Cambridge: Cambridge University Press, 2000); for World War II, see Götz Aly, *Endlösung: Völkerverschiebung und der Mord an den europäischen Juden* (Frankfurt: S. Fischer, 1995), among many other treatments.

48. Gyorgy, *Geopolitics*, 243. Haushofer's son, Albrecht, did not share the view of the others in his father's circle that the British Empire would disintegrate.

49. Karl Haushofer, "Die grösste Aufgabe," *Zeitschrift für Geopolitik* 18, no. 7 (1941): 369.

50. Colin Ross, "The 'Sun King' of America," *Zeitschrift für Geopolitik*, 18, no. 7 (1941): 399–403.

51. On the relations with the National Socialists, see J. Bendersrsky, *Carl Schmitt, Theorist for the Reich* (Princeton, NJ: Princeton University Press, 1983).

52. "Forms of Modern Imperialism in International Law" (1933), trans. Matthew Hannah, now included in Stephen Legg, ed., *Spatiality, Sovereignty and Carl Schmitt: Geographies of the Nomos* (New York: Routledge, 2011), 29–45. See also Legg's own essay "Interwar Spatial Chaos? Imperialism, Internationalism and the League of Nations" (ibid., 106–124). Schmitt particularly despaired that the real power of U.S. imperialism consisted of the fact that its victims accepted its vocabulary, and he asked Germans to see through

"the veil of words and concepts, of juridifications and moralization" ("Forms of Modern Imperialism," 44–45). In effect Schmitt was proposing from the Right the concept of "hegemony" that Antonio Gramsci was working out from the Left, but applying it to the national not the class struggle. We must save for another occasion a comparison between Gramsci's awed dismay at the American degradation of labor (Taylorism) and Schmitt's critique of America's formidable deterritorializing imperialism.

53. "*Grossraum* versus Universalism: The International Legal Struggle over the Monroe Doctrine," trans. Matthew Hannah, in ibid., 48. William Hooker's useful study *Carl Schmitt's International Thought: Order and Orientation* (Cambridge: Cambridge University Press, 2009), 126–155, has sharply criticized the idea of the *Grossraum* for its vagueness; its only function allegedly being to rescue the modern state from its new impotence. Despite the virtues of Hooker's work, in particular the long discussion of the later theory of the partisan, I find its criticism misplaced. Schmitt was writing in a context where the idea had taken on a general, if unattractive, resonance, and he deployed it to elaborate the great alternatives for imperialist rivalries as he discerned them.

54. See Carl Schmitt, *Land und See* (Stuttgart: Klett-Cotta, 1954), and the commentary by Claudio Minca, who emphasizes Schmitt's metaphysical horror of borderless spaces, in "Carl Schmitt and the Question of Spatial Ontology," in Legg, *Spatiality, Sovereignty and Carl Schmitt*, 162–181, esp. 170–178. The United States is the power that thrusts toward this borderless space—rolling back a bordered Europe toward the opening of Genesis: "The world was void and without form."

55. Carl Schmitt, *Land und Meer* (Stuttgart: Klett-Cotta, 1954).

56. Carl Schmitt, *Der Nomos der Erde im Völkerrecht des Jus Publicum Europaeum,* 4th ed. (Berlin: Duncker und Humblot, 1997), 48. For the meaning of nomos, see 36–48. I have translated *Hegung* as enclosure in this case, not bracketing.

57. Ibid., 48.

58. Ibid., 51, 55–56 ("*globales Liniendenken*"). The earlier such epochal creation had arisen from the great barbarian invasions at the end of the Roman Empire and followed from land invasions; the sixteenth-century and seventeenth-century *nomos* that would create the Jus Publicum Europaeum derived from oceanic as well as landed appropriation; adding the realm of the air would be part of the coming order—however, the terrestrial appropriation remained fundamental. Schmitt termed the Congo Act, signed at the 1884–1885 Berlin Conference the last effort at a common international-law treatment of colonial land, including a neutralized Congo basin (188–195).

59. Ibid., 50–51. Contrast with more conventional views of Spanish efforts at empire: Ludwig Dehio, *The Precarious Balance: Four Centuries of the European Power Struggle,* trans. Charles Fullman (New York: Knopf, 1962). For Schmitt, the Spanish Catholic jurist Vitoria was the major architect of the international law as it emerged in the sixteenth century.

60. Schmitt, *Nomos der Erde,* 162–163.

61. Ibid., 170.

62. Ibid., 171–172.

63. Ibid., 206.

64. Ibid., 210, 212. (The original is *"die bisher gelungene Hegung des Krieges."* Hegung is usually translated as "bracketing.")

65. Ibid., 213.

66. Ibid., 224–265.

67. Cited by Frances Stonor Saunders, "Stuck on the Flypaper: MI5 and the Hobsbawm File," *London Review of Books,* April 9, 2015, 9.

68. Dorothy Thompson, "On the Record: Hitler's World Strategy Is Now Russia's," a syndicated column, retrieved in this case from the *Pittsburgh Post-Gazette,* October 11, 1948. See also Dorothy Thompson, "On the Record: Russia's War Plan Follows Old Pattern of Geopolitics," August 16, 1950. From 1941 on she wrote perhaps close to twenty articles on geopolitics, citing Haushofer's malevolent influence during the war with Germany, and Mackinder's prescience in the Cold War.

69. Mackinder, *Democratic Ideals and Reality.*

70. See Kearns, "Imperial Geopolitics."

71. Nicholas Spykman, *America's Strategy in World Politics: The United States and the Balance of Power* (New York: Harcourt, Brace, 1942), 41. For the 1938 article: "Geography and Foreign Policy," *APSR* 32, nos. 1–2 (1938): 28–50 and 213–236; also Gyorgy, *Geopolitics,* 254.

72. For a good summary see Chiantera-Stutte, *Il pensiero geopolitico,* 159–169.

73. Robert Strausz-Hupé, *Geopolitics: The Struggle for Space and Power* (New York: G. P. Putnam's Sons, 1942); Robert Strausz-Hupé, *Protracted Conflict* (New York: Harper's, 1959).

74. Polelle, *Raising Cartographic Consciousness,* 102. The eminent geographer and theorist John Agnew has also tried to renew geopolitics in a neutral sense of political geography; see Agnew and Corbridge, *Mastering Space.*

75. Not only Americans picked up the term: see Y. M. Goblet, *Political Geography and the World Map* (London: George Philip and Son, 1955): "Political

geography is that part of human geography which deals with those political complexes which have a territorial component. To these complexes it is as biology is to living things" (17). It allegedly "admits of no a priori theory" (23) and was that science which was based on and summarized by a map (25). The applied science led to a history of an enlightened West, transcending colonialism and "leading humanity on the road to freedom" (292).

76. Jan Marius Otto Broek, "The German School of Geopolitics," in Fitzgibbon, *Global Politics,* 167–179, esp. 167–68; and Jan Marius Otto Broek, "Geopolitics and Political Geography," *Far Eastern Survey,* July 14, 1943, 143–145.

77. Steiner, "Relation," 4.

78. Ibid., 6.

79. Ibid., 14.

80. Derwent Whittlesey, *The Earth and the State: A Study of Political Geography* (New York: Henry Holt, 1944), iii. For "Immaturity," see 191–193.

81. Ibid., 11.

82. Ibid., 23.

83. See Derwent Whittlesey, "Haushofer: The Geopolitician," in *Makers of Modern Strategy,* ed. Edward Mead Earle (Princeton, NJ: Princeton University Press, 1941), 388–411; Derwent Whittlesey, Charles C. Colby, and Richard Hartshorne, *German Strategy of World Conquest* (New York: Farrar and Rinehart, 1942). For the popularization of geopolitics in the war, see Gerard Toal, *Critical Geopolitics: The Politics of Writing Global Space* (Minneapolis: University of Minnesota Press, 1996), 111–141. Mackinder's *Democratic Ideals and Reality* was reissued in 1942, with an introduction by the Australian Major George Fielding Eliot, who became quietly influential in the U.S. State Department under then Secretary George C. Marshall.

84. David Slater, "The Geopolitical Imagination and the Enframing of Development Theory," *Transactions of the Institute of British Geographers* 18, no. 4 (1993): 420.

85. See Agnew and Musara, *Making Political Geography,* vii. The authors referred to a 180-degree shift in the field since the 1890s (ix; see also 94–101).

86. Neil Smith, " 'Academic War over the Field of Geography': The Elimination of Geography at Harvard, 1947–1951," *Annals of the Association of American Geographers* 77, no. 2 (1987): 168. See also Neil Smith, *American Empire: Roosevelt's Geographer and the Prelude to Globalization* (Berkeley: University of California Press, 2003).

87. For Canada and the United States, see, in general, Charles Emmerson, *The Future History of the Arctic* (New York: Public Affairs, 2010), 177–197; Vasily

Burkhanov, *New Soviet Discoveries in the Arctic* (Moscow: Foreign Languages Publishing House, 1956); Pier Horensma, *The Soviet Arctic* (New York: Routledge, 1991).

88. John Roscoe, a major contributor to the effort, worked both for his dissertation and the CIA. See John Roscoe, "Antarctic Photogeography," in *Antarctica in the International Geophysical Year*, ed. Lawrence Gould (Baltimore, MD: American Geophysical Union, 1956); and for a survey, see David Day, *Antarctica: A Biography* (Oxford: Oxford University Press, 2013).

89. John Manning, "The 1939 Australian Map of Antarctica," *Globe*, August 1, 2010.

90. H. S. K Kent, "The Historical Origins of the Three-Mile Limi," *American Journal of International Law* 48, no. 4 (1954): 537–553.

91. See the survey by Anis H. Bajrektarevic, "Arctic and Antarctic: Two Poles—Different Scores: Similarities and Differences in Security Structures Surrounding the Two Polar Caps," *Geopolitics, History, and International Relations* 212 (2010): 165–232.

92. Philip E. Steinberg, Jeemy Tasch, and Hannes Gerhardt, with Adam Keul and Elizabeth A. Nyman, *Contesting the Arctic: Politics and Imaginaries in the Circumpolar North* (London: I. B. Taurus, 2015), 149.

93. See Eric Weitz, "From the Vienna to the Paris System: International Politics and the Engangled Histories of Human Rights, Forced Deportations, and Civilizing Missions," *The American Historical Review* 113, no. 5 (2008): 1314n1. "I would differ with Charles S. Maier by arguing that the defining feature of the nineteenth and twentieth centuries was not just a 'rescaling' of territoriality, but a profound emphasis on distinctive populations within clearly demarcated territories."

94. Jean Michel Hoerner, *Géopolitique des territoires: de l'Espace approprié à la suprématie de l'État-Nation* (Perpignan: Presses Universitaires de Perpignan, 1999).

95. From the preface by Christophe Codonnier to Paul Vidal de la Blache, *Principes de Géographie Humaine* (Paris: Utz, 1995), 22–23. For surveys of social geography or human geography, see Paul Claval, *Essai sur l'évolution de la géographie humaine* (Paris: Les Belles Letrres, 1964); and Paul Claval, *Principes de géographie sociale* (Paris: Editions M.-Th. Génin, 1973). For a survey of French geography traditions, see Jean-François Deneux, *Histoire de la pensée géographique* (Paris: Belin, 2008).

96. Vidal de la Blache, "Sens et objet de la géographie humaine," in *Principes de Géographie Humaine*, 31.

97. For circulation and iconography, see Jean Gottmann, *La politique des états et leur géographie* (Paris: Armand Colin, 1952); Jean Gottmann, *Megalopolis: The*

Urbanized Northeastern Seaboard of the United States (New York: Twentieth Century Fund, 1961).

98. See in particular Alan K. Henrikson, "The Iconography and Circulation of the Atlantic Community," and George Prevelakis, "The Relevance of Jean Gottmann in Today's World," both in *Ekistics / Oikistike: The Problems and Science of Human Settlements* 70, nos. 422–423 (2003): 270–294, and 294–304. This issue was the third devoted to Gottmann's work. I am grateful to both these authors for drawing my attention to the significance of Gottmann.

99. Yves Lacoste, *La géographie, ça sert, d'abord, à faire la guerre* (Paris: Maspéro, 1976); Deneux, *Histoire de la pensée géographique,* 150–151. See Lacoste's own account of the development of a geopolitical school, "La géographie, la géopolitique et le raisonnement géographique," *Hérodote* 146–147 (2012): 15–44.

100. Christian Grataloup, *Lieux d'Histoire: Essai de géohistoire systématique* (Montpélier: GIP RECLUS, 1996); valuable also as a bibliographic resource for the imposing French geographical output.

101. Among the vast number of studies that take this approach, across all the social-sciences, we can signal the works of John Agnew already cited, Saskia Sassen, *Territory-Authority-Rights: From Medieval to Global Assemblages* (Princeton: Princeton University Press, 2006); and Neil Brenner, ed., *Implosions/Explosions: Towards a Study of Planetary Urbanization* (Berlin: Jovis Verlag, 2014).

102. Cf. Jacques Donzelot, *L'invention du social: essai sur le déclin des passions politiques* (Paris: Fayard, 1984). Preoccupation with a bourgeois social order does not translate necessarily into the goal of advancing capitalism considered as restless economic advance. See Pierre Rosanvallon, *L'Etat en France de 1789 à nos jours* (Paris: Seuil, 1990), 216.

103. On international river governance bodies, see Francis B. Sayre, *Experiments in International Administration* (New York: Harper and Brothers, 1919); for the development of NGOs and international institutions in general, see the pioneering survey by Akira Iriye, *Global Community: The Role of International Organizations in the Making of the Contemporary World* (Berkeley: University of California Press, 2002).

104. Julian Clark and Alun Jones, "The Spatialities of Europeanisation: Territory, Government and Power in 'Europe,'" *Transactions of the Institute of British Geography* 33 (2008): 300–318; Hoerner, *Géopolitique des territoires,* 123–156.

105. See Timothy Nunan's study, *NGOs against Sovereignty: Afghanistan* (Cambridge: Cambridge University Press, 2016).

106. See Vanessa Ogle, "Archipelago Capitalism: Tax Havens, Money Markets, and the Other International Political Economy, 1930s–1980s," presented to the Weatherhead Initiative for Global History, Cambridge, Massachussetts, November 17, 2015—a first statement of ongoing research.

Conclusion

1. For the Schengen regime, see Daman Chalmers, Garth Davies, and Giorgio Monti, *European Union Law: Cases and Materials,* 2nd ed. (Cambridge: Cambridge University Press, 2010), esp. "EU Law and Non-EU Nationals," 484–533.

2. Giovanni di Lorenzo, "In Grenzen Wilkommen," *Die Zeit,* December 3, 2015, 1.

3. Rachel St. John, *Line in the Sand: A History of the Western U.S.-Mexico Border* (Princeton, NJ: Princeton University Press, 2011), 207, suggests "millions" of border crosssings per year. The Tiajuana-San Diego crossing counted 50 million persons in 2005; the Department of Homeland Security claims to process over a million incoming travellers and returning citizens a day. See www.dhs.gov/how-do-i-cross-us-borders.

4. For a rather dystopic view of local sovereignties as a portent of the future territorial order, see Timothy W. Luke, "Governmentality and Contragovernmentality: Rethinking Sovereignty and Territoriality after the Cold War," *Political Geography,* 15, nos. 6–7 (1996).

5. Based on Article 14 of the Universal Declaration of Human Rights in 1948, the 1951 Convention Relating to the Status of Refugees recognized the right of persons to seek asylum from persecution in other countries. Its original geographic and temporal limits (applying to Europe before 1951) were removed by the 1967 Protocol Relating to the Status of Refugees, and Resolution 2798 (XXI) adopted by the UN General Assembly. See Karel Vasak and Sidney Liskofsky, with the assistance of Stephen P. Marks, Jan Axelsson, and Thomas A. McCarthy, *The Right to Leave and to Return; Papers and Recommendations of the International Colloquium Held in Uppsala Sweden, 19–20 June 1972* (New York: American Jewish Committee, 1976). I am indebted to Samuel Moyn for this reference.

6. Michael Walzer argues for the right of a state to limit entrance because communities "depend upon closure" to maintain "the sense of relatedness and mutuality." See Michael Walzer, *Spheres of Justice: A Defense of Pluralism and Equality* (New York: Basic Books, 1983); As discussed in Linda Bosniak, *The Citizen and the Alien: Dilemmas of Contemporary Membership* (Princeton, NJ:

Princeton University Press, 2006), 40–43, which focuses primarily on the rights of aliens already admitted into the United States.

7. For the Bermuda and Evian conferences, see Arieh Tartakower and Kurt R. Grossman, *The Jewish Refugee* (New York: Institute of Jewish Affairs of the American Jewish Congress and World Jewish Congress, 1944).

8. "Global Trade after the Failure of the Doha Round," *New York Times,* January 1, 2016.

9. Charles S. Maier, *Among Empires: American Ascendancy and Its Predecessors* (Cambridge, MA: Harvard University Press, 2006), esp. chap. 3. For Europe's situation in particular, see Jan Zielonka, *Europe as Empire: The Nature of the Enlarged European Union* (Oxford: Oxford University Press, 2006), which discusses the EU as an analogue of empire. This seems exaggerated to me insofar as its internal ordering is concerned but has more validity perhaps when thinking about its global placement.

10. Saskia Sassen, *Guests and Aliens* (New York: New Press, 1999).

11. For critics who describe globalization in terms of a diffuse power of capital, see David Harvey, *The Condition of Postmodernity: An Enquiry into the Origins of Cultural Change* (Oxford: Blackwell, 1989). See also Michael Hardt and Toni Negri, *Empire* (Cambridge, MA: Harvard University Press, 2000).

12. See Kevin R. Cox, "'Globalization,' the 'Regulation Approach' and the Politics of Scale," in *Geographies of Power: Placing Scale,* ed. Andrew Herod and Melissa W. Wright (Oxford: Blackwell, 2002), 85–114. See also Eric Swyngedouw, "Neither Global nor Local: 'Globalization' and the Politics of Scale," in *Spaces of Globalization,* ed. K. R. Cox (New York: Guilford, 1967), 137–166; Bob Jessop, "Narrating the Future of the National Economy and the National State? Remarks on Remapping, Regulation and Reinventing Governance," in *State / Culture,* ed. George Steinmetz (Ithaca, NY: Cornell University Press, 1999), 378–405.

13. For example, Arjun Appadurai celebrates the global "imaginary" or *imaginaire* built on landscapes of finance, technology, media, and ideologies. See Arjun Appadurai, "Disjunction and Difference in the Global Cultural Economy," *Theory, Culture & Society* 7 (1990): 295–310; Arjun Appadurai, *Modernization at Large: Cultural Dimensions of Globalization* (Minneapolis: University of Minnesota Press, 1996).

14. Gilles Deleuze and Felix Guattari, *A Thousand Plateaus: Capitalism and Schizophrenia,* trans. Brian Massumi (London: Continuum, 1992), 382. The nomadic counterattack can generate the paradox of fascism. The fascist state is far less totalitarian than it is *suicidal.* "When fascism builds itself a totalitarian State, it is not in the sense of a State army taking power, but of a war

machine [the apparatus of violence assembled by the escapees of the state] taking over the State" (ibid., 230).

15. Deleuze and Guattari, *A Thousand Plateaus*, 202, 222. The authors follow another French meta-theoretician of state space, Paul Virilio, who identified the universal art of marking boundaries by lines and territories. See Paul Virilio, *L'insécurité du territoire* (Paris: Stock, 1975). For summaries, see Paul Patton, *Deleuze and the Political* (London: Routledge, 2000), 88–131; and James Der Derian, *Critical Practices in International Theory: Selected Essays* (London: Routledge, 2009).

16. Deleuze and Guattari, *A Thousand Plateaus*, 381–385: "If the nomad can be called the Deterritorialized par excellence, it is precisely because there is no reterritorialization *afterward* as with the migrant, or upon *something else* as with the sedentary (the sedentary's relation with the earth is mediatized by something else, a property regime, a State apparatus)" (381). See also Patton's gloss, *Deleuze and the Political*, 116–117. For Deleuze, the desert Bedouin or the barbarian tribe is the apparent prototype for the nomad, whereas Patton applies the idea of nomadic space to the colonial conquest and its appropriation of supposed *terra nullius*.

17. Deleuze and Guattari, *A Thousand Plateaus*, 508–509. Patton, *Deleuze and the Political*, 98–102.

18. William Butler Yeats, "The Second Coming," (1919) *The Collected Poems of W. B. Yeats*, ed. Richard Finneran, 2nd ed. (New York: Scribner's, 1996), 187.

19. See Thomas Friedman's visionary *The World Is Flat: A Brief History of the Twenty-First Century* (New York: Farrar, Strauss and Giroux, 2005).

20. See Seyla Ben Habib, Ian Shapiro, and Danilo Petranovic, eds., *Identities, Affiliations, and Allegiances* (Cambridge: Cambridge University Press, 2007).

21. For the effort, drawing on Carl Schmitt, to derive a ruthless reduction of political activity, see Giorgio Agamben, *Homo Sacer: Sovereign Power and Bare Life* (Stanford, CA: Stanford University Press, 1998). See also its sequel, *State of Exception*, trans. Kevin Attell (Chicago: University of Chicago Press, 2005).

22. The fundamental text was Hugo Grotius's *Mare Librum* (1609). See discussion in Chapter 1 of this book. For a new edition (though an old translation), see *The Free Sea*, trans. Richard Hakluyt, ed. David Armitage (Indianapolis: Liberty Fund, 2004). Cf. Philip Stephens's plea for London's secession from Great Britain (*Financial Times*, December 12, 2014, 11: "London should break free from Little England").

23. I am not equipped to follow the mathematics itself and must rely on summaries. For the scientific citations, see https://en.wikipedia.org/wiki/indes.php.?title=Quantum_nonlocality&oldid=687433577.

24. At the same time, the chief economic commentator of the *Financial Times* recognizes the backlash this cosmopolitanism can unleash. See Martin Wolf, "Losers are in Revolt against the Elites," *Financial Times,* January 26, 2016.

25. Theorists have suggested that, rightly understood, globalization involves a new focus on different scales of production and exchange and thus an expansion of awareness as much as changes in real activity. For important contributions, see the essays included in Andrew Herod and Melissa W. Wright, eds., *Geographies of Power: Placing Scale* (Malden, MA: Blackwell, 2002). Saskia Sassen emphasizes that the globalization of recent decades took place while national authority was increasing in many respects, certainly in terms of the balance of executive versus legislative power. See Saskia Sassen, *Migration, Rights, Territory* (Princeton, NJ: Princeton University Press, 2016).

26. Saskia Sassen, *Global City: London, New York, Tokyo* (Princeton, NJ: Princeton University Press, 1991). See also Neil Brenner, "Global Cities, Global States: Global City Formation and State Territorial Restructuring in Contemporary Europe," *Review of International Political Economy* 5, no. 1 (1998): 1–37.

27. On place, see the varied writings of John A. Agnew, *Globalization and Sovereignty* (Lanham, MD: Rowman and Littlefield, 2009); and with Luca Mascarà, *Making Political Geography* (Lanham, MD: Rowman, 2012), esp. 177–178.

28. Wordsworth "The Ruined Cottage," cited by Donna Landry, "The Geopolitical Picturesque," in *Land and Identity: Theory, Memory, and Practice,* ed. Christine Berberich, Neil Campbell, and Robert Hudson (Amsterdam: Rodopi, 2013), 96–97. For a suggestive inquiry into the emotional valence of places, especially for the migrants or exiles who have left them, see Svetlana Boym's *The Future of Nostalgia* (New York: Basic Books, 2001).

29. For the exposition of Heidegger as a philosopher of place in particular, see Edward Casey, *The Fate of Place: A Philosophical History* (Berkeley: University of California Press, 1998), 242–259.

30. For the theme of melancholy in Arcadia, see the classic essay on "Et in Arcadia Ego," by Erwin Panofsky in *Meaning and the Visual Arts* (Chicago: University of Chicago Press, 1963); Palestinians cited by Landry, "Geopolitical Picturesque"; E. P. Thompson, *William Morris, Romantic to Revolutionary* (London: Lawrence and Wishart, 1955); Raymond Williams, *The Country and the City* (Nottingham: Spokesman Books, 2011).

31. Jennifer Daskal, "The Un-Territoriality of Data," *Yale Law Journal* 125, no. 2 (2015): 397.

32. See Peter J. Spiro, *At Home in Two Countries: The Past and Future of Dual Citizenship* (New York: New York University Press, 2016). For the problem of reconciling dualism with one nationality, see Will Kymlicka, *Multicultural Citizenship: A Liberal Theory of Minority Rights* (Oxford: Clarendon Press 1995).

INDEX